Counter-Terrorism Laws and Freedom of Expression

Counter-Terrorism Laws and Freedom of Expression

Global Perspectives

Edited by
Téwodros Workneh and Paul Haridakis

LEXINGTON BOOKS
Lanham • Boulder • New York • London

Portions of the text in chapter 2, by Athina Karatzogianni and Andrew Robinson were previously published in “Schizorevolutions versus Microfacisms: The Fear of Anarchy in State Securitisation.” *Journal of International Political Theory*. Vol. 13. No. 3. October 2017.
Portions of the text in chapter 17, by Téwodros Workneh were previously published in “Development, democracy and digital freedoms: A critical analysis of state-sponsored internet censorship in Ethiopia.” *Internet Governance in the Global South*. Núcleo de Pesquisa em Relações Internacionais (NUPRI-USP). 2018.

Published by Lexington Books

An imprint of The Rowman & Littlefield Publishing Group, Inc.
4501 Forbes Boulevard, Suite 200, Lanham, Maryland 20706
www.rowman.com

6 Tinworth Street, London SE11 5AL, United Kingdom

British Library Cataloguing in Publication Information Available

Library of Congress Cataloging-in-Publication Data Available

ISBN 978-1-7936-2216-7 (cloth)
ISBN 978-1-7936-2217-4 (electronic)

Contents

Acknowledgments

When we embarked on this project in October 2019, little did we know the world would be afflicted by a once-in-a-century pandemic that upends livelihoods, causing tragedy and pain for so many individuals and families around the world. Like so many, the contributors of this anthology who hail from fifteen countries and five continents have experienced varying degrees of distress caused by COVID-19. Despite the real (and sensible) possibility of postponing or even suspending this project given the difficult circumstances created by the pandemic, our contributors pushed through and delivered remarkable scholarship. We would like to thank all our contributors for their dedication during the course of the last few months. Finally, we would like to thank Connor Wilcox and Harrison Lejeune for their valuable editorial assistance throughout the different development stages of the manuscripts.

PART I

INTRODUCTION

Chapter 1

Counter-terrorism Laws in the International Frame

Uncertain Times for Freedom of Expression

Téwodros Workneh and Paul Haridakis

The terrorist attacks of September 11, 2001, in the United States as well as other terrorist-related incidents in different parts of the world have caused profound changes in political, economic, and social relations globally. Nations have aggressively sought a wide range of mechanisms to proactively curb potential threats, such as strengthening controls on immigration, financial transactions, and communication flows. While arms of executive branches such as law enforcement bodies and even militaries are commonly part of the counter-terrorism apparatus, the authority under which such government entities operate is linked to the growing number of counter-terrorism laws worldwide. According to a report by Fionnuala Ni Aoláin, Special Rapporteur to the United Nations Secretary-General on the Promotion and Protection of Human Rights and Fundamental Freedoms while Countering Terrorism, between 2001 and 2018, at least 140 governments adopted counter-terrorism legislation (Human Rights Council 2019).[1] Counter-terrorism laws usually empower states to expedite the prosecution of alleged offenders by bypassing standard criminal jurisprudence processes (Donohue 2007; Neal 2012). While governments assert the need for such laws to counter terrorism and protect national security, critics argue counter-terrorism laws are prone to be misappropriated by state actors who routinely use such laws in non-terrorism domestic contexts. Regardless of the view accepted, laws designed to combat terrorism are being applied domestically in contexts not involving terrorism—such as governmental efforts to quash political dissent or restrict other forms of citizen expression (Baser, Akgönül, and Öztürk 2017; Cram 2006; Murray 2009).

The prominence of counter-terrorism laws across the world has had significant implications for the study of global terrorism from legal and policy perspectives, especially in terms of determining what does and does not constitute an act of terrorism. The executive delimitation of terrorism has been conditioned by Resolution 1373 of the United Nations Security Council that was issued on September 28, 2001, following the terrorist attacks on the United States earlier that month. The resolution, among other things, called on nations to criminalize acts of terrorism as well as the financing, planning, preparation, and support for terrorism. To expedite the directive, the Security Council created a new Counter-Terrorism Committee that was tasked with overseeing counter-terrorism actions adopted by member states. While the resolution directed member states to reinforce their counter-terrorism efforts, it did not provide a framework to define what constitutes an act of terrorism. Ramraj, Hor, and Roach (2015, 3) note that this left individual nations to define terrorism according to their contextual concerns. This approach is not unexpected given how international counter-terrorism law and policy involve multiple layers of actors and stakeholders as well as "interplay between international, regional and domestic sources of law" (ibid.).

The rather elastic conceptualization of terrorism coupled with the rise of counter-terrorism laws across nation-states has brought renewed concerns about infringement of basic human rights. Well-known post-9/11 counter-terrorism activities in Guantanamo Bay or American "black sites" and rendition locations around the world have demonstrated there is a thin line between curbing terrorist acts and violating the basic right to be free from torture and degrading treatment (Setty 2015). In addition to concerns over torture and degrading treatment, counter-terrorism efforts have also ignited debate on striking the right balance between thwarting terrorism and protecting freedoms of expression, association, and assembly (Schneiderman and Cossman 2002). Of critical importance here is how the UN Security Council's endorsement of counter-terrorism laws has created an added impetus for authoritarian governments to criminalize legitimate forms of domestic dissent. Today, many states, including those with well-established democracies, have aligned themselves with what came to be loosely known as the "war against terrorism" global front.[2] However, these states have intensified the use of their counter-terrorism apparatus, including legal frameworks, to curtail citizens' civil liberties, constrain freedom of the press, control civic organizations, and regulate communication systems.

Evidence from different parts of the world indicate many journalists, media practitioners, activists, and everyday citizens who disseminate alternative or critical political discourse are experiencing various forms of harassment, persecution, intimidation, and even legal prosecution under broadly framed terrorism charges sanctioned by state-sponsored counter-terrorism legislation. For example, in Ethiopia, the Anti-Terrorism Proclamation of 2009 has been used to prosecute several bloggers and journalists who were accused of writing about opposition groups designated by the government as terrorists (Kibret 2017; Workneh 2019). In the United States, despite a strong tradition of First and Fourth Amendment constitutional rights to free speech and privacy, government actors have routinely used provisions of the USA Patriot Act of 2001 to demand information about U.S. citizens, including journalists' sources (Podesta 2002). Saudi Arabia has aggressively used its anti-terrorism law to criminalize a wide range of peaceful expression that has subjected several individuals to different forms of retribution including capital punishment (Azoulay 2014).

This book is concerned with the impact of global counter-terrorism laws on communication, especially individual and institutional political speech. Almost all counter-terrorism laws incorporate language that affects communication, communication systems, media and/or media practitioners, and individual expression. In many instances, these laws define alleged terrorist speech, delineate the use of communication systems to disseminate said speech, and designate parameters to prosecute terrorists and networks of terrorism. At the same time, journalists, activists, and everyday media users around the world continue to experience varying degrees of state-sponsored harassment as a result of the broad interpretation of counter-terrorism laws that conflate terrorist expression with non-terrorist expression. Amid the rise of populist politics, nationalist political movements, and the retreat of the democratic order globally, the question about freedom of speech in the era of counter-terrorism frameworks is urgent. It is against this backdrop that we ask: What happens when a state-sanctioned legal framework aimed at protecting the public from terrorist activity—mostly perpetrated from foreign adversaries—is used internally against citizens? What are some of the consequences of using counter-terrorism laws that are prone to conflate freedom of expression with terrorist acts?

TERRORISM, COUNTER-TERRORISM, AND THE LAW

Although occurrences of terrorism date back to ancient epochs of human civilization and state formation, the term "terrorism" has entered popular public discourse recently.[3] While the media's framing of organizations such as the Irish Republican Army, Fuerzas Armadas Revolucionarias de Colombia, Lord's Resistance Army, and Euskadi Ta Askatasuna in news reports brought the terrorism lexicon to mainstream use in the 1970s and 1980s, it is arguably terrorist events that took place at the dawn of the new millennium that altered nearly all aspects of everyday life ranging from public gatherings, to airport security, to public policy. The 9/11 terrorist attacks in the United

States—arguably the most important exemplar in the modern conceptualization of terrorism—followed by the Madrid and London bombings of 2004 and 2005, respectively, ushered the era of "war on terrorism," which became the rallying cry of the United States and its allies in the post-communism era against purported enemies.

As referenced earlier, despite wide consensus among nations of the need to confront the threat of terrorism in the twenty-first century, reaching consensus on a definition of terrorism has been stubbornly elusive. In what is arguably the most comprehensive discussion regarding the rationales, debates, and implications of the various—and at times contesting—conceptualizations of terrorism, Schmid (2013b) details some of the influential attempts including those of the United Nations and the United States. Schmid further denotes how definitional disparities often arise from different actors' interpretation of terrorism's relationship (or lack thereof) with assassination, organized crime, civilian victims, and the state, among others.[4] In this sense, the difficulty of identifying a universally agreed-upon framework of what constitutes terrorism is unsurprising. There are several explanations for this vacuum, although most arguments can be summarized in five overarching propositions. First, most definitions of terrorism convey the underlying assumption that terrorist acts are inherently committed by non-state actors. Often, acts of violence perpetrated by the state are hardly referred to as "terrorism." The posture of the state in most conceptualizations of terrorism is that of a counter-terrorism agent. State violence is tolerated and justified through notions such as "monopoly of violence." The problem with this line of thinking is that it assumes states always operate under democratic norms of legal, moral, and ethical superiority, and "will do the right thing" (Claridge 1996; Jackson, Murphy, and Poynting 2010). Second, and relatedly, there is a lack of agreement on whether violence pertaining to resistance, liberation, and self-determination movements is akin to terrorism (Friedlander 1981; Ganor 2002; Halberstam 2002). Third, terrorism, as a subject of academic inquiry that cuts across various disciplines including international relations, political science, communication studies, legal studies, and many others is a subject of epistemological, ontological, axiological, and praxiological tensions (Jackson, Smyth, and Gunning 2009; Schmid 2013a). Fourth, state-sanctioned terrorism conceptualizations, which form important foreign policy tenets for many nations, are extremely politicized (Rees and Aldrich 2005; Stohl 1988). Fifth, and perhaps most importantly, domestic definitions of terrorism, which are predominantly influenced by internal struggles of political power, make it extremely difficult to conceptualize terrorism as a transnational phenomenon that cuts across borders, ideologies, and political orientations (Grozdanova 2014; Young 2006).

But why do we concern ourselves with the definitional exigencies of terrorism? After all, aren't consensus definitions not possible—even undesirable—in the case of other concepts studied in the humanities and social sciences such as culture, communication, spirituality, and so on? One rationale for those who seek to resolve the definitional disparities of terrorism rests upon pragmatic premises. To define what constitutes terrorism, in many instances, is to establish the contours of culpability, criminality, and punishment, which, in the case of the latter, could result in the death sentence. The existential implications of defining terrorism in a certain way are particularly relevant against the backdrop of how some liberation movements have historically been labeled and then criminalized as acts of terrorism by imperialists and minority-rule governments (e.g., Boehmer 2005). In addition, how do we account for state-sponsored violence in a context where the state often assumes a position of moral legitimacy and legal authority but abuses its power to crack down on dissent? This is, of course, not to suggest that a consensus definition of terrorism would alleviate any of these problems. The point here is that the universalistic-particularistic dialectic in defining terrorism and the way states choose to conceptualize terrorism—and make policies based on adopted definitions—affect us individually and collectively.

This very intricacy that marks conceptualizing terrorism is also reflected in debates revolving around counter-terrorism practices, strategies, and appraisal. Counter-terrorism strategies, targets, and legal frameworks are devised by state apparatuses in a manner that is consistent with acts identified by governments as constituting acts of terrorism. Given the disparities of attributing a common definition to terrorism, it is not surprising that the scope of counter-terrorism strategies in the international sphere is deeply varied (table 1.1). This is especially evident in how counter-terrorism laws are conceived and executed. Counter-terrorism laws constitute "the body of laws adopted by inter-governmental bodies and states to deter and punish terrorist acts, and to prevent terrorist groups from accessing resources that support their terrorist acts" (Burniske, Modirzadeh, and Lewis 2014, 3). By creating a perpetual state of emergency and giving extensive powers to states to respond to the said emergency, these laws have become pillars of state securitization. While creating a special class of legal frameworks to specifically target terrorism has become standard practice, the rationale for this route of securitization had been criticized. For example, Brownlie (2003) argues there should be no category of a law of terrorism and that terrorism cases should be conducted "in accordance with the applicable sectors of public international law: jurisdiction, international criminal justice, state responsibility, and so forth" (713). Criticism over the adoption of counter-terrorism laws has particularly highlighted how securitization legal

Table 1.1

Country	*Counter-terrorism legislation*
Afghanistan	Combat Against Terrorist Offences (2008)
Australia	Anti-terrorism Bill I,II,III (2004)
Bahrain	Protection of Community Against Terrorist Acts (2006, amended 2013, 2019)
Bangladesh	Anti-terrorism Act (2009, amended 2012, 2013)
Cameroon	Anti-terrorism Law (2014)
Canada	Proceeds of Crime (Money Laundering) and Terrorists Financing Act (2000, amended 2019); Anti-Terrorism Act (2015); Justice for Victims of Terrorism Act (2012)
China	Counterterrorism Law of the People's Republic of China (2015)
Egypt	Anti-Terrorism Law (2015, amended 2019)
Ethiopia	Anti-Terrorism Proclamation (2009, amended 2020)
India	Terrorist and Disruptive Activities (Prevention) Act (1985); Prevention of Terrorism Act (2002); Unlawful Activities Prevention Act (1967, amended 2019)
Indonesia	Anti-terrorism Law (2002); Eradication of Criminal Acts of Terrorism Law (2018)
Iraq	Iraqi Anti-Terrorism Law (2005)
Israel	Combatting Terrorism Law (2016); Prevention of Terrorism Ordinance (1948); Prevention of Funding of Terrorism Law (2005)
Jordan	Anti-Terrorism Law (2006)
Kazakhstan	Law on Counteraction of Legitimization (Laundering) of Incomes Received by Illegal Means, and Financing of Terrorism (2009, amended 2020); Law on Countering Terrorism (1999, amended 2017)
Kenya	Prevention of Terrorism Act (2012, amended 2014)
Malaysia	National Security Council Act (2016)
Maldives	Prevention of Terrorism Act (1990); The Anti-Terrorism Act (2015, amended 2019); Prevention of Money Laundering and Terrorist Financing Act (2017)
Morocco	Law to Combat Terror (2003)
Mozambique	Law to Combat Terrorism (2018)
Nigeria	Terrorism (Prevention) Act (2011, amended 2013)
Pakistan	Anti-terrorism Act (1997, amended 2014); National Counterterrorism Authority (NACTA) Act (2013); Investigation for Fair Trial Act (2014)
Philippines	Anti-Terrorism Act (2020), replaced the Human Security Act (2007); Terrorism Financing Prevention and Suppression Act (2012)
Qatar	Law on Combating Terrorism (2019)
Russian Federation	Federal Law No. 35-FZ on Counteraction of Terrorism (2006, amended 2014); Federal Law No. 115-FZ On Countering Money Laundering and the Financing of Terrorism (2006, amended 2014); Federal Law No. 114 FZ on Combating of Extremist Activity (2002, amended 2008)
Saudi Arabia	Law on Combating Crimes of Terrorism and its Financing (2017)

Country	*Counter-terrorism legislation*
South Africa	The Protection of Constitutional Democracy Against Terrorist and Related Activities Act (2004)
South Korea	The Act on Anti-Terrorism for the Protection of Citizens and Public Security (2016); Act on Prohibition Against the Financing of Terrorism (2008, amended 2014)
Sri Lanka	Prevention of Terrorism Act (1979)
Tanzania	Prevention of Terrorism Act (2002; amended 2019)
Tunisia	Law on Counter-Terrorism and Suppression of Money Laundering (2015)
Turkey	Law on Fight Against Terrorism (1991, amended 2010)
Uganda	Anti-Terrorism Act (2002; amended 2017)
United Arab Emirates	Federal Law on Combating Terrorism Offences (2014)
United Kingdom	Anti-Terrorism, Crime and Security Act (2001)/ Terrorism Act (2000)/ Counter-Terrorism and Security Act (2015)/Terrorism Prevention and Investigation Measures Act (2011) The Counterterrorism and Border Security Act (2019)
United States	Terrorist Expatriation Act (2010); Anti-terrorism and Effective Death Penalty Act (1996); International Emergency Economic Powers Act (2003); Immigration and Nationality Act; USA PATRIOT Act (2001); Homeland Security Act (2002); Homeland Security Appropriations Act (2007); Intelligence Reform and Terrorism Prevention Act (2004); National Intelligence Reform Act (2004); Terrorist Penalties Enhancement Act (2004); Terrorist Bombings and Financing Conventions Implementation Act (2002); Classified Information Procedure Act (1980); Military Commissions Act (2006); Protect America Act (2007); USA PATRIOT Act Additional Reauthorizing Amendments Act (2006); USA PATRIOT Improvement and Reauthorization Act (2005); Terrorism Risk Insurance Act (2002); Foreign Intelligence Service Act (1978, amended 2005)
Uzbekistan	The Law on Combating Terrorism (2000, amended 2019)

frameworks often come at the expense of undermining civil liberties (Head 2002; Michaelsen 2006; Neocleous 2007). From most states' perspectives, the prevailing assumption in contemporary counter-terrorism theory and practice is that security and liberty are inversely related, and that to guarantee the former, the latter may need to be compromised. Critics argue this either-or proposition between security and liberty, in addition to the false dichotomy it creates, depresses perspectives that emphasize security is ensured not in spite of liberty but because of it (e.g., Kielsgard 2005; Whittaker 2014). Most rights-focused approaches denote how counter-terrorism laws, by their very design of rationalizing the need for the creation of a state of emergency, tend to limit civil liberties as an inevitable price to pay to combat terrorism threats.

At the heart of this debate, and specifically pertinent to the object of this book, is how most counter-terrorism laws confine expressive rights and implicate communication as terrorism, and/or place controls on communication to effectively address terrorism. It is from this vantage point that we argue finding a proper balance between the application and practice of contemporary counter-terrorism law and protection of expressive rights invites a communication approach to critically assess these competing interests.[5]

WHY A COMMUNICATION APPROACH TO TERRORISM?

Every fall semester we offer *Communication and Terrorism*, an upper-undergraduate class, as one of the core courses of the global communication curriculum in the School of Communication Studies at Kent State University. Across a duration of fifteen weeks, the course typically aims to address four learning outcomes: (a) identifying the essential interplay between communication theory, communication practice, and the ways in which terrorist organizations gain public attention and recruit members; (b) discussing the efficacy and implications of government attempts to curb terrorist communication and influence or limit press coverage or terrorist incidents; (c) critically examining the messaging strategies and symbolism used by several terrorist organizations and state sponsors of terrorism, and how communication practices—including use of social media and branding strategies—are changing; and (d) identifying the impacts of media framing and popular culture on public understanding of terrorism. The class fills up quite quickly and attracts not only global communication majors but students from other disciplines.

We shared the anecdote here because we see it as a microcosm of the emergence of terrorism scholarship in the field of communication studies. The integration of terrorism as an object of inquiry in the field of communication studies has been generally lackluster. Traditionally, scholarship in terrorism has been housed in disciplines such as political science, peace and security studies, international studies, and legal studies. Most inquiries in these disciplines were concerned with the "what" of terrorism and with understanding the characteristics and manifestations of the phenomenon. As Archetti (2012) notes, the focus on descriptive scholarship in terrorism studies has come at the expense of neglecting explanatory research that attempts to understand the causes, processes, and consequences of terrorism. While descriptive inquiries are still important given the need to continuously engage with the rapidly evolving nature of the concept of terrorism amid the increasing fluidity, interdisciplinarity, and fragmentation of terrorism studies, explanatory inquiries are still underdeveloped.

Consequently, we argue process-focused, explanatory, and constructivist inquiries of terrorism found a sympathetic host in communication studies. In particular, we note two major rationales for the slow but perceptible ascent of terrorism research from the margins to the center. The first, we argue, is topical. Contemporary terrorism is an act performed, consumed, and conducted primarily through mediated communication. From the use of communication technologies by terrorist groups to media coverage of terrorism-related stories, communication has become an indispensable component of every terrorism incident. This has inevitably led communication and non-communication scholars alike to engage with terrorism as a communication phenomenon. The second rationale for the increasing interest in communication studies as an avenue for explanatory research in the study of terrorism is theoretical. This rationale denotes the communication turn in terrorism research is not only informed by the proliferation of communication technologies across households and individuals and the immediacy of dissemination they bring but also the existence of conceptual frameworks that explain said phenomena. From Marshal McLuhan's proposition of media ecology to Michael Shudson's sociology of news or emerging conceptualizations of affordances theories related to social media, the field offers a conducive atmosphere for contextual and process-based inquiries of terrorism. Even in the field of communication studies, however, terrorism scholarship is explored from a variety of approaches including, but not limited to, law and policy (Bosch 2012; Crelinsten 2002; Mayali and Yoo 2016), media technology and effects (Bassiouni 1981; Meleagrou-Hitchens, Alexander, and Kaderbhai 2017), discourse (Bartolucci 2012; Cloud 2004; Jackson 2005; Tuman 2009; Shaw 2012), radicalization and extremism (Chatfield, Reddick, and Brajawidagda 2015; Parker et al. 2019; Powers 2014), and freedom of expression (Baser, Akgönül, and Öztürk 2017; Cram 2009), among others.

While these strands of research demonstrate disagreement regarding the link between communication and terrorism, the nature, scope, and significance of the relationship are not quite clear-cut. On one hand, a good deal of scholarship approaches communication as an *instrument* of terrorism. Research in this area typically looks at how communication resources such as media technology, rhetorical techniques, and psychological dispositions are used to advance or counter terrorism. This area of research forms, loosely defined, the dominant paradigm of communication and terrorism scholarship. It fits the overall tenor of "strategic communication," an umbrella term in the field of communication studies denoting theory and practice emphasizing *purposeful* communication to advance a certain organizational mission (Hallahan et al. 2007). For example, by noting how "terrorist and violent extremist groups radicalize and recruit individuals through online propaganda, social media platforms, networking sites and traditional media," (United Nations Office of Counter-Terrorism n.d.) the United Nations Office of Counter-Terrorism unveiled the Secretary-General's Plan of Action to Prevent Violent Extremism,[6] a comprehensive document that singles out strategic communication as an essential tool to combat radicalization and extremism. By adopting strategic communication as an instrument of building a counter-terrorism narrative, the United Nations has in recent years elevated preemptive communication efforts on par with security-based counter-terrorism measures. "Since the rise of the Islamic State of Iraq and the Levant (ISIL)," the Office of Counter-Terrorism asserts, "concerted efforts have been undertaken to identify good practices in using *strategic communications* to prevent the appeal of violent extremism and terrorism" (United Nations Office of Counter-Terrorism n.d., emphasis added). The U.S. government also employs strategic communication across its military and public diplomacy units such as the Department of State, the Department of Defense, and the United States Agency for Global Media. For example, the Department of Defense's *Dictionary of Military and Associated Terms* defines strategic communication as:

> focused United States Government efforts to understand and engage key audiences to create, strengthen, or preserve conditions favorable for the advancement of United States Government interests, policies, and objectives through the use of coordinated programs, plans, themes, messages, and products synchronized with the actions of all instruments of national power. (United States Department of Defense 2016, 226)

Recently, the U.S. government identified strategic communication as one of the "most potent tools" as an integral part of America's counter-terrorism strategy (The White House 2018, 2). The "effects" tradition of approaching communication as an instrument of advancing (or curbing) terrorism continues to form the pillar of not only state-sponsored and think tank research but also most academic inquiries in the area (e.g., Aistrope 2016; Rothenberger 2017; Weimann 2015). However, a growing number of scholars are approaching the intersections between terrorism and communication with a more comprehensive and robust approach. This approach does not view terrorism's relationship with communication as one primarily informed by causality, effects, or strategic rationales. Rather than treating terrorism and communication as distinct variables defined by causal relationships, this perspective views terrorism *as* communication (see Archetti 2012). By viewing communication as the very essence of terrorism, this approach emphasizes interdependence over causality and context over effect. For some scholars, this perspective embodies what Spencer (2010) called the "constructivist turn" in terrorism research. Spencer (2010, 91) notes:

> Constructivist terrorism research is not so much interested in how the terrorist really is but how he is talked or written to be. Therefore, primary sources in the traditional sense and the focus on the terrorist have been replaced with the analysis of discourse and metaphors in particular which constitute the "new terrorist" in a certain way.

The focus on discourse, context, and lived experience is particularly relevant in contemporary inquiries involving mediated communication. The proliferation of everyday media technology, especially social media, which is characterized by ease of accessibility, instant sharing of information, or, as Negroponte (1996) notes, an overall omnipresence of "digitality," makes discourse a pivotal analytical tool of terrorism. In this regard, it is not surprising that scholarship that projects a constructivist optics is becoming more and more visible, as the contours of terrorism *as* communication research continue to spread through inquiries focusing on discourse (Boukala 2016; Fahmy 2019; Kelsey 2015; Połońska-Kimunguyi and Gillespie 2016), spectacle (Kellner 2015; Livingstone 2019), and mediatization (Cui and Rothenbuhler 2017; Ali and Khattab 2018; Solaroli 2011).

ORGANIZATION OF THE BOOK

The chapters in this book offer global perspectives on the interplay between counter-terrorism measures and civil liberties both from strategic and constructivist perspectives. In particular, the essays examine: (a) how the discourse around counter-terrorism laws is intertwined with the politics of state securitization; and (b) how the empowerment of state apparatuses, both in democratic and authoritarian contexts, is undermining journalism practice and citizen expression. In soliciting the chapters incorporated in this book, we were mindful about not only the Western bias in much prior terrorism scholarship but also that of communication studies (e.g., Chakravartty, Kuo, Grubbs, and McIlwain 2018; Ng, White and Saha 2020; Waisbord 2019; Wasserman 2020). Our intentional approach of incorporating internationally diverse authors and case studies has resulted in the review of topical issues pertaining to the various communicative elements of counter-terrorism laws in Africa, Asia, Europe, Latin America, North America, and Oceania.

The book is divided into three parts. Part I deals with the politics and discourse of counter-terrorism laws. The chapters in this section address issues of framing, discourse, and conceptualization of counter-terrorism laws from the perspectives of political orientation, regulation, and governance. In chapter 2, Athina Karatzogianni and Andrew Robinson critically engage with the relationship between state securitization and violence. By highlighting how state securitization fortifies an image of a state in existential crisis, the authors argue how anti-anarchist discourses are exploited to respond to network threats. The chapter also delves into the manifold footprints of state terror, and proposes the merits of desecuritizing society to put an end to the production and reproduction of terror involving state and network actors. In chapter 3, Eunice Castro Seixas deals with Portugal's recent bills concerning the fight against terrorism. Through critical discourse analysis, Castro Seixas examines parliamentary debates of these bills and examines discursive practices deployed for and against the approval of these bills by political representatives on the right and on the left. Specifically, Castro Seixas breaks down the different discursive strategies and performative versions of the debates in relation to national identity, either by constructing Portugal as a nation that has lagged behind other European countries or by projecting it as a nation of democratic rule of law that protects fundamental rights and freedoms. By analyzing provisions of counter-terrorism in Spain's Criminal Code of 1995, Isabel Serrano Maillo (chapter 4) probes the ramifications of some of the recent changes of regulating terrorism, especially as it relates to the aggravation of penalties for terrorist acts and the expansion of attitudes and actions that can be considered terrorism. The chapter outlines how recent reforms of the legislation limit freedom of expression, and how alleged perpetrators of terrorism are now not only those considered terrorists in the conventional sense of the word but also members of the civil society who are alien to violent action. In chapter 5, Nazli Bülay Doğan engages with political implications of cyberterrorism discourse in Turkey, and asks how the discourse of counter-terrorism functions within the meaning-making process of cybercrime for the Turkish state. In particular, Doğan discusses the relationship between hacktivism and cyberterrorism frames in the Turkish context and argues how the discourse of counter-terrorism by the Turkish state is instrumentalized to provide legitimacy for restrictive control over digital media and exclusive Internet governance. In another chapter that deals with discourses of counter-terrorism, Wei Sun (chapter 6) examines how Chinese-speaking netizens reacted to the Anti-Terrorism Law of the People's Republic of China. Through an examination of user reactions and interactions regarding China's counter-terrorism actions and laws on select news articles on the Voice of America (VOA) and the British Broadcasting Corporation (BBC), Sun offers insights on how Chinese netizens in China and overseas engage with popular foreign news platforms as alternative avenues of protest in response to increased Internet censorship in the homeland and the blurring of terrorism, separatism, and human rights advocacy. In chapter 7, Daniel

Oppermann outlines historical and contemporary debates on terrorism in Brazil and discusses the development of counter-terrorism legislation in the twentieth and twenty-first centuries. In doing so, Oppermann demonstrates how legal mechanisms adopted by authoritarian Brazilian governments in the twentieth century were deployed as mechanisms of control and repression of dissent under a broad and sweeping agenda of "fighting communism." Despite the absence of a major terrorism incident in Brazil, Oppermann argues the consideration of and debates over several counter-terrorism bills in the Brazilian parliament along the left-right political spectrum reflects the increasing politicization of terrorism in public discourse. Written from an attorney's perspective, in chapter 8, Rita Radostitz offers a rich, inside look at how the "war on terror" came to undermine U.S. commitment to human and civil rights through the CIA's control of information regarding its "Rendition, Detention and Interrogation" ("RDI") program and the proceedings in the Military Commissions at Naval Station Guantánamo Bay, Cuba. Radostitz argues how counter-terrorism measures have significantly abridged freedom of expression in the jurisprudence process involving Khalid Shaikh Mohammad, Khallad bin 'Atash, Ramzi Bin al Shibh, Ammar al Baluchi, and Mustafa al Hawsawi.

Part II focuses on the ways counter-terrorism laws have impacted journalistic practice globally. Specifically, it deals with the deployment of counter-terrorism laws in different countries, and how these laws undermined investigative journalistic practice with effects ranging from the imprisonment of reporters to self-censorship. The first chapter in this section (chapter 9) deals with the impact anti-terror and related legislation that have been introduced in Australia has had on journalism in that country. Through interviews conducted with journalists from across the spectrum of Australian news, Richard Murray, Rebecca Ananian-Welsh & Peter Greste argue Australian counter-terrorism laws have had a "chilling effect" and have weakened journalists' capacity to support and maintain Australia's democratic institutions. The authors highlight how senior Australian journalists have little faith this situation will improve in the wake of evermore restrictive legislation pushed through Australia's legislative chambers in recent years. Such legislation, the authors contend, offers a case of how Western democracies can weaken one of the primary pillars of accountability and oversight through securitization legislation. In chapter 10, Florence Namasinga Selnes provides a first-hand account of journalists in Uganda who face increasing government scrutiny and intimidation in relation to the provisions of the Anti-terrorism Act of 2002 and the Anti-terrorism (Amendment) Act of 2017. Grounded in the theoretical propositions of the sociology of journalism, Selnes interrogates the implications of counter terrorism regulations for journalism practice and how journalists perceive counter-terrorism laws in relation to their profession. By using document analysis of Uganda's counter-terrorism regulation and in-depth interviews with practicing journalists, Florence Namasinga Selnes details how counter-terrorism legislation is used to intimidate and harass journalists and media institutions that are targeted because of their critical coverage of the government. In a review of a case of India, Mohammad Imran Parray, in chapter 11, discusses how the enactment of counter-terrorism laws have adversely impacted forums of public discussion, reducing access to free information and threatening civil liberties. By exploring the use of counter-terrorism laws by the Indian state against members of the journalistic community, Parray shows how local journalists on the nation's fringes often resort to self-censorship. With a focus on the Kashmir region, Parray engages with evidence of how democratic states hide behind the veneer of security and counter terrorism arguments while imposing severe restrictions on free speech. In chapter 12, Peter Tiako Ngangum examines the redefinition of national security in Cameroon to incorporate the risk of terrorist actions undertaken by terrorist organizations, particularly the Boko Haram group. Ngangum contends that while the threat of terrorism and the rise of counter-terrorism legislation to combat terrorism are justified, the existence of arbitrary legislation and the vague, broad, and sweeping nature of such legislations remain potentially problematic to the protection of journalistic sources and other fundamental rights. This complexity is evident in Cameroon where the law on the suppression of acts of terrorism has been invoked to arrest, prosecute, and detain journalists, peaceful protesters, and Cameroon anglophone activists.

Finally, Part III addresses how counter-terrorism laws have targeted everyday citizens, social media activists, whistleblowers, and human rights advocates around the world. This section addresses how counter-terrorism laws affect citizen expression globally, and how this trend undermines democratic values in both authoritarian and democratic political contexts. Gabriela Martínez kicks off this section (chapter 13) by examining how counter-terrorism legal frameworks are used to silence citizens' dissent by targeting artists, activists, and institutions whose work is related to Peru's historical memory of the internal armed conflict. By focusing on specific sections of the Peruvian Penal Code ratified under the Presidency of Fernando Belaúnde Terry (1980–1985) and reaffirmed under subsequent governments including the most recent one in 2017, Martínez argues the tension between freedom of expression and the state's desire to restrict the range of that freedom signals an ongoing conflict between citizens and the state as demonstrated by the rich account the author presents concerning the cases of Lugar de la Memoria, la Tolerancia y la Inclusión Social, more commonly known as LUM, and artist and photographer Daniela Chacón. In chapter 14, Daniel Ortner critically engages with the Russian Federation's

2002 law "On Fighting Extremist Activity," also known as the Extremism Law. The law, which was originally adopted for combating the rise of Islamic fundamentalism or other extremist ideologies became a tool for banning religious literature, suppressing political dissent, confiscating property, and even jailing dozens of Jehovah's Witnesses merely for continuing to belong to their faith. In addition to the Extremism Law, the chapter also delves into the Yarovaya Law of 2016, a counter-terrorism and cybersecurity law with a provision that curtails missionary work. Ortner's account offers a rich discussion of how Russia's use of these laws undermines freedom of expression and freedom of religion in the name of national security. In the next chapter, Paul Haridakis (chapter 15) discusses how, even in a democracy with a strong constitutional foundation for protecting freedom of speech, such as the United States, those protections tend to be compromised when the government is confronted with an external threat such as terrorism. Haridakis outlines how policymakers in the United States have devoted considerable attention to counter-terrorism efforts in a proclaimed war on terrorism in the past twenty years, leading up to the imposition of various constraints on expressive activities. The chapter offers a reflection upon the tension between protecting internal freedoms and limiting them to advance a professed government interest in protecting national security. In addition, Haridakis addresses the important role of First Amendment rights to operate as a check on government abuse, particularly during times of crisis, and how that important check is thwarted when First Amendment rights of freedom of speech and the press are constrained or otherwise targeted. In chapter 16, Francesco Tamburini provides a historical analysis of counter-terrorism laws in Algeria. By outlining the rationales of the Algerian state to initially adopt counter-terrorism legislation to neutralize violent radical Islamism, Tamburini moves to discuss what he labels as the "soft strategy," a formula that the regime used to fight terrorist groups who aspired to create an Islamic state, but which also became an instrument to limit civil and political rights by targeting the regime's political opponents. Tamburini offers additional insights on recent developments regarding the Algerian government's use of Algerians' fear and psychological scars of the country's civil wars to justify anti-terrorism measures that often are deployed to consolidate the regime's power internally. Téwodros Workneh (chapter 17) looks at how the Ethiopian government has extensively used the provisions of the Ethiopian Anti-Terrorism Proclamation of 2009 to prosecute several Ethiopian citizens and organizations that were critical of the Ethiopian People's Revolutionary Democratic Front (ERPDF), Ethiopia's ruling party from 1991 to 2019. By framing the adoption and execution of Ethiopia's Anti-Terrorism Proclamation as an outcome of EPRDF's mechanism of control, Workneh demonstrates how the Ethiopian state has created a legal-rational bureaucracy that exploits terrorism narratives to stifle critical speech disseminated through both traditional and digital media platforms. In chapter 18, Shudipta Sharma discusses how counter-terrorism laws in Bangladesh were enacted by the government to curb terrorism threats and enhance de-radicalization processes. However, like the other instances in this book, politicians' use of citizens' fears to increase their power and control over society is evident in Bangladesh, as well. Several incidents discussed in this chapter demonstrate how the Bangladeshi government ignored its legal obligations to the Constitution and international agreements that guarantee peoples' right to freedom of expression. The author offers a critique of the broad and vague definition of several terms in the counter-terrorism legislation that creates opportunities for the state to abuse the laws and to stifle dissent and political opposition under the guise of protecting national security.

In chapter 19, we (Paul Haridakis and Téwodros Workneh) summarize some of the overarching themes of the different chapters that looked at the interplay between counter-terrorism laws and freedom of expression globally. We consider and discuss insights gained and what we can learn from the rise of counter-terrorism laws and whether we are safer, individually and collectively, from threats of terrorism by ceding civil liberties. We conclude by offering some remarks on the possibilities of ensuring security without curbing freedom of expression and the public sphere.

NOTES

1. For further insights on the scope and nature of these laws, see the Bureau of Counterterrorism's Country Reports on Terrorism (United States Department of State 2019).
2. See Van Munster 2004 for a discursive analysis of the U.S.-led rhetoric of "war on terrorism."
3. For a historical overview of terrorism from ancient civilizations to contemporary societies, see Law (2009).
4. Easson and Schmid (2013) compiled more than 250 academic, governmental, and intergovernmental definitions of terrorism, demonstrating the scale of interpretive disparities.
5. It should be noted that this table does not represent an exhaustive list of all countries that adopted counter-terrorism laws. The countries represented here have dedicated counter-terrorism legal frameworks which are deployed independently or in concert with other provisions incorporated in criminal and penal codes. Nations that have not adopted comprehensive counter-terrorism legal frameworks use provisions in their penal or criminal codes to prosecute charges related to terrorism.
6. See United Nations (2015).

REFERENCES

Aistrope, Tim. 2016. "Social Media and Counterterrorism Strategy." *Australian Journal of International Affairs* 70 (2): 121–38. https://doi.org/10.1080/10357718.2015.1113230.

Ali, Saira, and Umi Khattab. 2018. "Trans-Mediatized Terrorism: The Sydney Lindt Café Siege." *Global Media and Communication* 14 (3): 301–23. https://doi.org/10.1177/1742766518811367.

Archetti, Christina. 2012. *Understanding Terrorism in the Age of Global Media: A Communication Approach*. New York: Palgrave Macmillan.

Azoulay, Rivka. 2014. "Criminalizing Dissent: How Saudi Arabia's Counterterrorism Law is Used to Suppress Peaceful Opposition Movements." POMED. https://d1wqtxts1xzle7.cloudfront.net/35163599/POMED_brief.pdf?1413507581=&response-content-disposition=inline%3B+filename%3DCriminalizing_dissent_How_Saudi_Arabia_s.pdf&Expires=1603475114&Signature=KuCR~dQEcQxSL2TN9o290-cma83ljVZjQ-8qualssVkcV1BbJCRuMaIRPLFzzi8QhylBVXIo559HdI9QKq2kwjZTJ09tNc2OPcqzfm6QJRb602xNXAqxN-qbXmVX4muttyEMkb9MNkUSIzg8k2PqLBuWzb526RAtvUOFXqonAkxxYs-BSu95SSgJJhH3SaRak0TDfuI5xnz56e9xHYaXNvRVnpCuvn3hoGvJAPqzgs-50IAYvNtSeSGeq~1TjAyLUMQNZqg2yWYKB7p7-UT5fJnSH2CId8cQbo~J560og7m0NZaLPN9rWejQlIVbnI5cuKGTzGORYhTSWcTCfhMVKA__&Key-Pair-Id=APKAJLOHF5GGSLRBV4ZA.

Bartolucci, Valentina. 2012. "Terrorism Rhetoric under the Bush Administration: Discourses and Effects." *Journal of Language and Politics* 11 (4): 562–582. https://doi.org/10.1075/jlp.11.4.05bar.

Baser, Bahar, Samim Akgönül, and Ahmet Erdi Öztürk. 2017a. "'Academics for Peace' in Turkey: A Case of Criminalising Dissent and Critical Thought via Counterterrorism Policy." *Critical Studies on Terrorism* 10 (2): 274–96. https://doi.org/10.1080/17539153.2017.1326559.

Bassiouni, M. Cherif. 1981. "Terrorism, Law Enforcement, and the Mass Media: Perspectives, Problems, Proposals." *The Journal of Criminal Law and Criminology* 72 (1): 1–51. https://doi.org/10.2307/1142904.

Boehmer, Elleke. 2005. "Postcolonial Terrorist—The Example of Nelson Mandela." *Parallax* 11 (4): 46–55. https://doi.org/10.1080/13534640500331666.

Bosch, Olivia. 2012. "Critical Information Infrastructure and Cyber-Terrorism." In *Law, Policy, and Technology: Cyberterrorism, Information Warfare, and Internet Immobilization* edited by Pauline C. Reich and Eduardo Gelbstein, 31–40. Hershey, PA: IGI Global.

Boukala, Salomi. 2016. "Rethinking Topos in the Discourse Historical Approach: Endoxon Seeking and Argumentation in Greek Media Discourses on 'Islamist Terrorism.'" *Discourse Studies* 18 (3): 249–68. https://doi.org/10.1177/1461445616634550.

Brownlie, Ian. 2003. *Principles of Public International Law*. Oxford: Oxford University Press.

Burniske, Jessica, Naz Modirzadeh, and Dustin Lewis. 2014. "Counter-Terrorism Laws and Regulations: What Aid Agencies Need to Know." https://odihpn.org/wp-content/uploads/2014/11/NP_79_crc_string_FINAL.pdf.

Chakravartty, Paula, Rachel Kuo, Victoria Grubbs, and Charlton McIlwain. 2018. "#CommunicationSoWhite." *Journal of Communication* 68 (2): 254–66. https://doi.org/10.1093/joc/jqy003.

Chatfield, Akemi Takeoka, Christopher G. Reddick, and Uuf Brajawidagda. 2015. "Tweeting Propaganda, Radicalization and Recruitment: Islamic State Supporters Multi-Sided Twitter Networks." In *Proceedings of the 16th Annual International Conference on Digital Government Research*, 239–249. New York, NY, USA: Association for Computing Machinery. https://doi.org/10.1145/2757401.2757408.

Claridge, David. 1996. "State Terrorism? Applying a Definitional Model." *Terrorism and Political Violence* 8 (3): 47–63. https://doi.org/10.1080/09546559608427363.

Cloud, Dana L. 2004. "'To Veil the Threat of Terror': Afghan Women and the Clash of Civilizations in the Imagery of the U.S. War on Terrorism." *Quarterly Journal of Speech* 90 (3): 285–306. https://doi.org/10.1080/0033563042000270726.

Cram, Ian. 2006. "Regulating the Media: Some Neglected Freedom of Expression Issues in the United Kingdom's Counter-Terrorism Strategy." *Terrorism and Political Violence* 18 (2): 335–55. https://doi.org/10.1080/09546550600570184.

———. 2009. *Terror and the War on Dissent: Freedom of Expression in the Age of Al-Qaeda*. London and New York: Springer Science & Business Media.

Crelinsten, R.D. 2002. "Analysing Terrorism and Counter-Terrorism: A Communication Model." *Terrorism and Political Violence* 14 (2): 77–122. https://doi.org/10.1080/714005618.

Cui, Xi, and Eric Rothenbuhler. 2017. "Communicating Terror: Mediatization and Ritualization." *Television & New Media* 19 (2): 155–62. https://doi.org/10.1177/1527476417715685.

Donohue, Laura. 2007. *Counter-Terrorist Law and Emergency Powers in the United Kingdom, 1922-2000*. Dublin: Irish Academic Press.

Easson, Joseph, and Alex P Schmid. 2013. "250-plus Academic, Governmental and Intergovernmental Definitions of Terrorism." In *The Routledge Handbook of Terrorism Research*, edited by Alex P Schmid, 99–157. Routledge Handbooks. New York: Routledge.

Fahmy, Shahira S. 2019. "The Age of Terrorism Media: The Visual Narratives of the Islamic State Group's Dabiq Magazine." *International Communication Gazette* 82 (3): 260–88. https://doi.org/10.1177/1748048519843412.

Friedlander, Robert A. 1981. "Terrorism and National Liberation Movements: Can Rights Derive from Wrongs." *Case Western Reserve Journal of International Law* 13: 281.

Ganor, Boaz. 2002. "Defining Terrorism: Is One Man's Terrorist Another Man's Freedom Fighter?" *Police Practice and Research* 3 (4): 287–304. https://doi.org/10.1080/1561426022000032060.

Grozdanova, Rumyana. 2014. "'Terrorism'—Too Elusive a Term for an International Legal Definition?" *Netherlands International Law Review* 61 (3): 305–34. https://doi.org/10.1017/S0165070X14001351.

Halberstam, Malvina. 2002. "The Evolution of the United Nations Position on Terrorism: From Exempting National Liberation Movements to Criminalizing Terrorism Wherever and by Whomever Committed." *Columbia Journal of Transnational Law* 41 (3): 573–584.

Hallahan, Kirk, Derina Holtzhausen, Betteke van Ruler, Dejan Verčič, and Krishnamurthy Sriramesh. 2007. "Defining Strategic Communication." *International Journal of Strategic Communication* 1 (1): 3–35. https://doi.org/10.1080/15531180701285244.

Head, Michael. 2002. "Counter-Terrorism Laws: A Threat to Political Freedom, Civil Liberties and Constitutional Rights." *Melbourne University Law Review* 26: 666.

Human Rights Council. 2019. "Report of the Special Rapporteur on the Promotion and Protection of Human Rights and Fundamental Freedoms while Countering Terrorism on the Role of Measures to Address Terrorism and Violent Extremism on Closing Civic Space and Violating the Rights of Civil Society Actors and Human Rights Defenders." A/HRC/40/52. United Nations. https://www.ohchr.org/Documents/Issues/Terrorism/SR/A_HRC_40_52_EN.pdf.

Jackson, Richard. 2005. "Security, Democracy, and the Rhetoric of Counter-Terrorism." *Democracy and Security* 1 (2): 147–71. https://doi.org/10.1080/17419160500322517.

Jackson, Richard, Eamon Murphy, and Scott Poynting, eds. 2010. *Contemporary State Terrorism: Theory and Practice*. London and New York: Routledge.

Jackson, Richard, Marie Breen Smyth, and Jeroen Gunning, eds. 2009. *Critical Terrorism Studies: A New Research Agenda*. Routledge.

Kellner, Douglas. 2015. *Media Spectacle and the Crisis of Democracy: Terrorism, War, and Election Battles*. Routledge.

Kelsey, Darren. 2015. *Media, Myth and Terrorism: A Discourse-Mythological Analysis of the 'Blitz Spirit' in British Newspaper Responses to the July 7th Bombings*. London: Palgrave Macmillan.

Kibret, Zelalem. 2017. "The Terrorism of 'Counterterrorism': The Use and Abuse of Anti-Terrorism Law, The Case of Ethiopia." *European Scientific Journal* 13 (13): 1857–7881. https://doi.org/10.19044/esj.2017.v13n13p504.

Kielsgard, Mark D. 2005. "A Human Rights Approach to Counter-Terrorism." *California Western International Law Journal* 36: 249.

Law, Randall D. 2009. *Terrorism: A History*. Cambridge, UK/Maldon, MA: Polity.

Livingston, Steven. 2019. *The Terrorism Spectacle*. New York: Routledge.

Mayali, Laurent, and John Yoo. 2016. "A Comparative Examination of Counter-Terrorism Law and Policy Special Articles: SNU-JPRI-Berkeley." *Journal of Korean Law* 16 (1): 93–146.

Meleagrou-Hitchens, Alexander, Audrey Alexander, and Nick Kaderbhai. 2017. "The Impact of Digital Communications Technology on Radicalization and Recruitment." *International Affairs* 93 (5): 1233–1249. https://doi.org/10.1093/ia/iix103.

Michaelsen, Christopher. 2006. "Balancing Civil Liberties against National Security—A Critique of Counterterrorism Rhetoric." *University of New South Wales Law Journal* 29: 1.

Murray, Daragh. 2009. "Freedom of Expression, Counter-Terrorism and the Internet in Light of the UK Terrorist Act 2006 and the Jurisprudence of the European Court of Human Rights." *Netherlands Quarterly of Human Rights* 27 (3): 331–60. https://doi.org/10.1177/016934410902700302.

Neal, Andrew W. 2012. "Normalization and Legislative Exceptionalism: Counterterrorist Lawmaking and the Changing Times of Security Emergencies." *International Political Sociology* 6 (3): 260–276. https://doi.org/10.1111/j.1749-5687.2012.00163.x.

Negroponte, Nicholas. 1996. *Being Digital*. New York: Vintage Books.

Neocleous, Mark. 2007. "Security, Liberty and the Myth of Balance: Towards a Critique of Security Politics." *Contemporary Political Theory* 6 (2): 131–49. https://doi.org/10.1057/palgrave.cpt.9300301.

Ng, Eve, Khadijah Costley White, and Anamik Saha. 2020. "#CommunicationSoWhite: Race and Power in the Academy and Beyond." *Communication, Culture and Critique* 13 (2): 143–51. https://doi.org/10.1093/ccc/tcaa011.

Parker, David, Julia M. Pearce, Lasse Lindekilde, and M. Brooke Rogers. 2019. "Challenges for Effective Counterterrorism Communication: Practitioner Insights and Policy Implications for Preventing Radicalization, Disrupting Attack Planning, and Mitigating Terrorist Attacks." *Studies in Conflict & Terrorism* 42 (3): 264–91. https://doi.org/10.1080/1057610X.2017.1373427.

Podesta, John. 2002. "USA Patriot Act: The Good, the Bad, and the Sunset." *Human Rights* 29 (1): 3–7.

Połońska-Kimunguyi, Eva, and Marie Gillespie. 2016. "Terrorism Discourse on French International Broadcasting: France 24 and the Case of Charlie Hebdo Attacks in Paris." *European Journal of Communication* 31 (5): 568–83. https://doi.org/10.1177/0267323116669453.

Powers, Shawn Mathew. 2014. "Conceptualizing Radicalization in a Market for Loyalties." *Media, War & Conflict* 7 (2): 233–49. https://doi.org/10.1177/1750635214538620.

Ramraj, Victor V., Michael Hor, and Kent Roach, eds. 2005. *Global Anti-Terrorism Law and Policy*. Cambridge: Cambridge University Press.

Rees, Wyn, and Richard J. Aldrich. 2005. "Contending Cultures of Counterterrorism: Transatlantic Divergence or Convergence?" *International Affairs* 81 (5): 905–23. https://doi.org/10.1111/j.1468-2346.2005.00494.x.

Roach, Kent. 2015. "Comparative Counter-Terrorism Law Comes of Age." In *Comparative Counter-Terrorism Law*, edited by Kent Roach, 1–48. Cambridge: Cambridge University.

Rothenberger, Liane. 2017. "A Terrorist Group's Strategic Communication—The Case of the Red Army Faction." *International Journal of Strategic Communication* 11 (4): 286–305. https://doi.org/10.1080/1553118X.2017.1339191.

Schmid, Alex P. 2013a. "Introduction." In *The Routledge Handbook of Terrorism Research*, edited by Alex P Schmid, 1–37. Routledge Handbooks. Routledge.

———, ed. 2013b. *The Routledge Handbook of Terrorism Research*. New York: Routledge.

Schneiderman, David, and Brenda Cossman. 2016. "Political Association and the Anti-Terrorism Bill." In *The Security of Freedom*, edited by Ronald Daniels, Patrick Macklem, and Kent Roach, 173–94. Toronto: University of Toronto Press.

Setty, Sudha N. 2015. "The United States." In *Comparative Counter-Terrorism Law*, edited by Kent Roach, 49–77. Cambridge: Cambridge University Press.

Shaw, Ibrahim Seaga. 2012. "Stereotypical Representations of Muslims and Islam Following the 7/7 London Terror Attacks: Implications for Intercultural Communication and Terrorism Prevention." *International Communication Gazette* 74 (6): 509–24.

Solaroli, Marco. 2011. "Mediatized Conflicts, Performative Photographs and Contested Memory: The Abu Ghraib Scandal and the Iconic Struggle over the Meanings of the 'War on Terror.'" *Global Media and Communication* 7 (3): 245–50. https://doi.org/10.1177/1742766511427497.

Spencer, Alexander. 2010. "Constructivist Terrorism Research: The Role of Discourse and Predication." In *The Tabloid Terrorist: The Predicative Construction of New Terrorism in the Media*, edited by Alexander Spencer, 71–92. London: Palgrave Macmillan UK.

Stohl, Michael. 1988. *The Politics of Terrorism*, 3rd ed. New York: Marcel Dekker, Inc.

Tuman, Joseph S. 2009. *Communicating Terror: The Rhetorical Dimensions of Terrorism*. Los Angeles/London/New Delhi/Singapore/Washington DC: SAGE Publications.

United Nations General Assembly. 2015. "Plan of Action to Prevent Violent Extremism." United Nations. https://www.un.org/en/ga/search/view_doc.asp?symbol=A/70/674.

United Nations Office of Counter-terrorism. n.d. "Strategic Communication." Accessed October 7, 2020. https://www.un.org/counterterrorism/cct/strategic-communication.

United States Department of Defense. 2016. "Department of Defense Dictionary of Military and Associated Terms." https://fas.org/irp/doddir/dod/jp1_02.pdf.

United States Department of State. 2019. "Country Reports on Terrorism 2019." https://www.state.gov/wp-content/uploads/2020/06/Country-Reports-on-Terrorism-2019-2.pdf.

Van Munster, Rens. 2004. "The War on Terrorism: When the Exception Becomes the Rule." *International Journal for the Semiotics of Law* 17 (2): 141–53. https://doi.org/10.1023/B:SELA.0000033618.13410.02.

Waisbord, Silvio. 2019. *Communication: A Post-Discipline*. Cambridge: Polity.

Wasserman, Herman. 2020. "Moving from Diversity to Transformation in Communication Scholarship." *Annals of the International Communication Association* 44 (1): 1–3. https://doi.org/10.1080/23808985.2019.1706429.

Weimann, Gabriel. 2015. *Terrorism in Cyberspace: The Next Generation*. New York: Columbia University Press.

White House. 2018. "National Strategy for Counterterrorism of the United States of America." https://www.whitehouse.gov/wp-content/uploads/2018/10/NSCT.pdf.

Whittaker, David J. 2014. *Counter-terrorism and Human Rights.* London and New York: Routledge.

Workneh, Téwodros. 2019. "Counter-terrorism in Ethiopia: Manufacturing Insecurity, Monopolizing Speech." *Internet Policy Review* 8 (1). https://doi.org/10.14763/2019.1.1394.

Young, Reuven. 2006. "Defining Terrorism: The Evolution of Terrorism as a Legal Concept in International Law and Its Influence on Definitions in Domestic Legislation." *Boston College International and Comparative Law Review* 29: 23.

PART II

THE POLITICS AND DISCOURSE OF COUNTER-TERRORISM LAWS

Chapter 2

Schizorevolutions versus Microfascisms

The Fear of Anarchy in State Securitization

Athina Karatzogianni and Andrew Robinson

INTRODUCTION

This chapter investigates the role of "anarchy" in state securitization. First, we discuss state hierarchies' struggle with active and reactive anarchic networks, theorizing a state in existential crisis, which exploits anti-anarchist discourses to respond to network threats. In the second part, we illustrate with examples the use of fear of anarchy in hierarchical productive structures of securitization. As an "antiproduction assemblage," the state treats logics stemming from the "social principle" as a repressed Real, the exclusion of which underpins its own functioning. The scarcity and fear resulting from state terror ensure responses to this structural violence by reactive networks, while paradoxically also exacerbating reactive tendencies within social movements while having devastating effects on communication resources and freedom of expression. In the concluding part, we discuss visions of desecuritizing society, breaking away from majoritarian logics of control, and the coming of other worlds counterposed to the hierarchies producing and reproducing an eternal loop of state and network terror.

Contrary to the traditional international relations (IR) argument that there is "anarchy" in the international system, meaning that is there is no hierarchically superior, coercive power that can resolve disputes, enforce law, or order the system of international politics, the central starting point of this argumentation is that *there is no anarchy in the international system.* The world system is a hierarchical system, not an anarchic system and the fear of "anarchy" itself is used as a red herring by states, in the context of the antagonism between statist, hierarchical structures versus network social logics (both active and reactive). We suggest that the network form and "social principle" in Kropotkin's (1897) sense translate to statist thought as anarchy in the Hobbesian sense. The conceptualization of states as necessarily protective and industry promoting is a viewpoint untenable from a bottom-up point of view, yet pointing to the necessity of the state's integrative function for capitalism as an axiomatic system. This role is not productive but rather consists in separating active force from what it can do, to capture it for exploitation. As an "antiproduction assemblage," the state treats logics stemming from the "social principle" as a repressed Real, the exclusion of which underpins its own functioning.

Applying this analysis to the present day, we analyze the securitization discourse of "new threats" as a statist response to the uncertainty and fear brought on by the proliferation of opposing network forms of organization. This response is a statist form of terror attempting to fix network flows in place. The scarcity arising from capitalist/statist resource grabs and fear resulting from state terror ensure responses to this structural violence by reactive networks, while paradoxically also exacerbating reactive tendencies within social movements, creating a spiral of terror, and the very situation of global civil war which Hobbesian/Realist IR theory—reliant on the schema of states struggling for power in an anarchic international system—attempts to ward off.

Furthermore, this argumentation is based on a distinction between states and network movements, on one hand, and between two types of network, on the other. Elsewhere, we have conceptually divided networks into the affinity-active network form and the reactive network form (Karatzogianni and Robinson 2010). These derive from the distinctions between active (or schizoid) and reactive (or paranoiac) forces or desires in a Deleuze/Nietzsche synthetical theory (Karatzogianni and Robinson 2010). Reactive forces are associated with the closure of meaning and identity. Active desire subordinates social production to desiring production. Active forces are associated with difference and transformation: "only active force asserts itself, it affirms its difference and makes its difference an object of affirmation" (Deleuze 2006, 55–56). Active forces are connected to affirmative desire and reactive forces to nihilistic desire; affirmation and negation are "becoming-active" and "becoming-reactive," respectively (Deleuze 2006, 54). For Deleuze (2006), active forces are primary, as without them reactive forces could not be forces (2006, 41). Reactive force can dominate active force, but not by becoming active—rather, by alienating and disempowering it (Deleuze 2006, 57).

While open space is a necessary and enabling good from the standpoint of active desire, it is perceived as a threat by the state, because it is a space in which demonized others can gather and recompose networks outside state control. Hence, for the threatened state, open space is space for the enemy.

It is a space of risk, which needs to be mitigated. Given that open space is necessary for difference to function, since otherwise it is excluded as unrepresentable or excessive, the attempts to render all space closed and governable involve a constant war on difference, which expands into the fabric of everyday life. Horizontal networks flow around the state's restrictions, moving into residual unregulated spaces, gaps in the state's capacity to repress, across national borders, or into the virtual. Networks tend to take a reactive form when exposed to a hostile context. Similarly, Bourdieu (1998) argues that neoliberalism strengthens reactive networks by demoralizing and producing emotional turmoil (1998, 100), while Bauman (2000) links paranoiac social forces to insecurity. Baudrillard (2010) argues in *The Agony of Power* that every extension of hegemony is also an extension of terror: "Terror is multiplied by the grotesque profusion of security measures that end up causing perverse autoimmune effects: the antibodies turn against the body and cause more damage than the virus" (94).

Within this context, our discussion focuses on unraveling the interplay between security/insecurity, active/reactive, schizorevolutionary/microfascist, and autonomous desire/fear management in contemporary agency, state (in)security, and resistance movements. The key point is that reactive microfascist (in)security fear management discourses represent a distinct standpoint of the state, and *not* an orientation to protecting civilians or non-state actors. It represents an attempt by the state, to seize control of society, so as to operate social relations according to its own guiding principles. It is thus fundamentally against the interests of non-state social groups and networks. Or as Reid explains, "Deleuze does not simply mean that nomads employed warfare against the actual existing states they encountered but that they used war as a means to fend off the emergence of a state apparatus within their own societies" (Reid 2003, 63). Here, the difference is between forms of war that are codified by the state and "absolute war" defying state codification (Reid 2003, 74). The following section theorizes the state in existential crises to set up the fear of anarchy in securitization critique.

THE STATE IN EXISTENTIAL CRISIS

The statist idea of "anarchy," as seen in Hobbes (1996 [1651]), is actually a misperception of the affirmative power, the "power-to," of social networks and social movements. The state misperceives insecurity and disorder whenever its own perceptions do not yield an appearance of order. As Bergson (1998) argues, disorder is a false concept. It is a false perception arising from the recognition of a type of existence undesirable to or incompatible with one's own interests or needs. Disorder, therefore, is simply undesired order, from a certain point of view. Reality can be defined as disorderly relative to a particular project or set of practical needs. If disorder is relative to a point of view, then the point of view used in statist definitions is the state's own. The state perceives chaos or (bad) anarchy, not because there is no order, but because this order is incompatible with the state's own existence. For instance, Singer (1971, 232) describes "anarchy" in the statist sense as "one of the most fashionable words of our time," trotted out whenever those in power feel challenged. What was seen as anarchy in France in 1968, in Russia in 1917 and in many other situations is really a question of dual power (Singer 1971, 233–234). Dual power is parallel power—or power of non-state forces—brought to crisis point. It is a necessary part of social transformation. The effect of refusing to recognize dual power is the dehumanization of adversaries.

The state goes back 5000 years, and features of its basic logic have persisted from its earliest form to the present (Dean and Massumi 1992). Deleuze and Guattari (1987) theorize the state primarily as a repressive, "antiproductive" force. The state seeks to regulate speed, erecting barriers in the way of migratory packs (Deleuze and Guattari 1987, 386). It fragments the "parts" from each other to create a formal and empty unity (Deleuze and Guattari 1983, 212). Hence, the state is a machine for overdetermining, blocking, and subjugating social relations through violence (Deleuze and Guattari 1996, 254–255). State violence is "a violence that posits itself as pre-accomplished, even though it is reactivated every day" (Deleuze and Guattari 1987, 447). "The State machine and the machine of repression produce antiproduction, that is to say signifiers that exist to block and prevent the emergence of any subjective process on the part of the group" (Guattari 1984, 34). In addition to its own parts such as bureaucracies, it reintegrates the existing social segments as "organs of production" (Deleuze and Guattari 1983, 198), appropriating reality into its own system (1983, 210). Hence, the state does not originate but captures social flows and assemblages, decomposing their horizontal connections along the way. Societies, like people, end up torn between the two poles of active and reactive—the deterritorializing flows and the Urstaat (Deleuze and Guattari 1983, 260). These poles parallel what elsewhere are portrayed as the two poles of desire, the schizorevolutionary, and microfascist, or active and reactive poles.

This decompositive view of the state is shared by insurrectionist and autonomist authors. For instance, Gilles Dauvé (2000) argues that

> the substance of the state resides not in institutional forms, but in its unifying function. The state ensures the tie which human beings cannot and dare not create among themselves, and creates a web of services both parasitic and real. (28)

The irony of a British law which defines gathering together in a public place as "anti-social behavior," whereby the state poses as the source of society and guarantor against the "anti-social," when in fact it pursues and flourishes in the destruction of the social, demanding personal direct submission without intermediaries. The state is thus a source of constant social conflict, but blames this conflict on others: people engage in various activities without the state's permission, the state intervenes and then blames the people for the resultant fight (Ward 1982, 137). In Hardt and Negri's (2004) terms, "Modern sovereignty . . . does not put an end to violence and fear, but rather puts an end to civil war by organizing violence and fear into a coherent and stable political order" (239). Think of Prime Minister Theresa May's rhetoric after the London Bridge attacks and thirty-six hours before the polls opened before June 8, 2017, General Elections in the United Kingdom:

> And I mean doing more to restrict the freedom and the movements of terrorist suspects when we have enough evidence to know they present a threat, but not enough evidence to prosecute them in full in court. And if human rights laws stop us from doing it, we will change those laws so we can do it. (Mason and Dodd, 2017)

A similar theory of the state as viewing social life as risk can be found in Virilio. For him, the military class struggles against the "badly-defined collection of freedoms, risks and uncertainties" of spontaneity in an environment (Virilio 1990, 14), seeking to eliminate chance and contingency from social relations (1990, 18–19). War is the origin of totalitarianism because it has become an attempt to deny others' dialogue, the chance to rework perspectives, instead seeking to control the adversary by redefining their space (Virilio 1990, 17). In Virilio's (1990, 73) terms, the role of security discourse is to suppress the distinctness of civilian society and place it under military command. Today's warfare is "logistical." It does not simply fight an enemy on an existing terrain but seeks to rearrange space so as to prevent the enemy from acting (Virilio 1986 [1977], 117–118, 145). Applied against the military's own society, this leads to "endocolonialism," or the internalization of colonial power. Virilio (2000 [1998], 14) portrays everyday life as colonized or polluted by military ways of seeing, expressed through technologies such as surveillance cameras and disconnected images. Security scares become a kind of "orgy" allowing the release of otherwise repressed emotions (Virilio 1990, 68–69).

ANARCHY AND STATE SECURITIZATION

The state seeks to make societies "legible" (Scott 1999, 2). In doing so, it simplifies them both analytically, by ignoring the complexity, and materially, by imposing the categories it uses to simplify in practice (Scott 1999, 33, 81–82). Such simplifications

> represent techniques for grasping a large and complex reality; in order for officials to be able to comprehend aspects of the ensemble, that complex reality must be reduced to schematic categories. The only way to accomplish this is to reduce an infinite array of detail to a set of categories that will facilitate summary descriptions, comparisons, and aggregation. (Scott 1999, 77)

States, argues Scott, seek to turn "the population, space, and nature under their jurisdiction into the closed systems that offer no surprises and that can best be observed and controlled" (Scott 1999, 82). This is the matrix from which securitization emerges. It is arguably a re-emergence of the "reasons of state" studied by Foucault (2004) and Scott (1999).

Furthermore, Scott argues that such practices serve state, not social, interests. States simplify to serve state—not social—functions. This is similar to Foucault's (1984) argument that biopower seeks to render bodies useful for power (1984, 269). For example, the state seeks simplification so it can tax and conscript, and to head off rebellion (Foucault 1984, 2). The state lens brings into focus "certain limited aspects" of society that happen to interest the state (Foucault 1984, 11). State simplification is "necessarily schematic" and thus "ignores essential features of any real, functioning social order" (Foucault 1984, 6). The formal scheme ends up parasitic on everyday life to sustain it. Illegibility is relative to the state perspective. What seems illegible to the state is often entirely legible to locals within the context. For example, a complex set of customs of land ownership, redistribution, and mutual obligation effectively meets peasants' needs but is utterly incomprehensible to state lawmakers. Plasticity and adaptability are advantages for peasants, but problems for the state (Foucault 1984, 33–34).

Securitization is the pretext *par excellence* for both kinds of simplification. Practices such as lockdowns and roundups ignore, violate, and overwrite the density of the social spaces on which they are imposed and the needs and desires of those who inhabit these spaces. Risk management, for instance, simplifies complex lives into risk profiles based on aggregates, which might be irrelevant to the case at hand. This is the source of the recurring scandals of civilians being raided, searched, or interrogated based on random algorithmic data calculations (for a critique on digitization and social justice data activism, see Eubanks 2011, for securitization, digital activism debates, see Karatzogianni and Gak 2015; Karatzogianni and Robinson 2014).

State simplification renders swathes of social life as a Lacanian Real. In each case, "a whole world lying 'outside the brackets' returned to haunt [the] technical vision" (Scott 1999, 20), many of which are consequences of the state's tunnel-vision (Scott 1999, 21). In the case of securitization, this returning Real appears as the uncontrollable "black holes" and spiraling insecurity of the current period, as well as the failure of state initiatives such as the Iraq war. In the war on terror, "black holes," or illegibility, are seen as risk or insecurity (Innes 2008), zones of potential terrorism, crime, drug trafficking, human rights abuses (such as *female genital mutilation* (FGM)), and so on. As this assumption renders social life illegible, it leads to a cascading retreat into gated spaces. At root in this process of state terror is the pernicious fantasy of an entirely legible social order, fitting exactly with the state's perceptions—in other words, the denial of all autonomy to social forces. Legible, "securitized" space is fantasmatically "terrorist-free."

Securitization also goes hand-in-hand with insecuritization, or the creation of everyday fear to provide pretexts for control (Bigo 2000, 330). Securitization involves framing-out any claims, demands, rights or needs, which might be articulated by non-state actors. Such actors are simply disempowered, and either suppressed and "managed" or paternalistically "protected." Securitization tends to seek to control others by reducing or constraining their agency (e.g., situational crime management, which removes opportunities for crime), without engaging with others as actors in their own rights. The frame is fundamentally monological, recognizing no actors other than a managerial elite.

Securitization does not represent a response to an increase in existential threats to the state. Rather, it is a discursive shift toward framing all social problems and differences as "security" issues or "risks" that has created an illusion of expanding dangers. American unipolar dominance has led to shifts toward asymmetrical and unconventional warfare (Freedman 1998, 15; Kilcullen 2009, 25–26). The discourse of "new threats" frames issues such as armed opposition or "terrorism," organized crime, arms proliferation, and environmental problems as security issues (Gasteyger 1999, 77). As a result, the field of security studies "risks losing all focus" (Freedman 1998, 53). Securitization creates a field where certain social actors can expand their roles. It merges and de-differentiates militarism against external enemies and internal social regulation (Bigo 2000, 320). The resultant military functions may be carried out by the military, the police, or other social agencies, which are handed securitized tasks (e.g., teachers, doctors, and social workers commanded to implement prevent duties).

The expanded scope of the term "security" has irritated traditional security scholars, who see such issues as relatively insignificant compared to interstate rivalry (Mueller 2004, 110; Todd 2004) or even as pretexts for interstate hegemony (Mastanduno 2007). Furthermore, many of these "new" issues are not "new" at all (protest, armed rebellion, organized crime, and environmental damage have histories longer than capitalism), but newly securitized, sometimes connected to increased scope or internationalization. Securitization is primarily a framing issue—a question of the understanding of and appropriate response to social problems, and the capture of resources among different state agencies. Securitization effectively places the entire field of illegibility under the remit of the military/police apparatuses. On a global scale, failed states are seen as a threat to the United States or even as "engulf[ing] the rest of the world" (Eizenstat, Porter, and Weinstein 2005, 135). The approach typically blames local societies or states for "failure," ignoring the political-economic context (Jackson 2000, 296; Zartman 1995, 5) and replacing international dependency issues with internal capacity issues (Hill 2005, 149). Furthermore, it has been alleged that the category is unclear and selectively deployed (Boas and Jennings 2007, 478).

In this sense, Virilio (2012), the revelationary, in *The Administration of Fear*, talk of fear as a world and the management and administration of fear instead of confronting fear fundamentally:

> Fear is now an environment, a surrounding, a world. It occupies and preoccupies us. Fear was once a phenomenon related to localised, identifiable events that were limited to a certain timeframe: wars, famines, epidemics. Today, the world itself is limited, saturated, reduced, restricting us to stressful claustrophobia: contagious stock crises, faceless terrorism lightning pandemics, "professional" suicides. . . . Fear is a world, *panic* as a "whole." (14)

Framing social problems as "new threats" leads to militarized responses to social problems. The blurring of boundaries between state security and social problems leads to a zone of indistinction (Agamben 1998) in which anyone can become the enemy, the exceptions applying in wartime or colonies are applied across the state's terrain, and any area can become like a camp at any moment (Agamben 1998, 112). Lundborg (2016) explains Agamben's concept of the virtual—how life is potentially expendable and how this is to be resisted with the refusal to draw lines: "the lines that determine who is included and excluded through the actualization of the sovereign ban" (2016, 265). For example, the securitization of migration detracts from humanitarian and political-economic frames, drawing Agamben's lines, and leading to violent, repressive responses (Bigo 2000; Buonfino 2004), as is currently evident in the French state's responses to the jungle in Calais. Abolished in late 2016, it has been a battleground between active and reactive networks: local anti-refugee and pro-refugee protests have occurred reflecting the standoff between opposing actors in the European refugee and migrant crisis.

Zygmunt Bauman's (2000) analysis of the relationship between securitization and consumerism neatly summarizes our analysis here. In Bauman's (2000) argument, communities gate themselves off in a residue of an old utopia of a good society, which is without worry because of its basic sameness (92). Such a community is defined by what it excludes rather than what it contains and becomes "more secure but less free" (Bauman 2000, 94). What it refuses, in particular, is any kind of dialogue or negotiation across difference, and therefore any public interest or public sphere arising from negotiation (Bauman 2000, 100). This vision of community destroys any possibility of life in common. The more difference is excluded, the more threatening it looks (Bauman 2000, 106). Spaces that remain are marked by the "redundancy of interaction" to their functioning (Bauman 2000, 105). Bauman (2000) analyzes securitization as flight from contact with difference (105), rooted in neoliberal regimes of fluidity and uncertainty (2000, 108). Evans (2010) ups the ante by arguing that a new virtual economy of effect is at work in combination with a preemptive virtualization of terror "in which the self-propelling tendencies to provoke the virtual cause, will, through revealing its most catastrophic potential, set out the new conditions of the real" (2010, 9).

STATE TERROR PRODUCES NETWORK TERROR

At the intersection of the threatened state and the sources of its anxiety lies the collapse of marginal integration and "addition of axioms" in neoliberalism. Capitalism has been clenching its fists on the world for some time, yet many spaces and people are falling through its fingers. The formal sector of the economy is shrinking, leaving behind it swathes of social life marginalized from capitalist inclusion. Much of the global periphery is in effect being forcibly "delinked" from the world economy as inclusion through patronage is scaled down due to neoliberalism. For instance, "Sub-Saharan Africa has almost dropped out of the formal international economy" (Mann 2005, 55–56). Religious, militia, and informal economic organizations have replaced the state on the ground across swathes of Africa, and "whole regions have now become virtually independent, probably for the foreseeable future, of all central control" (Bayart et al. 1999, 19–20). These spaces are the locus of the state's fear of "black holes," where state power breaks down and insurgents can flourish (Innes 2008; Korteweg, 2008).

Viewed in affirmative terms, these excluded sites and people are associated with the network form. The past few decades have seen a proliferation of network-based movements—some emancipatory, others less so—drawing their membership from marginalized groups and creating autonomous zones in marginal spaces. In the South, such movements often grow out of the everyday networks of survival, which "provide an infrastructure for the community and a measure of functional autonomy" (Chatterjee 1993; Hecht and Simone 1994, 14–15; Lomnitz 1977). The discontented and excluded lie at the heart of today's asymmetrical wars. For instance, the Pakistani Taleban flourishes mainly among young people who do not receive "peace, income, a sense of purpose, a social network" from the established structure of tribal power (Giustozzi 2007, 39), while Watts (2007) has referred to what is known locally as the "restive youth problem" as central to the conflict in the Niger Delta.

Ignoring for the moment the distinctions among such movements, their vitality can clearly be traced to their networked and marginal loci. Resisting or eluding the terror state's grab for space, horizontal networks flow around the state's restrictions, moving into residual unregulated spaces, gaps in the state's capacity to repress, across national borders, or into the virtual. Repression drives dissent from open to clandestine forms, creating a field of diffuse resistance and deviance, which "returns" as intractable social problems and inert effects. Those with no place in social life, such as inner-city children, wage "jungle warfare" against the constraints of dominant discourse (Ward 1990 [1978], 89–90).

In a context where the state treats civilians (and especially marginal groups) as disposable, the formation of reactive networks offering security (economic security, fixed identities, military retaliation against dominant groups) is almost inevitable. If the marginal groups are treated as disposable, if the state threatens them and the social mainstream rallies to the state, then the marginal will look for human security to armed opposition groups, gangs, and reactive networks of all kinds. The state's misframing of its enemies as savage, absolute others and the corresponding, inverted form of this misframing aimed at the dominant group reinforce each other in a cycle of escalation. Actors joining ethnoreligious armed groups are often from the restive youth stratum who are left out of both the modern economy and the remnants of the traditional system. Reactive networks offer a mixture of wealth (from payments and opportunities for loot), power, identity (masculine and ethnoreligious), self-esteem, and something to believe in.

Within the system, reactive desire is the fear arising from state terror and it becomes fear of losing subsistence, if one is poor or losing property, and status if one is less poor, and outside it becomes fear of state repression and violence (McMarvill and los Ricos n.d., 15). The emotional effects of state terror on movements can be discussed in terms of the effects of experiences of oppression. In the work of David Matza (1964), for instance, everyday humiliation and indignity produce "moods of fatalism," which suspend constraints on action along with the sense of being a human agent. Material scarcity arising from capitalist/statist resource grabs can reinforce tendencies for networks to become reactive. With conditions of life put at risk, irrational mass attachments resurface, channeling in a distorted way the new class contradiction between included and excluded.

Reactive desire can take three different forms: as external blockage of active desire, as internal "repression" in the psychoanalytic sense and as desire itself when disempowered by repression (Deleuze 2006, 61). If movements respond to state terror by internalizing its effects, internalizing scarcity as an existential condition and fear as emotional, sexual, and bodily rigidity, they reproduce the affective form of state power, even while adopting the network form in their social interrelations. With reactive desire operating inside emergent networks, a split appears between affinity networks based on active desire and reactive networks, which give a central place to reactive desire. Affinity networks create and are sustained by what Sahlins terms "primitive affluence," a type of existential abundance. This way of experiencing the world is difficult to sustain amid state terror. However, there are different ways of responding to state-induced anxiety. The compositive energies of affinity are present in both types of networks. In internal structure, reactive groups rely on active energies and affinity. Hence, Marc Sageman's (2004) account of Wahhabi groups emphasizes the emotional force of the "small-world network" as their integrative force: ties of kinship, friendship, and discipleship create a strong emotional force of cohesion (2004, 107, 138). However, reactive networks also internalize statist–majoritarian conceptions of self. Reactive networks seek to psychologically recompose the self, acting-out violence against outsiders for the purpose of internal composition of the self and in-group (Theweleit 1987). They are defined by a refusal to identify with their actual life condition as minoritarian, networked, excluded, or marginal people. Instead, they hide behind a myth of belonging to a superior in-group, which should become the new master.

The passage from state terror to reactive network terror occurs through the graded stratifications, whereby majoritarian categories enter everyday life (Wallerstein 2004: 37–39). These stratifications, constructed around marked and unmarked terms, discursive exclusions and hierarchies, are products of the field of "ideology" or "fantasy" surrounding the state. Status groups, or "neoarchaisms" as Deleuze and Guattari (1983, 257–258) call them, occur at the intersection of states and networks and can attract either emancipatory or reactive forces. For instance, Pieterse (1998) argues that rigid ethnic identities arise from authoritarian institutions and political cultures and are an effect rather than a cause of conflicts based on "the politics of hard sovereignty." Outside such contexts, communities are neither denumerable nor exhaustive of identity (Chatterjee 1993, 223).

CONCLUSION: DESECURITIZING SOCIETY

If the security state is able to wrest control from global capital and from active and reactive networks, fascism is the likely outcome. In a new twist on the old Marxist tale of the means of production outstripping the social relations which produce them, capitalism now produces technologies that enable the exercise of diffuse power, at the same time as trying in increasingly paranoid ways to restrict them. The existing technologies vital to contemporary capitalism—such as the Internet, global travel, and financial flows—are already profiled as "risks" in securitization discourse (which in many ways reflects a backlash by the state against the loss of control suffered under 1990s liberalization). New technologies underpinning any economic revival—such as mass-market drones, artificial intelligence, three-dimensional (3D) printing, distributed ledger technologies, biological self-modification—pose even greater "risks" that may prove uncontrollable. If the deep state continues to see security as the bottom line, it may ultimately have to rupture with its global capitalist allies and impose a similar generalized chilling of social life and antiproduction against unregulated flows, including those unleashed by capitalism.

There are several alternatives, all of which require de-securitizing society. First, the system could switch from a subtraction to an addition of axioms approach, using social policy rather than securitization/militarization to respond to "risks." Second, people could seek security in diffuse rather than concentrated power, moving toward smaller-scale, more densely networked patterns of life and work, which reduce both the anxiety underpinning securitization and risks originating from global flows. Third, the securitization system itself is ineffective so new visions developed are needed for creating possibilities for trust building and conflict transformation in the situations of systemically produced scarcity which currently generate "risk." A Clastrean balance of power among diffuse social actors, or a situation of mutual tolerance based on a global ethic of valuing locality and diversity, might succeed in keeping relations among empowered diffuse groups largely peaceful.

On the other side, we should find hope in the proliferation of resistance among the excluded. We need to see in movements of the excluded the radical potential and not only the reactive distortions. To take Tupac Shakur's metaphor, we need to see the rose that grows from concrete, not merely the thorns. The problem is, rather, that many of the movements on the network side of the equation are still thinking, seeing, and feeling like states. Such movements are potential bearers of the other of the state form, of networks as alternatives to states, affinity against hegemony, abundance against scarcity. Hence, as Vaneigem (1967) argues, "[t]o work for delight and authentic festivity is barely distinguishable from preparing for a general insurrection" (1967, 50–51). It has been argued in utopian studies that fear and hope form part of a continuum, expressing "aspects of affective ambivalence" connected to the indeterminacy of the future (McManus, 2005). The type of hope needed is active and immanent, brought into the present as a propulsive force rather than deferred to the future. Deleuze and Guattari use the term "absolute deterritorialization" for this possibility.

In his work on conflict transformation, John Paul Lederach emphasizes the need to turn negative energies into creative energies and mobilizing hope against fear (Lederach, 2005; Lederach and Maiese 2009). How is this change in vital energies to be accomplished? Deleuze and Guattari (1983) invoke a figure of the shaman as a way to overcome reactive energies (1983, 67–68). They call for a type of revolutionary social movement "that follows the lines of escape of desire; breaches the wall and causes flows to move; assembles its machines and its groups-in-fusion in the enclaves or at the periphery," countering reactive energies (Deleuze and Guattari 1983, 277). As Zevnik (2016) discusses, disrupting scopic regimes involves moments of anxiety, where the anxious gaze puts one's identity and one's places in the social fantasy under question (2016, 133). Countering reactive energies while belonging to a hierarchical productive structure involves a dismantlement of the illusion, while "subjectification is never without a black hole in which its lodges its consciousness, passions and redundancies" (Zevnik 2016, 133).

Hence, it is in open spaces, safe spaces, and spaces of dialogue that hope can be found to counter the spiral of terror. This opening of space, this creation of autonomous zones, should be viewed as a break with the majoritarian logics of social control. The coming "other worlds" counterposed to the spaces of terror are not an integrated "new order," but rather a proliferation of smooth spaces in a horizontality without borders. These "other worlds" are being built unconsciously, wherever networks, affinity, and hope counterpose themselves to state terror and the desire for fixed identity be it national, ethnic, religious, or cultural. It is in the incommensurable antagonism between the autonomous zones of these "other worlds" and the terror state's demands for controlled spaces to serve capital that the nexus of the conflicts of the present and near-future lies.

REFERENCES

Agamben, Giorgio. 1998. *Homo Sacer: Sovereign Power and Bare Life* (trans. D Heller-Roazen). Stanford, CA: Stanford University Press.

Baudrillard, Jean. 2010. *The Agony of Power*. (trans. A Hodges). Los Angeles, CA: Semiotext(e).

Bauman, Zygmut. 2000. *Liquid Modernity*. Cambridge: Polity Press.

Bayart, Jean-François, Stephen Ellis, and Béatrice Hibou. 1999. *The Criminalization of the State in Africa*. Oxford: James Currey.

Bergson, Henri. 1998. *Creative Evolution*. New York: Dover Publications.

Bigo, Didier. 2000. "When Two Become One: Internal and External Securitisations in Europe." In *International Relations Theory and the Politics of European Integration: Power, Security and Community*, edited by Morten Kelstrup and Michael Charles Williams, 171–204. London: Routledge.
Boas, Morten, and Kathleen M. Jennings. 2007. "Failed States' and 'State Failure': Threats or Opportunities?" *Globalizations* 4 (4): 475–485.
Bourdieu, Pierre. 1998. *Acts of Resistance: Against the Tyranny of the Market* (trans. R Nice). New York: The New Press.
Buonfino, Allesandra. 2004. "Between Unity and Plurality: The Politicization and Securitization of the Discourse of Immigration in Europe." *New Political Science* 26 (1): 23–49.
Chatterjee, Partha. 1993. *The Nation and Its Fragments*. Princeton, NJ: Princeton University Press.
Dauvé, Gilles. 2000. *When Insurrections Die*. London: Antagonism Press.
Dean, Kenneth and Brian Massumi. 1992. *First and Last Emperors: The Absolute State and the Body of the Despot*. New York: Autonomedia.
Deleuze, Gilles. 2006. *Nietzsche and Philosophy* (trans. H Tomlison). New York: Columbia University Press.
Deleuze, Glles and Felix Guattari. 1983. *Anti-Oedipus*. London: Athlone Press.
———. 1987. *A Thousand Plateaus* (trans. B Massumi). London: Athlone Press.
———. 1996. *What Is Philosophy?* (trans. H Tomlison and G Birchill). New York: Columbia University Press.
Eizenstat, Stuart, John Edward Porter, and Jeremy Weinstein. 2005. "Rebuilding Weak States." *Foreign Affairs* 85 (1): 134–146.
Eubanks, Virginia. 2011. *Digital Dead End: Fighting for Social Justice in the Information Age*. Cambridge, MA: The MIT Press.
Evans, Brad. 2010. "Terror in All Eventuality." *Theory & Event* 13 (3). Available at: https://doi.org/10.1353/tae.2010.0009.
Foucault, Michel. 1984. *The Foucault Reader* (ed. P. Rabinow). New York: Pantheon Books.
———. 2004. *Society Must Be Defended*. Harmondsworth: Penguin Books.
Freedman, Lawrence. 1998. "International Security: Changing Targets." *Foreign Policy* 110: 48–64.
Gasteyger, Curt. 1999. "Old and New Dimensions of International Security." In *Towards the 21st Century: Trends in Post-Cold War International Security Policy*, edited by Kurt R. Spillmann and Andreas Wenger (Volume 4 of Studien zu Zeitgeschichte and Sicherheitspolitik), 69–108. Bern: Peter Lang.
Giustozzi, Antonio. 2007 *Koran, Kalashnikov and Laptop: The Neo-Taliban Insurgency in Afghanistan 2002–2007*. London: C. Hurst & Co.
Guattari, Felix. 1984. *Molecular Revolution: Psychiatry and Politics* (trans. R Sheed). Harmondsworth: Penguin Books.
Hardt, Michael and Antonio Negri. 2004. *Multitude*. New York: Penguin Books.
Hecht, David and Maliqalim Simone. 1994. *Invisible Governance: The Art of African Micropolitics*. New York: Autonomedia.

Hill, Jonathan. 2005. "Beyond the Other? A Postcolonial Critique of the Failed State Thesis." *African Identities* 3 (2): 139–154.
Hobbes, Thomas. 1996 [1651]. *Leviathan*. Cambridge: Cambridge University Press.
Innes, Michael A. 2008. "Protected Status, Sacred Sites, Black Holes and Human Agents: System, Sanctuary and Terrain Complexity." *Civil Wars* 1: 1–5.
Jackson, Robert H. 2000. *The Global Covenant: Human Conduct in a World of States*. Oxford: Oxford University Press.
Karatzogianni, Athina and Martin Gak. 2015. "Hack or be Hacked: The Quasi-totalitarianism of Global Trusted Networks." *New Formations: A Journal of Culture/Theory/Politics* 84–85: 130–147.
Karatzogianni Athina and Andrew Robinson. 2010. *Power, Resistance and Conflict in the Contemporary World*. London; New York: Routledge.
———. 2014. "Digital Prometheus: WikiLeaks, the State–network Dichotomy, and the Antinomies of Academic Reason." *International Journal of Communication* 8: 2704–2717. Available at: http://ijoc.org/index.php/ijoc/issue/view/10#more4.
Kilcullen, David. 2009. *The Accidental Guerrilla*. Oxford: Oxford University Press.
Korteweg, Rem. 2008. "Black Holes: On Terrorist Sanctuaries and Governmental Weakness." *Civil Wars* 1: 60–71.
Kropotkin, Peter. 1897. "The State and Its Historic Role." Accessed December 1, 2020. https://www.panarchy.org/kropotkin/1897.state.html.
Lacan, Jean. 2007. *Ecrits*. New York: W. W. Norton & Company.
Lederach, John Paul. 2005. *The Moral Imagination: The Art and Soul of Building Peace*. Oxford: Oxford University Press.
Lederach, John Paul, and Michelle Maiese. 2009. "A Circular Journey with a Purpose." *New Routes* 14: 7–10.
Lomnitz, Larissa Adler. 1977. *Networks and Marginality: Life in a Mexican Shantytown*. New York: Academic Press.
Lundborg, Tom. 2016. "The Virtualization of Security: Philosophies of Capture and Resistance in Baudrillard, Agamben and Deleuze." *Security Dialogue* 47 (3): 255–270.
McManus, Susan. 2005. *Fictive Theories: Towards a Deconstructive and Utopian Political Imagination*. Basingstoke: Palgrave Macmillan.
McMarvill, Brian and Rob Los Ricos. n.d. "Empire and the End of History." *Green Anarchist* 67: 13–15.
Mann, Michael. 2005. *Incoherent Empire*. London; New York: Verso Books.
Mason, Rowena and Vikram Dodd. 2017. "I'll Rip up Human Rights Laws that Impede New Terror Legislation." *The Guardian*, June 6, 2017. https://www.theguardian.com/politics/2017/jun/06/theresa-may-rip-up-human-rights-laws-impede-new-terror-legislation.
Mastanduno, Michael. 2007. "Preserving the Unipolar Moment: Realist Theories and US Grand Strategy after the Cold War." *International Security* 21 (4): 49–88.
Matza, David. 1964. *Delinquency and Drift*. New York: Wiley.
Mueller, John. 2004. *The Remnants of War*. New York: Cornell University Press.
Negri, Antonio. 1998. "Archaeology and Project: The Mass Worker and the Social Worker." In *Revolution Retrieved: Selected Writings on Marx, Keynes, Capitalist*

Crisis, and New Social Subjects 1967–83, edited by Antonio Negri, 199–228. London: Red Notes.

Pieterse, Jan Nederveen. 1998. "Sociology of Humanitarian Intervention: Bosnia, Rwanda and Somalia Compared." In *World Orders in the Making: Humanitarian Intervention and Beyond*, edited by Jan Nederveen Pieterse, 230–26. Basingstoke: Macmillan Publishers.

Reid, Julian. 2003. "Deleuze's War Machine: Nomadism against the State." *Millennium: Journal of International Studies* 1: 57–85.

Sageman, Marc. 2004. *Understanding Terror Networks*. Philadelphia, PA: University of Pennsylvania Press.

Scott, James. 1999. *Seeing Like a State: How Certain Schemes to Improve the Human Condition Have Failed*. New Haven, CT: Yale University Press.

Singer, Daniel. 1971. *Prelude to Revolution: France in May 1968*. Chicago, IL: Haymarket Books.

Theweleit, Klaus. 1987. *Male Fantasies* (2 volumes). Minneapolis, MN: University of Minnesota Press.

Todd, Emmanuel. 2004. *After the Empire*. Washington, DC: Columbia University Press.

Vaneigem, Raul. 1967. "The Revolution of Everyday Life: Impossible Participation or Power as the Sum of Constraints." Accessed December 2, 2020. http://library.nothingness.org/articles/SI/en/pub_contents/5.

———. 1986 [1977]. *Speed and Politics*. New York: Semiotext(e).

———. 1990. *Popular Defense & Ecological Struggles* (trans. M. Polizzotti). New York: Semiotext(e).

———. 2000 [1998]. *The Information Bomb*. London: Verso Books.

Virilio P (2012) *The Administration of Fear* (trans. A Hodges). Los Angeles, CA: Semiotext(e).

Wallerstein, Immanuel. 2004. *World-Systems Analysis: An Introduction*. Durham, NC: Duke University Press.

Ward, Colin. 1982. *Anarchy in Action*. London: Freedom Press.

———. 1990 [1978]. *The Child in the City*. London: Freedom Press.

Watts, Michael. 2007. "Petro-insurgency or Criminal Syndicate? Conflict & Violence in the Niger Delta. *Review of African Political Economy*." 114: 637–660.

Zartman, William I. 1995. *Collapsed States: The Disintegration and Restoration of Legitimate Authority*. Boulder, CO: Lynne Rienner.

Zevnik, Andreja. 2016. "The Politics of the Face: The Scopic Regime and the (Un-)masking of the Political Subject." *Journal for Cultural Research* 20: 122–136.

Chapter 3

Parliamentary Discussion of Counter-terrorism in Portugal

Discourses on the Right and on the Left

Eunice Castro Seixas

INTRODUCTION

The growing interest in the analysis of terrorism and counter-terrorism from the perspective of discourse is quite evident, especially within critical terrorism studies (de Graaf and de Graaff 2010; Jackson 2015; Smyth, Gunning, Jackson, Kassimeris, and Robinson 2008). However, in the European context, scholarly inquiries have focused mainly on the United States or the European Union (EU) (e.g., Bartolucci 2014; Baker-Beall 2009; Jackson 2005, 2007) while less attention has been paid to the political and parliamentary debates and discourses on this subject in relation to nation-states.[1] However, such analysis is key to understanding the impact of national security cultures vis-à-vis the supranational actors such as the EU or the UN. Securitization, which has been a key aspect of counter-terrorism discourses and policies, is not similar in European and national contexts. This is because, in the case of the former, "the relationship between that discourse and the reception, discussion, legitimization and actualization of policy proposals and changes is less clear" (Neal 2009, 336–337). This makes the links between the securitization entities and the European public much more uncertain than in the case of national contexts. Nevertheless, there are also many parliamentary debates at the national level that do not attract either the media's or the public's attention. Predictably, the issue of terrorism and counter-terrorism tends to attract more media attention when terrorist attacks occur, and not necessarily when important law proposals are discussed in national legislative assemblies.

In the case of Portugal, which, unlike other European countries, has not been a target of international terrorist attacks, important laws and policies related to terrorism have mostly gone unnoticed by the public. This gap warrants a critical analysis of the parliamentary debates on terrorism at the national level. On one hand, the Portuguese case may be particularly interesting to analyze the right-left divide in regard to the issue of terrorism because Portugal already presents low levels of right-left anchoring and polarization (Freire and Belchior 2011). On the other hand, the absence of international terrorist attacks within the national territory of Portugal could have prevented a shift in political attitudes toward the right, as has happened in other countries (e.g., Gries and Yam 2020). It is against this background that I seek to uncover the main discursive constructions of counter-terrorism in Portugal. By adopting a sociopolitical strand of critical discourse analysis (CDA) (see Fairclough 1992), I will demonstrate how members of parliament (MPs) from the right and the left mobilize certain discursive constructions while arguing for or against the enforcement of counter-terrorism laws and strategies. These discursive constructions are analyzed within the context of the terrorist attacks that took place in the United States and Europe in tandem with Portugal's positioning in relation to supranational institutions such as the EU, NATO, and UN as well as big powers involved in the fight against terrorism.

I will start by briefly outlining the major discursive constructions on the subject of terrorism and counter-terrorism since 9/11 to situate the relevance of the Portuguese case for both its specificity and complexity in relation to global trends. I will then present the methodology and the main findings of the current inquiry that focuses on Portugal's parliamentary plenary sessions that addressed the issue of terrorism/counter-terrorism at length. I will conclude by discussing some of the potential implications of these findings for Portugal. In doing so, I will offer some insights based on comparisons with other contexts and propose the furthering of studies that focus on parliamentary discourses on terrorism and counter-terrorism.

DISCOURSES ON TERRORISM AND COUNTER-TERRORISM AFTER 9/11

In the past two decades, both the United States and the EU have become key political actors in the fight against terrorism and in promoting specific discursive constructions on the subject. Identity claims have been central to these discourses, culminating often in Manichean formations of good versus evil and "us" versus "them." Most notably, under the Bush administration in the United States, the issue of terrorism became a top government agenda where it was proclaimed as a threat to civilization, freedom, and democracy (Devetak 2005; Jackson 2005; Rai 2004). Such discourse has been cardinal in legitimizing aggressive and extra-legal counter-terrorist strategies (Jarvis 2009). Specifically, a preemptive war was portrayed as both the right to self-defense and as a kind of crusade to civilize the barbarian other (Jackson 2007; Kellner 2004; Leudar, Marsland, and Nekvapil 2004).

In the aftermath of 9/11, several EU countries have partly distanced themselves from the United States' global "War on Terror," especially concerning the invasion of Iraq. In fact, the EU has remained consistent in constructing terrorism as a criminal phenomenon instead of a war-like aggression, as proposed by the United States (Monar 2015). Nonetheless, in addition to a strong focus on criminalizing terrorism, the EU counter-terrorism strategy also contains a preventive aspect related to "combating radicalization and recruitment into terrorism, empowering mainstream opinion and promoting security, justice and democracy" (Eijkman and Schuurman 2011, 6). This preventive pillar emerged progressively important as, in the aftermath of the terrorist attacks that took place in Europe, the EU also became a securitizing agent, grounded in a discourse that regarded terrorism—and often "the migrant other"—as a threat to the European society (Baker-Beall 2009). Hence, like the United States, some EU countries such as the UK (prior to Brexit) and France incorporated surveillance and control of "the internal other" in the domestic sphere (Amore 2006, 2009; Baker-Beall 2009; Pantazis and Pemberton 2009; Ragazzi 2014). With the "War on Terror," a new "dispositive of precautionary risk" has emerged and brought about "new rationalities of government that require that the catastrophic prospects of the future be tamed and managed" (Aradau and Van Munster 2008, 24). This type of "preemptive security" was based on "a strong urge to criminalize not only those who actually cause harm, but also those merely suspected of being harmful" (Ericson 2008, 57).

Political discourse has been key in legitimizing the deployment of such apparatuses. Political discourse on countering terrorism is nonetheless mediated by ideological positioning, with the left wing traditionally stressing liberty and the inviolability of human rights, and the right wing stressing the need for security. In this regard, achieving the right balance between liberty and security has become an ideological trope and a recurrent rhetorical device in political discussions after 9/11 (Waldron 2003). However, this rhetorical device has been criticized for presupposing a commitment to security rather than a real balance between security and liberty (Bronitt 2008; Eckersley 2007; Freeman 2005; Neocleous 2007; Zedner 2005). It has also served to instigate a "logic of security" that dominates political discourse by delegitimating any political debate on issues construed as matters of security (Neocleous 2007). Within counter-terrorist policies, this logic of security has been linked to the emergence of a center-right political consensus in the UK (Pantazis and Pemberton 2012).

Thus, if some authors suggest that terrorism is, especially since 9/11, among the international issues that have been furthering a left-right polarization (Farneti 2012), other studies propose the opposite: that the advent of terrorist attacks in the United States and in Europe has eliminated differences between the left and right. For example, this scenario was evident in the UK as it pertains to British political discourse in relation to Muslims and Islam (Allen 2010). Also, in France, in the wake of the terrorist attacks that occurred in 2015, human rights tropes traditionally used by the left were re-signified by President François Hollande to justify the new anti-terror policies (Bogain 2017). Similarly, in Canada, a discourse that linked security to freedom enabled and legitimized the emergence of new modalities of governance through security (Bell 2011). Furthermore, some studies have suggested that, ideology is one among several factors explaining why political actors choose specific counter-terrorism policies (Eder, Libiseller, and Schneider 2020)[2] while others noted terrorism attacks can also shape individual-level ideologies (Gries and Yam 2020).

In general, these different findings suggest that the role of ideology and specifically of the right/left divide in the political discourse on the War on Terror is a complex one. It is against this backdrop that the importance of analyzing national discourses on terrorism and counter-terrorism as it relates to the interplay among ideology, national identity, geopolitics, and biopolitics becomes apparent. Such discursive formations not only allow for specific counter-terrorist measures but they also contribute to the constitution of self and others' relationships in the domestic and the international sphere.

THE RELEVANCE OF THE PORTUGUESE CASE

Portugal is considered one of the most peaceful countries of the world, occupying the third place in the 2019 Global Peace Index of (Institute for Economics and Peace 2019) and ranking 138 out of 163 in the 2019 Global Terrorism Index (Institute for Economics and Peace 2019). The fact that Portugal has been spared from international terrorist attacks thus far may lead some to expect less support for strong securitizing policies and a more pronounced left-right divide on the matter. However, recent studies have indicated that Portuguese citizens have low levels of left-right attitude anchoring. This means that the meanings attributed to the left-right divide are not clear or structured. According to Freire and Belchior (2011), among other factors, the low levels of polarization at the party system level and the blurring of ideological boundaries by parties and governments at both aisles of the political spectrum can be relevant in explaining these findings. Freire and Belchior (2011) further note that there are important mismatches between deputies and citizens in terms of the meaning of the "right" and the "left," and in terms of left-right self-placement, especially regarding ideological positioning toward "authoritarian-libertarian" issues. In view of these characteristics, the analysis of the Portuguese case gains relevance in the current international context for its specificity within Europe (as a country that has been spared of terrorist attacks) as well as for its complexity regarding the left-right anchoring placement and the discrepancies between citizens and MPs. The latter issue prompts us to interrogate the reception and understanding of political communication and parliamentary debates by citizens.

It is important to briefly contextualize this study in political and economic terms. Politically, the period of the corpus (from 2001 to 2017) comprises six legislatures and eight constitutional governments, in which the center-left Socialist Party (PS) and the Social Democrats conservative party (PSD) have been alternating in holding power. In 2015, however, a new government took power in Portugal, led by António Costa of the PS. The PS was supported by agreements with three parties on the left: the Portuguese Communist Party (PCP), the Left Block (BE "Bloco de Esquerda"), and the "Os Verdes" ecological party. This leftist coalition was given the nickname of "Geringonça."[3] The present PS government, still led by António Costa, maintains an understanding with the parties of the former "Geringonça," although this cooperation is sustained through non-written agreements. Economically, Portugal has gone through a serious economic crisis, having asked for international assistance from the "Troika"[4] in 2011. This was followed by a period of austerity measures from 2011 until 2014. Since then, the economy has gradually recovered.

During these past decades, the Portuguese parliament has passed important laws and resolutions on counter-terrorism following a progressive political recognition of terrorism as a global threat that can also strike in Portugal. This was acknowledged in 2013 in the National Defense Strategic Concept as well as by the National Strategy to Combat Terrorism (ENCT) in 2015. The ENCT

> undertakes to respect the European Convention on Human Rights and Fundamental Freedoms of the Council of Europe, the originating law of the European Union, the Charter of Fundamental Rights of the European Union, the constitutional principles of the Portuguese State, and is inspired by the United Nations Resolutions and the European Union's counter-terrorism policy. (SGMAI 2015)

Thus, the centrality of the EU for the Portuguese fight against terrorism is quite clear. Indeed, the first paragraph of the ENCT makes an explicit reference to terrorism as "one of the most serious threats to the livelihood of European area of freedom, security and justice and the democratic rule of law." Moreover, the preamble of this strategy gives salience to the transborder cooperation within the EU and the commitments of Portugal in compliance with the Union's anti-terrorism policy. The ENCT itself seems to mimic the four pillars of the EU Counter Terrorism Strategy although it adds a new first pillar—detect—"which is the early identification action of potential terrorist threats, by acquiring the knowledge essential for effective combat."

On a more specific note, the Portuguese strategy also reflects a political will to increase collaboration between the Armed Forces and the Security Forces and Services, and the recognition of the importance of the intelligence in the fight against terrorism (Folgado 2016). Subsequently, a proposal to revise the Framework Law of the Information Services of the Portuguese Republic (SIRP) in 2015 reinforced the will to strengthen the capacities of these services, although that would be rejected by the Constitutional Court. In reality, the issue of intelligence will remain one of the most controversial issues in the parliamentary debate, and a key one for analyzing the right-left divide.

METHODOLOGY

To analyze Portuguese parliamentary debates on terrorism, I relied on the full transcription of the plenary sessions of the Portuguese parliament, which is available in the Diários da Assembleia da República (Diaries of the Assembly of the Republic, hereafter "DAR"), Series I.[5] Specifically, I focused on the plenary sessions where the issue of terrorism and counter-terrorism was discussed at considerable length, starting from the period following September 11, 2001, to the present. The decision of starting the analysis from 9/11 was based on the verification that the issue of terrorism did not appear significantly in the Portuguese parliament before this date.[6] The keyword "terrorism" was used in the search for the diaries, and, subsequently, a selection was made based on the number of times this word appeared in the DAR. Only plenary sessions with ten or more references to "terrorism" were included in the corpus. In total, seventeen plenary sessions were analyzed that dealt with specific debates on terrorism and counter-terrorism. These include three plenary sessions in 2001, two in 2002, four in 2003, three in 2004, one in 2008, two in 2015, and two in 2017.

The transcriptions of the plenary sessions were read repeatedly, and coding was made with the aid of the NVivo 9 software. The analysis sought to uncover the main discursive constructions mobilized by each of the parties during the sessions. Then, these constructions were compared against the right-left political spectrum, as well as throughout the time.

From a sociological approach, discourse analysis requires an understanding of the historical and sociopolitical context in which discourses are embedded. Discourse is understood here as "a practice not just of representing the world, but of signifying the world, constituting, and constructing the world in meaning" (Fairclough 1992, 64). Bell (2011, 17) notes:

> Discourse analysis is not simply concerned with "studying words" or rhetoric (though this may be involved) but also examines representations of the world and how these representations became possible. It asks which sensibilities, under-interrogated beliefs, or claims to history are necessarily invoked to create particular discursive representations.

In deploying CDA, attention is paid not only to the discourses but also to the conditions of the emergence of these constructions within the national and international political context. This specifically includes the role played by the main national as well as supranational actors (EU, NATO, and UN) in the fight against terrorism, and the terrorist attacks in the United States and Europe.

PARLIAMENTARY DEBATES ABOUT TERRORISM IN PORTUGAL (2001–2019)

The first analysis of the corpus reveals that parliamentary interest on the issue of terrorism does not always follow the time sequence of the main terrorist attacks in Europe; neither does the parliamentary agenda pertaining to this issue correspond to the need for an internal transposition of EU directives, which have their own deadlines.

The 9/11 attacks on the Twin Towers and the Pentagon in the United States did raise a lot of attention on the subject with three plenary sessions held in 2001 where terrorism was debated at length. This debate continued throughout 2002 and 2003, focusing particularly on the war against Iraq and the Portuguese presence in it, which was criticized by all the left-wing parties. Indeed, 2003 is the year that appears most represented in the corpus considered in the current inquiry, with four plenary sessions where the issue of terrorism was debated at length.

The terrorist attack of March 11, 2004, in Madrid also further instigated a parliamentary debate on the issue of terrorism, which is not surprising due to Portugal's geographical, historical, and cultural proximity to Spain. However, after April 1, 2004, the discussion shifted to foreign policy that brought back the question of the war in Iraq. The next plenary session discussing terrorism did not occur until February 6, 2008. Between these two dates, Al Qaeda attacked the London metro on July 7, 2005, causing 56 deaths and 700 injuries. There were no significant terrorist attacks in Europe in 2008 but the issue of counter-terrorism was debated at the plenary session of February 6, which focused on the transposition of two EU directives dealing with the implementation of the use of the financial system and activities and professions specially designated for the purpose of money laundering and terrorist financing. Following this plenary session, a deeper discussion of terrorism in the Portuguese parliament only occurred years later in 2015. 2015 was a particularly deadly year for France, with the attack on the satirical publication "Charlie Hebdo" in January, and, later in November, the assault on Bataclan concert hall in Paris that caused 130 deaths and more than 350 injuries. However, the plenary sessions where "terrorism" appeared a greater number of times were held on March 4 and July 1, 2015, before the attack at Bataclan. In the plenary session of March 4, several important law proposals with the aim of adjusting the Portuguese legal framework to the threat of terrorism were discussed. The plenary session of July 1, 2015, focused on a law proposal to strengthen the SIRP to address the threat of terrorism.

In 2016, despite the deadly terrorist attacks that occurred in Brussels, Belgium, and Nice, France, there occurred no plenary sessions where the issue of terrorism was key. However, in 2017, terrorism was discussed at length in two plenary sessions, on May 11 and 17. These came a few days before the attack on the Ariana Grande concert in Manchester, UK. At the plenary session of May 17, 2017, several bills, which related primarily to a tighter control of immigration services to prevent the entry and stay in national territory of foreigners convicted of the crime of terrorism, presented by CDS-PP, were debated. The discussion also included access to traffic data, location, or other related data of communications by officials and agents of the SIRP. Several draft resolutions proposed by CDS-PP were also discussed. These concerned the issues of airport security; specific training in detecting, preventing, and combating terrorism provided to security forces performing functions of proximity policing; and the preparation of the strategies and action plans resulting from the National Strategy to Combat Terrorism. Finally, Law Proposal no. 79/XIII (2nd) on the special regime for access to basic data and electronic communications traffic data by the SIRP was discussed. The latter recommended an increase in the power of intelligence services to access telecommunications of citizens to prevent security and terrorist threats.

After 2017, there were several plenary sessions mentioning the issue of terrorism. These sessions, however, did not inspire in-depth discussions. Although they were not included in the corpus, it is important to note that the plenary session of September 18, 2018, discussed and approved bill 139/XIII/3rd (Gov) with favorable votes from the PSD, PS, CDS-PP, and the

Party of People, Animal and Nature (PAN) parties and abstentions from the BE, PCP, and Os Verdes. This bill changes the Law to Combat Terrorism, transposing the EU Directive 2017/541. It extends and specifies the criminalization of terrorist activities, including receiving training for terrorism. It also seeks to incorporate in the Portuguese internal legal system the recommendation from the Financial Action Task Force and from the UN Security Council concerning the financing of terrorism. An amendment to the national Law to Combat Terrorism is thus proposed, to criminalize not only the financing of terrorist acts but also of terrorist organizations or individual agents.

In sum, the parliamentary agenda on the issue of terrorism cannot be seen as a mere reaction to the terrorist attacks in the United States and Europe, although some of these attacks have raised much more discussion than others. The same applies to the EU directives, with some being more controversial than others. Although issues are often raised (especially by the left-wing parties) regarding some of the specifics of these directives, there is a general mood in favor of an affirmative vote. This is why it is important to look deeper into the discursive constructions on the subject, which more clearly show the divisions within the Portuguese parliament. Below, three main discursive constructions focusing on the response to terrorism are presented. The first of these discursive constructions relates to the strategic use of fear in the counter-terrorism discourse. The second concerns the dialectics between security and freedom. Finally, the third construction concerns the discursive presentation of Portugal within the supranational institutions of the EU, UN, and NATO.

RESPONDING TO TERRORISM: FEAR AS A DOUBLE DISCURSIVE FORMATION

Fear is a word used frequently by members of both right and left parties when talking about terrorism and counter-terrorism. However, the manner in which fear is invoked is different depending on the political party under consideration. Right-wing parties such as the PSD and CDS-PP pronounce the importance of not showing fear in the face of terrorism. This is linked to the discourse of emergency, that is, the claim that there is a need for urgent measures against terrorism, and that these require acting in a firm manner and without fear. Such discursive formation implies the defense of a militarized response to terrorism, as seen in the justification of the Portuguese presence in Iraq by the ex-Prime Minister Durão Barroso, who represented the PSD government:

> The Iraqi regime continues to challenge legality and the United Nations. The international community can only have a firm attitude, founded on the

primacy of convictions and the clarity of principles. . . . We are for peace and international law. But let there be no ambiguities: if diplomatic channels are exhausted, there is no neutrality between tyranny and democracy, between dictatorship and freedom, between totalitarianism and the rule of law, among those who defend human dignity and those who, by violence, defy, violate and repress human rights. (Assembly of the Portuguese Republic Plenary Session 2003)

The speaker criticizes "false neutralities," evoking the position of Portugal during the Second World War (a time when Portugal was under an authoritarian, autocrat, and state corporatist regime ruled by António de Oliveira Salazar),[7] to distance himself from it: "That is why Portugal can have a firm and clear position and not take refuge in supposed neutrality. I do not want to see my country, as it did in the old regime, in a position of neutrality between Nazism and democracy" (Assembly of the Portuguese Republic Plenary Session 2003).

By demanding urgent actions, the proponents of this discourse are effectively preventing deeper reflection and debate. Furthermore, according to this discursive formation, failure to act equals being complicit with terrorism. As Figueiredo Lopes, Minister of the Interior, put it, "Who hesitates, who yields to fear, favors terrorism. Who is firm, convinced, and determined helps to combat terrorism. . . . Unity, firmness, and cooperation" (Assembly of the Portuguese Republic Plenary Session 2004). It should be noted that this "over-arching Manichean frame of good versus evil" or "either you are with us or you are with the terrorists" is not a new discursive strategy as it was often employed by U.S. president George W. Bush in his defense of the "War on Terror." This discourse prevailed beyond the immediate post-9/11 context, prompting a growing concern for security in Europe. Through this discourse of emergence and by declaring any debate related to terrorism a state issue, the right preemptively de-legitimated any divergence.

This is the case especially when debating a highly controversial issue such as intelligence services as it can be seen in the statements of Luis Marques Guedes, Ministry of Presidency and of Parliamentary Issues in 2015:

It is a fact that this has been a field of broad debate and some divergence of opinion, to a large extent conditioned by historical stigmas or misunderstandings related to the respective activities of each of the services. However, in view of the current picture of enormous threats and uncertainties that characterize the international system and 30 years after the establishment these services, the political consensus has finally emerged as to the need to strengthen national information in order to make it possible to meet the real needs of the State. I welcome the Socialist Party's sense of responsibility in this matter, which is not

> a partisan matter, but a matter of state and of the defense of freedom and democracy. (Assembly of the Portuguese Republic Plenary Session 2015)

By relying on vague claims of threat and uncertainty and putting forward arguments such as "the current situation of enormous threats and uncertainties that characterize the international system" as definitive, the words of Luis Marques Guedes are effectively opening the door toward exceptionalism and securitization.

For the left, "having no fear" means something quite different. It means the strength to continue to live as before, without giving in to "the trap of hatred and war." Responding to terrorism with violence is interpreted as becoming as bad as the terrorists. The emphasis here is not on security, but on solidarity, and on sustaining "a culture of peace." Again, this discourse about peace, although important in the aftermath of 9/11, extends beyond that attack, as can be seen in a statement by José Luís Ferreira, MP from the party "Os Verdes," in 2015:

> On matters that we consider important in the fight against terrorism, we refer to the need for the Government to make a commitment to actively engage within the European Union and other international organizations in promoting peace policies between peoples and states; we refer to the need to take measures to combat terrorist financing through offshore and other unclear practices; we mention the need to see in schools an important stage in this fight, especially when we talk about preventing violence. (Assembly of the Portuguese Republic Plenary Session 2015)

The left's discourse focuses on multilateral negotiations for promoting international peace and preventing global instability and war, which are perceived as the major causes of terrorism. However, at the same time, leftist parties do not disregard other types of measures to fight terrorism, such as repressive measures to combat terrorist financing and social/educational actions to prevent violence.

SECURITY VS FREEDOM AND SECURITY AS FREEDOM

The dialectics between security and freedom appear throughout these parliamentary debates, with the left parties criticizing the trend toward securitization and militarization and warning against using terrorism as an excuse for imperialism, war, and the violation of citizens' rights. Both the PCP and BE specifically criticize the United States for its incoherence and hypocrisy in the fight against terrorism, denouncing its contribution to global instability, and the violations of human rights in Guantanamo. Below, we find an example of such criticism by António Filipe, MP from the PCP:

> What we mean by this is that the states that have supposedly legislated the most to combat terrorism have been the least consistent and, in some cases, have actually behaved like Dr. Frankenstein, that is, they create creatures that then turn against the creator. We have many examples of this. We still remember that in the 1980s, Bin Laden was a freedom fighter and the terrorist was Nelson Mandela. The second aspect to be emphasized is that, in order to combat terrorism effectively, erratic drifts must be avoided. We had many erratic drifts: since 2001, we have had and have Guantánamo; we had the Patriot Act; we had secret prisons in Europe; we had secret CIA flights; we had wars in Iraq, in Libya, in Syria; and we had the creation of the Islamic State, which is inseparable from the consequences of these wars. (Assembly of the Portuguese Republic Plenary Session 2015)

Often, the left also raises concerns regarding the constitutionality of the EU directives as they are transposed to the Portuguese legal framework. This is the case of Odete Santos, MP from the PCP at the plenary session of October 18, 2001, when the government presents a draft law establishing the system of sanctions applicable to cases of noncompliance with sanctions imposed by EU regulations.

> Mr. President and MPs, we agree with the fight against terrorism, not only by using weapons of criminal repression but also in other ways, and these, unfortunately, worldwide, have not been followed up. In my opinion, the law that comes out of this House must be concerned not to incur in unconstitutionalities that endanger the diploma itself. (Assembly of the Portuguese Republic Plenary Session 2001)

This same concern was raised in 2017 by MP José Manuel Pureza from the BE in relation to the proposal to strengthen the power of intelligence services to access sensitive and communication data:

> Mr. President and MPs, Members of the Government: The debate that we have been having presents itself as being about the fight against terrorism, but one cannot hide the debate that we are actually having here today, which is about limitations, lawful and unlawful limitations to fundamental rights and freedoms in accordance with the Constitution. (Assembly of the Portuguese Republic Plenary Session 2017)

The right, on the other hand, resolves this dilemma between security and freedom by claiming that security, positively re-signified as a right, is in itself a condition of freedom and democracy, while freedom is negatively defined as a release from threat (Bell 2011; Tsoukala 2006). Within this discursive formation, "strong institutions" are needed to protect the freedom of all the citizens, as suggested by Luis Marques Guedes, the Minister of the Presidency and Parliamentary Affairs in July 1, 2015, when arguing for strengthening the capacity of the intelligence services:

> Ladies and gentlemen, fellow MPs, a constitutional state needs strong institutions to protect the freedoms and guarantees it offers its citizens. The exercise of the properly proportionate and supervised democratic authority is the guarantee of those freedoms. This is the area per excellence of the mission of the intelligence services. Strengthening their capacity to exercise it is to strengthen our own freedom. (Assembly of the Portuguese Republic Plenary Session 2015)

In relation to this issue of metadata, it is interesting how the PS, through MP Jorge Lacão, joins the right wing in constructing the situation as a threat to national security to approve exceptional measures:

> In that sense, Mr. Deputy António Filipe, what we have said here is that we are completely available for constitutionality checks, because we believe in them. But we said more: that, in view of the situation that must be guaranteed for the defense of the security of the State, of society and of people, and in view of the very serious risks that the societies of our time are faced with, it is important to assess whether it is possible to make an interpretation update on the possibility of accessing sensitive data. (Assembly of the Portuguese Republic Plenary Session 2015)

The PS thus endorses exceptional measures that can be considered within the framework of preemptive security, justifying such measures solely on the basis of vague and abstract notions of global "serious risks" and not on specific risks affecting Portugal.

RESPONDING TO TERRORISM: PORTUGAL WITHIN THE EU, NATO, AND UN

Although there is a consensus in the Portuguese parliament regarding the need for international and multilateral cooperation in the fight against terrorism, it is possible to observe differences along the right-left political spectrum. On the right, the PSD and CDS-PP emphasize the responsibilities of Portugal within supranational institutions, especially the EU and NATO. Furthermore, these parties specifically argue for a transatlantic cooperation with the United

States. The Portuguese government's signature of the U.S.-led "coalition of the willing" that supported the invasion of Iraq in 2003 (at that time a PSD government led by Durão Barroso) was heavily criticized by the left parties at the national parliament, including the PS. The PSD and CSD-PP, on the other hand, justified this participation by presenting the issue as a war between tyranny and democracy, and stressing Portuguese responsibilities toward its allies, the United States and the United Kingdom.

Subsequently, when Europe became the target of terrorist attacks, and when the EU started developing its own counter-terrorist approach, the right continued to advocate a cooperation with the United States. Terrorism was depicted by MP Telmo Correia from the CDS-PP as "a threat that must be countered through the union of Europeans and strong transatlantic ties" (Assembly of the Portuguese Republic Plenary Session 2004).

Grounded in a discourse of emergency, right-wing parties also argued for a fast transposition of EU directives on terrorism laws, construing any delay as bad for the reputation of Portugal. This position is evident, for example, in the plenary session of February 6, 2008, when PSD MP Patinha Antão spent a great part of his intervention criticizing the government's delay in transposing the EU directives on the implementation of the use of the financial system and activities and professions specially designated for the purpose of money laundering and terrorist financing.

> The first question we would like to place to you is this: why is the government not tabling the draft law until the end of December, which means that the legislative procedure has already come to an end, because the Assembly will have to consider the bill and has a program of hearings, which is already established? Naturally, when the process is over, Portugal will be, in the context of the countries that are to transpose this directive, regrettably behind schedule. (Assembly of the Portuguese Republic Plenary Session 2008)

Also for the PS, the position of Portugal relative to other EU countries in the fight against terrorism is a determining factor in pushing for a fast transposition of the EU directives, as can be observed in the following statement of MP Helena Terra, February 6, 2008:

> Mr. President, Mr. and Mrs. MPs, the legislative options contained in this government proposal maintain the political coherence of other legislative proposals which have now been adopted and which in a report by the Financial Action Task Force on money laundering and the financing of terrorism made it possible to place Portugal in second place in relation to the rest of Europe in terms of the effectiveness of this fight. (Assembly of the Portuguese Republic Plenary Session 2008)

On the other hand, parties at the left of the PS were much more willing to question the United States and support a "European perspective on terrorism." This position is accompanied by a critique of United States foreign policy as a cause of global instability and growing fundamentalism. In this respect, Portuguese participation in the Iraq war is criticized for blindly following George W. Bush's policies on the basis of false information regarding the presence of weapons of mass destruction in Iraq. Hence, MP Luís Fazenda from the BE, on March 17, 2004, asks: "What is the political and moral legitimacy of an international coalition founded on serial lies? Serial liars and serial killers!" (Assembly of the Portuguese Republic Plenary Session 2004). Subsequently, parties at the left of the PS are also much more inclined to question EU directives on the basis of their potential violation of human rights, as enshrined in the Portuguese Constitution.

DISCUSSION

The three discursive constructions presented above should be understood jointly and as forming two different political discourses on terrorism: a right-wing discourse and a left-wing discourse. The right-wing (PSD and CDS-PP) discourse is primarily anchored on the construction of a climate of fear and emergency. Second, it emphasizes Portugal's responsibilities in relation to the supranational institutions of which it is a member (especially the EU and NATO), and on the duty of solidarity toward its democratic allies (UK and the United States). Security becomes a condition for protecting democracy and freedom from the global threat of terrorism. Securitization is thus producing a certain idea of freedom and not just limiting it. This is consistent with effective discourses of securitization within liberal democracies (Bell 2011).

The left discourse—mostly represented by the PCP, BE, and Os Verdes, but also in some degree by the new party PAN[8]—is not so clear nor assertive in its interpretation and response to the terrorism threat, as it is very much a "negative" discourse constructed against the right-wing discourse against fear, the war, securitization, and U.S. imperialism. Its main "positive" contribution is its focus on the causes of terrorism, but this is again done by pointing the finger toward the United States and the latter's responsibility in contemporary global instability.

PS positioning appears to be less coherent and less stable compared to the other parliamentary groups, and it does not fit completely in either of these discourses. In in the aftermath of 9/11, although the PS joined the left's critique of Bush's preemptive war, it seemed to have progressively shifted toward more to the right regarding the need to prioritize security over human rights, and the emphasis on a fast internal transposition of EU directives.

Perhaps this positioning represents a case of "terrorism envy" (Zulaika 2010, 248–250), which denotes the idea that the absence of a terrorism risk could be perceived as political irrelevance. Involvement in counter-terrorism would thus serve to guarantee the political relevance of the country under consideration in the international sphere.

CONCLUSION

In this chapter, I sought to uncover the main discursive constructions of counter-terrorism in the Portuguese parliament in the post-9/11 period. One of the first conclusions of this analysis is that these discourses are not new as they resonate with other international frames on terrorism. Thus, even if Portugal has until now been spared of terrorist attacks, the political discourse on the part of the right-wing parties reflects a global tendency toward "preemptive security," grounded on the normalization of emergency and the legitimation of exceptionalism. Such discourse has legitimized the reduction of freedoms in other European countries, affecting predominantly specific groups of migrant populations, racialized and religious communities, and activists. The difference between Portugal and these other European countries, like the UK or France, may lie more on the targeting of specific population groups as objects of state surveillance and regulation. Indeed, while, for example, the UK counter-terrorist legislation has targeted specifically Muslims, who were designated as the "enemy within" and constructed as a "suspect community" (Pantazis and Pemberton 2009; Mythen, Walklate, and Khan 2009), in Portugal the Muslim population is very small and has raised few if any concerns. Consequently, at the level of counter-terrorist policies, and understanding these from the perspective of governance (Bell 2011), Portugal may have been focusing more on the control of migrants in general, which are for the most part (although not entirely), Christians. But there is also a growing concern on the left with the question of the metadata and the sharing of these data with other countries within counter-terrorism obligations of international cooperation. This issue of metadata signals a preemptive approach to security that, as Murphy (2014, 169) argues, "treats the population as a whole as potential suspects and makes them subject to surveillance and systems of control." It means that the idea is not so much to target specific groups for surveillance but to place everyone under surveillance.

Another interesting aspect of these discourses is that they did not change much over time. This could mean that there is an ideological consistency within the Portuguese parliamentary groups in the last decades, which contradicts other studies suggesting that Portugal presents low levels of right-left polarization at the party system level (Freire and Belchior 2011). There is, as stated before, one exception to this ideological consistency, which is the PS discourse. The PS has shown less coherence in its positioning as it has become progressively closer to the right than to the left in its discourse. As reported in the findings, the party's position in favor of the law on the meta-data, wherein the MPs evoke vague global and societal threats for justifying their support to exceptional and anti-Constitutional measures, is a good case in point here.

One distinctive aspect of these discourses might be related to Portugal's strategy in foreign, security, and defense policies, which has relied on a balancing act between different security organizations in an attempt to "being simultaneously Atlantic and European" (Robinson 2016, 135). This is evident when some MPs pledge alliance to the EU and the United Nations as well as to NATO, seemingly regarding these institutions as complementary in spite of the tensions between and within them. At the same time, for the parties in power (either PS or PSD), these discourses seem to reveal a docile positioning regarding the big powers (the United States and UK) and the supranational institutions, which are rarely criticized.

Finally, critical terrorism studies have been more interested in deconstructing discourses on the "War on Terror" and preventive security, paying less attention to discourses that are critical of these propositions. This chapter gives an important contribution in this regard by presenting the example of the Portuguese parliamentary groups on the left. In general, Portuguese left-wing parties' discourse on terrorism tends to present itself as a reactive discourse built argumentatively in opposition to the right. This finding is in line with other studies in other national contexts that show that the left has been unable to respond to the right's reframing of the dialectic between security and freedom (Tsoukala 2006), and that the left loses identity when the trope of human rights is used to legitimate anti-terror policies (Bogain 2017). These characteristics may weaken the effectiveness of the left-wing discourse as a convincing alternative to the right-wing discourse. In the Portuguese case, the ambiguous positioning of the PS sometimes with the left and sometimes with the right contributes to weaken the cohesiveness of the left bloc.

Subsequent studies should focus on the reception of parliamentary debates by the general public to grasp the latter's level of interest in the subject of terrorism and counter-terrorism. This is particularly important in view of recent findings of mismatches between MPs and the electorate regarding issues of left-right self-placement and meaning (Freire and Belchior 2015). For a progressive discourse on terrorism to develop, it is necessary to foster both academic and public debate on this matter. Thus, more studies on Portuguese political communication and parliamentary discourses on terrorism are required. But we also need to make sure that parliamentary debates are clarified and commented on by the media, which facilitate the discussion produced by lawmakers and have the power to help the public understand the debates. Last, the political changes that have taken place in Portugal during the past decade, either in terms of a government formed by an unexpected coalition at the left (the so-called "Geringonça") or the new parties that have recently gained representation in the parliament (at the left and the right) might have had an important impact on the parliamentary activity and political communication at the level of the right-left polarization. In this regard, it is important to mention André Ventura, the leader of the extreme-right party, CHEGA, who got a seat in the parliament in the 2019 legislative elections. Ventura's populist discourse on a variety of issues has been attracting a lot of media and public attention. Its impact on the political debate regarding the fight against terrorism is yet to be analyzed.

NOTES

1. Some exceptions are Andrew Neal's (2012) and Jarvis and Legrand's (2016) analysis of UK Parliamentary debates and counter-terrorism lawmaking.
2. According to this study, other important factors explaining Austrian political actors' positioning regarding counterterrorism include a sense of ownership and anticipated political gains.
3. In the Portuguese language, the word "geringonça" has several meanings: an unsound and easily flawed construction; a complicated apparatus; something that works at cost. Figuratively speaking, it can mean a complex and unreliable structure or an idea that is improvised and works with difficulty (Infopedia 2020). The Portuguese governmental coalition that became known as "Geringonça" expresses a sentiment related to all these meanings, as it was an improbable and improvised solution that many doubted could work at all.
4. "Troika" is the name by which the group composed by the European Central Bank, the European Commission, and the International Monetary Fund became known.
5. The Diary of the Assembly of the Republic is the official journal of the Assembly. Series I contains "a faithful and complete account of what happens at each plenary meeting" (Assembleia da República n.d.).
6. Since the democratic elections of 1976, Portugal has not been the target of any terrorist attacks, either transnational or internal. There were, however, some internal terrorist attacks—from both extreme-left and -right groups—in the period between the "Carnation Revolution" (April 25, 1974) that ended the dictatorship of António de Oliveira Salazar, and the democratic elections of 1976. This period became known as the "Ongoing revolutionary Period" (Periodo Revolucionário em Curso–PREC).
7. This political regime was called "Estado Novo" and prevailed in Portugal for forty-one uninterrupted years, from the approval of the 1933 Constitution until its overthrow by the Revolution of April 25, 1974.
8. PAN, the Party of Persons, Animals, and Nature, become represented in the Portuguese Parliament in 2015 with one MP elected by Lisbon.

REFERENCES

Assembly of the Portuguese Republic. 2001. "REUNIÃO PLENÁRIA DE 18 DE OUTUBRO DE 2001/Series1-Number 14." Lisbon, Portugal: A DIVISÃO DE REDAÇÃO E APOIO AUDIOVISUAL. Accessed April 25, 2020. http://debates.parlamento.pt/catalogo/r3/dar/01/08/03/014/2001-10-18.

———. 2003. "REUNIÃO PLENÁRIA DE 31 DE JANEIRO DE 2003/Series1-Number 82. Lisbon, Portugal: A DIVISÃO DE REDAÇÃO E APOIO AUDIOVISUAL." Accessed April 25, 2020. http://debates.parlamento.pt/catalogo/r3/dar/01/09/01/082/2003-01-31.

———. 2004. "REUNIÃO PLENÁRIA DE 17 DE MARÇO DE 2004/Series1-Number 64. Lisbon, Portugal: A DIVISÃO DE REDAÇÃO E APOIO AUDIOVISUAL." Accessed April 25, 2020. http://debates.parlamento.pt/catalogo/r3/dar/01/09/02/064/2004-03-17.

———. 2008. "REUNIÃO PLENÁRIA DE 6 DE FEVEREIRO DE 2008/Series1-Number 44. Lisbon, Portugal: A DIVISÃO DE REDAÇÃO E APOIO AUDIOVISUAL." Accessed April 25, 2020. http://debates.parlamento.pt/catalogo/r3/dar/01/10/03/044/2008-02-06.

———. 2015. "REUNIÃO PLENÁRIA DE 4 DE MARÇO DE 2015/Series1-Number 57. Lisbon, Portugal: A DIVISÃO DE REDAÇÃO E APOIO AUDIOVISUAL." Accessed April 25, 2020. http://debates.parlamento.pt/catalogo/r3/dar/01/12/04/057/2015-03-04.

———. 2015. "REUNIÃO PLENÁRIA DE 1 DE JULHO DE 2015/Series1-Number 105. Lisbon, Portugal: A DIVISÃO DE REDAÇÃO E APOIO AUDIOVISUAL." Accessed April 25, 2020. http://debates.parlamento.pt/catalogo/r3/dar/01/12/04/105/2015-07-01.

———. 2017. "REUNIÃO PLENÁRIA DE 17 DE MAIO DE 2017/Series1-Number 88 Lisbon, Portugal: A DIVISÃO DE REDAÇÃO E APOIO AUDIOVISUAL." Accessed April 25, 2020. http://debates.parlamento.pt/catalogo/r3/dar/01/13/02/088/2017-05-17.

———. n.d. "Diário Da Assembleia Da República." Accessed December 7, 2020. https://www.parlamento.pt/DAR.

Allen, Chris. 2010. "Fear and Loathing: The Political Discourse in Relation to Muslims and Islam in the British Contemporary Setting." *Politics and Religion Journal* 4 (2): 221–236.

Amoore, Louise. 2006. "Biometric Borders: Governing Mobilities in the War on Terror." *Political Geography* 25 (3): 336–351.

Amoore, Louise. 2009. "Algorithmic War: Everyday Geographies of the War on Terror." *Antipode* 41 (1): 49–69.

Aradau, Claudia and Rens Van Munster. 2008. "Taming the Future: The Dispositif of Risk in the War on Terror." In *Risk and the War on Terror*, edited by Louise Amoore and Marieke de Goede, 23–40. London and New York: Routledge.

Baker-Beall, Christopher. 2009. "The Discursive Construction of EU Counter-Terrorism Policy: Writing the 'Migrant Other,' Securitisation, and Control." *Journal of Contemporary European Research* 5 (2): 188–206.

Bartolucci, Valentina. 2014. "Security vs. Liberty: The Discourse on Terrorism in the United States and Morocco and Its Societal Effects." *Democracy and Security*, 10 (1): 1–21.

Bell, Colleen. 2011. *The Freedom of Security Governing Canada in the Age of Counter-terrorism*. Vancouver: UBC Press.

Bogain, Ariane. 2017. "Security in the Name of Human Rights: The Discursive Legitimation Strategies of the War on Terror in France." *Critical Studies on Terrorism* 10 (3): 476–500.

Bronitt, Simon. 2008. "Balancing Security and Liberty: Critical Perspectives on Terrorism Law Reform." In *Fresh Perspectives on the "War on Terror,"* edited by Miriam Gani and Penelope Mathew, 65–83. Canberra: Australian National University Press.

de Graaf, Beatrice, and Bob de Graaff. 2010. "Bringing Politics Back in: The Introduction of the "Performative Power" of Counterterrorism." *Critical Studies on Terrorism* 3 (2): 261–275.

Devetak, Richard. 2005. "The Gothic Scene of International Relations: Ghosts, Monsters, Terror, and the Sublime after September 11." *Review of International Studies* 31 (4): 621–643.

Eckersley, Robyn. 2007. "Security, Liberty and the Myth of Balance: Towards a Critique of Security Politics." *Contemporary Political Theory* 6 (2): 131–149.

Eder, Franz, Chiara Libiseller, and Bernhard Schneider. 2020. "Contesting Counter-Terrorism: Discourse Networks and the Politicisation of Counter-Terrorism in Austria." *Journal of International Relations and Development*. https://doi.org/10.1057/s41268-020-00187-8.

Eijkman, Quirine, and Bart Schuurman. 2011. "Preventive Counter-Terrorism and Non-Discrimination in the European Union: A Call for Systematic Evaluation." *The International Centre for Counter-terrorism (ICCT)–The Hague* 2 (5).

Ericson, Richard. 2008. "The State of Preemption: Manging Terrorism Risk through Counter Law." In *Risk and the War on Terror*, edited by Louise Amoore and Marieke de Goede, 57–76. London and New York: Routledge.

Fairclough, Norman. 1992. *Discourse and Social Change*. Cambridge: Polity Press.

Farneti, Roberto. 2012. "Cleavage Lines in Global Politics: Left and Right, East and West, Earth and Heaven." *Journal of Political Ideologies* 17 (2): 127–145.

Freire, André, and Ana Maria Belchior. 2011. "What Left and Right Means to Portuguese Citizens." *Comparative European Politics* 9: 145–167.

———. 2015. "Ideological Representation in Portugal: Congruence between Deputies and Voters in terms of Their Left-right Placement and Its Substantive Meaning." In *Election, Leadership, and Political Representation in Portugal: Essays on Parliament, Media, Voluntary Associations, Parties, Politics, and Voting*, edited by André Freire and José Manuel Leite Viegas. New York: Edwin Mellen.

Folgado, Pedro Naves. 2016. "Portugal e o combate ao terrorismo—a Estratégia Nacional." *Proelium* 7 (11): 335–347.

Freeman, Michael. 2005. "Order, Rights, and Threats: Terrorism and Global Justice." In *Human Rights in the "War on Terror,"* edited by Richard Wilson, 37–56. Cambridge: Cambridge University Press.

Gries, Peter, and Paton Pak ChunYam. 2020. "Ideology and International Relations." *Current Opinion in Behavioral Sciences* 34: 135–141.

Infopédia. 2020. "Geringonça." In *Infopédia—Dicionários Porto Editora*. https://www.infopedia.pt/dicionarios/lingua-portuguesa/geringon%C3%A7a.

Institute for Economics & Peace. 2019. "Global Peace Index 2019: Measuring Peace in a Complex World." Accessed April 25, 2020. https://www.economicsandpeace.org/wp-content/uploads/2020/08/GPI-2019web.pdf

Jackson, Richard. 2005. "Security, Democracy, and the Rhetoric of Counter-Terrorism." *Democracy and Security* 1 (2): 147–171.

———. 2007. "An Analysis of EU counterterrorism Discourse post-September 11." *Cambridge Review of International Affairs* 20 (2): 233–247.

———. 2015. "The Epistemological Crisis of Counterterrorism." *Critical Studies on Terrorism* 8 (1): 33–54.

Jarvis, Lee. 2009. "The Spaces and Faces of Critical Terrorism Studies." *Security Dialogue* 4 (1): 5–27.

Jarvis, Lee, and Tim Legrand. 2016. "Legislating for Otherness: Proscription Powers and Parliamentary Discourse." *Review of International Studies* 42 (3): 558–574.

Kellner, Douglas. 2004. "9/11, Spectacles of Terror, and Media Manipulation." *Critical Discourse Studies* 1 (1): 41–64.

Leudar, Ivan, Victoria Marsland, and Jirí Nekvapil, 2004. "On Membership Categorization: 'Us,' 'Them,' and 'Doing Violence' in Political Discourse." *Discourse & Society* 15 (2–3): 243–266.

Monar, Jörg. 2015. "The EU as an International Counter-terrorism Actor: Progress and Constraints." *Intelligence and National Security* 30 (2–3): 333–356.

Murphy, Cian. 2014. "Counter-Terrorism Law and Policy—Operationalisation and Normalisation of Exceptional Law after the 'War on Terror.'" In *EU Security and Justice Law: After Lisbon and Stockholm*, edited by Diego Acosta Arcarazo and Cian Murphy, 168–185. Oxford: Hart Publishing.

Mythen, Gabe, Sandra Lyn Walklate, and Fatima Khan. 2009. "'I'm a Muslim, but I'm not a Terrorist': Risk, Victimization and the Negotiation of Risky Identities." *The British Journal of Criminology* 49 (6): 755–771.

Neal, Andrew W. 2009. *Exceptionalism and the Politics of Counter-terrorism: Liberty, Security and the War on Terror*. London: Routledge.

———. 2012. "Terrorism, Lawmaking, and Democratic Politics: Legislators as Security Actors." *Terrorism and Political Violence* 24 (3): 357–374.

Neocleous, Mark. 2007. "Security, Liberty and the Myth of Balance: Towards a Critique of Security Politics." *Contemporary Political Theory* 6: 131–149.

Pantazis, Christina, and Simon Pemberton. 2009. "From the 'Old' to the 'New' Suspect Community. Examining the Impacts of Recent UK Counter-Terrorist Legislation." *The British Journal of Criminology* 49 (5): 646–666.

———. 2012. "Reconfiguring Security and Liberty: Political Discourses and Public Opinion in the New Century." *The British Journal of Criminology* 52 (3): 651–667.

Ragazzi, Francesco. 2014. "Policed Multiculturalism? The Impact of Counter-terrorism and Counter-radicalization and the 'End' of Multiculturalism." In

Counter-Radicalisation: Critical Perspectives, edited by Christopher Baker-Beall, Charlotte Heath-Kelly, and Lee Jarvis, 170–188. London: Routledge.

Rai, Amit S. 2004. "Of Monsters: Biopower, Terrorism and Excess in Genealogies of Monstrosity." *Cultural Studies* 18 (4): 538–570.

Robinson, Steven. 2016. "Still Focused on the Atlantic: Accounting for the Limited Europeanization of Portuguese Security Policy." *European Security* 25 (1): 134–58. https://doi.org/10.1080/09662839.2015.1090430.

SGMAI. 2015. "Estratégia Nacional de Combate Ao Terrorismo." 2015. https://www.sg.mai.gov.pt/Noticias/Paginas/Estrat%C3%A9gia-Nacional-de-Combate-ao-terrorismo-.aspx.

Smyth, Marie Breen, Jeroen Gunning, Richard Jackson, George Kassimeris & Piers Robinson. 2008. "Critical Terrorism Studies–an Introduction." *Critical Studies on Terrorism* 1 (1): 1–4.

Tsoukala, Anastassia. 2006. "Democracy in the Light of Security: British and French Political Discourses on Domestic Counter-terrorism Policies." *Political Studies* 54 (3): 607–627.

Waldron, Jeremy. 2003. "Security and Liberty: The Image of Balance." *The Journal of Political Philosophy* 11(2): 191–210.

Zedner, Lucia. 2005 "Securing Liberty in the Face of Terror: Reflections from Criminal Justice." *Journal of Law & Society* 32 (4): 507–533.

Zulaika, Joseba. 2010. "The Terror/Counterterror Edge: When Non-terror Becomes a Terrorism Problem and Real Terror cannot be Detected by Counterterrorism." *Critical Studies on Terrorism* 3 (2): 247–260.

Chapter 4

Anti-terrorism Regulations and Freedom of Speech in Spain

Isabel Serrano Maillo

INTRODUCTION

Spain has experienced terrorist acts that spanned over several generations. Arguably the most significant terrorism-affiliated entity in the past few decades in Spain had been Euskadi Ta Askatasuna (ETA), a group that, between its beginnings in 1958 and the definitive end of its armed activity in 2011, committed 2,472 terrorist attacks that claimed the lives of 829 people (including soldiers, politicians, civilians, and children) and injured 2,597 individuals. ETA aspired for the construction of a socialist state in the Basque Country and sought independence from Spain and France. During its early years, it had the support of the Basque population because it was one of the many organizations that opposed the Franco dictatorship. Once the Constitution was approved, it lost a great deal of Basque popular support, although it always had the political appeal of the Herri Batasuna political party headed by Arnaldo Otegui. In addition to ETA, others of lesser impact had been involved in terrorism activities. These include Grupos de Resistencia Antifascista Primero de Octubre (GRAPO)[1] and Terra Lliure,[2] which were responsible for the deaths of 84 people and injuries to 200 individuals (which resulted in 5 people being killed), respectively. In the past two decades, terrorist threats in Spain have emerged from jihadist groups that claimed the lives of 209 people and injured more than 2,000 individuals. Orchestrated by Abu Dujan al Afgani, who called himself Al Qaeda's military spokesman in Europe, a notable example of these terrorist acts includes the Madrid train bombings of March 11, 2004, that killed 193 people. Most recently, the Islamic State of Iraq and the Levant, also known as Daesh, used vehicles to run over crowds of people in Barcelona on August 17, 2017.

Spain adopted counter-terrorism measures in response to these incidents and other potential threats of terrorism. The Spanish approach in upholding counter-terrorism legislation is markedly different from experiences in other countries such as the United States or the United Kingdom. The United Kingdom, for example, has a history of deploying anti-terrorism legislation since the 1970s to quell nationalist movements under the premise that terrorist activities warrant a state of exception (Carrasco Andino 2019, 88). In the United States, as Pillar (2001, 10) notes:

> Every tool used in the fight against terrorism has something to contribute, but also significant limits to what it can accomplish. Thus, counterterrorism requires using all the tools available, because no one of them can do the job. Just as terrorism itself is multifaceted, so too must be the campaign against it.

In Spain, anti-terrorism measures have been embedded in ordinary legislation (Tenorio Sánchez 2010, 183). As Álvárez Conde and González (2006, 2) state:

> Terrorism is not a circumstantial, but a structural phenomenon, which is why the fight against it can neither be of a military nature (the case of the United States), nor can it be carried out by adopting exceptional and extraordinary laws (the case of the United Kingdom), but instead through ordinary legislation, in accordance with the principles inherent in a State governed by the rule of law.

Although there are some precedents for autonomous anti-terrorism laws in Spain,[3] anti-terrorism regulation has generally been included in the Criminal Code. However, we can find some independent laws that include legal consequences for those who, in a nonviolent manner, commit or promote acts of terrorism. The Law 6/2002, June 27, 2002, on Political Parties (LOPP), for example, holds that a political party can be held liable for "giving express or tacit political support to terrorism, legitimizing terrorist actions for the achievement of political ends outside peaceful and democratic channels, or exculpating and minimizing their meaning and the violation of fundamental rights that they entail."[4] This specific article has given rise to several court rulings on issues of great relevance to constitutional law. Specifically, the issue of whether failure to condemn terrorist attacks implies tacit support for terrorists has been controversial. In other words, holding actors liable for non-condemnation of terrorists invites a debate on whether such ruling infringes upon freedom of speech. The Spanish courts were unanimous on this point, indicating that freedom of speech includes both the right to express an opinion and the right not to do so. Silence alone, therefore, cannot be considered irrefutable evidence of support for terrorism if it is not accompanied by other acts. However, the high court noted that when it comes to political formations, "the requirement that organizations and groups that seek to participate in public institutions must carry out an unequivocal and concrete rejection of terror must be accepted as reasonable, proportional and adequate" (Supreme Court Ruling STS 27 March 2003, 75[5] and Constitutional Court Ruling STC 5/2004, January 16, 2004, 104).[6]

What this implies for those who view terrorist speech in the same vein as terrorist acts, among other things, is when they speak of terrorist acts, they do not only mean those aimed at killing and injuring others. Terrorist acts may reside in the realm of words or behavior that induces others to commit these acts, glorifies those who have committed them, or humiliates those who saw their own people die or who were direct victims of terror. This proposition embraces the notion that even if these are acts that do not physically kill, the public nonetheless needs to be protected from them since they are actions that attack psychologically and offend the democratic and constitutional values that prevail in a democratic society (see Fernández Martínez 2010, 44; Ruiz Landáburu 2002, 82).

This view of "speech as terrorism" sets the tone of the preamble to Spain's Law 2/2015 of 30 March 2015, which amended the Criminal Code on terrorism. It states:

> International terrorism of a jihadist nature is characterized precisely by the incorporation of these new forms of aggression, consisting of new instruments of recruitment, training or indoctrination in hatred, to be used cruelly against all those who, in their extremist and violent ideology, are described as enemies. These new threats must therefore be combated with the most effective tool that democracies can use against the totalitarian fanaticism of terrorists: the law. (Organic Law 2/2015, 1)[7]

It can be inferred that this type of discourse is sanctioned as terrorism despite not directly incurring action, say, in a form of physical deaths. Yet, sometimes, it is difficult to discern if any of these actions are nothing more than expression of an opinion (especially when it is a question of expressions made by subjects outside the terrorist environment). When opinions are reprehensible and despicable, should they get protection under premises of freedom of expression?

In this chapter, I analyze how these actions typified as terrorism in Spanish legislation can place an excessive limit on freedom of expression. These are behaviors that consist of extolling or justifying terrorist violence ("spoken terrorism") carried out by people outside the terrorist environment whose words are not intended to provoke violence. I will discuss what is understood by spoken terrorism before I briefly examine the Spanish legislation on freedom of expression. In doing so, I will propose how conflicts should be resolved in this field. Finally, I will review various judicial cases of individuals convicted of terrorism due to jokes, messages on Twitter, and other platforms of mediated communication.

"SPOKEN TERRORISM"

In the context of this chapter, the term "spoken terrorism" refers to all those crimes that Spanish legislation typifies as terrorism crimes, specifically those that do not involve physical attacks. These include speech that encourages, justifies, or applauds terrorists and their acts. The intent here is not to analyze all the actions that may constitute a terrorism offense but to examine the rationales and ramifications of expressions that are categorized as a crime of terror. Three concepts are particularly important here: apology, glorification, and justification of terrorism (Criminal Code, Article. 578).[8] Apology, glorification, and justification are very similar concepts. According to the Dictionary of the Royal Academy of the Spanish Language, apology is considered "speech in word or in writing, in defense or praise of someone or something" (RAE 2020). Glorification, on the other hand, denotes "action of glorifying" (RAE 2020); *glorifying,* in this sense, signifies *exaltation,* which, in turn, is interpreted as *enlargement* or an act of increasing, making something great, praising, exaggerating, or raising someone to a higher degree or dignity. Finally, justification is the "action and effect of justifying," with the intent "to prove something with convincing reasons" (RAE 2020). In Spanish law, each of these concepts has its distinctive elements, although differentiating one type of conduct from another can be difficult. While all of them are based on the expression of an idea, the objective of each is different:

> "The statement, before an audience of persons or by any means of diffusion, of measures or doctrines that extol the crime or exalt its authors. The apology will only be considered criminal if it serves as a form of provocation and if, by its nature and circumstances, it constitutes a direct incitement to commit a crime"; *Glorification*, on the other hand, consists of praising and justifying the conduct and crimes committed by terrorists, giving the appearance of lawfulness to behavior that is prohibited by the law; Finally, *justification* of terrorism consists of approving of the conduct of terrorists, considering that there are valid reasons for them to behave the way they did. Glorification and justification do not seek to directly provoke terrorist violence, but instead reinforce and support "very serious criminal acts and the sustainability and perpetuation of such acts." (Criminal Code, Article 18)

All these different types of conduct have essential elements in common: they are aimed at penalizing expressions of approval for the conduct of terrorists, albeit to different degrees. To be punishable, these expressions ought to be carried out in person before an audience that listens to the actor's expressions or through a media outlet. In addition, the act must incite violence in some way, directly as in apology, or indirectly as in the other cases. This interpretation is contradictory and is not always effective in determining which of these crimes we are dealing with. In fact, it is common for the courts to condemn terrorism under the generic formula of "glorification and justification," either because the two types of conduct coincide or because it is not easy to distinguish between them.

The crime of humiliating the victims of terrorism or their families has a different meaning since it involves carrying out acts that discredit, belittle, or humiliate these individuals. According to the Dictionary of the Royal Academy of Spanish Language, *discredit* means "the reduction or loss of reputation of persons." A closely related term, *disrepute*, refers to "contempt" or "dismissal." Another one, *humiliation*, denotes "hurting someone's self-esteem or dignity." These are behaviors that seek to vilify, mock, or ridicule those who have suffered the consequences of terrorist acts or their families. For the conduct to be punishable under these circumstances, it is not necessary that it be done publicly (Dolz Lago 2013, 4). This conduct is directly related to the crime of insult, "action or expression that harms the dignity of another person, undermining his fame or attacking his own esteem" (Criminal Code, Article 208), or with less severe offenses against honor as regulated by civil legislation.[9]

The crime of apology was already included in the version of the Criminal Code that existed in 1995, while the crimes of glorification, justification, and humiliation of victims were included in the reformed Criminal Code in 2000. The reform of this article came at a time when terrorist attacks by ETA were frequent, which indicates it was intended to have a preventive role. However, the reform was highly criticized (e.g., Alonso Rimo 2010, 37) as it sanctioned behaviors that did not really affect the protected legal good as crimes, thus causing "a deficit of freedom" (Cancio Meliá 2002, 26).

After the reform of 2015, the penalties for these behaviors were increased to three years in prison (previously prison sentences were for one to two years) "when the acts were carried out through the dissemination of services or content accessible to the public through the media, the Internet, or through electronic communications services or through the use of information technologies" (Criminal Code, Article 578, 2). This expansion of cases, together with the fact that the punishment is more severe if they are disseminated through traditional media or the Internet, has led to the conviction of rap singers and a Facebook and Twitter user (e.g., Hasel has been sentenced to nine months in prison for exalting terrorism;[10] Valtonyc has been sentenced to three years and six months in prison;[11] and Facebook and Twitter user Fernando de Reyna was sentenced to one year of prison for the crime of humiliating victims of terrorism[12]). This situation has led to a debate about whether recent reforms are limiting freedom of speech unfairly and disproportionately, especially considering how participation in online networks is increasingly common (Tapia Rojo 2016, 3). This controversy has arisen because many of those condemned, after the inclusion of these new crimes, are not people linked to terrorist movements and are not involved in violent action. Statements that until recently were mere jokes or more or less accurate personal opinions can now be punished. The lack of consensus between the legislator and the courts and the disparity of criteria found in the jurisprudence, as we will see later, does not help the current situation as well. This has clear implications for freedom of speech, which, despite not being an absolute and unlimited right, must be given special or at least meaningful protection.

FREEDOM OF SPEECH IN SPANISH LAW

Freedom of speech in Spain is a fundamental right and consists of the right to "freely express and disseminate thoughts, ideas and opinions by word, writing or any other means of reproduction" (Spanish Constitution Article 20, 1, a). It is not an absolute right as Mir Puig and Corcoy Bidasolo (2012, 13) point out, but it is a preferential right in the sense that it has few internal limits (only that which is expressed as being of public interest and not offensive). Thus, all opinions of public interest that are not injurious will be protected. It should be noted that in Spain's legislation, freedom of speech (to disseminate ideas) is a different right from the right to information (to issue and receive truthful information). Freedom of speech is a broader right because it does not require that opinions be truthful. This does not mean that "anything goes," but that the scope of protection of opinions is very broad. This is because the purpose of this right is the creation of free public opinion, which is necessary to shape and maintain a solid foundation for democracy (Magdaleno Alegría 2007). Freedom of speech does not only protect friendly and neutral opinions but also negative ones, however offensive and despicable they may be. As George Orwell said in his *Rebellion on the Farm* (1945), "If freedom means anything, it is the right to tell others what they do not want to hear." But where is the limit?

The most powerful interpreter of this right in Spain is the Constitutional Court. Its first rulings on freedom of speech date back to 1980. Since then, it has continued to modulate the meaning of this right. In relation to freedom of speech and the class of crimes pertaining the current topic (although the case law is very recent), this court has issued several rulings that consider that "freedom of expression includes freedom of criticism even when it is tasteless and may annoy, disturb or displease those who address it, since pluralism, tolerance and the spirit of openness require it, without which there is no democratic society."[13] It must be understood, therefore, that "freedom of speech applies not only to the dissemination of ideas or opinions welcomed or considered to be harmless or indifferent but also to those which are contrary to, conflict with or disturb the State or any part of the population" (*De Haes and Gijsels v. Belgium* 1997, §49).

But as I pointed out at the beginning, freedom of speech is not an unlimited right, so we must again ask, where is the limit? Can this right justify conduct that is covered by criminal law? Obviously not. Messages that are criminalized are not protected by this right. But it is essential to define their contours in a tangible way to prevent freedom of speech from being so constrained by the law that it goes so far as losing its reason for being. In fact, the 2000 legislation did not intend that the reform of Article 578 of the Criminal Code would restrict freedom of speech, as is shown in the preamble to Law 7/2000 that states:

> It is not a question, with all evidence, of prohibiting the praise or defense of ideas or doctrines, even if these deviate from or even call into question the constitutional framework, nor, even less, of prohibiting the expression of subjective opinions on historical or current events. On the contrary, this is about something as simple as pursuing the exaltation of terrorist means, which are radically illegitimate from any constitutional perspective, or of the perpetrators of these crimes, as well as the particularly perverse conduct of those who slander or humiliate the victims while increasing the horror for their relatives. (Law 7/2000 amending Criminal Code 2000)

So, what is there to consider in determining what should and should not be condemned? Not only should the words be considered, but also the speaker's intention and the context in which those words are being used. This implies including elements as highly subjective as intentionality. However, this is also the understanding of our Constitutional Court when it says:

> In this type of crime, it is important not only the *literal meaning* of the words spoken, but also the *meaning* or *intention* with which they have been used, since it is clear that language ordinarily allows for various interpretations and, for the purposes of establishing responsibility for an offense of glorification of terrorism, it is necessary to clearly determine which of the possible meanings has been used in each specific occasion. (STC 112/2016 2016, 6)[14]

WHEN SHOULD FREEDOM OF SPEECH PREVAIL OVER "SPOKEN TERRORISM"?

To answer this question, we must start from an essential principle: judges cannot make an extensive interpretation of criminal rules that limit freedom of speech in an excessive manner:

> The criminal judge must always bear in mind their constitutional content so as not to run the risk of making criminal law a deterrent to the exercise of freedom of expression, which is undoubtedly undesirable in a State governed by the rule of law. . . . That is how things stand, and the judicial body must assess this, as a matter of principle prior to the application of the criminal law and also taking into account the circumstances of the case, whether the conduct which it prosecutes constitutes a lawful exercise of the fundamental right of freedom of speech and, consequently, if it is justified by the prevailing value for freedom of expression. (Constitutional Court Ruling STC 177/2015, July 22, 2015, 6)[15]

While keeping this principle in mind, answering the question posed is hardly an easy task, considering the case law. The Supreme Court has ruled on this matter in fifty or so judgments (Santiago Ramírez and Cotobal 2019). Many of the convictions were the result of tributes to terrorists who had died, who were in prison, or who had been released. However, the disparity of criteria is evident. On one hand, it is common for the Supreme Court to modify the sentences issued by the lower court, namely the National Audience (as of September 2020, of the fifty sentences issued by the Supreme Court, eighteen modify those issued by the National Audience). On the other hand, there is a high percentage of individual votes issued in sentences on these matters. This is mainly due to the difficulty in establishing the limits in those actions that should be protected by freedom of expression. Thus, there are repeated sentences (affecting similar cases) that consider interference to be legitimate and many others that assert the opposite. Obviously, there is no doubt that when there is a real risk of generating violence (such as in the case of apology), such discourse must be prohibited, and the conduct punished. There is a broad consensus that freedom of speech should be limited when it

> carries the risk that terrorist acts may be committed. In each individual case, the specific circumstances of each case, such as the perpetrator and the recipient of the message, as well as the context in which the act was committed, should be taken into account when considering whether such a risk has materialized. The significance and credibility of this risk should also be considered when applying the provision on public provocation in accordance with national law. (European

Union Directive 2017/541 of the European Parliament and of the European Council 2017, §10)

This implies the significance of assessing the context, the sender, the receiver, and the possibility of actual violence. Doubt in these cases arises in relation to those behaviors that, without resulting in a real risk of provoking terrorist violence, are framed within what we have been calling "spoken terrorism," referring to the crimes of the glorification and justification of terrorism. In light of the difficulties in establishing the limit on the extent to which a given conduct may be considered to be protected by freedom of speech or may constitute a crime, the courts have repeatedly stated that the facts must be carefully evaluated both to determine whether the conduct is criminal and, if so, to determine the penalty as provided by the Criminal Code. All objective and subjective circumstances must be carefully considered to decide whether freedom of speech prevails over conduct that glorifies or justifies violence. Many of the Supreme Court's rulings insist on the need of balancing interests, thereby highlighting the difficulties in resolving the issues on which they must rule: condemnation for glorification, justification of terrorism, humiliation of the victims, or acquittal on the grounds that the subject has acted under the constitutional right to freedom of speech. Thus, as the Constitutional Court states, *consideration is going to be an essential element*, since "the absence of this prior examination to which the criminal judge is obliged or its performance without including the connection of the conduct being prosecuted with the content of fundamental rights and public freedoms is not constitutionally admissible" (Constitutional Court Ruling STC 177/2015 2015, 6).[16]

So far, the answer appears to be that the limitation of freedom of speech cannot be considered as the general rule. It is, however, only legitimate when, after studying the case and making a correct balancing of all the facts and circumstances, the expressions or acts carried out may pose a real risk of provoking terrorist violence directly or indirectly. Speech can also be litigated when there is a real risk for individuals, the rights of third parties, or the system of freedoms itself. In all other cases, freedom of speech shall prevail.

This statement would lead us to believe that only apology should act as a limit to freedom of speech. In contrast, glorification or justification is unlikely to be used to bring about limits to freedom of expression if they are made outside of a terrorist context and without the intention of generating violence. Some circumstances that do not seem to be in the spirit of the law of Spanish jurisprudence are habitual references to the justification of punishments produced when "moral support," "praise for terrorists," and so on, is evident. This seems to be clear from a 2017 Supreme Court ruling. In this case, Jose Ángel and Ovidio were convicted of exalting terrorism by posting many messages extolling and publicizing ISIS/Daesh attacks and crimes on Facebook over a period. After reviewing the case, the Supreme Court ruled that:

> Criminal penalties linked to conduct that incites or advocates terrorism may be justified in limiting freedom of speech when it can be inferred that such conduct poses a risk to national security, territorial integrity or public security, the defense of order or the prevention of crime . . . either as moral support for the activity—through the glorification of the activity itself . . . or as moral support for the ideology through the praise of those who carry out the activity by glorifying its authors. (Supreme Court Ruling STS 221/2017, March 29, 2017, 5)[17]

In a different ruling, the Supreme Court stated that:

> The criminal sanctioning of conduct that glorifies terrorism, as sanctioned in Article 578, implies a legitimate interference in the authors' freedom of speech insofar as it can be considered as a manifestation of hate speech by favoring or encouraging, even indirectly, a situation of risk for persons or rights of third parties or for the system of freedoms itself. (Supreme Court Ruling STS 378/2017, May 25, 2017, 3)[18]

Thus, we can see how the courts, in the interest of justifying the limitation of expressions and opinions that fall outside those that pose a real risk, have introduced a new element into the equation: hate.

HATE SPEECH, FREEDOM OF SPEECH, AND "SPOKEN TERRORISM"

The relationship between hate speech and free speech is one of the most debated in political communication and civil liberties legal literature. Lately, in Spain, one perspective regarding this issue is that hate is commonly invoked to condemn all kinds of behavior and opinions that are not considered to be politically correct. This is probably the result of the inclusion in the Criminal Code of Article 510, which defines hate crimes as:

> Conduct that directly or indirectly encourages, promotes or incites hatred on the grounds of membership of a group, for racist or anti-Semitic reasons or for reasons of ideology, religion or belief, family situation, membership of an ethnic group, race or nation, national origin, sex, sexual orientation or identity, or on grounds of gender, illness or disability. (Criminal Code, Article 510)

As suggested in the previous section, courts also have invoked "hate speech" to justify limitations on freedom of speech on terrorism grounds. For example, the Constitutional Court itself has indicated that the sanctioning of actions that responds to the glorification or justification of terrorism "supposes a legitimate interference in the scope of the freedom of expression of its authors insofar as they can be considered as a manifestation of the discourse of hatred because they promote, encourage, even indirectly, a situation of risk for persons or rights of third parties or for the system of freedoms itself" (Constitutional Court Ruling STC112/2016, 2016, 12). Some authors have argued that the crimes defined in Criminal Code, Article 578, should be considered as "hate crimes in the field of terrorism" (Bernal del Castillo 2016, 19) while others place them "within the crimes of hate based on so-called hate speech" (Arroyo Chamber 2017, 216).

It also needs to be pointed out that the behaviors cited in Article 578 of the Criminal Code ought to have manifestation that makes them punishable because hate alone cannot be punished by law:

> Criminal law cannot prohibit hatred, it cannot punish the citizen who hates. As if that were not enough, the word speech, even in its most simple grammatical meaning, evokes a rational act of communication whose punishment should not be made dependent on the feeling that animates the person who utters it. (Supreme Court Ruling STS 334/2018, July 4, 2018, 7)[19]

It is possible to consider these behaviors within the "discourse of terrorist hatred" when they come from environments or contexts marked by terrorism and violence or if the words are pronounced by subjects who come from that environment, and when the intention (whomever the sender is) is to effectively extol or justify violence. It is difficult to justify the limitation of freedom of speech with subjects who do not belong to these groups or to others close to them, and whose intention is clearly different. Obviously, it will not always be easy to discern the context in which we find ourselves or the intention of the sender of the message. Avoiding the expansion of the catalog of hate speech without limit is necessary.

CONVICTIONS OF MEMBERS OF CIVIL SOCIETY FOR SPOKEN TERRORISM

It is essential to look at some specific cases to see how the rule on spoken terrorism offenses has been applied. Some of those prosecuted have been rappers, comedians, Twitter users, and so on. This situation has generated a wave of opinions contrary to restrictions against freedom of expression encouraged by the fallacious idea that freedom of speech includes "everything." This position has been sustained by the dissolution of the terrorist group ETA in 2011, which has made the possibility of encouraging violence more remote.

Today, there is a certain social tolerance of this type of message in Spain (including messages that justify certain terrorist violence; messages that make jokes about terrorism victims; or messages that encourage individuals to commit an attack against politicians or people who are not to their liking). However, even though ETA is no longer operational, the generation of terrorist violence is still a possibility.

One of the convictions that received the most media coverage was that of the rapper Valtonyc. In 2017, he was sentenced to three and a half years in prison for the crime of glorifying terrorism, threats, and insults to the king (the sentence was ratified by the Supreme Court, Ruling STS 397/2018, February 15, 2018).[20] The National Audience determined that the lyrics of Valtonyc's songs

> goes beyond the expression of coincidence with political objectives, solidarity with prisoners, or camaraderie born of ideological ties and which carry praise, not only of political objectives but of the violent means employed by the aforementioned terrorist organizations and their members and contains an incitement to its reiteration. (SAN 2017, 10)

Furthermore, the court determined that "the aforementioned contents are not covered by the freedom of speech or dissemination of opinions invoked by the defendant and his defense" (STS 2018, 11). Some of the lyrics for which Valtonyc was convicted incorporate language such as: "a shot in the forehead from your boss is justified or there is always hope that he will be kidnapped by some GRAPO" (STS 2018, 3); "we want fear to knock on your doors with flames" (STS 2018, 3); or "that a PP bus with loaded nitroglycerine will explode" (referring to the Popular Party)[21] (STS 2018, 3); "but hey, we have rubber2 and amonal,[22] and so we will arrive a day that exploiters will fly, as high as right-wing workers who are now businessmen, I will cut their necks as they cut expenses" (STS 2018, 5).

Consider the case of César Strawberry, a rap singer. He was sentenced by the Supreme Court (Ruling STS 4/2017, January 18, 2017).[23] He was convicted of posting tweets like: "Ortega Lara[24] should be kidnapped now" (STS 2017, 3) or "how many should follow the flight of Carrero Blanco"[25] (STS 2017, 3). He was acquitted by the Constitutional Court in 2020 (Ruling STC 35/2020, February 25, 2020).[26]

Yet, in another instance, the Audiencia Nacional Court sentenced Cassandra Vera in 2017 for the crime of glorifying terrorism in the form of humiliating the victims through thirteen mocking messages published on Twitter that were about Carrero Blanco (SAN 514/2017, March 29, 2017).[27] The Supreme Court acquitted her in 2018,[28] finding that "they [the tweets] did not contain any acidic comments targeting the victim of the attack or express hurtful, lacerating or outrageous phrases or comments against their person or any specific aspect of their public or private life" (STS 95/2018 2018, 21).

These are just some examples as there are many other cases that make us wonder whether or not this type of message should be considered within the crime of glorification of terrorism, especially given we are dealing with people who are neither directly nor indirectly linked to terrorist environments, and whose intention is not to generate violence in any way. It is also essential to bear in mind that their messages refer to terrorist groups that are currently inactive.

ON PENALTIES

Regarding spoken terrorism, the Spanish Criminal Code stipulates penalties ranging from one to three years in prison. The judge may also decide during sentencing to legally disqualify the person for the exercise of charge or public employee for a period that he or she determines. Furthermore, it is considered an aggravating circumstance if the facts show that the act was carried out with publicity, that is, if it was disseminated through the media or any other information technology. This is also the case when the facts seriously disturb the public peace or create a serious feeling of insecurity or fear in all or part of the society. As a precautionary or definitive measure, the judge may order the destruction of all materials used (documents, recordings, etc.). If the message has been perpetrated through digital means, the judge may request the deletion of illicit contents both from websites and search engines.

In the discussion of penalties, it is important to consider the principle of proportionality (Cuerda Arnau 2007, 109). The penalty imposed should be proportional to the damage caused. It is, therefore, highly relevant to take this principle into account when an exaggerated limitation of certain fundamental rights may be at stake. It is also necessary to avoid a punitive expansion that may affect other rights (Bernal del Castillo 2016, 17), including violating the right to freedom of speech (Alonso Rimo 2010, 77). Thus, to ensure the proportionality of penalties, each specific case must be assessed.

It should also be kept in mind that the tendency of the courts is to impose the penalty at its lowest limit: one-year imprisonment, with a few cases resulting in prison sentences of one year and six months. Two-year imprisonment is exceptional. It should be noted that, in Spain, imprisonment exceeding two years for such offenses is not permissible. If a sentence exceeds two years, it is because it is not the only crime committed by the subject or because the subject is a repeat offender.

It should also be noted that in the event that the judge or court is not clear about whether freedom of speech protects the subject from being prosecuted for the crime (i.e., doubt as to whether the conduct is punishable or not), freedom of speech shall prevail, that is, the conduct will go unpunished, not because freedom of expression is a fundamental right but because of the principle of *in dubio pro reo*. In other words, in case of doubt, the judge or court must acquit.

On the issue of "cases of doubt," it is a consolidated doctrine of the Spanish Constitutional Court in relation to the glorification/justification of terrorism that judicial work must be individualized by studying the circumstances of each case. The conflict between spoken terrorism and freedom of expression is evident, which means it will be necessary to analyze both the specific phrases or expressions and the time and place where it is pronounced to determine whether or not it is a crime (Constitutional Court Ruling STC 112/2016, June 20, 2016)[29]. In other words, when faced with doubt, the principle *in dubio favor libertatis* must be respected: "In case of doubt, in favor of freedom" (Supreme Court Ruling STS 748/2015, February 19, 2015, 8).[30]

CONCLUSION

In light of the discussion thus far, freedom of speech should be considered a preferential, though not unlimited, right. Freedom of expression also should protect extreme opinions, even when they may be considered despicable by society at large. However, there are certain behaviors that are not protected by this right, particularly when the objective is generating violence insofar as they are oriented toward it and provoke it. Proving intention is not enough as there must also exist a real possibility of creating violence. Thus, the apology of terrorism must be condemned as a verbal act of terrorism since the aim of such behavior is precisely to provoke others to generate more terrorist violence. As for the crime of humiliation to the victims, it should be considered subsumed as a crime of defamation (not within the crimes of verbal terrorism). Thus, the crime of humiliation to the victims should be included at the request of a party, that is, they are only investigated if the offended party requests that they should. Consequently, simple jokes (although unfortunate or even unpleasant) should be exempt from prosecution. In this case, the law should be modified, since, in the existing one, some types of jokes can be considered spoken terrorism.

As for the crimes of glorification and justification, the answer is not so simple. Any opinion, idea, or expression that is not aimed at generating violence should be protected by freedom of speech, but not those that are susceptible to generating violence in a palpable way (Galán Muñoz 2018, 293). This involves, as some authors (e.g., Mira Benavent 2018, 318) note, analyzing the type of person who sends the message (it is not the same to be a politician, a religious leader, or a political activist as a simple citizen with many or few followers who are active on social networks); the context (there are differences if the terrorist group in question is still active or not); the recipient (it is not the same if the public receiving the message is a group of sympathizers of these pro-terrorist messages as opposed to citizens who are alien or even opposed to these messages); and intentionality (the individual who seeks to convince, recruit or encourage violence will not be treated the same as one who gives an opinion).

NOTES

1. First of October Antifascist Resistance Group (GRAPO) is a Spanish terrorist organization born in Galicia in 1975 with the aim of establishing a "popular and federative republic" in Spain (Jiménez 1992, 113). They are considered a terrorist group by the European Union (European Union 2004) and the United States (United States Department of State 2005).
2. Terra Lliure or "Free Land" was a Spanish terrorist organization founded in 1978 and dissolved in 1991. Its objective was to build a socialist Catalonia independent of Spain. Some of its leaders and militants subsequently joined the Esquerra Republicana de Catalunya (ERC), which required them to explicitly renounce terrorism as a condition of enrollment). See Piñol (1991).
3. Some examples include Decree-Law 10/1975 of August 26, on the prevention of terrorism; Organic Law 11/1980 of December 1, on the cases provided for in Article 55.2 of the Spanish Constitution (CE) (on the actions of armed gangs or terrorist elements); and Law 9/1984 of December 26, known as the anti-terrorist law.
4. LOPP, Article 9, 3, a.
5. Tribunal Supremo. 2003. "Sentencia, de 27 de marzo de 2003, del Tribunal Supremo sobre la ilegalización de los partidos políticos Herry Batasuna, Euskal Herritarrok y Batasuna." DERECONS (Red Académica de Derecho Constitucional). https://dialnet.unirioja.es/servlet/articulo?codigo=3418456.
6. STC 5/2004, January 16, 2004, §18 (Resolution of the appeal filed by Batasuna against its illegalization) http://hj.tribunalconstitucional.es/de/Resolucion/Show/5010.
7. Organic Law 2/2015 amending the Organic Law 10/1995 of the Penal Code Regarding Crimes of Terrorism. 2015. https://www.boe.es/boe/dias/2015/03/31/pdfs/BOE-A-2015-3440.pdf.
8. In recent times, several initiatives have been presented to repeal Article 578 of the penal code. The last one, in March 2020, was proposed by the Parliamentary Group Unidas Podemos. If it were to be repealed, the exaltation or justification of terrorism could be punished, according to Art. 579, if there is evidence of incitement of terrorist acts. Humiliation of victims would be a crime of defamation.
9. Law 1/1982, May 5, 1982, on Civil Protection of the Right to Honor, Personal and Family Privacy and Self Image.
10. SAN 8/2014, March 31, 2014.http://www.poderjudicial.es/search/AN/openCDocument/c277b83324185873f820b9f14c5b14b4e72d6b2c0fb88c03. In this resolution, a rap singer was sentenced to nine months of imprisonment.

11. STS 397/2018, February 15, 2018. http://www.poderjudicial.es/search/indexAN.jsp. In this resolution, a rap singer was sentenced to three years and six months in prison.

12. SAN 25/2017, December 11, 2017.http://www.poderjudicial.es/search/AN/openCDocument/c277b83324185873b2bf057e5c710c89094a1ef10f1fb978. In this resolution, a Facebook and Twitter user was sentenced to one year of prison for the crime of humiliating victims of terrorism.

13. STC 177/2015, of July 22. https://www.boe.es/boe/dias/2015/08/21/pdfs/BOE-A-2015-9392.pdf. Promoted by Jaume Roura Capellera and Don Enric Stern Taulats against the sentence that condemns them for a crime of insulting the Crown for the public burning of the portrait of the Kings.

14. STC 112/2016, June 22, 2016. https://www.boe.es/diario_boe/txt.php?id=BOE-A-2016-7289. Promoted by Tasio Erkizia Almandoz against the sentence that condemns him for a crime of exalting terrorism and hate speech by the public praise of an author of terrorist activities.

15. STC 177/2015, July 22, 2015. http://hj.tribunalconstitucional.es/docs/BOE/BOE-A-2015-9392.pdf. Promoted by Jaume Roura Capellera and Don Enric Stern Taulats against the sentence that condemns them for a crime of insulting the Crown for the public burning of the portrait of the Kings.

16. Ibid.

17. STS 221/2017, March 29, 2017. https://supremo.vlex.es/vid/676592769. In this resolution, a man was sentenced for exalting Islamic terrorism to one year and three months in prison.

18. STS 378/2017. May 25, 2017. https://supremo.vlex.es/vid/680381361. The Supreme Court revoked the one-year prison sentence that the National Court imposed on a Facebook user for messages wishing that "hopefully" ETA and GRAPO will return: it was the first case in which the Supreme Court reversed a sentence.

19. STS 334/2018. July 4, 2018. (In this resolution, a judgment of the National Court was annulled, in which a man was sentenced to one year in prison for exalting terrorism in social networks.) http://www.poderjudicial.es/search/index.jsp.

20. STS 397/2018, February 15, 2018.http://www.poderjudicial.es/search/AN/openCDocument/cac2ec927df2ac24599e4e9439214f9125b594b67952d9a8. In this resolution, the sentence imposed in the SAN 494/2017, February 21, 2017, is confirmed.

21. The Popular Party is a conservative liberal Spanish political party located between the center-right and the political right. It ruled between 1996 and 2004 with José María Aznar and between 2011 and 2018 with Mariano Rajoy. It is currently the party of the political opposition to the Government.

22. Rubber2 and amonal are the types of explosives that ETA commonly used in its attacks.

23. STS 4/2017, January 18, 2017. https://supremo.vlex.es/vid/661459257. In this resolution, a singer was sentenced for exalting terrorism.

24. Ortega Lara is a retired Spanish prison official who was kidnapped by the terrorist organization ETA for 532 days between 1996 and 1997.

25. Luis Carrero Blanco was the president of the Spanish Government with Francisco Franco. He was assassinated by ETA in 1973.

26. STC 35/2020, February 25, 2020. https://www.boe.es/diario_boe/txt.php?id =BOE-A-2020-4120. The Constitutional Court annulled a sentence of the Supreme Court in which a man was sentenced for exalting terrorism through social networks. He considers that his right to freedom of expression was violated.

27. SAN 514/2017, March 29, 2017.http://www.poderjudicial.es/search/AN/Ope nDocument/ df20f64a08082024/20170330. A Twitter user, Cassandra, was convicted of humiliating the victims because of jokes.

28. STS 95/2018, February 26, 2018. https://ep00.epimg.net/descargables/2018/03 /01/efce456d8d321e7c99d1746413da7e79.pdf. In this resolution, the judgment of the National Court about Cassandra's case was annulled.

29. Ratification of a sentence for praising terrorism for a subject from the terrorist environment. For more, see https://www.boe.es/diario_boe/txt.php?id=BOE-A-2016 -7289.

30. STS 748/2015, February 19, 2015.http://www.poderjudicial.es/search/doAct ion?action=contentpdf&databasematch=TS&reference=7323856&links=%221374 /2014%22&optimize=20150313&publicinterface=true. Condemnatory sentence against rap singer Hasse for exalting terrorism.

REFERENCES

Alonso Rimo, Alberto. 2010. "Apología, enaltecimiento del terrorismo y principios penales." *Revista de Derecho Penal y Criminología* 4 (3): 13–80.

Álvárez Conde, Enrique, and Hortensia González Rodríguez. 2006. "Legislación antiterrorista comparada después de los atentados del 11 de septiembre y su incidencia en el ejercicio de los derechos fundamentales." *Revista Real Instituto El Cano de Estudios Internacionales y Estratégicos* 7: 1–10.

Bernal del Castillo, Jesús. 2016. "El enaltecimiento del terrorismo y la humillación a sus víctimas como formas del discurso del odio." *Revista de Derecho penal y Criminología* 16 (3): 13–43.

Cámara Arroyo, Sergio. 2017. "El concepto del delito de odio su comisión a través del discurso del odio. Especial referencia al conflicto con la libertad de expresión." *Anuario de Derecho Penal y Ciencias Penales* 70: 139–225.

Cancio Meliá, Manuel. 2002. "Derecho penal del enemigo y delitos de terrorismo en el Código penal español después de la LO 7/200." *Jueces para la Democracia*, 44: 19–26.

Cano Paños, Miguel Ángel. 2016. "Odio e incitación a la violencia en el contexto del terrorismo islamista. Internet como elemento ambiental." *InDret: Revista para el análisis del Derecho* 4: 2–37.

Cararsco Andino, Mª del Mar. 2019. "Derechos fundamentales y legislación antoterrorista. ¿Qué hemos perdido por el camino?" *Estudios Penales y Criminológicos* 39: 59–105. http://dx.doi.org/10.15304/epc.39.5766.

Cuerda Arnau, María Luisa. 2007. "Proporcionalidad penal y libertad de expresión: la función dogmática del efecto desaliento." *Revista General de Derecho Penal*, 8.

———. 2008. "Terrorismo y libertades políticas." *Teoría y Derecho: Revista de pensamiento jurídico* 3: 61–97.

Dolz Lago, Manuel Jesús. 2013. "Delito de descrédito, menosprecio o humillación víctimas del terrorismo: diferencias con el delito de enaltecimiento o justificación en los delitos de terrorismo." *Diario La Ley* 8152.

European Union. 2004. "Official Journal of the European Union, Vol. 47." April 3, 2004. https://eur-lex.europa.eu/legal-content/EN/TXT/?uri=OJ:L:2004:099:TOC.

Fernández Martínez, Juan Manuel. 2010. "Enaltecimiento del terrorismo." *Revista Aranzadi Doctrinal* 10: 37–44.

Galán Muñoz, Alfonso. 2018. "El delito de enaltecimiento terrorista. ¿Instrumento de lucha contra el peligroso discurso del odio terrorista o mecanismo represor de repudiables mensajes de raperos, twitteros y titiriteros?" *Estudios Penales y Criminológicos* 38: 1–60. http://dx.doi.org/10.15304/epc.38.5127.

Jiménez, Fernando. 1992. "Spain: The Terrorist Challenge and the Government's Response." *Terrorism and Political Violence* 4 (4): 110–130. https://doi.org/10.1080/09546559208427176.

Magdaleno Alegría, Antonio. 2007. "Libertad de expresión, terrorismo y límites de los derechos fundamentals." *Revista de Derecho Público* 69: 181–218. https://doi.org/10.5944/rdp.69.2007.9023.

Mir Puig, Santiago and Mirentxu Corcoy Bidasolo (Dirs). 2012. *Protección penal de la libertad de expresión e información*. Valencia: Tirant lo Blanch.

Mira Benavent, Javier. 2018. "El delito de enaltecimiento del terrorismo, el de humillación a las víctimas del terrorismo y la competencia de la Audiencia Nacional: ni delito, ni terrorismo, ni competencia de la Audiencia Nacional." In *Terrorismo, sistema penal y derechos fundamentales,* edited by AlbertoAlonso Rimo, María Luisa Cuerda Arnau, and Antonio Hernández Fernández, 299–330. Valencia: Tirant lo Blanch.

Orwell, George. 1945. *Rebellion on the Farm.* Madrid: Austral.

Piñol, Angels. 1991. "Terra Lliure renuncia a la violencia y anuncia que sus militantes ingresarán en Esquerra Republicana." *El País*, July 5, 1991. https://elpais.com/diario/1991/07/06/espana/678751218_850215.html.

Pillar, Paul. 2001. "The Instruments of Counterterrorism." *An Electronic Journal of the U.S. Department of State* 6 (3): 10–13.

RAE (Royal Spanish Academy). 2020. Dictionary of the Royal Academy of the Spanish Language. http://www.rae.es.

Ramos Vázquez, José Antonio. 2008. "Presente y futuro del enaltecimiento y justificación del terrorismo." *Anuario Facultad de Derecho Universidad de Coruña* 12: 771–795.

Rollnert Liern, Goran. 2014. "Incitación al terrorismo y libertad de expresión: el marco internacional de una relación problemática." *Revista de Derecho Político* 91: 231–262.

Ruiz Landáburu, Mª José. 2002. *Provocaión y apología: delitos de terrorismo.* Madrid: Colex.

Santiago Ramírez, Vanessa, and Víctor Cotobal. 2019. *Enaltecimiento del terrorismo. Análisis jurisprudencial y policial del artículo 578 del Código penal.* Madrid: Colex.

Soto García, Mercedes. 2012. "Los límites de la libertad de expresión en el debate político." *Revista de Derecho Comunitario Europeo* 42: 575–591.

Tapia Rojo, María Eugenia. 2016. "Análisis de la estrategia comunicativa del terrorismo yihadista. El papel de las redes sociales." *Instituto Español de Estudios Estratégicos* 2: 1–15.

Tenorio Sánchez, Pedro. 2010. *Constitución, derechos fundamentales y seguridad.* Madrid: Thomson/Civitas.

Teruel Lozano, Germán. 2015. "La libertad de expresión frente a los delitos de negacionismo y de provocación al odio y a la violencia: sobras y luces en la reforma del Código penal." *InDret*: *Revista para el análisis del Derecho* 4: 1–51.

Teruel Lozano, Germán. 2018. "Internet, incitación al terrorismo y libertad de expresión en el marco europeo." *InDret*: *Revista para el análisis del Derecho* 3: 1–34.

US Department of State. 2005. "Country Reports on Terrorism 2004." https://2009-2017.state.gov/j/ct/rls/crt/c14818.htm.

Chapter 5

Counter-terrorism Gone Digital

Framing Cybercrime in Turkey

Nazli Bülay Doğan

INTRODUCTION

This chapter deals with the political implications of cyberterrorism discourse in Turkey.[1] In parallel, it asks how the discourse of counter-terrorism functions within the meaning-making process about cybercrime for the Turkish state. Based on a qualitative study, I explore how the Turkish judicial system perceives cyberterrorism through data generated from interviews involving a Turkish hacktivist group charged with terrorism in the 2010s. In this line of inquiry, my research question is based on the functionality of the counter-terrorism discourse on the Internet.

I will start by discussing the context of Turkish politics, terrorism, and counter-terrorism. Then, I will review discussions of cyberterrorism within their sociopolitical contexts. Next, I will examine how the case of diverse frames of cybercrime, terrorism, and cyberterrorism concretize the contemporary perspective of the Turkish state as they relate to counterterrorism practices in the digital realm.

TERRORISM AND COUNTERTERRORISM IN TURKEY: A CONTEXT

Terrorism and counterterrorism have been central topics in the Turkish political agenda for at least the past forty years. Since the rise of terrorism discourse, issues of national security, civil liberties, and state control intermingle to influence the greater Turkish sociopolitical context in profound ways. This discourse finds its source dating back to the military coup of 1980 and the subsequent promulgation of the Anti-Terror Law (TMK) in 1991.

In the pre-coup political atmosphere, Turkey was shaken by political polarization between the working class and those who wanted to maintain the status quo against the former's rising political demands. The military coup of 1980 erased the political regime which was built on the struggle of the working class (Savran 1987, 153). After taking over political power on September 12, 1980, the armed forces dissolved the parliament and deposed the cabinet, and all political parties and some trade union confederations were suspended. This period was also characterized by arrests and mass trials against leftists and extreme right-wing militants, with hundreds of leftists dismissed, imprisoned, and tortured as the result of the coup.[2]

Another decisive result of this coup for Turkey was the development of neoliberal conservative policies. Very similar to Chile's case of 1973, the military coup of 1980 in Turkey was a deliberate strategy of "shock doctrine" aimed to support neoliberal free-market policies (Klein 2007). In line with the worldwide rise of neoliberal political current, the leftist political presence was largely erased both discursively and physically from the Turkish political scene.

The severe judicial atmosphere created by the military coup quickly became the concretization of what the German criminal law professor Günther Jakobs names as the "enemy criminal law" (Rosenau and Temel 2008, 393–396). This perspective divides the population between normal citizens—who stay as citizen even though they commit a crime—and enemies—who must be fought against. During the 1980s, enemy criminal law consolidated its existence through legislation related to counterterrorism. In the post-coup Turkey, this meant prisoners of conscience spent years under arrest (Kanar 2015, 188–189).

Within this context, political offenses were transformed irreversibly to terrorism in Turkish criminal discourses. Political crime as a concept was ignored in favor of an enlarged terror frame which was constructed based on the neglect of actors' motivations (Bayraktar 2015, 149). In the subsequent period, the Turkish state developed a zero-tolerance authoritarian policy against leftists and Kurdish dissidents while economic liberation discourse and free markets rhetoric shaped the political agenda under the pretense of liberty. This counterterrorism strategy would result in a civil war and the massacre of leftist and Kurdish militants during the dark days of the 1990s. This was the political atmosphere in which the Turkish Anti-terror Law was promulgated in 1991. Article 1 of the Anti-Terror Law defined terrorism as:

> Any criminal action conducted by one or more persons belonging to an organization with the aim of changing the attributes of the Republic as specified in the Constitution, the political, legal, social, secular, or economic system, *damaging the indivisible unity of the State* with its territory and nation, *jeopardizing the*

> *existence of the Turkish State* and the Republic, *enfeebling, destroying or seizing the State authority*, eliminating basic rights and freedoms, *damaging the internal and external security of the State*, the public order or general health, is defined as terrorism. (Turkish Anti-Terror Law 1991, Article 1, emphasis added)

With an explicit emphasis on harm toward the state as the decisive element to define terrorism, the written legal definition of terrorism actually suggests a non-framing due to its broad interpretable nature. The absence of demarcations that differentiate terrorist acts from non-terrorist acts results in the ambiguity to define terrorism. In this case, rather than a written legal definition, the framing of terror relies heavily on agreed-upon names that can be seen as "folk devils," which are actors "defined as a threat to societal values and interests" (Cohen 1972, 9).

In the Turkish context, reference to terror is fed by "moral panics," which can be defined as public indignation fanned by the media (Young 1971, 37) about aforementioned survivors of the 1980 coup—the Kurdish movement and the armed socialist and communist groups active in the 1990s using extralegal political methods. These outlawed organizations challenge the monopoly of violence of the Turkish state. The Kurdistan Workers' Party (PKK) is the primary armed political organization struggling for the Kurdish movement for more than 30 years.[3] DHKPC (Revolutionary People's Liberation Party/Front) is a Marxist-Leninist organization that has used arms since its formation in 1994.[4] Imagined as "folk devils," these groups are constructed as responsible actors for many of the potential or imagined threats in Turkey.

Folk devils' most common representation is the image of "domestic enemies" whose supposed main purpose is to keep the country from developing. The quest for development is a popular political discourse for the past few centuries in Turkey. Together with the modernization myth, the developmentalist ideal is one of the cornerstones of the Turkish official discourse (Özbek 2003, 235). In this discourse, domestic and foreign enemies appear as scapegoats—entities that are to be blamed if Turkey could not reach the foreseen development level (Cinar 2017, 62).

Amnesty International (AI) published a report criticizing Article 8 of the Anti-Terror Law which outlawed all "separatist" statements "irrespective of the method or intention" were risen (Amnesty International 1991, 4). These methods included "written or spoken propaganda, assemblies, demonstrations, and marches" (Turkish Anti-Terror Law 1991, Article 8). AI considered this perspective as a tool to intimidate and eliminate political dissidence (Amnesty International 1994). Moreover, AI claimed that "the imprecise nature" of the charges included in Article 8 could be used as a pretext for graver violations of the right to freedom of opinion and expression (Amnesty International 1995, 14). Human Rights Watch (2002) shared these concerns by stressing that the Anti-Terror Law punished many nonviolent actors such as pacifists and those who are critical of political violence under the premises of Article 8.

After a decade marred with controversy, the 2000s brought about a more relaxed atmosphere for Turkey concerning terrorism discourse. This atmosphere was mostly influenced by the unilateral cease-fire declared by PKK in 2000. Consequently, terrorism discourse receded in Turkey in the following years. This coincided with the coming into power of the Justice and Development Party (AKP) in 2002. As an actor performing within the neoliberal period fueled by populist ideologies, AKP was considered as the representative of moderate Islam. In its quest of consolidating its power, AKP conducted reforms in line with the International Monetary Fund's (IMF) conditionalities and the European Union's (EU) harmonization laws. AKP followed the post-coup political orientation of Turkish capitalism, which had moved toward global integration by the end of the 1990s. However, this consensus between international neoliberal institutions and the AKP around "requirements of the ascendant market-oriented internationalization" brought along the "consolidation of neoliberal authoritarian statism," which is characterized by the overgrowth of the executive branch of the state apparatus to manage capitalist contradictions (Oğuz 2009, 17–18). AKP conducted many reforms related to freedom of expression in the 2000s such as the promulgation of Press Law No. 5187 and amendments to the Anti-Terror Law. In 2003, the notorious Article 8 of the Anti-Terror Law was abolished, and, therefore, the last vestige of the so-called "thought crimes" were supposed to be eliminated within the sixth reform package (Ozbudun 2007, 184). However, the repressive reactions of the government in these years showed how reforms and repressions were concomitant and complementary sides of AKP's governmentality (Erensü and Alemdaroğlu 2018).

The instrumentalization of the Anti-Terror Law is a perfect example for understanding the repressive practices of the AKP government during its "liberal" period. From 2006 to 2017, several amendments were made to the law. These amendments broadened the range of crimes that were considered as terrorist offenses, extended lengths of punishment, and, in several instances, restrained the right to fair trial. The rising number of terror convicts included political dissidents, media agents, students, and human rights activists. The number of convicts escalated from 273 to 12,897 between 2005 and 2011 (Erensü and Alemdaroğlu 2018, 22–23). In the following years, the repressive practices took the shape of violent suppression of protests and strikes alongside increasing persecution of dissidents and journalists.

Even though terrorism discourse was already a mainstream agenda in Turkey before 2000, 9/11 fueled its relevance to new heights as evidenced by the escalating numbers of terror convicts. Despite a seemingly liberal political atmosphere in Turkey during that time, the AKP government's repressive practices about the enlargement of terror charges were no doubt encouraged by this rise of the war on terror discourse.

In the 2010s, important national events significantly influenced the course of the terrorism discourse. The Gezi protests of 2013, which were a part of the wave of anti-austerity movements and anti-governmental uprisings in the 2010s ranging from the Arab uprisings to the Occupy movements, became the symbol of public discontent in Turkey against the AKP government.[5] The year 2013 then witnessed another political crisis for then-prime minister Recep Tayyip Erdoğan's Party. Before the end of the year, the political agenda of Turkey was again shaken, now with an explicit conflict between the Gülen Community and AKP via a corruption scandal.[6] The last event that would shape the terrorism discourse and the counter-terrorism perception in Turkey would be the end of the Peace Process between the PKK and the Turkish state.[7] This would result in military campaigns in Kurdish cities and the corrosion of the rule of law, especially in political reactions related to these campaigns. These crises would become the roots of the aggravated terrorism discourse in Turkey by the second half of the 2010s.

In parallel with these crises, AKP diminished the separation of powers, weakened the role of the legislative power, and took the judiciary's power under its control (Erensü and Alemdaroğlu 2018, 17). It is at this time that Recep Tayyip Erdoğan would begin to use terror frames as enlarged and influential labels to incrementally include HDP, the Gülen Community, and many leftist dissidents under the umbrella term of "unarmed terrorists" by the beginning of 2016 (Diken 2016). Erdoğan would declare: "There is no difference between terrorists and those who gave order to (influence) the terrorists by using its position, its pen and its title. An academic, a journalist, the director of an NGO are also terrorists" (Diken 2016, translation by author).[8] This broadened definition of a "terrorist" is actually in line with the Anti-Terror Law's provisions. Per Article 2 of the Anti-Terror Law, terrorist offenders are "persons who, not being a member of a terrorist organization, commit a crime in the name of the organization, are also considered as terrorist offenders and shall be punished as members of such organizations" (Turkish Anti-Terror Law 1991, Article 2).

It is crucial to emphasize the coherence between the Anti-Terror Law of 1991 and the speech of Recep Tayyip Erdoğan, as it demonstrates the continuity of the terror discourse in Turkey against the perspective defending the sudden authoritarianism turn of AKP in the 2010s. In other words, the contemporary enlargement of the terrorism label by the AKP government is not something new: Erdoğan and its political party contributed to this legacy with several examples. The Turkish state preserved and applied the enemy criminal law approach on terrorism through the State Security Courts (DGMs) founded in the post-coup atmosphere (1982), the Specially Authorized Courts (ÖYMs) founded in place of DGMs that were abolished the same day in 2004, and Specialized Courts, this time (2015), in place of ÖYMs that were abolished in 2014 (Birgün 2015). Consequently, for more than thirty years, "Turkey has never regained normalcy after 1980; it has existed *as a state of exception*" (Kars Kaynar 2017, 33, emphasis in original). The uninterrupted criminalization of political opposition via the continuous presence of exceptional courts indicates how institutions of constitutional states and parliamentary democracies can be regular apparatuses to suppress political oppression (35).

The criminalization of those who are not members of a terrorist organization is a crucial topic in terrorism discourse in Turkey. The counter-terrorism measure of the state created a large enough scope to include as many citizens as possible into its terrorist label. Alongside the category of the active supporters of terrorism, the 1990s created another category of citizens, a type who could be easily deceived and who constantly need to be protected: those who "support terrorist organizations *not* on purpose" (Üstel 2008, 304, emphasis in original). Here, the terrorism discourse frames not only the active agents and their supporters but also the potential audience. By the 2010s, this "unwitting support to terror" framing would fade and would be merged into the "unarmed terrorists" category.

In the summer of 2015, the regular usage of violence as a political tool by ideologically diverse groups such as the Islamic State of Iraq and the Levant, also known as the Islamic State of Iraq and Syria (ISIS), Kurdistan Freedom Hawks (TAK),[9] and the Turkish state have left major marks on the Turkish political trajectory. This context would peak with the military coup attempt in July 2016 and the state of emergency declaration following this attempt which lasted until January 2018.[10] In the end, the proliferation of terror frames and the criminalization of dissidents became part of a larger "a process of rapid democratic retrenchment" and "growing authoritarianism" (Baser, Akgönül, and Öztürk 2017, 3).

DEFINING CYBERTERRORISM

The digital realm has become a crucial site of the debate surrounding terrorism and counterterrorism discourse in Turkey and many other countries in the world. Terrorism is indeed one of "The Four Horsemen of the Info-pocalypse" (Assange et al. 2012, 43). Nation-states and supranational political institutions constantly voice their concerns about terrorism through information and communication technologies (ICTs). The construction of cyberterrorism discourse is part of the wider issues of national security, civil liberties, and state control of ICTs. However, cyberterrorism discourse is strongly linked to fears from cybercrime, which is crystallized in the form of spectral hackers.

The relationship between hackers, hacktivists, and cyberterrorists is a long-debated issue.[11] In some sources, the category of cyberterrorists provides definition to hackers and hacktivists, as a diverging limit. In others, the two categories intermingle easily. In the frequently cited work by Denning (2001), cyberterrorism refers to "the convergence of cyberspace and terrorism. It covers politically motivated hacking operations intended to cause grave harm such as loss of life or severe economic damage" while hacktivism is defined as "operations that use hacking techniques against a target's internet site with the intent of disrupting normal operations but not causing serious damage" (241). The ambiguity of defining *the severity* of the damage is a problematic issue that transforms cyberterrorism to an all-inclusive concept. As a result, while internet technology can stand as an ideal medium to facilitate "threats" of terror attacks, the same technology provides tools for authorities—especially governments—to exert wider control over crime and public use of the internet; and these controls are based on perceived threat of terror (Wykes and Harcus 2009, 216). How the mass media became major constituents in the construction and the promulgation of this discourse (Thatcher 2006), how mobilizing fear through moral panics of cyber-terror is instrumentalized to promote social control (Bowman-Grieve 2015), and how hacktivism came to be labeled as cyberterrorism (Klein 2015; Vegh 2005; Vlavo 2015) are central themes in critical cyberterrorism studies. Yet, cyberterrorism is quite popular since its coining in the 1990s (Collin 1996). To understand the interest in cyberterrorism discourse, a look at the history to the 2000s would be essential. Cyberterrorism discourse has been particularly amplified in the post 9/11 period as mixed labels like "cyber-vandals, hackers, or potential cyberterrorists" began to be used to refer to political hacker groups, especially in the American media (Vegh 2005, 10).

The threat perception of digital technologies is undoubtedly related to its crucial place in today's global economy. The beginning of the 1990s was marked by a rapid restructuring of the internet on "starkly neoliberal lines" (Schiller 1999, 12). Such commercialization was in line with the neoliberal restructuring of the global economy. As the network of networks, the Internet became the perfect tool for the unconstrained movement of capital. In parallel, the crisis deepened the vulnerability felt from network technologies upon which neoliberal globalism heavily depends. Nation-states were considered the most vulnerable actors in this digital transformation.

Were the states really the losers of the digital race? Or were they once again the authors and enforcers of the new system?[12] Cyberattacks allegedly involving states indicate the latter. *Stuxnet*, the cyberattack on the nuclear program of Iran allegedly supported by the United States and Israel, is the first known malware to cause physical damage to the critical infrastructure of a country (Jarvis, Macdonald, and Whiting 2015, 71). However, to perform these alleged cyberattacks—and due to the lack of knowledge about ICTs among traditional state agents—states turn to hackers and adopt them as vigilante groups who in turn facilitate the indirect crime control on the Internet (Wykes and Harcus 2009, 221).

Here comes the image of the hacker as a source of anxiety about ICTs. When states and corporations began to acknowledge the capability of hackers, the fear from them became much more concrete. In the beginning, hacking had been described as "the imaginative re-appropriation of technology's potential within countercultural and oppositional communities" (Jordan and Taylor 2004, 5). Eventually, however, hackers began to be framed as criminals. Their perception turned from the "talented nerds" (Krapp 2005, 71) to those who perform "illicit, illegal or unwanted computer intrusion" (Jordan and Taylor 2004, 5). This transformation was in accordance with the centrality of ICTs in the global political economy. Hacking was criminalized because of the potential that hackers are vested with and the risk that they pose. When information-oriented research and production processes were becoming the characteristic of all major businesses, the old hacker motto of "all information should be free" came to be considered "subversive infringements on the rights of enterprise" (Schiller 1999, 76).[13] Following that, the framing of hackers' as criminals was concretized via this opposition to corporate and governmental interests in the 1990s (Nissenbaum 2004, 195). The mainstream media and culture solidified this representation of hackers as "omnipotent technological wizards" (Steinmetz 2016, 181). By the 2000s, governments, law enforcement, the computer security industry, businesses, and the media begin to actively construct hacking as cybercrime and hackers as folk devils (Yar 2006, 23). In this process, hackers were demonized to justify increases in security, surveillance, and punishment (Nissenbaum 2004, 199–200), leading to construction of the "unquestioning assuredness" in public opinion about "the seriousness of what hackers have done" (Wall 2012, 4–7). In this context where the Internet was incrementally perceived as a criminal space, distorted imagery about hackers fed the panic over technology, crime, terrorism, and economic losses. This resulted in the legitimization of security institutions (Steinmetz 2016, 214). The conflation of cybercriminals with cyberterrorists legitimized new forms of surveillance on the Internet by applying terrorism legislation against large populations. Specifically, such legislation targeted political protesters who were labeled as "domestic extremist" or "domestic terrorist" (Feigenbaum 2011, 86).

Legislative and executive practices deeply influence these counter-terrorism practices in the digital realm. While the legislative powers abstain from defining cyberterrorism, various executive powers willingly establish offices specialized in cybercrime and cyberterrorism. The United States had its first Office of Cybersecurity and Communications under the Bush administration in the post-9/11 period; the UK had its own cybersecurity office in 2009 (Vlavo 2015, 5). Turkey established the Department of Cybercrime under Turkish National Police in 2011. Two conventions by the Council of Europe stand as important documents about cyberterrorism, without explicitly using the term, namely the Convention on Cybercrime (2001) and the Convention on the Prevention of Terrorism (2005). Even though these documents do not possess legislative or executive powers, the former is important for being the "first international instrument" to be used against crimes committed via the Internet (Marsili 2018, 9).

In Turkey, there is still not a legal document defining cyberterrorism, as is the case in many other countries. Yet, the charges of being a supporter of terrorist organizations would be instrumentalized to control the political discourse in every social media platform, especially on Twitter. Most notably, the heavy use of social media platforms during such pivotal moments as the Gezi protests triggered the heavy surveillance of the digital realm by the Turkish state. This surveillance would be performed by law enforcement agents, citizen-informers, and political trolls sponsored directly by the AKP. Demonization campaigns initiated by AK Trolls would profoundly shape the online political atmosphere in Turkey after 2016 (Bulut and Yörük 2017; Saka 2018). This way, snitching was institutionalized in the digital realm (Yesil, Sözeri, and Khazraee 2017, 16). Results of these new counter-terrorism tactics would include the detention of political dissidents (BBC 2018; Evrensel 2019) and the political intimidation of every social media platform's users. Internet surveillance system became an indispensable part of the "authoritarian surveillant assemblage" in Turkey during this period (Topak 2019, 11).

In addition to the containment politics applied on social media platforms, another area in which counter-terrorism practices have been applied in the digital realm are hacking incidents. Hacking is supposedly covered through Article 243 (unlawfully accessing a data processing system) and Article 244 (preventing the functioning of a system and deletion, alteration or corrupting of data) on the Turkish Penal Code (TPC). The only implication of the "damage to critical infrastructure" that can refer to cyberterrorism is present in Article 244, which declares: "Where this offence is committed in relation to a data processing system of a public institution or establishment, bank or institution of credit, then the penalty to be imposed shall be increased by one half" (Turkish Penal Code 2004, Article 244). Yet, this indirect link in legal documents does not prevent the framing of hacking incidents with the terrorism discourse in Turkey.

Amid all the ambiguities surrounding cyberterrorism and the lack of its legal definitions, the perception of executive and judicial actors involved in cyberterrorism becomes crucial to understand how the categories of cybercrime, terrorism, and cyberterrorism intersect through counter-terrorism measures in Turkey, and how the criminalization processes serve to strictly control the Internet.

METHODOLOGY

Judicial processes always play a central role in the construction of criminalization. In the absence of clear legal definitions, this role becomes much more critical, as *RedHack*'s legal case exhibits. *RedHack* is a political hacker group that fueled the discussion in Turkey about how to define cyberterrorism and how to distinguish terrorism from activism in the digital realm. Founded in 1997, *RedHack* became highly popular following the Gezi protests of 2013. As a self-identified Marxist-Leninist hacktivist group (Mahir 2013), it is the first hacker group to be put on trial and charged with terrorism in Turkey. For that reason, how this group is perceived is a litmus test for understanding how the Turkish state defines terrorism in the digital realm.[14]

In the summer of 2017 and winter of 2018/2019, I conducted a total of twenty-five semi-constructed in-depth interviews with people who worked in cybercrime and terrorism-related judicial processes as experts, law enforcement agents, and lawyers or prosecutors in Turkey.[15] Eight of the twenty-five interviewees involved individuals who worked in judicial cases about *RedHack*.

During the interviews, interviewees were asked how they defined specific concepts (cybercrime, hacking, cyberterrorism, terrorism). As the interviews were not totally structured, idiosyncratic questions appeared in each interview. Questions about *RedHack* were added to concretize their perceptions about aforementioned concepts. In terms of interviewee recruitment, I tried to be as inclusive as possible by considering diversity in age, profession, and political position. Also, interviewees range from active duty to inactivity and retirement. Their distinctive feature is their specialization in cybercrime or terrorism. As there is no official specialization in cyberterrorism, responses about this category varied enormously among interviewees. In reporting interview data, I will use generic labels such as "LEA" (law enforcement agent) to refer to informants anonymously. Each interviewee is assigned a number that distinguishes them from other interviewees (e.g., LEA 1, LEA 2, Prosecutor 1, Prosecutor 2, etc.).

ANALYSIS

When coding and analyzing the data generated from the interviews, specific crime frames emerged in the discourse of executive and judicial actors. The use of these frames exhibited important characteristics about the perception of cyberterrorism in Turkey. In addition, it demonstrated the specific circumstances counter-terrorism practices took the place of cybercrime discourse.

Fear of Cybercrime and Perception of Incompetence by Executive and Judicial Actors

For many interviewees, the fear of cyberterrorism was deeply connected to the perceived characteristics of cybercrime. One of the main characteristics of this fear was the ubiquity of cybercrime. As one interviewee noted: "Nobody has a personal life. Cell phones are chips. There is a system controlling every one of them" (Prosecutor 1, personal communication, 2019). Seeing every technological device as a threat exhibited the hysteria of "potential victimness," a characteristic of "the postmodern fascination with crime" (Jewkes 2004, 28).

In that line, every technological development—and relatedly, every cybercrime threat—seemed to precede the establishment of laws. This made the threat of cybercrime an omnipotent and uncontrollable force. Faced with these threats, interviewees expressed perceived incompetency either for themselves or for the state. Law enforcement was one of the frequent targets that interviewees blamed for their incompetence about ICTs. This incompetence was much more than just the inability to effectively address the threats posed by ICTs in cybercrime and cyberterrorism. It seemed more like an incompetence to adapt to Internet technology.

Interviewed lawyers were extremely critical about the incompetence of law enforcement agencies, as well as the lack of expertise of prosecutors and judges. Prosecutors specializing in cybercrime also complained about the technical difficulties of finding cybercriminals in given circumstances. The ambiguity gave rise to the perception of powerful yet invisible cybercriminals, which were crystallized in the image of hackers. This anxiety against cybercriminals nourished another anxiety: the anxiety of "falling behind." This falling behind is sometimes imagined against cybercriminals, and, in other times, against legal actors of the digital realm–other nation-states.

In both cases, it is closely related to the lack of knowledge, knowledge about how ICTs work.

Cyberwar scenarios and conspiracy theories about how ICTs could be used for "harming the country" appeared several times during the interviews. Attacks to the infrastructure of the country, disabling its power plants and structures, demolishing its communication and transportation networks, and damaging airline companies and hospitals emerged as cyber-paranoias, scenarios that did not happen but *could* happen in Turkey from the perspective of executive and judicial actors. This perspective self-justified the need for patriotic hackers against dangerous and *bad* hackers who are the enemies of the country.

War on Domestic Enemies

As the history of counter-terrorism in Turkey exhibits, the terrorism discourse grounds itself often on the long-established concerns about foreign and domestic enemies. This was echoed in the digital realm. The Turkish state allegedly uses patriotic hacker groups to defend its own ideology against these alleged enemies under the rhetoric of "defending the interests of the state" (LEA 2, personal communication, 2018). For example, *Ayyıldız Tim* is a patriotic hacker group founded in 2002. The group defines its mission as "voluntary lobbying against cyber-attacks targeting Turkey," and proclaims "statism" as its ideological cause with an explicit reference to one of the six official principles of Kemalism.[16] The group aims to protect state institutions, statesman, and "our" moral values (Ayyıldız Tim n.d.). *Ayyıldız Tim* has an explicit ideological affinity with the Turkish state. Many privileges accompany this affinity. Even though it is a hacker organization that performs website attacks—illegal acts according to the Turkish Penal Code's Article 244—the group make calls for recruits through its website and Twitter accounts. Most notably, the group broadcasts propaganda on national TV channels (Ayyildiz Tim 2016) without undergoing any judicial process.

Some interviewees think that the activities of patriotic hackers refer to counter-guerilla[17] working against enemy hacker groups (LEA 5, personal communication, 2018; LEA 6, personal communication, 2019). These are not considered as cyberterrorists by the Turkish state.[18] The real cyberterrorists are political hackers who do not share the state's ideology and those who allegedly want to harm the country, the state, and the people—as overlapping categories. In line with the nationalist ideology of Turkish patriotic hackers, an emphasis on *the harm to the country* becomes decisive to define bad hackers within the discourse of nationalist protectionism. In this perspective, it is not the other countries' patriotic hackers who are defined as terrorists. Rather, these are mostly the "domestic enemies" who are considered as terrorists and/ or cyberterrorists.

Who Is the Enemy?

An important characteristic of such state enemies is the crucial issue of data leaks. *RedHack* stands as a perfect example. The group defaced hundreds of public websites (and few company websites) to protest an event, support offline protests, or commemorate murdered leftists. Their first known leak was from the Ankara Police Directorate website in 2012 through which they publicized information about citizen informants who had sent emails to the police directorate (Radikal 2012a). In 2016, *RedHack* came to the fore once again with their alleged hacking of the email account of the Minister of Energy, Berat Albayrak (Birgün 2016). The most politically delicate issue from these emails was the close relationship between Albayrak and Powertrans, an oil company implicated in deals with oil produced by ISIS (Independent 2016). Such data leaks would trigger judicial processes about *RedHack* in which charges of terrorism would appear.

In line with these acts of *RedHack*, "stealing documents" appeared in many interviews, as a critical point to describe cyberterrorism. Although not identified as a physical harm or a cause for disability, the critical possession of data appears as harming the state. "E-state structure, data. It is the most valuable thing, data. That means the cause (*dava*) of a country" (LEA 5, personal communication, 2018). The attributed centrality of data by the interviewees reflects the informationalism argument presented by Castells (2001) which posits that processing information became the main driver of economic, political, and social systems.

The ghost of the leftist political violence and its armed opposition to the state also appeared within the interviews for defining cyberterrorism. Repertoire selection of the leftist groups like "throwing a Molotov cocktail" (Prosecutor 3, personal communication, 2019) and "placing a bomb in a bank" (Prosecutor 1, personal communication, 2019) were mentioned as analogies to label data theft and bringing down of ICT systems as acts of cyberterrorism. However, the summoning of the communist folk devils was not popular anymore in the Turkish news media. For example, CNN Türk's website used a humorous tone when reporting the prosecutor's office specializing in cybercrime's decision to consider *RedHack* as a terrorist organization based on the latter's hammer and sickle logo and their possession of a manifesto (CNN Türk 2012). Many news outlets would report the decision with the same satirical tone (Odatv 2012; Radikal 2012b; Sabah 2012; SoL 2012). In the end, due to the aforementioned absence of the legal definition of cyberterrorism, interviewees defined cyberterrorism according to their own ideology and through their own imagination. Mostly, this imagination was constructed based on the agreed-upon Turkish state's definition of terrorism and terrorists.

Imagining Cyberterrorism with Agreed-Upon Terrorists

The absence of a description for cyberterrorism in legal texts creates a maneuvering area for state agents to enlarge the definition of terror in the digital realm. The ambiguity of defining cyberterrorism is overcome with hypothetical relations formed between cyberterrorists and *agreed-upon* terrorists. For example, LEA 6 (personal communication, 2019) notes: "If they have connections with terrorist organizations that would harm the system of the state, then the law considers this notion as terror."

Interviewees used many folk devils from Turkish political history to designate cyberterrorists: "Leftist terrorist organization, DHKP-C, MLKP,[19] they do propaganda through ICTs, they collect militants to their organizations. Fuat Avni,[20] he is right-wing terrorist" (LEA 7, personal communication, 2019). Here, the appearance of the organizations that the Turkish state accepts as terrorists is critical to define cyberterrorism. Cyberterrorism exists through its relationship with offline terrorism, and, at the same time, terrorism exists through its relationship with the state. In these relations, the concept of *support* becomes a crucial issue echoing the terrorism discourse of Turkey since the 1980s. Similar to how "support to terrorist organizations" is central for defining the general terrorism discourse, it is fundamental in defining the terrorism discourse in the digital realm, too. Judicial processes about the hacker group *RedHack* exhibit perfect examples of this tendency.

During the first judicial process related to data leaks from Ankara Police Directorate performed by *RedHack*, those who followed and liked the group were charged as being members of *RedHack*. Alongside cybercrime charges defined in Article 243, Article 244, and Article 334 (securing prohibited information), charges of being terrorist offender (Turkish Anti-Terror Law 1001, Article 2), being part of a terrorist organization (Turkish Anti-Terror Law 1001, Article 7), and establishing organizations for the purpose of committing crimes or committing an offense on behalf of an organization, although not being a member of that organization (Turkish Penal Code 2004, Article 220), appeared in the indictment (Ankara Chief Public Prosecutor's Office 2012). In the decision of this case, the charges of terrorism took the shape of alleged relations with organizations that the Turkish judiciary acknowledged as terrorists. This charge was based upon the support of *RedHack* for Marxist-Leninist-Maoist leftist and separatist groups. In this language, the prosecutor declared that *RedHack*'s members are committing a crime in the name of terrorist organizations without being members. The judge of the lawsuit declared *RedHack* as an illegal organization, without claiming it as a terrorist organization (Ankara Heavy Penal Court no. 7 2015). That decision exhibited how alleged terror offenses on the Internet were resulting not from the acts but from perceived relations with agreed-upon terrorists. However, none of the suspects were sentenced at the end of the five years (Ankara Heavy Penal Court no. 7 2015). Terrorism charges against *RedHack* ensured long periods of arrests (Cumhuriyet 2015; Diken 2017; Sputnik Türkiye 2016) and repetitive detentions with mistreatment allegations (Cumhuriyet 2016) in each judicial process in the following years.[21] These usual "side-effects" of counter-terrorism exhibited how preventive judicial measures were used as punishment tactics by the Turkish state.

In later lawsuits, those who faced trial were people who were charged not for being members of *RedHack* but for being supporters of the group. They include, for example, a private from the Turkish army who allegedly shared the leaked information (Amasya Heavy Penal Court 2016) or journalists who allegedly propagated for the group (Istanbul Chief Public Prosecutor's Office 2017, 4–9). Similar terrorism charges appeared in judicial documents in each case. These charges enlarged the traditional periphery of counter-terrorism practices of the Turkish state: they targeted their audience more than the alleged suspects of the criminal activity. However, even though the periphery of suspects was expanding, the origin of the charges was strictly focused on the folk devils of Turkey.

Some interviewees who were critical of the terror framing of *RedHack* were aware of how the Turkish state was framing *RedHack* in relation to agreed-upon terrorists: "It is up to who did it. If PKK does it, it is terror. If it is a hacker, it is not a terrorist act. For that reason, they tried to connect the (*RedHack*'s) case (to PKK)" (Lawyer 9, personal communication, 2019). Alongside the effort to consider *RedHack* as a terrorist organization and act against it with counter-terrorism measures, there was an avoidance of naming it as a cyberterrorist organization.

Legibility of the Digital Realm

In societies influenced deeply by rapidly changing ICTs, social realities become *illegible* to the state in their raw form. To be able to transform these realities into legible and controllable facts, states need to create myths by administrative, judicial, and coercive powers even though these myths would never fit the realities (Scott 1998, 24). In the legibility effort of the Turkish state, hackers—those who use the affordances provided by ICTs—are haunting figures. For that reason, most law enforcement agents were careful to frame *RedHack* not as a hacker group or cyberterrorist organization but as a familiar terrorist organization. Subsequently, the state transformed political hackers into more familiar and more controllable figures—into the figure of terrorists.

All dissidents, not just political hackers, risk falling into the category of terrorists through the tactical reaction of the state to contain dissidence. Terrorism is still a source of moral panics in Turkey. For that reason, it is still a useful instrument for the state to criminalize dissidence. That is how the Turkish state controls and contains the digital realm. Consequently, the political atmosphere of Turkey driven by the prevalence of the discourse of "terrorists without arms," the historical anxieties about leftist radicalism and Kurdish nationalism, the international popularity of the terrorism discourse, and the paranoia of cyberterrorism fortifies the terror labeling in the digital realm and constructs the backbone of digital counter-terrorism practices.

CONCLUSION

When she was asked to define political hacking, Prosecutor 3 (personal communication, 2019) had responded: "I hardly saw political hacking." Actually, the judicial case of *RedHack* on which Prosecutor 3 worked was the first case including terrorism charges in an act of unlawfully accessing a data processing system—a case that could easily be considered as political hacking. Yet, in the digital realm, the official discourse of the Turkish state does not allow *politics* to survive. Similar to how the terrorism discourse in Turkey absorbed the conceptualization of political crimes in the 1980s and in the early 1990s, it is presently used once again to absorb the political opposition through ICTs. Following the demonization of the politically motivated crime, the Turkish state, motivated by political interests, attempted to label cybercrime as an act of terrorism. The state activates the older moral panics of terrorism to contain the popular influence of a hacktivist group.

Per this perception, hacktivism, as a specific digital activism type that combines hacking and activism, becomes a crucial site where the discourse of counter-terrorism gets accentuated through a feeling of vulnerability caused by hackers. Capitalizing on this scenario, actors from the Turkish judicial system benefit from a rich mixture of political history and popular imagery to promote a discourse of counter-terrorism for cybercrime. This discourse reflects the political crisis in Turkey, evokes residual anxieties of the Turkish state, and aligns oneself with global trends of cyberterrorism. In the end, this discourse of counter-terrorism is instrumentalized to provide legitimacy for restrictive control over social media and exclusive internet governance to the detriment of citizens.

How the Turkish state benefits from the extendible nature of the terrorism discourse and carries out counter-terrorism measures in the digital realm challenges the techno-fetishist optimism which posits technological development would bring democracy. This case study from Turkey exhibits how the digital realm becomes an arena of struggle between the legitimacy of the political dissidence and the discourse of counter-terrorism. Further research is undoubtedly needed to deepen scholarship about the terrorism discourse in Turkey to understand the criminalization of political hacking in the larger political discourse. Moreover, research about the implications of cyberterrorism discourse in other contexts would provide an international lens to compare the impact of intrinsic and common factors about repressive counter-terrorism practices on the Internet. Certainly, states' effort to contain dissidence through the instrumentalization of the terrorism discourse is not a new phenomenon; nor is it peculiar to the Turkish context. For that reason, beyond digital and beyond local, this study offers a critical and contextualized approach in the diversifying scholarship of terrorism studies.

NOTES

1. I am indebted to everyone who supported me during my doctoral research from which this chapter was born. Especially, I am deeply grateful to Michael Ben Sims for his careful proofreading and to the editors of this book for their detailed review.
2. For detailed information, see Zürcher (2005, 278–288).
3. For more, see Yegen (2016).
4. DHKPC (Revolutionary People's Liberation Party/Front) takes its origin from another Marxist-Leninist fraction belonging to the pre-1980 tradition (Ersan 2014, 357–425).
5. Ercan and Oğuz (2014) define the Gezi protests as "a resistance against the commodification of urban space, nature and everyday life for the reproduction of capital, as well as the conservative authoritarianism of the party in power, the AKP" triggered by an urban regeneration project (114).
6. The religion-based Gülen Community was the former political ally of AKP, before their conflict peaked in the alleged Corruption Leaks in December 2013. Known as the *Tape Scandal* it was based upon tapes leaked in social media platforms. These tapes allegedly belonged to top political figures from the AKP.
7. Between 2013 and early 2015, the PKK and the Turkish state both declared the negotiations for a peace agreement. Negotiations failed in Spring 2015 and after the general elections—in which The Peoples' Democratic Party (HDP) formed mostly by Kurdish politicians gained an unexpected success while AKP lost its majority in the Parliament—and the armed conflict resumed (Yegen 2016, 16).
8. This speech of Erdoğan targeted "Academicians for Peace" who signed a call for action to the Turkish state to stop the violence against civilians in Kurdish regions.
9. Kurdistan Freedom Hawks (TAK) is an armed, ultra-nationalist, Kurdish organization.

10. After the failed military coup attempt by the Gülen Community in 2016, a state of emergency was declared. The government put in jail many dissidents for months, even those who were ideologically opposed to the coup attempters. After this date, Gülen Community began to be called FETÖ/PDY (Fethullahçı Terror Organization/ Parallel State Structure) in official sources.

11. At the risk of simplifying, I define hacktivism as political hacking in the scope of this work.

12. This discussion follows the role of states as authors and enforcers of the neoliberal system. See Panitch and Gindin (2005, 101).

13. The motto "all information should be free" is originally from Himanen (2001).

14. For detailed information see Doğan (2019a) and Doğan (2019b).

15. Even though lawyers and prosecutors need to have a Law education, not every lawyer can be a prosecutor in Turkey.

16. Kemalism—derived from the name of the founding political leader of the Turkish Republic, Mustafa Kemal—is an ideology developed in the 1930s. Its basic principles are republicanism, secularism, nationalism, populism, statism, and revolutionism (or reformism).

17. Counter-guerilla groups were allegedly behind these illegal activities in the name of the Turkish state against leftist, Kurdish, and dissident groups, which had its peak in the 1990s (Serdar 1994).

18. Those who positively framed patriotic hackers acknowledged that they could be categorized as cyberterrorists by other nation-states. The relativity of the concept was accepted outside national borders.

19. Similar to DHKP-C, MLKP (Marxist–Leninist Communist Party) is another leftist political group that uses extralegal methods including paramilitary ones as acts of combat.

20. Fuat Avni was an anonymous Twitter account. This highly popular account was one of the main channels from which the Corruption Leaks of AKP were posted.

21. For detailed information about judicial processes about RedHack, see Doğan (2019b).

REFERENCES

Amasya Heavy Penal Court. 2016. *Gerekçeli karar (Reasoned decision).*

Amnesty International. 1991. "Amnesty International's Principal Concerns in Respect of Turkey's New Anti-Terror Law." Accessed December 3, 2020. https://www.amnesty.org/en/documents/eur44/129/1991/en.

———. 1994. "Amnesty International's Concerns in Turkey." Accessed December 1, 2020. https://www.amnesty.org/download/Documents/180000/eur440501994en.pdf.

———. 1995. "Unfulfilled Promise of Reform." Accessed December 1, 2020. https://www.amnesty.org/en/documents/EUR44/087/1995/fr.

Ankara Chief Public Prosecutor's Office. 2012. *İddianame (Indictment).*

Ankara Heavy Penal Court no. 7. 2015. *Gerekçeli Karar (Reasoned Decision).*

Assange, Julian, Jacob Appelbaum, Andy Müller-Maguhn, and Jérémie Zimmermann. 2012. *Cypherpunks, Freedom and the Future of the Internet*. New York: OR Books.

Ayyildiz Tim. 2016. "Interview with Kanal A." Accessed May 7, 2020. https://www.youtube.com/watch?v=laBc-Yz8Gak.

———.n.d. "Ayyildiz Tim." Accessed June 12, 2020. https://ayyildiz.org/.

Baser, Bahar, Samim Akgönül, and Ahmet Erdi Öztürk. 2017. "'Academics for Peace' in Turkey: A Case of Criminalizing Dissent and Critical Thought via Counterterrorism Policy." *Critical Studies on Terrorism* 10 (2): 274–296.

Bayraktar, Köksal. 2015. "Siyasal Suç ve Terör Eylemleri." In *Türkiye'de Hukuku Yeniden Düşünmek*, edited by Halil İnanıcı, 141–150. Istanbul: Iletişim.

BBC. 2018. "'Zeytin Dalı aleyhinde paylaşım' operasyonu: Halkevleri Eş Genel Başkanı Aktaş dahil 18 gözaltı kararı." Last modified February 22, 2018. https://www.bbc.com/turkce/haberler-dunya-43152591.

Birgün. 2015. "Özel Yetkili Mahkemeler geri geliyor." Last modified February 17, 2015. https://www.birgun.net/haber/ozel-yetkili-mahkemeler-geri-geliyor-75251.

Birgün. 2016. "RedHack, Enerji Bakanı'nın Mail Hesabını 'Hack'lediğini Duyurdu." Last modified September 23, 2016. https://www.birgun.net/haber-detay/redhack-enerji-bakani-nin-mailhesabini-hack-ledigini-duyurdu-129163.html.

Bowman-Grieve, Lorraine. 2015. "Cyberterrorism and Moral Panics." In *Terrorism Online, Politics, Law and Technology*, edited by Lee Jarvis, Stuart Macdonald, and Thomas M. Chen, 86–106. New York: Routledge.

Bulut, Ergin and Erdem Yörük. 2017. "Digital Populism: Trolls and Political Polarization of Twitter in Turkey." *International Journal of Communication* 11: 4093–4117.

Castells, Manuel. 2001. "Epilogue: Informationalism and the Network Society." In *The Hacker Ethic and the Spirit of the Information Age*, edited by Pekka Himanen, 155–178. New York: Handom House Trade Publishers.

Celik, Serdar. 1994. "Turkey's Killing Machine: The Contra-Guerrilla Force," *Kurdistan Report* 17. Accessed December 3, 2020. http://www.hartford-hwp.com/archives/51/017.html.

Cinar, Meral Uğur. 2017. "'Gelişirken': Türkiye örneğinden hareketle iktisadi kalkınma söylemleri ve demokrasi ilişkisini yeniden düşünmek." *ODTÜ Gelişme Dergisi* 44: 47–67.

CNN Türk. 2012. "RedHack terör örgütüymüş!" Last modified July 6, 2012. https://www.cnnturk.com/2012/bilim.teknoloji/teknoloji/07/06/redhack.teror.orgutuymus/667919.0/index.html.

Cohen, Stanley. (1972) [2011]. *Folk Devils and Moral Panics. The creation of the Mods and Rockers*. London: Routledge.

Collin, Barry C. 1996. "The Future of Cyberterrorism," Paper presented at *the 11th Annual International Symposium on Criminal Justice Issues*, University of Illinois at Chicago. http://afgen.com/terrorism1.html.

Council of Europe Convention on Cybercrime. 2001. Accessed November 12, 2020. https://rm.coe.int/1680081561.

Council of Europe Convention on the Prevention of Terrorism. 2005. Accessed November 22, 2020. https://www.coe.int/en/web/conventions/full-list/-/conventions/treaty/196.

Cumhuriyet. 2015. "Redhack'te 9 ay hapis, 3 yıl dava: Sonuç beraat. Last modified March 17, 2015. http://www.cumhuriyet.com.tr/haber/turkiye/231774/Redhack_te_9_ay_hapis__3_yil_dava__Sonuc_beraat.html.

———. 2016. "Taylan Kulaçoğlu gözaltında gördüğü işkenceyi anlattı: Tecavüzle tehdit ettiler." Last modified October 6, 2016. http://www.cumhuriyet.com.tr/haber/turkiye/611114/Taylan_Kulacoglu_gozaltinda_gordugu_iskenceyi_anlatti__Tecavuzle_tehdit_ettiler.html.

Denning, Dorothy E. 2001. "Activism, Hacktivism, and Cyberterrorism: The Internet as a Tool for Influencing Foreign Policy." In *Networks and Netwars: The Future of Terror, Crime, and Militancy*, by John Arquilla and David Ronfeldt, 239–288. California: Rand. https://www.rand.org/content/dam/rand/pubs/monograph_reports/MR1382/MR1382.ch8.pdf.

Diken. 2016. "Erdoğan muhaliflere çattı: Ya bizim yanımızda olacaklar ya teröristlerin." Last modified March, 2016. http://www.diken.com.tr/erdogan-faturayi-akademisyenlere-kesti-ya-bizim-yanimizda-olacaklar-ya-teroristlerin/.

———. 2017. "RedHack davası: Tunca Öğreten ve Mahir Kanaat'e tahliye kararı." Last modified December 6, 2017. http://www.diken.com.tr/redhack-davasi-tunca-ogreten-ve mahirkanaate-tahliye-karari/.

Doğan, Bülay. 2019a. Contextualizing Hacktivism: The Criminalization of Redhack. *CARGC Paper 10*. Philadelphia, USA: CARGC Press.

———. 2019b. "Framing Hacktivism: The Criminalization of Redhack in Turkey." PhD diss, Koç University.

Emniyet Genel Müdürlüğü Siber Suçlarla Mücadele Daire Başkanlığı. "Hakkımızda." Accessed December 26, 2020. https://www.egm.gov.tr/siber/hakkimizda2.

Ercan, Fuat and Şebnem Oğuz. 2014. "From Gezi Resistance to Soma Massacre: Capital Accumulation and Class Struggle in Turkey." *Socialist Register* 51: 114–135.

Erensü, Sinan and Ayça Alemdaroğlu. 2018. "Dialectics of Reform and Repression: Unpacking Turkey's Authoritarian 'Turn.'" *Review of Middle East Studies* 52 (1): 16–28.

Ersan, Vehbi. 2014. *1970'lerde Türkiye Solu*. İstanbul: İletişim Yayınları.

Evrensel. 2019. "Sosyal medyada Suriye operasyonu karşıtı paylaşım yapanlara operasyon." Last modified October 17, 2019. https://www.evrensel.net/haber/389059/sosyal-medyada-suriye-operasyonu-karsiti-paylasim-yapanlara-operasyon.

Feigenbaum, Anna. 2012. "Security for Sale! The Visual Rhetoric of Marketing Counter-terrorism Technologies." *The Poster* 2 (1): 75–92.

Himanen, Pekka. 2001. *The Hacker Ethic and the Spirit of the Information Age*. New York: Random House Trade Publishers.

Human Rights Watch. 2002. *Questions and Answers: Freedom of Expression and Language Rights in Turkey*. Accessed November 22, 2020. https://www.hrw.org/legacy/press/2002/08/turkeyqa041902.htm.

Independent. 2016. “Email Cache Proves Turkish Oil Minister’s Links to Isis Oil Trade, WikiLeaks Claims.” Last modified December 7, 2016. https://www.independent.co.uk/news/world/middle-east/wikileaks-turkey-isis-oilminister-email-cache-leaks-claims-a7460736.html.

Istanbul Chief Public Prosecutor’s Office. 2017. *İddianame (Indictment).*

Jarvis, L., Macdonald, S., and Whiting, A. (2015). “Constructing Cyberterrorism as a Security Threat: a Study of International News Media Coverage.” *Perspectives on Terrorism*, 9 (1): 60–75.

Jewkes, Yvonne. 2004. *Media and Crime.* London: Sage Publications.

Jordan, Taylor and Paul A. Taylor. 2004. *Hacktivism and Cyberwars: Rebels with a Cause?* New York: Routledge.

Kanar, Ercan. 2015. “Siyasi Davalar Yargı Pratiği ve Dürüst Yargılanma Hakkı.” In *Türkiye’de Hukuku Yeniden Düşünmek*, edited by Halil İnanıcı, 165–200. Istanbul: Iletişim.

Kars Kaynar, Ayşegül. 2017. “Political Trials and the Second Jurisdiction of the State: Normalcy of the Exception.” In *Contemporary Turkey at a Glance II, Turkey Transformed? Power, History, Culture*, edited by Meltem Ersoy and Esra Ozyurek, 25–37. Wiesbaden: Springer.

Klein, Adam G. 2015. “Vigilante Media: Unveiling Anonymous and the Hacktivist Persona in the Global Press.” *Communication Monographs* 82 (3): 379–401.

Klein, Naomi. 2007. *The Shock Doctrine: The Rise of Disaster Capitalism.* New York: Metropolitan Books/Henry Holt and Company.

Krapp, Peter. (2005). “Terror and Play, or What Was Hacktivism?” *Grey Room* 21 (8): 70–93.

Marsili, Marco. 2018. “The War on Cyberterrorism, Democracy and Security” Democracy and Security (published online).

Nissenbaum, Helen. 2004. “Hackers and the Contested Ontology of Cyberspace.” *New Media & Society* 6 (2): 195–217.

Odatv. 2012. “Red Hack terör listesine alındı.” Last modified July 7, 2012. https://odatv.com/redhack-teror-listesine-alindi-0707121200.html.

Oğuz, Şebnem. 2009. “The Response of the Turkish State to the 2008 Crisis: A Further Step in Neoliberal Authoritarian Statism.” *The Crisis, Interdisciplinarity and Alternatives, Third International Research Workshop of the International Initiative for Promoting Political Economy*. Ankara: METU.

Özbek, Nadir. 2003. “Alternatif tarih tahayyülleri: Siyaset, ideoloji ve Osmanlı-Türkiye tarihi.” *Toplum ve Bilim* 98: 234–254.

Ozbudun, Ergun. 2007. “Democratization Reforms in Turkey, 1993 2004.” *Turkish Studies* 8 (2): 179–196.

Panitch, Leo, and Sam Gindin. 2005. “Superintending Global Capital.” *New Left Review* 35: 101–123.

Radikal. 2012a. “Ankara Emniyeti ‘Çökertildi’.” Last modified February 28, 2012. http://www.radikal.com.tr/turkiye/ankara-emniyeti-cokertildi-1080108/.

———. 2012b. “Redhack resmen terör örgütü ilan edildi.” Last modified July 6, 2012. http://www.radikal.com.tr/turkiye/redhack-resmen-teror-orgutu-ilan-edildi-1093352/.

Mahir Ç. 2013. *RedHack Canlı Söyleşisi—ODTÜ*. https://www.youtube.com/watch?v=B1rUbJ5Pm7k.

Rosenau, Henning and Erhan Temel. 2008. "Jakobs'un Düşman Ceza Hukuku Kavramı Hukukun Düşmanı." *Ankara Üniversitesi Hukuk Fakültesi Dergisi* 57: 391–402.

Sabah. 2012. "Redhack terör listesine giriyor." Last modified July 5, 2012. https://www.sabah.com.tr/gundem/2012/07/05/redhack-teror-listesine-giriyor.

Saka, Erkan. 2018. "Social Media in Turkey as a Space for Political Battles: AKTrolls and Other Politically Motivated Trolling." *Middle East Critique*: 1–17.

Savran, Sungur. 1987. "1960, 1971, 1980: Toplumsal Mücadeleler, Askeri Müdahaleler." *Tez 6*: 132–168.

Schiller, Dan. 1999. *Digital Capitalism. Networking the Global Market System*. Cambridge: The MIT Press.

Sendika.org. 2018. "İzmir'de "sosyal medya" operasyonu: Çok sayıda gözaltı." Last modified January 23, 2018. https://sendika63.org/2018/01/izmirde-sosyal-medya-operasyonu-cok-sayida-gozalti-469754/.

Scott, James C. 1998. *Seeing like a State*. New Haven: Yale University Press.

SoL. 2012. "RedHack 'Terör örgütü' ilan edildi." Last modified July 6, 2012. http://haber.sol.org.tr/devlet-ve-siyaset/redhack-teror-orgutu-ilan-edildi-haberi-56680.

Sputnik Türkiye. 2016. "Utku Kalı beraat etti." Last modified February 4, 2016. https://tr.sputniknews.com/turkiye/201602041020641921-utku-kali-reyhanli-mit-tirsuriye/.

Steinmetz, Kevin. 2016. *Hacked, A Radical Approach to Hacker Culture and Crime*. New York: New York University Press.

Thatcher, Sarah E. H. 2006. "The Hunt for the Paper Tiger: The Social Construction of Cyberterrorism." PhD diss, London School of Economics and Political Science.

Topak, Özgün E. 2019. "The Authoritarian Surveillant Assemblage: Authoritarian State Surveillance in Turkey." *Security Dialogue* 50 (5): 454–472.

Turkish Anti-Terror Law. 1991. Accessed November 12, 2020. https://www.legislationline.org/download/id/3727/file/Turkey_anti_terr_1991_am2010_en.pdf

Turkish Penal Code. 2004. Accessed November 12, 2020. http://www.ilo.org/dyn/natlex/natlex4.detail?p_lang=en&p_isn=77393&p_count=96544.

Üstel, Füsun. 2008. *"Makbul Vatandaş"ın Peşinde*. Istanbul: Iletişim.

Vegh, Sandor. 2005. "The Media's Portrayal of Hacking, Hackers, and Hacktivism Before and After September 11." *First Monday* 10 (2). https://firstmonday.org/ojs/index.php/fm/article/download/1206/1126?inline=1.

Vlavo, Fidele. 2015. "Framing Digital Activism: The Specter of Cyberterrorism." *First Monday* 20 (10). https://doi.org/10.5210/fm.v20i10.6139.

Wall, David S. 2012. "The Devil Drives a Lada: The Social Construction of Hackers as Cybercriminals." In *Constructing Crime*, edited by Christiana Gregoriou, 4–18. London: Palgrave Macmillan.

Wykes, Maggie and Daniel Harcus. 2009. "Cyber-terror: Construction, Criminalisation and Control." In *Handbook of Internet Crime*, edited by Yvonne Jewkes and Majid Yar, 214–229. Cullompton: Willan.

Yar, Majid. 2006. *Cybercrime and Society*. London: SAGE Publications.

Yegen, Mesut. 2016. "The Turkish left and the Kurdish question." *Journal of Balkan and Near Eastern Studies* 18 (2): 157–176.

Yesil, Bilge, Efe Kerem Sözeri, and Emad Khazraee. 2017. "Turkey's Internet Policy after the Coup Attempt: The Emergence of a Distributed Network of Online Suppression and Surveillance." *Internet Policy Observatory*. https://repository.upenn.edu/cgi/viewcontent.cgi?article=1021&context=internetpolicyobservatory.

Young, Jock. 1971. "The Role of the Police as Amplifiers of Deviancy, Negotiators of Reality and Translators of Fantasy: Some Consequences of our Present System of Drug Control as Seen in Notting Hill." In *Images of Deviance*, edited by Stanley Cohen, 27–61. Harmondsworth: Penguin.

Zürcher, Erik J. 2005. *Turkey: A Modern History*. London: I. B. Tauris.

Chapter 6

Chinese-Speaking Netizens' Comments on VOA's Coverage of China's Counter-terrorism Laws and Freedom of Speech

Wei Sun

INTRODUCTION

Following the 9/11 terrorist attacks against the United States, more than 140 countries adopted counter-terrorism laws. Of these, 130 countries' counter-terrorism laws adopt language that restrains citizens' right to free expression (Callamard 2017). Combined with cybersecurity laws, the result has been citizens from many countries encountering greater censorship and less freedom of expression (Callamard 2017; Liu 2015; Pan 2015). The counter-terrorism measures stated in the laws have strengthened governmental power and control but might have violated human rights (Williams 2014). Currently, "the massive (meaning indiscriminate, disproportionate) nature of state digital surveillance makes it an important tool of censorship through the chilling effect it creates by precluding or preventing the exploration of dissent, controversial ideas, and reaching out to certain groups of people" (Callamard 2017, 131). Globally, censorship has become more "privatized, personal, and technologically grounded" (Callamard 2017, 132). Because terrorist organizations use technology, especially popular social media sites to promote terrorist ideologies and activities, cyber-terrorism has become a new and fast-growing threat that government agencies target (Reeves 2016; Wu 2019).

Scholars have argued whether there is a public definition of terrorism and the difference between terrorism and other violent crimes (Goldberg 2009; Liu 2010; Ortner 2016). Liu (2015) summarized several characteristics of terrorism: (1) It directly targets civilians/ non-combatants; (2) It seeks to achieve some goal by creating terror in a population; (3) It directly targets one victim to coerce another; (4) It aims to achieve some political goal—especially that of "destabilizing (or maintaining) an existing political or social order"; (5) It aims to call public attention to the perpetrator's cause (260). Under the name of national security, many Western countries, including the United States, Belgium, France, Germany, Portugal, Romania, Sweden, the Netherlands, and the United Kingdom, have allowed their intelligence agencies to collect citizens' private information on a large scale (The Law Library of Congress 2016). In response to this trend, human rights organizations have raised concerns over governments' violation of citizens' basic rights to privacy (Ortner 2016; Paye 2014; Purbrick 2017; Stoughton 2019). In Europe, the controversy over re-publishing or banning cartoons depicting the Islamic prophet Muhammad in the Danish *Morgenavisen Jyllands-Posten* newspaper led to protests, arson, and violence in 13 countries and caused the deaths of 139 people. However, the question of whether the controversial re-publishing or banning is a terroristic act or expression of freedom is unanswered (Eko and Hellmueller 2018; Mchangama 2017; Modood et al. 2006). Each country has its own interpretations and regulations concerning what is considered free speech or terrorism propaganda (Bhabha 2018; Tsesis 2017). The way in which other countries handled controversial issues was often cited by Chinese authorities as a defense for China's policies (Purbrick 2017).

Social media has been easy access for citizens all over the world to participate in democracy. However, the criticism and protests expressed on social media may intensify the tension between the government and its citizens (Hu and Yang 2019). The term "netizens" is commonly used in China to refer to "self-actualizing" citizens who have created public citizenship in cyberspace (Robertson 2009, 287). Chinese Internet and mobile phone users are now more than 1.7 billion (China Internet Network Information Center 2017). Chinese government agents are believed to hire an "Internet Water Army" (social media militia) disguised as grassroots commenters to lead public opinion (Chen 2018; Kanat 2012; Yu et al. 2015; Zhang 2018). While the Chinese government may use the convenience of netizens to agitate against international anti-China activities, the government officials are also fearful of netizens' free expression on political matters. There is a thin line between the encouraged free expression on some topics and censorship of others (Beech et al. 2015). This study aims to shed light on Voice of America's (VOA) Chinese-language media coverage and netizens' reactions to freedom of speech issues and China's Counter-Terrorism Law. Specifically, it attempts to explain Chinese-speaking netizens' interests in international counter-terrorism reporting.

Since the 1990s, China has claimed that the country experienced several terrorist attacks on its territory and asserted certain notorious militant members of the East Turkestan Islamic Movement (ETIM) received training and support from radical Islamists (Buckley 2015; Sun 2010). On December 27, 2015, the 18th Session of the Standing Committee of the 12th National People's Congress passed the Counter-Terrorism Law of the People's Republic of China (hereafter Law) (Clarke 2018; Counterterrorism Law 2015). Article 3 of the Law defines terrorism as "any proposition or activity that, by means of violence, sabotage or threat, generates social panic, undermines public security, infringes upon personal and property rights, or menaces state authorities and international organizations, with the aim to realize political, ideological and other purposes" (para. 4). In 2016, the National Cyberspace Security Strategy (hereafter, Strategy) was implemented. Article 12 of the Strategy states that all individuals and organizations should comply with the government's order, and not use the network to conduct any activity which

> endangers national security, honor and interest, incites to subvert the state power or overthrow the socialist system, incites to split the country or undermine national unity, advocates terrorism or extremism, propagates ethnic hatred or discrimination, spreads violent or pornographic information, fabricates or disseminates false information.

Both the Law and the Strategy aim to safeguard China's national sovereignty and suggest that China's global counter-terrorism efforts are intertwined with its national counter-separatism strategies. The news of the passing of the Law was immediately covered by major Western media outlets such as *Reuters*, *The Washington Post*, and *The New York Times*. Critics feared that China was overreacting, and the Law was deemed controversial (Denyer 2015; Wong 2016; Wu 2019). The international community voiced great concerns about the Chinese government's blurring of the difference between terrorism, separatism, and human rights advocacy (Campbell 2019; Denyer 2015).

Since media organizations in China operate under the Communist Party's close watch, there is no actual freedom of speech under the government's tightening Internet policy. As a result, many Chinese intellectuals obtain news reports about China from Western online media outlets. For example, the international Chinese-language programs of British Broadcasting Corporation (BBC) and VOA are consumed by Chinese netizens in China and overseas. Chinese netizens' responses to Western media reporting on China's Counter-Terrorism Law and their interpretations of the Law versus freedom of expression can be understood by analyzing user comments on Western media websites. VOA provides a public audience forum that gives Chinese-speaking netizens an opportunity to comment on their coverage of the Law. This chapter represents an attempt to understand how Chinese-speaking netizens react to Western media reports on China's Counter-terrorism Law, and make sense of audiences' meaning-making process. In doing so, I will first provide an overview of the literature on China's war on terrorism, China's Internet regulation, and online political participation. Then I will explain how the data was collected and analyzed for this study and the findings and implications of the research.

CHINA'S WAR ON TERRORISM

China's anti-terrorism campaign started in 2001 right after 9/11. From the beginning, it linked the East Turkestan Islam Movement to international terrorist groups, and asked the U.S.-led campaign to incorporate this localized problem in China into its global efforts (Clarke 2010; Cunningham 2012; Denyer 2015; Pike 2006; Wu 2019). Four months after 9/11, Wang Yi, then vice minister of the Ministry of Foreign Affairs of China, spoke at the 39th Munich Security Conference (MSC). Wang (2002) claimed China was a victim of terrorism. Wang asserted that the East Turkistan terrorists had long been trained, armed, and funded by international terrorist organizations such as Al Qaeda. He proposed a new security concept which "focuses on safeguarding national sovereignty, unity and territorial integrity while serving economic construction, and striving to ensure a stable international environment, especially a good surrounding environment" (para. 4). Wang's speech explained China's anti-terrorism policy as maintaining societal stability, promoting a peace-seeking foreign policy, and applying defensive military strategies.

China has experienced attacks by Uighur [also spelled as Uyghur] separatists, such as eight people being killed by knife assaults in the Xinjiang Autonomous Uyghur Region (hereafter Xinjiang) in 2017, and a car which drove into a crowd on Tiananmen Square in Beijing in 2013. Incidents like these were called terrorist threats (BBC News 2020). Quotes by Xinjiang's leader, Quanguo Chen, provide examples for the Chinese authority's justification to fight terrorism with the encouraging support of the public. Chen is quoted saying his local government would use any force to "bury the corpses of terrorists in the vast sea of a people's war" (Gracie 2017, para. 2). It is believed by the United Nations and international human rights organizations that China has detained over a million Uighurs in re-education camps. However, China denied the accusation, and claimed that Uighurs voluntarily attended vocational schools to combat terrorists and religious extremists (Nebehay 2018). A well-known Uighur geographer, Tashpolat Tiyip, was once president of a university and known as a model scholar, even receiving an honorary degree from France's École Pratique des Hautes Études. He was arrested and secretly tried on the charge of separatism and was sentenced to death (Illmer 2019).

The Chinese government's strategy in linking terrorism, separatism, and human rights advocacy has caused criticism from the international community. In addition to ETIM, separatists from Tibet, Xinjiang, and Taiwan have been regarded as three threats to China's sovereignty (Chung 2002; Wayne 2009; Wong 2009). As Denyer (2015) notes:

> [China] has exploited a genuine terrorist threat to further empower its repressive state-security apparatus. It is, they say, invoking the dangers of violent extremism to justify and expand already a harsh crackdown on civil rights and to punish foreign information technology companies that refuse to play by its rules. (para. 2)

Tanner and Bellacqua (2016) have studied the U.S. and China counterterrorism cooperation and acknowledged that the two countries hold different legal and ideological values. The disagreement between the two countries is formed based on different views on security interests of "the nature and causes of terrorism and social violence in China" (5).

CHINA'S INTERNET REGULATIONS AND ONLINE POLITICAL PARTICIPATION

China entered the Internet age in the late 1990s. By 2016, half of the population was using the Internet (China Network Information Center 2017). The number of mobile phone users reached 601.8 million in 2017. In 2020, 904 million people, or nearly 60% of the population, uses the Internet. The Internet and its increased access through smartphones led to the creation of new forums for the transmission of information, which has challenged the Chinese government's authority over peoples' communication. On December 15, 2019, China's State Internet Information Office publicized the "Provisions on the Governance of the Online Information Content Ecosystem." Article 7 of Chapter 2 of the Provisions indicates: "Online information content producers shall employ measures to prevent resist content [such as] . . . improper comments on natural disasters, major accidents, or other disasters" (State Internet Information Office of China 2019, para. 1–4).

Speaking or writing the truth could be regarded as criminal conduct which intends to overthrow the government, and such conduct is often considered terrorism. Chinese leaders have publicly criticized and humiliated well-known online celebrities who violated the no free-expression regulations. When comments are posted online which criticize the government, the posting netizen could be monitored and arrested. After a year-long Hong Kong protest, the China government passed the Hong Kong National Security Law in June 2020. The law is intended to give the government more power over the people of Hong Kong. The newly passed law has been criticized since it denounces the protests in Hong Kong as separatism and terrorist activities, which has led to the jailing of journalists, punishment for critical news outlets, blocking of digital communication, criminalizing peaceful online expression, restricting artistic and academic free expression, and a crackdown on religious communities (Cook 2020). Hong Kong, a former British colony, has been allowed certain freedoms different from policies in the Mainland, referred to as "one country, two systems" (Grossman 2019, para. 1) since its return to China in 1997. Hong Kong citizens were assured to have their own governance in the economy, legal system, and administration (Grossman 2019). For more than two decades, Hong Kong residents have enjoyed more democracy and freedom of expression compared to Chinese citizens in the Mainland. This is a vivid example that the Chinese government can enact new legislation anytime when it is deemed needed, in the name of national security.

China also has been criticized for restricting free access to the Internet by strengthening a firewall system (O'Brien 2019). According to O'Brien, "the Great Firewall is a system of surveillance and blocking technology that prevents Chinese citizens from viewing websites outside the country" (para. 1). The Chinese government considers the Internet as a "sovereign" entity that should be fully under the control of the government (O'Brien 2019, para.1). Through the firewall, the Chinese government not only silenced the dissidents in China but also extended the restriction to Chinese immigrants overseas.

The expanded restrictions angered and united Chinese intellectuals, dissidents, and human rights activists in protesting the government's actions. However, protests within Chinese territory are often suppressed, and those involved are often arrested (Wong 2016; Wu and Wong 2019). In a report to the U.S.-China Economic and Security Review Commission, Tanner and Bellacqua (2016) have summarized China's strategies and policies of counter-terrorism, and its effort in international cooperation. They indicated the most controversial effort of China

> is to press regional security partners to deport PRC citizens and former citizens that China regards as potential threats back to China. China also seeks cooperation against on-line extremism, overseas recruitment, trafficking into China, and political cooperation with Uighur activist groups. (5)

Since the Chinese government maintains full online censorship through an Internet documentation system, Chinese citizens can only join Western social networks through a virtual private network (VPN) to circumvent censorship

(Denyer 2017; Sun 2019). Even though certain Chinese online forums allow public reactions, comments criticizing the government, or its leaders are swiftly removed. It is in this context that Western online media platforms such as VOA became a public sphere where any Chinese-speaking netizens could participate freely in online discussions.

VOA was created in 1942. Funded by the U.S. Congress, VOA is the largest U.S. international broadcaster to more than 275 million people in more than 40 languages. VOA is one of the few government-owned news agencies in the United States (Allen 2004; Heil 2003). According to the Smith-Mundt Act, VOA is not allowed to broadcast directly to American citizens so that the public is protected from the government's propaganda (Metzgar 2012; Palmer and Carter 2006; Voice of America n.d.). According to the broadcaster, VOA

> has committed to providing comprehensive coverage of the news and telling audiences the truth. Through World War II, the Cold War, the fight against global terrorism, and the struggle for freedom around the globe today, VOA exemplifies the principles of a free press. (Voice of America n.d., para. 2)

VOA's Chinese Department started radio broadcasting to China from the very beginning of VOA operations in 1942. Presently, VOA Chinese broadcasts to the Chinese-speaking population in China and the diaspora. The VOA Chinese website was created on September 11, 2001, and aims to separate its content from its TV and radio broadcasts.

RESEARCH PROCEDURES AND DATA ANALYSIS

This research employs a qualitative textual analysis method. Qualitative research methods examine the meanings associated with messages rather than the frequencies in which message variables occur. The textual analysis focuses on stories and storytelling in a specific context (Gatson 2011). The current research adheres to Riessman's (2002) recommendations in examining thematic content and narrative structure in an online setting. Specifically, this method is used to interrogate VOA's coverage of the Chinese Counter-terrorism Law and how Chinese-speaking netizens react to that coverage through their comments. The texts analyzed for this study are articles and user comments found in the VOA online archive (https://www.voachinese.com/) concerning counter-terrorism. Since September 2001, 113 articles about counter-terrorism in China were posted. For this study, the search period was from December 2015, when the Law was passed, to January 2020, when this research was conducted, resulting in twenty-three articles (see Table 6.1). There are between 5 and 139 netizen user comments under each media report.

Table 6.1 VOA Chinese Reports on Chinese Counter-terrorism Law and Freedom of Speech

	Title	Byline	Date of Publication	Number of comments
1	China tries to dispel foreign concerns over China's Counter-terrorism Law	VOA	12/23/2015	5
2	China: U.S.-based Counter-terrorism Law does not affect freedom of speech	Ye Lin	12/24/2015	51
3	China's "Counter-terrorism Law" attracts much attention and controversy	VOA	12/28/2015	21
4	French reporter Guo Yu: China distorts my anti-terrorism report	Lin Sen	12/28/2015	135
5	How does China's anti-terrorism law affect media companies and individuals?	Huang Liling	12/29/2015	27
6	China's "Anti-Terrorism Law" Arouses Concerns in Western Countries	VOA	12/29/2015	23
7	About Obama's State of the Union Address	Han Lianchao	1/15/2016	29
8	It's time for the United States to reconsider its China policy	Han Lianchao	1/25/2016	185
9	Amnesty International says China's human rights situation worsens	VOA	2/24/2016	13
10	Current affairs talk: Amnesty International severely criticizes China's human rights	Yu Zhou	2/24/2016	16
11	Human Rights Watch calls on China to reform human rights violations laws	VOA	3/1/2016	12
12	Human rights groups question China's abuse of crimes against national security	VOA	3/17/2016	7
13	2016 Report on Religious Freedom	Li Yihua	5/2/2016	12
14	India Sees No Evil City Management	Han Lianchao	6/14/2016	26
15	Freedom of the Net vs. Anti-Terrorism: The United States wants to be a good role model for China	VOA	7/23/2016	8
16	U.S. anti-terrorism agencies also control anti-foreign propaganda: China and Russia are the focus	Ye Lin	1/4/2017	58
17	U.S. Human Rights Report 2016 focuses on China's crackdown on lawyers	VOA	3/4/2017	19
18	Tricks of global news censorship, Chinese measures attract attention	Mo Yu	4/25/2017	40

(*Continued*)

	Title	*Byline*	*Date of Publication*	*Number of comments*
19	China's National Human Rights Report: Human Rights Cause Guided by Xi Jinping Thought	Wan Bing	11/6/2018	139
20	Two sides of Xi Jinping's handling of Xinjiang	Jin Zhe	11/28/2019	15
21	U.S. law related to Xinjiang triggers strong reaction from China	Ye Bing, Mu Feng	12/4/2019	17
22	China condemns U.S. Uyghur human rights policy bill, saying Uyghur students have all graduated	VOA	12/9/2019	29
23	Amnesty International annual report praises young people for fear of suppression, says China's human rights setback	VOA	1/30/2020	4

User comments of the articles were examined to uncover salient themes of VOA's Chinese-language website and netizens' reactions to China's Counter-Terrorism Law and freedom of speech issues. After I coded and categorized the user comments associated with the twenty-three articles from the VOA archive, four recurring themes were identified: debates over China's Counter-Terrorism Law; human rights issues; U.S., international, and China relations; and Chinese President Xi Jinping and the issue of Xinjiang.

ANALYSIS

Debate over the Counter-terrorism Law

Five out of the twenty-three selected articles directly targeted the Counter-terrorism Law (Articles 1–5). They were all published in December 2015, the same month the Law was passed. The first article titled "China Tries to Dispel Foreign Concerns over China's Counter-Terrorism Law" discussed both China and U.S. government officials' explanation and reaction to the new Law. The Chinese government assured that technology companies should not worry about China's new counter-terrorism law. The government stressed that the Law is intended to prevent and investigate terrorist activities and will not affect the intellectual property rights of enterprises. Despite assurances from the Chinese government, the Law generated concerns in Western countries as fears of Chinese authorities requiring foreign companies to submit sensitive information such as encryption keys grew. The five comments under this article were light-hearted. One commenter joked about how naïve the VOA is. Another said, in a satiric tone:

> For foreign companies that don't listen to our party's words, our usual approach is to crack them down severely. For example, Microsoft has become more and more obedient after changing its president. The style of its behaviors is quite similar to our Baidu, Tencent, and 360, and thus has won our favor.

Baidu, Tencent, and 360 are all major social networking companies in China. The commenter obviously was criticizing Microsoft for surrendering to China.

In the second article entitled "China: U.S.-based Counter-terrorism Law does not Affect Freedom of Speech," the Law is defended and compared to other countries' laws. The article indicates that elements of U.S. laws were referenced during the drafting of China's Counter-Terrorism Law. Hong Lei, a spokesman for the Chinese Foreign Ministry, said at a press conference on December 23, 2015: "In its relevant laws such as the Communications Assistance for Enforcement Law, the United States explicitly requires relevant companies to assist law enforcement personnel in conducting lawful interception and provide decryption support for encrypted communications" (para. 1). Furthermore, the article explained the U.S. law required telecommunication operators and telecommunications equipment manufacturers to design or modify their equipment, facilities, and services to ensure compliance with applicable laws. The implicit meaning was that since the United States could require telecommunication operators to obey their demands, and, as such, China could also do so without judgment. An important factor to consider here is that the Law was enacted against the background of the popularity of digital telephone exchanges, which concerned law enforcement tapping would be difficult. This law required telecommunications operators and telecommunications equipment manufacturers to design or modify their equipment, facilities, and services to ensure that, while the technology is developing, government monitoring can proceed normally. User comments diverge under this article, supporting U.S. concerns and endorsing the Chinese law. One commenter questioned the legislative standpoint of the Law, blaming China for always finger-pointing to the United States for any domestic trouble: "The Communist Party of China does not fight terrorism. It is basically to strengthen their stability and legalize surveillance of dissidents, human rights lawyers, and petitioners!" Another commenter defended the Law, arguing the United States would always bully China on almost anything:

> Even if the anti-terrorism law of the United States is copied in its entirety, the United States will still raise its nose and eyes. Because the gangster logic of the United States is to allow the United States to set fire but not allow Chinese to twinkle!

The third article, "China's Counter-Terrorism Law Attracts Much Attention and Controversy," discussed the definition of terrorism in the Law, aiming to confront violence which creates social panic and endangers the public. Chinese officials argued that terrorism is a real threat and that anti-terrorism tasks including those stipulated in the Counter-terrorism Law should be carried out. However, the U.S. State Department criticized this new law by arguing it further restricts freedom of the press, speech, assembly, and religion. This view was shared by Chinese netizens who are critical of the Law. For some commenters under this article, the Law is just a new way of weaponizing the legal system to control the Chinese people: "The current anti-terrorism is similar to the class struggle during the Cultural Revolution. . . . Only now it is replaced with a new label: 'Counter-Terrorism.' Wherever the Communist Party's philosophy of struggle was used, its people suffered." Other commenters defended the Chinese government's position and described U.S. criticism of China's anti-terrorism measures as hypocritical. For example, one comment represents a commonly held belief among pro-Chinese government groups: "In recent years, the United States has 'expressed concerns' about everything China has done. I don't think it is necessary. If the United States is worried about other countries' affairs so much, why not mind its own business"? This type of messaging—the idea that one needs to self-interrogate before judging others—has been widely observed in the Chinese government's communication. In United States–Sino relations, Chinese officials often respond to U.S. accusations by saying the latter should look itself in the mirror. If racial discrimination and political protests still exist in the United States, then U.S. leaders should not criticize China's human rights records before fixing their own problems.

Human Rights and Counter-terrorism

Nine articles discussed China's human rights issues and argued that because of the Counter-terrorism Law, China's human rights records have worsened (Articles 9, 10, 11, 12, 13, 14, 17, 19, 22). For example, Article 9, "Amnesty International Says China's Human Rights Situation Worsens," stated:

> A series of new laws focusing on national security have been drafted or implemented, posing a huge threat to human rights. The government has launched a nationwide mass crackdown on human rights lawyers and activists as systematic harassment and intimidation continues. (para. 4)

The harassment and intimidation included the arrest of five women for planning an anti-sexual harassment initiative on International Women's Day and authorities' increased control over the Internet, mass media, and academia. Religious practices are banned in Xinjiang, Tibet, and other provinces. One commenter was obviously a dissident. He was outraged and called the Communist Party a bandit, and attributed his unemployment and divorce to the persecution:

> The Communist bandit has bloody terrorist rules against the common people. I am a member who lives in a bandit zone. I was unemployed due to the corruption of the Communist bandit. I am deeply disgusted with their rules and often commented at VOA's website. My ex-wife was deeply frightened by my free speech . . . she chose to divorce me.

Another netizen thought both the U.S. and China's human rights records were bad but felt that the United States did not take terrorism attacks against China seriously. This netizen believes Xinjiang terrorists and ISIS terrorists are a threat to the two countries. The United States, the commenter argues, should not always criticize China:

> If Amnesty International believes that China's human rights situation has deteriorated, then China can send Xinjiang terrorists to the United States, let them organize terrorist operations with 'Islamic State' terrorists and Al Qaeda in the United States, let the United States continue to face terrorist destruction and let Americans taste what is a terrorist threat.

In Article 12, "Human Rights Groups Question China's Abuse of Crimes against National Security," VOA raised concerns over Human Rights Watch through a statement questioning China's recent convictions for "endangering national security" (para. 1). The statement said that China's prosecutions involving national security and terrorism doubled in 2015, reflecting the government's increased crackdown on peaceful dissidents. "China's conviction rate in 2015 remained at 99%. Of the more than 1.2 million people on trial, only 1,039 were acquitted" (para. 2). The article cited Human Rights Watch's report on the issue, saying that cases involving crimes against national security and terrorism are difficult to defend in Chinese courts. Persons detained on related charges are usually held in isolated confinement for several months and are barred from meeting with family members and lawyers. They are forced to hire government-appointed lawyers during the trial. In addition, Chinese state media are increasingly broadcasting videos of detainees confessing guilt for political activities. The Chinese government has detained hundreds of Uighur Muslims and sent them to secret camps of "indoctrination" (Nebehay 2018).

The U.S., International, and China Relations

Six articles discussed U.S., international, and China relations (Articles 4, 6, 8, 14, 15, 16). Article 8, "It's Time for the United States to Reconsider Its China Policy" was written by Han Lianchao, VOA's visiting fellow from the politically conservative Hudson Institute. In this article, Han praised Taiwan as a democratic country that has become a model for developing countries. Han applauded Taiwan's progress in democracy, freedom, human rights, and the legal system, by noting Taiwan has truly entered the ranks of modern advanced countries. He then criticized China's Taiwan policy that has forced Taiwan to a dead-end in the international arena. It should be noted that, under the "One China" policy, Taiwan is not allowed to be recognized. As such, Taiwanese international contributions have not been welcome, and Taiwan was isolated from forging international relations.

The one hundred eighty-nine comments under this article from all over the region showed netizens were really stirred up by Han. There is name-calling on each side, and serious discussion of Taiwan's presidential election, China's Taiwan policy, and opinions on independence or unification. One netizen scolded the writer strongly:

> What a mean man this writer is? If it is for the sake of your own survival, you can ignore the death of the entire Chinese nation. If you have the ability, why not go to Taiwan to be elected as a president, and then declare Taiwan's independence?

Another person admitted that as a Mainlander, he/she could not agree to let Taiwan become an independent country: "Taiwan's independence has not considered the interests of the Mainland, so why should the Mainland consider Taiwan's interests? The United States will only consider its own interests." Other comments were involved in naming calling: "Insightful. With the exception of the shameful Wu Mao (Communist fans), all Chinese (including members of the Communist Party of China) agree to unite China with the Three People's Principles."

In Article 15, "Freedom of the Net vs. Anti-Terrorism: The United States Wants to Be a Good Role Model for China," VOA stated that after the terrorist attack in San Bernardino, California, in 2016, the U.S. Federal Bureau of Investigation (FBI) tried to crack the suspect's encrypted iPhone by asking the Apple company to comply, sparking a debate about anti-terrorism and protecting citizens' privacy. At the same time, U.S. senators and experts pointed out that countries such as China and Russia circumvent counter-terrorism measures to restrain freedom of expression. Of the eight comments available under this article, one netizen echoed the sentiments of Article 15, arguing that counter-terrorism has been misused in other countries and the United States should set a good example:

> Centralized countries, such as China and Russia, use the name of counter-terrorism to suppress online speech and suppress dissidents. . . . It is necessary to strike a balance between counterterrorism and protecting citizens' privacy. Set a good example.

Another netizen cited plenty of technical information to prove that the U.S. government and authorities are not as concerned about protecting their citizens' basic rights as they claim, and alleged they perform actions to monitor information. This netizen posted five long comments on how U.S. governmental agencies collect information from citizens. In one comment, he said that the FBI attempted to develop applications to gather information from social networks such as Facebook and Twitter:

> The FBI Center for Strategic Information and Operations (SOIC) is inviting technology companies on the website to provide feasible solutions and estimate costs for the development of reliable social media monitoring procedures . . . to quickly and automatically collect information publicly posted by users on social networks.

Article 16, "U.S. Anti-terrorism Agencies also Control Anti-foreign Propaganda: China and Russia are the Focus," revealed that the U.S. State Department's Global Engagement Center (GEC), which was established in March 2016, was originally designed to counter propaganda from foreign terrorist organizations such as "Islamic State" and "Al Qaeda." The article mentioned that the Anti-Foreign Propaganda and Anti-Fake Information section of the 2017 National Defense Authorization Act, which was passed by both Houses of Congress and signed into force on December 23, 2016, states that the U.S. State Department coordinates with the Department of Defense to establish an information warfare against foreign governments. A spokesman for the GEC at the State Department told VOA that, under the requirements of this bill, GEC will increase its anti-foreign propaganda function while continuing its original anti-terrorist information dissemination work. In response to this article that generated fifty-eight comments, both supportive and critical comments are observed. For example, one recurring theme is that the United States is justified to take these actions because foreign countries could influence the U.S. election and alleged the Chinese government infiltrated Western social media with the aim of swaying public opinion. One comment reads:

> Now the Chinese Communist Party not only propagates through CCTV and other mouthpieces to attack Western democratic systems, but also organizes a

> large number of overseas Chinese students to pretend to be foreigners to guide public opinion on Facebook and Twitter.

In contrast, other commenters emphasized the Chinese government's actions are consistent with those of the U.S. government's trajectories, which, again, circles back to the "hypocrisy" line of argument that is routinely deployed by proponents of the former. According to one commenter:

> No matter how difficult, just be equal. The Chinese Communist Party does not allow the American media to land or broadcast in China, the Chinese Communist Party is not allowed to land or broadcast in the United States. Everyone must follow the principle of reciprocity.

Chinese President Xi Jinping and the Xinjiang Issue

Five articles (Articles 18, 19, 20, 21, 22) fall into this category including those that criticized current Chinese President Xi Jinping, mocked Chinese media censorship, and defended the U.S. advocacy and law on Uighur ethnic group members. Article 19, "China's National Human Rights Report: Human Rights Cause Guided by Xi Jinping Thought," reports the United Nations' Human Rights Council conducted the third Universal Periodic Review of China's human rights situation in Geneva on November 6, 2018, and that the Chinese government submitted a national report. The report states that there is no universal human rights development path in the world and that China's human rights cause has always been guided by Xi Jinping's thought which "takes the path of human rights development with Chinese characteristics." Of the 139 comments submitted in response to this article, one stated that although Xi's pictures and words always fill the headlines of the newspaper, too little attention is given to the fact that people are monitored all the time:

> Xi Jinping has the thought of "dictators." He wanted to [control] newspapers, radio stations, all available propaganda tools. . . . Even when sending a WeChat message, we are intimidated . . . your right to speak is deprived, but no one ever told you what was considered "wrong."

Another netizen criticized the United States instead, using the same "mind your own business" viewpoint:

> The United States withdrew from human rights organizations itself, constantly crossfired within their own government, threw bombs all over the world, and threatened to shoot at refugees. But in return, it has a crooked attitude as to how Xi Jinping's thoughts can guide human rights. What a shame!

Article 21, "U.S. Law Related to Xinjiang Triggers Strong Reaction from China" reported that the U.S. House of Representatives overwhelmingly passed the "Uyghur Human Rights Policy Act" (para. 1), and how the Chinese Foreign Ministry spokesman responded. The spokesperson urged the United States to immediately correct its mistake [of passing the Act] and stop using the Xinjiang-related issue to interfere in China's internal affairs. Similarly, Article 22, "China Condemns U.S. Uyghur Human Rights Policy Bill, Saying Uyghur Students have All Graduated" is critical of the United States. Together, the two articles generated thirty-eight comments. Netizens exchanged insults, and several did not use fake identities. Using an online fake name is common among Chinese netizens. Because no one knows who is behind the fake name, people gain anonymity and some sense of privacy so their expressions online would have fewer personal restrictions and are less likely to result in consequences (Salahuddin 2010). One of several similar comments claimed the goal is to obliterate Muslim identity in re-education camps in Xinjiang: "In the current re-educational camps, it is mandatory to learn 'national' language, so-called Mandarin. . . . If they cannot graduate [from the camp], they cannot regain their freedom." In contrast, another netizen lambasted the United States by arguing "the U.S. killed more Muslims in the world. The U.S. has the most Muslim blood on its hands."

Article 18, "Tricks of Global News Censorship, Chinese Measures Attract Attention," reported that the Committee to Protect Journalists cited new dangers and new threats facing journalists and free independent media. China's censorship has long included routine means of blocking journalists' social media accounts and shutting down news sites and detaining journalists. This type of censorship goes as far as blocking journalists' other daily activities, depriving them of employment opportunities, and barring them from participating in mainstream social activities. Some of the forty comments following this article are harsh accusations against VOA, including the following:

> What is the purpose of VOA's compilation of this issue? Is it acceptable for a free press in democratic countries to entertain these ideas or touting authoritarian brutal rule, blocking Internet freedoms. . . . The editors are seriously wrong. China is taking a brand-new approach to deal with people who are free and equal. . . . The Chinese Communist Party will never follow the path of democracy.

DISCUSSION, LIMITATIONS, AND CONCLUDING REMARKS

The previous section provided data drawn from VOA's online reporting on China's Counter-Terrorism Law and netizen's comments on these reports.

There are some key takeaways that can be discussed here. One important insight that can be drawn from the analysis relates to whether VOA is presenting American views or propagandizing to foreign countries (see Heil 2003; Metzgar 2012; Smith and Despard 1991). From VOA's perspective, China has created a very restrictive environment for journalism practice and expressive rights. Allowing user comments is one way to provide a forum for netizens to express their opinions on news from China. As Jungreis (2018) writes:

> China is known for the depth and reach of its censorship operations. Thousands of websites have been blocked in the country, inspiring the phrase "the Great Firewall of China." Foreign journalists are routinely detained for their reporting, and virtually all domestic media capable of reaching a mass audience is tightly regulated. (para. 7)

Under these circumstances, netizens who follow and comment on VOA reporting have displayed conflicting interests and diverse views using anonymous names to protect themselves from future persecution online or repercussions upon return to the Chinese Mainland. Under most articles, there are crossfire arguments, name-calling, debates, defensive opinions, and attacks. Netizens could be from any Chinese-speaking region such as Hong Kong, Taiwan, Mainland China, or the diaspora. They hold different political beliefs, values, and attitudes which are shaped by their experiences inside and out of China. Depending on the online host of information about Chinese laws and policies, Chinese netizens may show homogeneous support for China's Counter-Terrorism Law. For example, there was universal support from commenters on the article "A Prosperous Nation" on *The People's Daily*, considered to be the voice of the Communist Party, as critical comments are not allowed to be posted (see Sun 2019). However, on the VOA website, netizens are less constrained and either lean toward China or the United States. They are more likely to express criticism of the Law on a site not hosted in China.

One implication of this study is that counter-terrorism is of national interest, and it is difficult to persuade a nation to accept a definition made by another nation. User comments seemingly supporting the Law and critical of the United States suggest that the United States has issues to solve internally before criticizing China's policies and practices. The United States and China each operate under different juridical and political systems. To achieve total understanding and cooperation on issues of terrorism within the differing systems is not an easy task.

Another key takeaway is that netizens are divided on understanding and commenting on the VOA reports on counter-terrorism and free speech issues.

Dunn and his associates (2016) have studied word choice, such as terrorism, violence, and patriotism, in newspaper articles which could lead the audience to perceive war differently, demonstrating the power of national media in influencing people. Labeling an incident as one associated with terrorism by media or government officials makes the incident more dangerous and worrisome for netizens. Chinese government agents are believed to hire an "Internet Water Army" (social media militia) disguised as grassroots commenters to lead public opinion (Chen 2018; Kanat 2012; Yu et al. 2015; Zhang 2018). The hired "Internet Water Army" is capable of posting comments on the VOA website. The netizen under Article 15 who had posted five long comments to "expose" the American government's hypocrisy or double standard on free expression, for example, echoes the policies of the Chinese government directly.

Finally, the study offered important insights regarding netizens' comments about Western governments' roles in China's counter-terrorism actions. In China, media coverage of global counter-terrorism has been intensive. International news reporting has been an essential part of Chinese national TV and newspapers. When provoked by Western media, China usually takes a defensive–offensive strategy, blasting Western media and exposing failings of foreign governments. Mistrust between Western media and China has existed for years (Sun 2019). The ideological difference is a significant obstacle hindering mutual understanding on many issues such as human rights, freedom of speech, and counter-terrorism strategies. VOA netizens whose ideology leans toward China's government applauded China's Counter-Terrorism Law and criticized the U.S. government's intervention in China's internal affairs. Unlike in China, netizens who use the VOA website can make comments freely online, enjoying the right of free speech. Conversely, in China, criticism of President Xi Jinping and his administration is censored, and the commenters' mobile phones and Internet use are tracked, often resulting in severe consequences for individuals with critical views (Velghe 2019).

There are limitations to this study. First, demographic information about the users commenting on VOA articles is unavailable. Consequently, it is not possible to know the exact motivations of netizens who post commentary. Second, it is not possible to know whether VOA Chinese TV and VOA online have the same or different audiences. Some netizens may have multiple online identities and post repeated comments on VOA articles. Third, due to China's Internet censorship, the VOA website is banned in China, so users in Mainland China would have to use a VPN to circumvent the firewall and it is unknown how many of the commenters are located in the Mainland and how many are located throughout the diaspora. Future studies may address the issue by comparing more Chinese-language websites hosted by both China and Western countries.

By examining user comments on VOA articles regarding China's Counter-Terrorism Law from its enaction, this study provides insight into the online user comments of Chinese netizens concerning the Law. User comments are unlikely to be posted on websites hosted within China as the government monitors commentary closely or restricts user comments that are not supportive of the government. It is in this context that VOA and other media organizations fill this vacuum by hosting important public service online forums that provide space for people to post their opinions of news in China and abroad. The study also reminds us that citizens are easily controlled by governmental policies that state they are preventing or protecting the citizenry from terroristic acts. It is difficult for netizens to counter an official governmental narrative that its borders need protection from those willing to cause death and destruction. Additionally, while cooperation across borders and governments to combat terrorism is beneficial, justification of official policies and newly enacted laws because other countries have similar practices can hinder human rights and prevent citizens from expressing their opinions freely.

REFERENCES

Allen, Craig. 2004. Review of "Voice of America: A History (by Alan Heil)." *Journalism and Mass Communication Quarterly* 81 (1): 221–224. https://doi.org/10.1177%2F107769900408100113.

Amnesty International. 2019. "UN: Act to End China's Mass Detentions in Xinjiang." Accessed December 15, 2020. https://www.amnesty.org/en/latest/news/2019/02/un-act-to-end-china-mass-detentions-xinjiang/.

BBC News. 2020. "The Uighurs and the Chinese State: A Long History of Discord." *BBC News* July 20, 2020. https://www.bbc.com/news/world-asia-china-22278037.

Beech, Hannah, Yongqiang Gu, Victor Luckerson, and Sam Frizell. 2015. "The Other Side Of the Great Firewall." *TIME Magazine* June 22, 2015. https://time.com/magazine/south-pacific/3917933/june-22th-2015-vol-185-no-23-asia-europe-middle-east-and-africa-south-pacific/.

Bhabha, Faisal. 2018. "The Spies Who Hate Us: Official Misdeeds and Sowing Distrust in Canadian National Security." *University of New Brunswick Law Journal* 69: 160–197. https://papers.ssrn.com/sol3/papers.cfm?abstract_id=3273224.

Buckley, Chris and Keith Bradsher. 2018. "China Moves to Let Xi Stay in Power by Abolishing the Term Limit." *The New York Times* February 15, 2018. https://www.nytimes.com/2018/02/25/world/asia/china-xi-jinping.html.

Callamard, Agnes. 2017. "The Control of 'Invasive' Ideas in a Digital Age." *Social Research* 84 (1): 119–145. https://muse.jhu.edu/article/659226/pdf.

Campbell, Joel. 2019. "Terrorism and Counter-Terrorism in China: Domestic and Foreign Policy Dimensions." *International Affairs* 95 (5): 1197–1199. https://doi.org/10.1093/ia/iiz153.

Chen, Na. 2018. "Guns for Hire: China's Social Media Militia Engage on Command." *Sixth Tone* March 12, 2018. http://www.sixthtone.com/news/1001904/guns-for-hire-chinas-social-media-militia-engage-on-command.

China Network Information Center. 2017. CNNIC: Thriving After 20 Years' Effort, Serving as Cornerstone on the Internet. Accessed June 5, 2019. https:///cnnic.com.cn/AU/MediaC/rdxw/2017/201706/t20170609_69333.htm.

Chung, Chien-peng. 2002. "China's 'War on Terror': September 11 and Uighur Separatism." *Foreign Affairs* May/June 2002. https://www.foreignaffairs.com/articles/asia/2002-07-01/chinas-war-terror-september-11-and-uighur-separatism.

Clarke, Michael. 2010. "Widening the Net: China's Anti-Terror Laws and Human Rights in the Xinjiang Uyghur Autonomous Region." *The International Journal of Human Rights* 14 (4): 542–558. https://doi.org/10.1080/13642980802710855.

———. 2018. *Terrorism and Counter-Terrorism in China: Domestic and Foreign Policy Dimensions*. Oxford: Oxford University Press.

Cook, Sarah. 2020. "Hong Kong Warning Signs, US Protest Coverage, Citizen Defiance." *China Media Bulletin*. Accessed November 12, 2020. https://freedomhouse.org/report/china-media-bulletin/2020/hong-kong-warning-signs-us-protest-coverage-citizen-defiance-june.

Counterterrorism Law of the People's Republic of China (Order No. 36 of the president of the PRC). 2015. Accessed December 12, 2020. http://en.pkulaw.cn/display.aspx?id=4a6094a588ac744ebdfb&lib=law&SearchKeyword=counterterrorism&SearchCKeyword=.

Cunningham, Christopher P. 2012. "Counterterrorism in Xinjiang: The ETIM, China, and the Uyghurs." *International Journal on World Peace* 29 (3): 7–50. https://go.gale.com/ps/anonymous?id=GALE%7CA305747379&sid=googleScholar&v=2.1&it=r&linkaccess=fulltext&issn=07423640&p=AONE&sw=w.

Denyer, Simon. 2015. "China's New Anti-terrorism Law Provokes Anger in the US, Concerns at Home." *The Washington Post,* March 5, 2015. https://www.washingtonpost.com/world/asia_pacific/china-invokes-terrorism-as-it-readies-additional-harsh-measures/2015/03/04/1e078288-139c-497e-aa8a-e6d810a5a8a2_story.html.

Dunn, Kevin Mark, Rosalie Atie, Michael Kennedy, Jan A. Ali, John O'Reilly, and Lindsay Rogerson. 2016. "Can You Use Community Policing for Counter Terrorism? Evidence from NSW, Australia." *Police Practice and Research* 17 (3): 196–211.

Eko, Lyombe and Hellmueller, Lea. 2018. "To Republish or Not to Republish: The 'Je Suis Charlie' Mohammed Cartoon and Journalistic Paradigms in a Global Context." *International Communication Gazette* 80 (3): 207–229. https://doi.org/10.1177/1748048517727220.

Gatson, Sarah N. 2011. "The Methods, Politics, and Ethics of Representation in Online Ethnography." in *Collecting and Interpreting Qualitative Materials*, edited by Norman K. Denzin and Yvonna S. Lincoln, 513–528. New York: Sage Publications.

Gracie, Carrie. 2017. "'All-out Offensive' in Xinjiang Risks Worsening Grievances." *BBC News* March 2, 2017. https://www.bbc.com/news/world-asia-china-39137420.

Grossman, Derek. 2019. "One Country, Two Systems, Lots of Problems: Beijing's Soft Sell to Taiwan and Hong Kong is Falling Apart." *Foreign Policy*, June 21, 2019. https://foreignpolicy.com/2019/06/21/one-country-two-systems-lots-of-problems/.

Goldberg, David. 2009. "Europe Bans Terrorist Media: What Sort of Antidote to Poisonous Voices?" *Cardozo Journal of International & Comparative Law* 17 (3): 445–469.

Heil, Alan L. Jr. 2003. *Voice of America: A History*. New York: Columbia University Press.

Hu, Jieren and Yang Zheng. 2019. "Social Media, State Control and Religious Freedom in China." *Political Theology* 20 (5): 382–391. https://doi.org/10.1080/1462317X.2019.1624038.

Illmer, Andreas. 2019. "Tashpolat Tiyip: The Uighur Leading Geographer Who Vanished in China. *BBC News*, October 11, 2019. https://www.bbc.com/news/world-asia-china-49956088.

Jungreis, Max. 2018. "China Eyes Banning Foreign Online News." *VOA News*, September 20, 2018. https://www.voanews.com/east-asia/china-eyes-banning-foreign-online-news.

Kanat, Kilic Bugra. 2012. "'War on Terror' as a Diversionary Strategy: Personifying Minorities as Terrorists in the People's Republic of China." *Journal of Muslim Minority Affairs* 32 (4): 507–27. https://doi.org/10.1080/13602004.2012.746179.

Law Library of Congress. 2016. "Foreign Intelligence Gathering Laws." Accessed May 13, 2020. https://www.loc.gov/law/help/intelligence-activities/intelligence-gathering.pdf.

Liu, Renwen. 2015. "A Description and Analysis of Chinese Anti-Terrorism Criminal Legislation." *Renmin Chinese Law Review: Selected Papers of the Jurist* 3: 120–41.

Mchangama, Jacob. 2016. "Freedom of Expression and National Security." *Society* 53 (4): 363–367. https://doi.org/10.1007/s12115-016-0029-1.

Metzgar, Emily T. 2012. "Public Diplomacy, Smith-Mundt and the American Public." *Communication Law & Policy* 17 (1): 67–101. https://doi.org/10.1080/10811680.2012.633807.

Modood, Tariq, Randall Hanse, Erik Bleich, Brenda O'Leary, and Joseph H. Carens. 2006. "The Danish Cartoon Affair: Free Speech, Racism, Islamism, and Integration." *International Migration* 44 (5): 3–62. https://doi.org/10.1111/j.1468-2435.2006.00386.x.

Nebehay, Stephanie. 2018. "U.N. Says it has Credible Reports that China Holds Million Uighurs in Secret Camps." *Reuters*, August 10, 2018. https://www.reuters.com/article/us-china-rights-un/u-n-says-it-has-credible-reports-that-china-holds-million-uighurs-in-secret-camps-idUSKBN1KV1SU.

O'Brien, Danny. 2019. "China's Global Reach: Surveillance and Censorship Beyond the Great Firewall." *The Electronic Frontier Foundation*, October, 10 2019. https://www.eff.org/deeplinks/2019/10/chinas-global-reach-surveillance-and-censorship-beyond-great-firewall.

Ortner, Daniel. 2016. “Conscientious Offenders: Russia’s Ban on ‘Extremist’ Religious Literature, and the European Court of Human Rights.” *Virginia Journal of International Law* 56 (1):147–183.

Palmer, Allen, and Edward Carter. 2006. “The Smith-Mundt Act’s Ban on Domestic Propaganda: An Analysis of the Cold War Statute Limiting Access to Public Diplomacy.” *Communication Law and Policy* 11 (1): 1–34. https://doi.org/10.1207/s15326926clp1101_1.

Pan, Xinrui. 2015. “Collation and Thoughts of Perfection About Laws of Anti-Terrorism: From the Ninth Amendment to the Anti-Terrorism Law (Draft) Commentary.” *China Legal Science* 3 (6): 101–122.

Paye, Jean-Claude. 2014. “Merging the Law of War with Criminal Law.” *Monthly Review: An Independent Socialist Magazine* 66 (3): 128–135. https://doi.org/10.14452/MR-066-03-2014-07_8.

Pike, George H. 2006. “Global Reach of Anti-Terrorism Laws.” *Information Today* 23 (1): 17–19.

Purbrick, Martin. 2017. “Maintaining a Unitary State: Counter-Terrorism, Separatism, and Extremism in Xinjiang and China.” *Asian Affairs* 48 (2): 236–56. https://doi.org/10.1080/03068374.2017.1313595.

Reeves, Jeffrey. 2016. “Ideas and Influence: Scholarship as a Harbinger of Counterterrorism Institutions, Policies, and Laws in the People’s Republic of China.” *Terrorism and Political Violence* 28 (5): 827–847. https://doi.org/10.1080/09546553.2014.955915.

Riessman, Catherine Kohle. 2002. *Narrative Methods for the Human Sciences*. Thousand Oaks, CA: Sage Publications.

Robertson, Margaret. 2009. “Young ‘netizens’ Creating Public Citizenship in Cyberspace. *International Research in Geographical & Environmental Education* 18 (4): 287–293.

Salahuddin, K M Rehan. 2010. “Fake Identities and Social Networks.” *China.org.cn*, August 4, 2010. http://www.china.org.cn/opinion/2010-08/04/content_20638651.htm.

Smith, Gaaddis, and Lucy Edwards Despard. 1991. “The Voice of America: Propaganda and Democracy.” *Foreign Affairs* 70 (3): 168–168.

State Internet Information Office of China. 2019. “Provisions on the Governance of the Online Information Content Ecosystem.” Accessed September 13, 2020. https://www.chinalawtranslate.com/en/provisions-on-the-governance-of-the-online-information-content-ecosystem/.

Stoughton, Corey. 2019. “Free Expression, Pre-Crime and Counter-Terrorism Legislation.” *Political Quarterly* 90 (3): 416–421. https://doi.org/10.1111/1467-923X.12738.

Sun, Degang. 2010. “China and Jihad Network.” *Journal of the Middle East & Africa* 1 (2): 196–207. https://doi.org/10.1080/21520844.2010.517036.

Sun, Wei. 2019. “China’s National Media Coverage of Counter-Terrorism and its Netizens’ Reactions.” In *Global Media Representation and International Community Perception,* edited by Emmanuel K. Ngwainmbi, 163–187. London, UK: Palgrave MacMillan.

Tanner, Murray, Scot Tanner, and James Bellacqua. 2016. "China's Response to Terrorism." Accessed April 17, 2020. https://www.uscc.gov/sites/default/files/Research/Chinas%20Response%20to%20Terrorism_CNA061616.pdf.

Tsesis, Alexander. 2017. "Terrorist Speech on Social Media." *Vanderbilt Law Review* 70 (2): 651–708. https://scholarship.law.vanderbilt.edu/vlr/vol70/iss2/4/.

Velghe, Pieter. 2019. "'Reading China': The Internet of Things, Surveillance, and Social Management in the PRC." *China Perspectives* 2019 (1): 85–89. https://doi.org/10.4000/chinaperspectives.8874.

Voice of America. n.d. "Mission & Values." Accessed December 23, 2020. https://www.insidevoa.com/p/5831.html.

Wang, Yi. 2002. "New Challenges and New Concepts: International Anti-Terrorism Struggle and China's Policy." The 39th Munich Security Conference, Munich, Germany. Accessed December 20, 2020. https://www.fmprc.gov.cn/123/wjdt/zyjh/t4658.htm.

Wayne, Martin I. 2009. "Inside China's War on Terrorism." *Journal of Contemporary China* 18 (59): 249–61. https://doi.org/10.1080/10670560802576018.

William, George. 2014. "Anti-Terrorism Laws and Human Rights." *Review of Constitutional Studies* 19 (2): 127–145.

Wong, Edward. 2016. "Xi Jinping's News Alert: Journalists Must Serve the Party." *The New York Times*, February 23, 2016. https://www.nytimes.com/2016/02/23/world/asia/china-media-policy-xi-jinping.html.

Wong, Edward. 2009. "China Sees Separatist Threats." *The New York Times*, January 20, 2009. https://www.nytimes.com/2009/01/21/world/asia/21china.html.

Wu, Chunying, and Juan Wang. 2019. "Analysis of Cyberterrorism and Online Social Media." *Advances in Social Science, Education and Humanities Research* 351: 925–927. https://doi.org/10.2991/mmetss-19.2019.189.

Yu, Louis Lei, Sitaram Asur, and Bernardo A. Huberman. 2015. "Trend Dynamics and Attention in Chinese Social Media." *American Behavioral Scientist* 59 (9): 1142–1156.

Zhang, Qibin. 2018. "Disclosing the Business 'Internet Water Army': You Pay, We Post." *CCTV News*, February 5, 2018. http://m.news.cctv.com/2018/02/05/ARTI5T9viL8A5yYnwbpWm2Om180205.shtml.

Chapter 7

Terrorism and Counter-terrorism Legislation in Brazil

Daniel Oppermann

INTRODUCTION

Historically, Brazil has a relatively calm public discourse on terrorism. Although it is attentive to debates and incidents happening in different parts of the world, the country itself has not been a target of extensive terrorist attacks comparable to those happening in other parts of the world (Raza 2007, 165). Neither is terrorism, as it is discernible in many high-income countries in the North today, considered by the Brazilian population or public representatives a serious threat to the country. However, this should not hide the fact that Brazil is suffering from serious acts of violence in all of its five regions. Per United Nations data, Brazil is categorized as one of the few countries worldwide with disproportionately high homicide rates (UNODC 2019, 18). The public debates on violence in Brazil are mostly related to organized crime and social inequality. Nevertheless, fear of terrorist attacks in the global North and discussions on terrorism especially after the 9/11 attacks in the United States also had an impact on the public discourse of terrorism in Brazil (Cepik 2010; da Cunha 2010; Zúquete 2017). In this sense, it is important to interrogate whether the current public discourse on terrorism in Brazil is a reflection of reality in Latin America or the reflection of the impact of Western debates on the region.

To understand the specific characteristics of terrorism discourses in Brazil, it is necessary to look at a number of historical developments in the country including the political and social conflicts of the early twentieth century when increasing labor movements were labeled a threat by the traditional and oligarchic leaders. For example, the National Security Law, which was passed in 1935, was used to restrict and criminalize the political left which has since been lumped under "communists." Throughout the following decades the official understanding of terrorism remained related to the political opposition from the left, although, in specific instances, security laws were also applied against the radical right. A high point of political repression occurred during the military regime (1964–1985) when the state used torture and murder against members of the political opposition (Brazil 2014; Gaspari 2002; Skidmore 1988). The radicalization of that epoch also became visible through militant and armed groups on the left, who, in addition to being categorized as terrorist by the regime, were instrumental in introducing the discourse on state terrorism.

The discourses on state security and terrorism in Brazil and the legal acts developed within this framework frequently aimed at the limitation of basic rights including freedom of speech or the freedom of political organization and manifestation. After democracy had finally overcome the military regime in the late 1980s, the newly elected democratic governments tried to abstain from the topic of terrorism. This is partly because some among them had suffered from the military regime which had categorized them as terrorists and/or communists. Since then, terrorism has become a topic the Brazilian public was primarily observing on television related to violent acts in other regions of the world. The so-called war on terror initiated by the United States after the 9/11 attacks in New York was remote from the Brazilian reality. Much more present, though, was and still is the impact of urban violence by drug organizations, militias, and the military police (Cano and Duarte 2012; de Santis Feltran 2012; French 2013; Rodrigues 2015). Nevertheless, the debates on terrorism appeared back on the political agenda in recent years (Buzanelli 2013). Ironically, it was President Dilma Rousseff, who, in 2016, forty-six years after suffering torture from the military regime, signed the new Brazilian counter-terrorism law that partly criminalized her own political supporters (Brazil 2016a). The following sections will address historical and contemporary debates on terrorism in Brazil and discuss the development of counter-terrorism legislation and its impact on freedom of expression in the twentieth and twenty-first century.

PUBLIC DEBATES ON TERRORISM IN BRAZIL

In public and academic debates in Brazil, the risk of terrorist attacks is classified as low but not impossible (Cepik 2010; Lasmar 2015). Authors discussing the topic are frequently framing their debates in a manner that is akin to the way terrorism is conceived in the global North. Although recent scholarship in the global North focuses on right-wing extremists as possible terrorist threats, the past twenty years were dominated by a fear of religious terrorism. The focus on religiously motivated attacks conducted by groups and individuals who belong to or sympathize with organizations such as Al Qaeda, the Islamic State, Boko Haram, and related groups are influencing the framing of the Brazilian public and academia in regard to terrorism threats. Per this logic, however, there are in fact no notable terrorist attacks happening in Brazil. And the question that often occurs during these debates is whether the country could become a target in the future. Since there is no evidence to predict the occurrence of such attacks, this question is difficult to assess. But since traditional security studies are accompanied by a substantial level of pessimism, the answer is never negative (Diniz 2004). When looking over the scope of contemporary Western debates on terrorism, which for many years were highly influenced by anti-Islamic rhetoric, it is possible to identify more specific characteristics of the discourse on terrorism in Brazil.

In the Latin American context, Brazil has a specific role due to its geographic size, its large population, and its economic strength. Although the country has gone through unstable moments of economic trajectory marked by growth, stagnation, or recession, it remains the largest and strongest economy in the Latin American region since 2005, followed (with a significant distance) by Mexico, Argentina, Colombia, and Chile. It should be noted that throughout the second half of the twentieth century, several countries in the region suffered from military dictatorships that were backed especially by the United States in their former campaigns against the spreading of "global communism" (Fico 2008; Skidmore 1988). Also, Brazil had to pay a high price for these campaigns that resulted in a military coup in 1964, followed by political repression against opposition leaders and other individuals as well as torture, killings, or disappearing of numerous individuals. In 2020, more than thirty years after the end of the military dictatorship, many details about the victims of the regime are still unclear. Following the National Truth Commission (Comissão Nacional da Verdade, CNV), a group installed in 2011 by the Brazilian government under then-president Dilma Rousseff (who herself was imprisoned and tortured as a student during the military regime), 434 individuals were killed or disappeared for political reasons between 1946 and 1988, before, and during the military regime (Brazil 2014). Per official reports, about 20,000 people were tortured during the military regime (Brazil 2009, 173).[1]

Contemporary discussions on terrorism in Brazil are partly related to not only historical precedents but also to contemporary nondemocratic actors that invoke the threat of "global communism" in the country. Therefore, "communists" are often identified as members of left-wing organizations, specific political parties (mostly social-democratic, socialist, and communist parties), social movements, NGOs, students, and intellectuals in and outside of public universities in the country (Raza 2007, 167). In addition to these antiquated forms of political thought and its contemporary recurrences, there are additional actors that were identified throughout the late twentieth and in the early twenty-first century that are part of the contemporary discourse on terrorism in the country. Among them are radical religious groups and movements, right-wing extremists often identified as *Integralistas* (a movement inspired by Italian fascism since the 1930s), criminal organizations such as Primeiro Comando da Capital (PCC), Comando Vermelho (CV), and the militias as well as numerous individual cases (Cano and Duarte 2012; de Santis Feltran 2012; Rodrigues 2015).

TWENTIETH CENTURY TERRORISM DEBATES IN BRAZIL

To discuss terrorism and political violence in Brazil during the twentieth century, there are two important historical epochs that need to be taken into consideration. The first is the era of Getúlio Vargas, who ruled the country from 1930 to 1945 and again from 1951 to 1954. The second is the military regime that ruled from 1964 to 1985.

Both epochs are associated with political instability and state coups followed by undemocratic rule in which political opposition was fiercely suppressed and legal mechanisms were developed to justify the oppression of dissidence. Rulers in both epochs are also associated with support for extreme right-wing orientations and support of anti-communist ideologies (whereas "communism" again serves as an umbrella term for any kind of left-wing politics). Nevertheless, these two types of dictatorships, as they are perceived today, have taken different positions in contemporary public thought in Brazil. While the military regime is clearly labeled a dictatorship by almost 80% of the population (Gielow 2020), the Vargas regimes are often excused for having created institutions and specific mechanisms or regulations like the labor law *Consolidação das Leis do Trabalho* which is still in force today.

In April 1935, the National Security Law, also known as the "monster law" for its repressive character (see Groppo and Laclau 2010, 252), came into force (Brazil 1935a). Over the following decades, this law was revised or substituted several times. Its current version was signed in 1983. Although the National Security Laws were partly addressing terrorism and can be referred to as early anti-terrorism laws in Brazil, a more specific counter-terrorism law was signed in 2016 as will be discussed later in this chapter.

The objective of the 1935 National Security Law was to shield the first government of Getúlio Vargas from political opponents (Skidmore 2007, 42). Vargas, himself a putschist who had come to power by force shortly before, was supported by groups of oligarchs and militaries with whom he shared the fear of an increasing workers movement that had grown in the country over the previous decades. The workers' movement used strikes as a means to achieve their political interest of improved living and working conditions.

The workers' movement was made up of heterogeneous groups which were partly inspired by anarchist movements and later also by supporters of the Russian Revolution of 1917. While anarchist movements considered the state itself as an organization that had to be removed together with private property to overcome the exploitation of the working people, the communist movement later accepted the state as a means to bring political, economic, and social change to the working population. In 1922, a section of the workers' movement founded the Communist Party of Brazil (Partido Comunista do Brasil and later Partido Comunista Brasileiro, PCB). The party was banned in the same year by then-president Epitácio Pessoa who feared economic and political disadvantages for him and his well-situated supporters in case the working population would accelerate their activities by forming a political party. The fear of an organized communist or socialist workers movement has passed on through generations in Brazil. Even in 2020, the word "communist" is still used by very conservative parts of the population to publicly denounce individuals or organizations that are not favoring conservative or right-wing viewpoints. At the same time, members of the political left use the term "fascist" to characterize right-wing and conservative groups.

When Vargas came to power, he was, like his predecessors, concerned about political groups questioning not just the distribution or handling of political power but also the comfortable living conditions he and his oligarchic supporters had compared to the majority of the population in the country. Vargas, who had little respect for election results and was driven by fear of social reforms that could harm him and his backers, decided to pass the security law that helped him prosecute those who would act against the state in a way he himself had done previously.

The law focused on and defined crimes against political and social order. Its main focus was to address a number of activities that could threaten the political and social order of the time, its representatives, and institutions (Fernandes 2009). It restricted individuals, parties, and other organizations or groups that tried to influence public servants and security forces to act against the current order by applying different means considered to be illegal. This included, among other things, the dissemination of specific publications (including those containing what was labeled as false information supposedly spreading fear among the population), the creation of conflict between social classes (labeled as "hate" in the law), the utilization of strikes to achieve political goals unrelated to working conditions, and the unregulated production, possession, and distribution of weapons of warfare including explosives. Specific attention was also given to foreign organizations in the country and professors who were suspected of using their positions at work to undermine the current order of the country.

Given the political situation of Brazil in the 1930s, the law was clearly targeting political actors surrounding the workers movement and especially organizations such as the Communist Party, which, since its foundation in 1922, was outlawed several times. Political repression was kept high after members of the Communist Party and other left-wing organizations tried to overthrow the Vargas government in November 1935. The objective of the National Security Law of 1935 was later strengthened and extended by additional documents such as law 136 (Brazil 1935b) and decree-laws 431 (Brazil 1938) and 4766 (Brazil 1942).

After Vargas's dictatorial regime from 1937 to 1945 (*Estado Novo*) ended, he later came back to power in 1951. Since he came out first in the elections, he did not need to use force for a third time to become president. His rule ended after political turbulences, with him committing suicide in August 1954 leaving a letter in which he painted a portrait of himself as a friend of the working people and victim of uncontrollable circumstances. Vargas professed he was defending the country and himself against foreign interests which he identified in the financial and economic sector. In his final letter, he compared these foreign forces with birds of prey, animals that kill and eat their victims. He wrote about sacrificing himself, offering his blood and his life "in a holocaust" to save the people against foreign animals that came to "suck dry" the country (Vargas 1954). Such anti-Semitic stereotypes about foreign, not clearly identified forces with high purchasing power, invading countries like animals and behaving like parasites can be observed for centuries in many parts of the world. Vargas's fear of secret communist operations and conspiracies can also be found in his earlier personal notes (Peixoto de Paula Marques 2014, 643). A year before Vargas gave up against the "foreign animals," the new Security Law 1802 (Brazil 1953) was passed to substitute the 1935 edition (Fernandes 2009).

During the military regime (1964–1985), the political opposition in Brazil suffered violent repression on different levels. Targets of the military regime were mostly but not exclusively left-wing individuals, union activists, or political groups which were often labeled as communists. On the international level, Brazil participated in Operation Condor, an alliance of secret services in South and North America to investigate, torture, and kill members of the political opposition. Blakeley and Raphael (2016, 344) have categorized campaigns within Operation Condor as examples of limited state terrorism defined as "one-off events and small-scale terror directed at one group or sector or a series of small operations."[2]

An important part of the ideological framework for political repression in Brazil was the National Security Doctrine developed by the Brazilian

War College *Escola Superior de Guerra* (ESG). Following Zúquete, "this doctrine set forth a narrative that transformed politics into a battlefield, a sort of domestic warfare, against the insidious, all-out 'revolutionary war' (a total war) permanently being perpetrated by enemies of the State" (Zúquete 2017, 277). Throughout the years of the military regime, parts of the political opposition turned into armed guerrilla groups fighting the military government. The conflicts between armed groups and the government forces were used by the regime to justify the violent repression of the political opposition. Terrorism was a term used by both sides to describe the actions of the opponent.

In March 1967, decree-law 314 came into force which was considered a new National Security Law based on the doctrine of the ESG (Brazil 1967). In September 1969, it was substituted by the more extensive decree-law 898 (Brazil 1969). This new security law designated left-wing actors and international workers movements as enemies of the state by focusing on "adverse psychological warfare" and "revolutionary warfare" (ibid). While "adverse psychological warfare" was roughly defined in the law as propaganda and political activities to motivate third parties (including foreigners) to act against the national interest, "revolutionary warfare" was described as an internal conflict inspired by "an ideology" or supported from outside the country. Interestingly, even in 2020, more than fifty years after the passing of the decree-law and thirty-five years after the end of the military regime, there are still numerous occasions when foreigners are watched with suspicion or are made responsible by both the political right and the left for conflicts or problems occurring in Brazil. However, a public discourse on xenophobia or anti-Semitism is not taking place.

In 1978, law 6620 became the new National Security Law (Brazil 1978). It was substituted by law 7170 in 1983 (Brazil 1983). Similar to its predecessors, the 1983 law was entitled to address crimes against national security and the political and social order. As Zúquete (2017, 278) notes, it was "more liberal and democratic than its predecessors, with a more limited concept of national security. This law, still in force today, is currently viewed as a relic of the military regime that should be adapted to the new democratic context" (Zúquete 2017, 278).

Besides the National Security Law in its manifold versions, a central document of the military regime to increase pressure on political opponents was Institutional Act 5, commonly known in Brazil as AI5. "In the Brazilian collective political imaginary, this Act has remained as the epitome of political repression under military dictatorship" (Zúquete 2017, 278). AI5 was one of the seventeen acts which were installed over the first five years of the military regime. AI5 enabled dictatorial measures to be used by the president of the Republic including the power to close down essential institutions like the National Congress, legislative assemblies in all parts of the country, the power to restrict political rights for any citizen including the right to vote and to be elected, the power to prohibit any political manifestation, the power to conduct surveillance of citizens, and the power to enforce restrictions on freedom of movement (Brazil 1968). In October 2019, deputy Eduardo Bolsonaro, son of President Jair Bolsonaro, mentioned in an interview that a new AI5 could be useful again to respond to the contemporary political opposition from the left (Bergamo 2019).

TWENTY-FIRST-CENTURY TERRORISM DEBATES IN BRAZIL

The experience of the military regime that left its marks on Brazilian politics and society throughout the 1990s and the early 2000s is also visible in contemporary debates in the country. Notwithstanding the lack of a wider and deeper debate on the occurrences of the 1960s to 1980s (which have got more attention through the establishment of the Truth Commission as discussed above), the memories of torture and state violence against a political opposition labeled as terrorists by the old regime made new democratic governments refrain from attempts to repeat the same discourse. Terrorism was not considered a topic worth discussing with the same enthusiasm as it happened in other parts of the world. Even the attacks on the World Trade Center in New York on September 11, 2001, did not cause the same political reactions that happened in North America or Europe. The social-democratic governments of the Workers Party (PT) that came to power for the first time in history in 2003, where they stayed until the controversial impeachment of Dilma Rousseff in 2016, were not willing to join the Western discourse of labeling individuals belonging to specific religions, nationalities or descendants as political extremists. Several members of the Brazilian government back then were among those who experienced the military regime's harassment. Dilma Rousseff herself was tortured by the regime as a student and member of a revolutionary opposition group in the early 1970s. The increasing stigmatization of Muslims or people of Arab descent, which is common in many Western countries, especially since the early twenty-first century, was rejected by the Brazilian governments of that time. A relatively small but nevertheless well-recognized part of Brazilian society has roots in a number of Arab countries. Furthermore, a large number of political activist movements on the left who supported the PT governments were using tactics that conservatives often consider as politically radical. Among them is the internationally known landless movement *Movimento dos Trabalhadores Rurais Sem Terra* which is in permanent conflict with landowners and the agrobusiness because of several land occupations throughout the country.

Although the then-president Lula da Silva (PT) demonstrated support and solidarity to the victims of terrorist attacks in the West, Brazil did not actively join alliances that responded with war and destruction in a number of Asian and African countries. The political priorities in Brazil remained hunger reduction and social developments, especially for the lower-income population. Also, Brazil was not directly confronted with terrorist attacks similar to those in the North (Cepik 2010). The most visible issues of public security in Brazil have been the different facets of organized crime, mostly related to drug trafficking organizations and the militias who started as self-proclaimed anti-drug-gang organizations which then developed their own illicit activities in the neighborhoods under their control (Bartolomé and Ventura Barreiro 2020; Brancoli and Vasquez 2016; Dias and Darke 2016; Ramos da Cruz and Ucko 2018).

However, the occurrences in the North have not left Brazil completely untouched. This became visible especially during debates on one of the so-called tri-border regions (Argentina-Brazil-Paraguay) where investigators identified activities of religious groups classified as extremists (da Cunha 2010; Raza 2007) and possible threats in the context of some of the international sports events that the country hosted like the FIFA World Cup in 2014 and the Olympic Games in 2016 (Buzanelli 2013). In addition, the large political manifestations in the country that started in 2013 (Carlos Brandão and de Paula Brito 2014) and which partly turned into violent clashes with the military police, coupled with individual cases like the public debate around Cesare Battisti[3] (Folha de São Paulo 2019) and the attempted murder of Jair Bolsonaro during his election campaign in 2018 (Folha de São Paulo 2018), became part of the Brazilian discourse on terrorism.

It is important, though, to distinguish between the public discourse on terrorism and actual terrorist activities. Battisti was accused of specific terrorist activities in Italy in the 1970s. The attack on Bolsonaro was committed by a socially isolated individual who was a former member of the socialist PSOL party and later became an active evangelical Christian. Following investigations, however, there was no clear political background for the crime. He was later declared *non compos mentis* by the court (Canofre 2019). Nevertheless, this does not change the fact that he did not commit such a violent act in his closer environment but chose a Presidential candidate as his target.

There are a number of additional cases like the killing of deputy Marielle Franco and her driver Anderson Gomes in Rio de Janeiro in 2018 or the bomb attack on the comedy group Porta dos Fundos in Rio de Janeiro in 2019. Both received national and some international attention. Between January 2016 and August 2020, 125 elected politicians or election candidates were victims of assassinations or attempted murder in Brazil (Lauris and Hashizume 2020). Most cases of assassinations of political representatives in the country do not receive wider attention in the national or international media. These numbers have almost doubled after the election of President Jair Bolsonaro (from 17 to 32), reaching the same level of cases (30 to be precise) as the year of the impeachment of Dilma Roussef (ibid).

In 2016, the Brazilian government under Dilma Rousseff agreed to sign the first counter-terrorism law (in Brazil also referred to as the anti-terrorism law) that was intensely discussed in parliament. Although terrorism was somehow addressed in the 1983 National Security Law and was also part of the organized crime legislation, the 2016 law (13.260/2016) had a more exclusive focus on terrorism (Brazil 2016a).

Per the new law, terrorism was understood as an act by one or more individuals with the objective of causing terror through different means including the use, possession, and transportation of explosives or toxic and nuclear material. The motivations defined by the law are prejudices of different kinds including xenophobia, racism or ethnic, and religious preconceptions. A passage that included political motivation as a foundation for terrorist activities was vetoed by the Office of the President. Also, passages regarding the damaging of public and private property were removed (Brazil 2016e).

The draft law was criticized by representatives of civil society and the United Nations due to specific paragraphs criminalizing political manifestations and social movements (Martins and Marques 2016) as well as conflicts with international human rights (Terenzi 2016). Although critical passages were removed before the law was signed by Dilma Rousseff in March 2016, opponents of the law continued to be critical of the legislation. In a public statement, Amnesty International in Brazil lamented the passing of the law and questioned its necessity by referring to recent attempts to criminalize political manifestations in Brazil through the National Security Law of the military regime (Anistia Internacional 2016). Following this argumentation, the 2016 anti-terrorism law could deteriorate the right to freedom of expression and political manifestation. In fact, since then, different attempts were made by members of parliament to edit the anti-terrorism law with the objective of making it more restrictive.

After the law was signed in March 2016, different members of parliament handed in amendments bills. Some of these amendments attempted to reintroduce parts that were vetoed by President Rousseff before; others sought to criminalize specific political groups or movements. Two amendment bills to reintroduce vetoed sections were PL 5065/2016 (Brazil 2016b) and PLS 272/2016 (Brazil 2016d). Both were published in relatively short periods of time after the signing of the actual law. PL 5065/2016 was handed in by deputy Edson Moreira in April 2016 followed by Senator Lasier Martins's project PLS 272/2016 in July of the same year. The first aimed at including political, ideological, social, and criminal motivations in the list of items defining terrorism in addition to proposing a number of alterations regarding attacks on more or less critical infrastructure and public institutions including prisons which are frequently damaged during insurgencies, often by members of organized crime. The second bill refers to damages caused to private and public property, distinguishing attacks on means of transportation (in Brazil urban violence often includes burning buses of the public transportation system) and politically motivated attacks on IT systems. Furthermore, the bill criminalizes individuals supporting those who committed acts of terrorism as defined in the law. The legislation also makes it an offense for those who offer support individuals, groups, or acts defined as terrorist through different means of dissemination. For example, the Internet is explicitly mentioned in the bill. Sharing or "liking" posts on social media about land occupations in the countryside or about social unrest in the cities could be considered illegal and the Internet user could be sent to prison for four to eight years. Individuals found guilty of damaging the turnstile of a metro station during one of the frequent manifestations against fare hikes or of stealing products from plundered supermarkets during social unrest could be classified as terrorists and sent to prison for twelve to thirty years. They would fall into the same category as individuals or groups responsible for the explosion of buildings or similar acts of violence.

In addition to these, another two bills were presented to parliament in May 2016 and June 2020 that are affecting the anti-terrorism law. The May 2016 bill (PL 5358/2016) by deputy Eduardo Bolsonaro targeted public support for communism and conflicts between social classes (Brazil 2016c). Following this bill, the support of conflictual situations between social classes should be considered terrorist when occurring in a number of specific situations. Furthermore, the bill suggests the removal of one section from the current law which exempts political manifestations, social movements, union activities, and other gatherings or groups from the definition of terrorism. Besides that, the bill aims at criminalizing compliments and support for acts of terrorism and communist governments. The objective of the bill is clearly stated in its header section ("to criminalize the support for communism") and also in its justification in which Bolsonaro incriminates journalists, artists, teachers, and others who openly or secretly support "communist regimes" responsible for the killing of "more than 100 million people" (Brazil 2016c). Following Bolsonaro, "members of criminal groups" have tried to establish a "dictatorship of the proletariat" in the time of the "so called military regime" (ibid). In justifying his draft law, Bolsonaro stated that "lie[s] [were] . . . the oxygen of these [communist] villains." Following this pronouncement, the leaders of what he identified as "communist" movements were *using lies to manipulate innocent people* while many of those people (the voting population) had in fact "good intentions." Furthermore, he downplayed acts of torture "supposedly" committed by militaries during the military dictatorship after 1964, holding those imprisoned and tortured responsible for what was done to them (Brazil 2016c).

In addition to the anti-terrorism law, the Bolsonaro bill also affects law 7716/1989 (Brazil 1989). Here, his bill aims at criminalizing the support of conflictual situations between social classes. Furthermore, the bill suggests the prohibition of hammer and sickle in any kind of object produced, sold, or distributed in the country, "or any other means" in favor of spreading Nazism or communism (Brazil 2016c). The current edition of law 7716/1989 is known as an anti-racism law, which, among other things, prohibits the production and distribution of swastika symbols in the country. Following the Bolsonaro bill, producers and distributors of red flags, red stars, or similar symbols of the political left shall be fined and/or sentenced to prison for 2–5 years.

The June 2020 bill (PL 3019/2020) was presented by deputy Daniel Silveira, a former member of the military police and a political freshman from Rio de Janeiro who was elected to the federal parliament in 2018 for the first time in the course of the pro-Bolsonaro movement. In the year of his election, Silveira received larger attention for publicly breaking a sign in memory of deputy Marielle Franco who had been assassinated a few months before. His first mandate was marked by verbal and physical aggressions in and outside of parliament against political opponents, the media, and what he identified as "antifa" and "communists." The bill he presented mainly consisted of the denomination of groups known as antifas, antifascists, or organizations "with similar ideologies" as terrorist organizations (Brazil 2020).

By October 2020, all of the four bills presented above were still being analyzed in parliament. Representatives of civil society have so far addressed mostly the 2016 bills, which, per Amnesty International, are: "proposals [which] will have a particular impact on the rights to freedom of expression and peaceful assembly if passed. Changes to the anti-terrorism law contain vague and overly broad definitions that could be used to arbitrarily prosecute anyone who expresses their opinions publicly or who protests peacefully on the streets" (Amnesty International 2017). In fact, the current version of the anti-terrorism law serves as a platform for conservatives and right-wing extremists trying to delegitimize, if not criminalize, political opponents. While clearly undemocratic and unconstitutional bills like the 2020 proposal have little chance to get too far in parliament, some of the 2016 bills could seriously endanger democratic rights in Brazil. The current discussions on counter-terrorism legislation in the country also show that the fear of terrorism as it was under debate in the North, especially after 9/11, does not exist in

Brazil. Some Brazilian lawmakers and also extremists are clearly interested in using this debate to impose restrictions on freedom of expression and fundamental rights in the country.

CONCLUSION

Public security is one of the biggest challenges for Brazilian politics and society. The debates around violence are multifaceted and they are a dominant factor in the life of citizens who can frequently accompany it not just through the media but also throughout their daily routines. In some of the larger urban centers, the sound of gunfire can be a common background noise in many neighborhoods. In other neighborhoods, and especially in several low-income areas that are dominated by criminal organizations, citizens are directly affected by this type of violence. Terrorism, however, as it is discussed in Western academia and the public, is not the origin of these circumstances. While for the past twenty years the major drivers of these debates in the global North were principally looking at religiously motivated organizations and networks (and nowadays partly at right-wing extremists as well), Brazil is struggling with massively armed criminal organizations that are partly controlling prisons and selected residential areas all over the country, with some already starting making their way into different parliaments. And while the discourse on these types of violence is clearly prevalent, there is a much smaller discourse on terrorism or political violence which is related to the debates on organized crime.

To better understand the debates around political violence, terrorism, and corresponding legislations and their impacts on freedom of expression, it is important to look at the historical circumstances of the Vargas era when the first National Security Law was passed as a response to the growing workers movement in the country. The importance of the communist movement and the communist party of that time, combined with the fear of the conservative forces in power who advocate any political opposition on the left—irrespective of being reform oriented or revolutionary—could endanger the political and economic status quo, led to an ideological simplification and to an aggregation of all nonconservative left-wing politics under the umbrella term of communism. This simplification helped to construct communism as a major threat to Brazil's traditional society which later partly embraced the military regime in the 1960s. Contemporary supporters of the old military regime are driven and motivated by anti-communist attitudes and rhetoric used to disqualify and criminalize progressive and reform-oriented forces in the country.

Although there is no substantial terrorist threat in Brazil in the sense of terrorism as it is framed in the global North, the decision was taken to pass a counter-terrorism law in 2016, which, similar to the National Security Laws, was used as a platform by conservative and reactionary actors to criminalize political actors or movements on the left. The political discourse on religiously motivated terrorism in the global North was a welcome opportunity to advance the agenda of restricting political rights in Brazil. Prominent examples are the draft laws that were presented to parliament with the objectives of criminalizing "communism-supporting" symbols or "the antifa." This is compounded by efforts to remove passages from the counter-terrorism law currently exempting activities in the context of political manifestations, social movements, unions, religious groups, and others from the legal definition of terrorism. Following the widespread understanding of categorizing anything from the democratic center-left to the radical left as "communist" (and nowadays sometimes as "antifa"), a large part of the political landscape in Brazil, including civil society organizations, could be classified as terrorist if such amendments were to be approved in parliament. The same could happen to social movements, political manifestations, unions, and other forms of political and social mobilization.

The experience of the Brazilian discourse on terrorism and counter-terrorism legislation exemplifies how public or international security debates initiated in one part of the world can lead to a restriction of basic rights and freedom of expression in other parts of the world. Although Brazil has not found solutions so far to resolve the existing problems of criminal violence that are overtly present in the country for decades, lawmakers opted for passing additional legislation focusing on security issues that can hardly be identified. The recent debates surrounding the counter-terrorism law have made clear that, contemporarily, there is no objective of protecting the population from an actually existing threat but to create new mechanisms to reduce public space for reform-oriented politics that could improve the living conditions for large parts of the population. The challenge for Brazil is not the lack of legislation but the lack of action to identify, agree upon, and address the roots of the violence that is keeping public life in check. Debates on counter-terrorism are merely distracting from what really is at stake. Once such debates are used to criminalize reform-oriented political actors, they often turn out to be counterproductive.

NOTES

1. For a more detailed analysis of this era, see Skidmore (1988), Gaspari (2002), and Dreifuss (2008).
2. More extensive analysis of Operation Condor can be found at McSherry (2002), McSherry (2005), and Dinges (2005).

3. Cesare Battisti is an Italian citizen who escaped from an Italian prison in the 1980s where he was kept for membership in a politically motivated left-wing armed group called Armed Proletarians for Communism (Proletari Armati per il Comunismo) and related accusations. He was later also accused of participation in politically motivated assaults that caused the death of four individuals. Battisti objected to the verdicts. He fled prison and Italy in the 1980s and spent the following decades in several countries. For more than ten years, he lived in Brazil where he received the status of a political refugee. This decision taken during the government of President Lula da Silva was publicly discussed and caused concern among conservatives in Brazil and within the Italian government who for several years was requesting Battisti's extradition. In 2018, President Michel Temer signed the extradition order. Battisti was arrested in Bolívia in 2019 and brought to Italy where he confessed his crimes including the participation in the killings he was accused of. He received life imprisonment and is detained in Italy.

REFERENCES

Amnesty International. 2017. "Brazil: New Amnesty Campaign Will Fight Back as Congress Considers Legal Changes That Flagrantly Attack Human Rights." *News* (blog). July 31, 2017. https://www.amnesty.org/en/latest/news/2017/07/brazil-new-amnesty-campaign-will-fight-back-as-congress-considers-legal-changes-that-flagrantly-attack-human-rights/.

Anistia Internacional. 2016. "Nota Pública: Anistia Internacional Lamenta Aprovação de Projeto de Lei 2016/15 Que Tipifica Crime de Terrorismo No Brasil." *Notícias* (blog). February 25, 2016. https://anistia.org.br/noticias/nota-publica-anistia-internacional-lamenta-aprovacao-de-projeto-de-lei-201615-que-tipifica-crime-de-terrorismo-brasil/.

Balloussier, Anna Virginia. 2018. "Movimentos Temem Que Até 'like' Baste Para Virarem Terroristas No Governo Bolsonaro." *Folha de São Paulo*, June 12, 2018. https://www1.folha.uol.com.br/poder/2018/12/movimentos-temem-que-ate-like-baste-para-virarem-terroristas-no-governo-bolsonaro.shtml.

Bartolomé, Mariano César, and Vicente Mario Ventura Barreiro. 2020. "Narcotráfico En América Del Sur Más Allá Del Bloque Andino: Los Casos de Argentina y Brasil." *Revista Relaciones Internacionales, Estrategia y Seguridad* 14 (1): 205–22.

Bergamo, Mônica. 2019. "Eduardo Bolsonaro Diz Que Se Esquerda Radicalizar, Resposta Pode Ser 'Um Novo AI-5.'" *Folha de São Paulo*, October 31, 2019. https://www1.folha.uol.com.br/colunas/monicabergamo/2019/10/eduardo-bolsonaro-diz-que-se-esquerda-radicalizar-resposta-pode-ser-um-novo-ai-5.shtml.

Blakeley, Ruth, and Sam Raphael. 2016. "Understanding Western State Terrorism." In *Routledge Handbook of Critical Terrorism Studies*, edited by Richard Jackson, 339–59. New York: Routledge.

Brancoli, Fernando, and Pedro Henrique Vasquez. 2016. "Deconstructing Automatisms: Milicia Practices and Neopentecostal Formations in Rio De Janeiro." *Brasiliana: Journal for Brazilian Studies* 4 (2): 112–133.

Brazil. 1935a. *L 38/1935*. http://www.planalto.gov.br/ccivil_03/LEIS/1930-1949/L0038.htm.

———. 1935b. *L 136/1935*. http://www.planalto.gov.br/ccivil_03/LEIS/1930-1949/L0136.htm.

———. 1938. *L 431/1938*. http://www.planalto.gov.br/ccivil_03/Decreto-Lei/1937-1946/Del0431.htm.

———. 1942. *L 4766/1942*. http://www.planalto.gov.br/ccivil_03/decreto-lei/1937-1946/del4766.htm.

———. 1953. *L 1802/1953*. http://www.planalto.gov.br/ccivil_03/leis/1950-1969/l1802.htm.

———. 1967. *L 314/1967*. http://www.planalto.gov.br/ccivil_03/Decreto-Lei/1965-1988/Del0314.htm.

———. 1968. *Ato Institucional No 5*. http://www.planalto.gov.br/ccivil_03/ait/ait-05-68.htm.

———. 1969. *L 898/1969*. http://www.planalto.gov.br/ccivil_03/decreto-lei/1965-1988/del0898.htm.

———. 1978. *L 6620/1978*. http://www.planalto.gov.br/ccivil_03/leis/1970-1979/L6620.htm.

———. 1983. *L 7170/1983*. http://www.planalto.gov.br/ccivil_03/leis/l7170.htm.

———. 1989. *L 7716/1989*. http://www.planalto.gov.br/ccivil_03/leis/l7716.htm.

———. 2009. "PNDH-3, Programa Nacional de Direitos Humanos." Secretaria Especial dos Direitos Humanos da Presidência da República (Brasília).

———. 2014. *Comissão Nacional da Verdade: Relatório (Vol 1)*. Brasília.

———. 2016a. *L 13260/2016*. http://www.planalto.gov.br/ccivil_03/_Ato2015-2018/2016/Lei/L13260.htm.

———. 2016b. *PL 5065/2016*. https://www.camara.leg.br/proposicoesWeb/fichadetramitacao?idProposicao=2082470.

———. 2016c. *PL 5358/2016*. https://www.camara.leg.br/proposicoesWeb/fichadetramitacao?idProposicao=2085411.

———. 2016d. *PLS 272/2016*. https://www25.senado.leg.br/web/atividade/materias/-/materia/126364.

———. 2016e. *Mensagem No 85*, de 16 de março de 2016 http://www.planalto.gov.br/CCIVIL_03/_Ato2015-2018/2016/Msg/VEP-85.htm.

———. 2018. "Relatório Final—Comissão Externa Destinada a Acompanhar, No Rio de Janeiro, as Investigações Referentes Aos Assassinatos Da Vereadora Marielle Franco e Do Sr. Anderson Pedro Gomes—CEXVRIO." Brasília: Câmara dos Deputados.

———. 2020. *PL 3019/2020*. https://www.camara.leg.br/proposicoesWeb/fichadetramitacao?idProposicao=2254171.

Buzanelli, Márcio Paulo. 2013. "Porque é Necessário Tipificar o Crime de Terrorismo No Brasil." *Revista Brasileira de Inteligência (ABIN)*, no. 8: 9–19.

Cano, Ignacio, and Thais Duarte. 2012. *No Sapatinho: A Evolução Das Milícias No Rio de Janeiro (2008-2011)*. Rio de Janeiro, RJ: LAV, Laboratório de Análise da Violência (LAV-UERJ).

Canofre, Fernanda. 2019. "Juiz Decide Que Adélio Bispo Tem Transtorno Mental e é Inimputável." *Folha de São Paulo*, May 27, 2019. https://www1.folha.uol.com.br/poder/2019/05/juiz-decide-que-adelio-bispo-tem-transtorno-mental-e-e-inimputavel.shtml.

Carlos Brandão, Priscila, and Vladimir de Paula Brito. 2014. "Terrorismo, inteligência e mecanismos legais: desafios para o Brasil." In *Políticas de defesa, inteligência e segurança*, edited by Carlos S Arturi, 168–86. Porto Alegre: UFRGS Ed.

Cepik, Marco. 2010. "Combate Ao Terrorismo e Estado No Brasil: Avaliação Crítica e Sugestões Preliminares." In *Terrorismo e Relações Internacionais: Perspectivas e Desafios Para o Século XXI*, edited by Mônica Herz and Arthur Bernardes do Amaral. Rio de Janeiro: Editora PUC.

Cunha, Ciro Leal M. da. 2010. *Terrorismo Internacional e Política Externa Brasileira Após o 11 de Setembro*. Brasília: Fundação Alexandre de Gusmão.

Davis, Stephen R. 2018. *The ANC's War against Apartheid: Umkhonto We Sizwe and the Liberation of South Africa*. Bloomington, IN: Indiana University Press.

Dias, Camila Nunes, and Sacha Darke. 2016. "From Dispersed to Monopolized Violence: Expansion and Consolidation of the Primeiro Comando Da Capital's Hegemony in São Paulo's Prisons." *Crime, Law and Social Change* 65 (3): 213–225.

Dinges, John. 2005. *The Condor Years: How Pinochet and His Allies Brought Terrorism to Three Continents ; with a New Afterword by the Author*. New York: New Press.

Diniz, Eugenio. 2004. "Considerações Sobre a Possibilidade de Atentados Terroristas No Brasil." In *II Encontro de Estudos: Terrorismo*, edited by Brasil, 15–45. Brasília: Gabinete de Segurança Institucional.

Dreifuss, René Armand. 2008. *1964, a conquista do Estado: ação política, poder e golpe de classe*. Petrópolis: Vozes.

Ellis, Stephen. 2013. *External Mission: The ANC in Exile, 1960-1990*. Oxford; New York, NY: Oxford University Press.

Fernandes, Reginaldo. 2009. "Um Breviário Da Lei de Segurança Nacional (LSN): Do Estado Novo Aos Primeiros Anos Do Regime Militar (1930-1969)." *Diversitas (USP)*.

Feyyaz, Muhammad. 2019. "Terrorism Can and Should Be Defined. But How?" *Strategic Analysis* 43 (4): 310–327.

Fico, Carlos. 2008. *O Grande Irmão: Da Operação Brother Sam Aos Anos de Chumbo: O Governo Dos Estados Unidos e a Ditadura Militar Brasileira*. Rio de Janeiro: Civilização Brasileira.

Finnane, Mark. 2015. "The Munich Olympics Massacre and the Development of Counter-Terrorism in Australia." *Intelligence and National Security* 30 (6): 817–836.

Folha de São Paulo. 2018. "Bolsonaro Leva Facada Durante Ato de Campanha Em Juiz de Fora," June 9, 2018. https://www1.folha.uol.com.br/poder/2018/09/bolsonaro-leva-facada-durante-ato-de-campanha-em-juiz-de-fora.shtml.

———. 2019. "Quem é Cesare Battisti; Entenda o Caso," January 13, 2019. https://www1.folha.uol.com.br/poder/2019/01/quem-e-o-cesare-battisti-entenda-o-caso.shtml.

French, Jan Hoffman. 2013. "Rethinking Police Violence in Brazil: Unmasking the Public Secret of Race." *Latin American Politics and Society* 55 (4): 161–181.

Gaspari, Elio. 2002. *A Ditadura Envergonhada*. As Ilusões Armadas. São Paulo, Brazil: Companhia das Letras.

Gielow, Igor. 2020. "Para 78%, Regime Militar de 1964 Foi Uma Ditadura." *Folha de São Paulo*, June 27, 2020. https://www1.folha.uol.com.br/poder/2020/06/para-78-regime-militar-de-1964-foi-uma-ditadura.shtml.

Goertz, Stefan. 2019. *The New Terrorism: Actors, Strategies and Tactic*. 1st edition. New York: Springer.

Groppo, Alejandro, and Ernesto Laclau. 2010. *The Two Princes: Juan D. Perón and Getulio Vargas: A Comparative Study of Latin American Populism*. Colección Poliedros. Villa Maria: Eduvim.

Guttmann, A. 2018. "Combatting Terror in Europe: Euro-Israeli Counterterrorism Intelligence Cooperation in the Club de Berne (1971–1972)." *Intelligence and National Security* 33 (2): 158–175.

Jongman, Albert, and Alex Schmid. 1984. *Political Terrorism: A New Guide to Actors, Authors, Concepts, Data Bases, Theories, & Literature*. London: Transaction Publishers.

Kumar, Deepa. 2020. "Terrorcraft: Empire and the Making of the Racialised Terrorist Threat." *Race & Class* 62 (2): 34–60.

Laqueur, Walter, and Christopher Wall. 2018. *The Future of Terrorism: ISIS, Al-Qaeda, and the Alt-Right*. New York: Thomas Dunne Books.

Lasmar, Jorge Mascarenhas. 2015. "A Legislação Brasileira de Combate e Prevenção Do Terrorismo Quatorze Anos Após 11 de Setembro: Limites, Falhas e Reflexões Para o Futuro." *Revista de Sociologia e Política* 23 (53): 47–70.

Lauris, Élida, and Maurício Hashizume. 2020. "Violência Política e Eleitoral No Brasil. Panorama Das Violações de Direitos Humanos de 2016 a 2020." Curitiba: Terra de Direitos & Justiça Global.

Lewis, Olivier. 2017. "Conceptualizing State Counterterrorism." In *The Palgrave Handbook of Global Counterterrorism Policy*, edited by Scott Nicholas Romaniuk, Francis Grice, Daniela Irrera, and Stewart Tristan Webb, 3–37. London: Palgrave Macmillan.

Martins, Paula, and Camila Marques. 2016. "O Velho Álibi Do Combate Ao Terrorismo." *Carta Capital*, February 25, 2016. https://www.cartacapital.com.br/sociedade/o-velho-alibi-do-combate-ao-terrorismo/.

McKinley, Dale T. 2018. "Umkhonto We Sizwe: A Critical Analysis of the Armed Struggle of the African National Congress." *South African Historical Journal* 70 (1): 27–41.

McSherry, J. Patrice. 2002. "Tracking the Origins of a State Terror Network: Operation Condor." *Latin American Perspectives* 29 (1): 38–60.

———. 2005. *Predatory States: Operation Condor and Covert War in Latin America*. Lanham: Rowman & Littlefield Publishers.

Peixoto de Paula Marques, Raphael. 2014. "Repressão Política e Anticomunismo No Primeiro Governo Vargas: A Elaboração Da Primeira Lei de Segurança Nacional." *Revista Jurídica Da Presidência* 15 (107): 631–665.

Ramos da Cruz, Claudio, and David H. Ucko. 2018. "Beyond the Unidades de Polícia Pacificadora: Countering Comando Vermelho's Criminal Insurgency." *Small Wars & Insurgencies* 29 (1): 38–67.

Raza, Salvador. 2007. "Terrorism in the Southern Cone." In *The Ideological War on Terror: Worldwide Strategies for Counter-Terrorism*, edited by Anne Aldis and Graeme P. Herd, 163–178. London: Routledge.

Rodrigues, Thiago. 2015. "Drug-Trafficking and Security in Contemporary Brazil." In *World Politics of Security*, 234–250. XII Forte de Copacabana Conference. International Security: A European—South American Dialogue. Rio de Janeiro: Konrad Adenauer Stiftung.

Santis Feltran, Gabriel de. 2012. "Governo Que Produz Crime, Crime Que Produz Governo: O Dispositivo de Gestão Do Homicídio Em São Paulo (1992–2011)." *Revista Brasileira de Segurança Pública* 6 (2): 232–255.

Schmid, Alex. 2004. "Terrorism—The Definitional Problem." *Case Western Reserve Journal of International Law* 36 (2): 375.

———. 2011. "The Definition of Terrorism." In *The Routledge Handbook of Terrorism Research*, edited by Alex Schmid, 39–157. New York: Routledge.

Shanahan, Timothy. 2016. "The Definition of Terrorism." In *Routledge Handbook of Critical Terrorism Studies*, edited by Richard Jackson, 223–246. New York: Routledge.

Simpson, Thula. 2009. "'Umkhonto We Sizwe, We Are Waiting for You': The ANC and the Township Uprising, September 1984—September 1985." *South African Historical Journal* 61 (1): 158–177.

Skidmore, Thomas. 1988. *The Politics of Military Rule in Brazil, 1964-85*. New York: Oxford University Press.

———. 2007. *Brasil: De Getúlio a Castelo*. São Paulo: Ed Paz e Terra.

Svendsen, Adam. 2010. *Intelligence Cooperation and the War on Terror: Anglo-American Security Relations after 9/11*. New York: Routledge.

Terenzi, Gabriela. 2016. "ONU Critica Aprovação Do Projeto Da Lei Antiterrorismo Pelo Congresso." *Folha de São Paulo*, February 26, 2016. https://www1.folha.uol.com.br/poder/2016/02/1743863-onu-critica-aprovacao-do-projeto-da-lei-antiterrorismo-pelo-congresso.shtml.

UNODC. 2019. "Global Study on Homicide: Homicide Trends, Patterns and Criminal Justice Response (Booklet 2)." UNODC Vienna.

Vargas, Getúlio. 1954. "Carta Testamento," August 23, 1954. https://www2.camara.leg.br/atividade-legislativa/plenario/discursos/escrevendohistoria/getulio-vargas/carta-testamento-de-getulio-vargas.

Zúquete, José Pedro. 2017. "Counterterrorism in Brazil: From Dictatorship to Democratic Times." In *The Palgrave Handbook of Global Counterterrorism Policy*, edited by Scott Nicholas Romaniuk, Francis Grice, Daniela Irrera, and Stewart Tristan Webb, 275–294. London: Palgrave Macmillan.

Chapter 8

How 9/11 Changed America and How We (Can) Talk about It

Torture and the Guantanamo Military Commissions

Rita Radostitz

INTRODUCTION

This chapter will provide a view of how the United States' response to the attacks of September 11, 2001, and the counter-terrorism policies enacted thereafter, have damaged human rights, civil rights, and civil liberties—from the perspective of one attorney, working on the defense team of one defendant charged in the Military Commissions at Naval Station Guantánamo Bay, Cuba.[1] The views expressed here are mine and mine alone—they do not reflect the views of the Department of Defense, the U.S. Government, or any agency or instrumentality thereof. And, my views are all based upon unclassified, open-source materials; nothing I write should be interpreted as in any way confirming or denying classified material.[2]

The Palestinian poet Mourid Barghouti wrote:

> It is easy to blur the truth with a simple linguistic trick: Start your story from "Secondly." . . . Start your story with "Secondly," and the world will be turned upside-down. Start your story with "Secondly," and the arrows of the Red Indians are the original criminals and the guns of the white men are entirely the victims. It is enough to start with "Secondly," for the anger of the black man against the white to be barbarous. Start with "Secondly," and Gandhi becomes responsible for the tragedies of the British.[3]

My goal here is to ensure that the story of the attacks of September 11, 2001, and the U.S. government's response to them, does not begin with

Secondly. For most Americans, the story of September 11 starts on a sunny Tuesday morning when we first heard about planes flying into the World Trade Center in New York, the Pentagon, and a field in Pennsylvania. But many across the globe recognized the attacks as a reaction to the history of Western involvement in Muslim countries; a complex history filled with dispossession, generations of Western colonialism, and the deaths of hundreds of thousands of innocent children.

Before I go on, I want to acknowledge that the attacks devastated the lives of the families of the 2,976 people who died that day, and many more who have died from cancer and other diseases after working in the debris of the fallen buildings. We can never forget what they suffered in the aftermath of that Tuesday morning, and nothing I write should be interpreted as seeking to diminish their suffering or their loss. My focus is, instead, on what was done by the U.S. government after the attacks, and how that, too, forever changed American lives, and also lives around the world.

In the months after the terrorist attacks of September 11, 2001, decisions were made at the highest levels of the U.S. government[4] that led to a fundamental shift in human and civil rights in this country. The U.S. PATRIOT Act[5] implemented significant changes to privacy laws and increasing the ability of the government to spy on its own citizens.[6] Further, with regard to the arrest and charging of those believed to be responsible for the attacks, President George W. Bush authorized "secret indefinite detention and the use of coercive interrogations."[7] The U.S. government also took the position that those captured would not be given the protections of the Geneva Conventions and their additional protocols.[8] And instead of relying on the tried and true systems of federal or military courts-martial proceedings, the Bush Administration—and the Obama Administration after it—created a system of military commissions where a cloak of "national security" imposes limits and curtails what should be a free and open trial.[9]

This chapter will be one attorney's view of how the "war on terror" came to undermine the United States' commitment to human and civil rights through the CIA's control of information regarding its "Rendition, Detention and Interrogation" ("RDI") program and the proceedings in the Military Commissions at Guantanamo. It uses my language to describe what I have observed, and learned about first hand. It will explore how counter-terrorism measures have significantly abridged freedom of expression in the jurisprudence process, through the lens of the litigation in the Military Commission at Guantanamo Bay, Cuba, in response to the charges against five individuals: Khalid Shaikh Mohammad, Khallad bin 'Atash, Ramzi Bin al Shibh, Ammar al Baluchi, and Mustafa al Hawsawi.[10]

POST 9/11 POLICIES AND THE GUANTANAMO MILITARY COMMISSIONS

At the risk of starting with "Secondly," I begin with what happened immediately after the attacks of September 11 that led to the creation of the military commissions on Guantanamo, addressing the question: How the trial of those alleged to be responsible for the attacks of September 11 ended up being held at an island prison, on land stolen from a sovereign power. The answer to that question informs the answer to another important question: Why have those alleged to be responsible for the worst terrorist attack in our country's history not yet been tried? Why, in 2020, has the trial not even come close to finishing pretrial proceedings? The answers to those questions begin with secret, incommunicado detention, and torture.

In the aftermath of the attacks of 9/11, the U.S. government quickly determined that the attacks had been planned by a group known as Al Qaeda, which was believed to be led by Osama bin Laden.[11] Intelligence reports over the prior year had provided information that bin Laden was planning an attack on the United States, but many government officials felt that there was not yet "concrete, actionable" intelligence.[12] President George W. Bush was briefed on September 6, 2001, about the possibility of an imminent Al Qaeda attack.[13] Yet, nobody seemed to know what the attack might look like, when it might happen, or whether there was any way to prevent it. At the time, President Bush did not seem to take the threat assessment very seriously.

And then, five days later, four planes were hijacked and flown into the Twin Towers of the World Trade Center in New York, the Pentagon in Washington D.C. and—after passengers on the fourth flight intervened—a field in Pennsylvania (rather than the intended target, which is sometimes reported to be the U.S. Capitol Building; other times, the White House).[14] This was the largest attack on U.S. soil in the history of the country, and 2,976 people lost their lives.

In his address to the nation the evening of the attacks, President Bush said:

> Today, our fellow citizens, our way of life, our very freedom came under attack in a series of deliberate and deadly terrorist acts.
>
> . . .
>
> The search is underway for those who are behind these evil acts. I've directed the full resources of our intelligence and law enforcement communities to find those responsible and to bring them to justice. We will make no distinction between the terrorists who committed these acts and those who harbor them.[15]

And so began the narrative that these attacks were the beginning of a war against the United States by "Islamic Terrorists." That narrative continued when President Bush again addressed the nation on the eve of war to be waged against Afghanistan: "Tonight we are a country awakened to danger and called to defend freedom. Our grief has turned to anger, and anger to resolution."[16] However, even then, President Bush noted: "Whether we bring our enemies to justice, or bring justice to our enemies, justice will be done."[17]

The question is, when and how did that commitment to justice morph into a twisted tale of torture and cruel, inhumane and degrading treatment?

Government Authorization of Torture

In the weeks after the September 11 attacks, assistant U.S. attorney general and director of the Office of Legal Counsel Jay Bybee and deputy assistant attorney general John Yoo drafted a series of memorandum and sent them to White House Advisor Alberto Gonzalez and William J. Haynes II, General Counsel for the Department of Defense. These memos colloquially referred to as the "Torture Memos," asserted that the protections of the Geneva Conventions did not apply to detainees from the war in Afghanistan, and—incorrectly—assert that the definitions of torture in both statutory and international law do not prohibit physical and mental harm unless it results in "organ failure, impairment of bodily function, or even death" and that mental harm must last for "months or even years before it is considered torture."[18] These policies formed the basis for the RDI program, which was implemented just a few months later.[19] What happened after that was—and to a large extent still is—shrouded in secrecy, hidden behind black bars of redaction and protected by the "National Security" or "State Secrets" Privilege.[20]

As early as 2003, many nongovernmental organizations (NGOs) and some foreign governments started investigating what was happening to those captured in Afghanistan, and information about the torture program started leaking out. At first, the information was ignored, or disbelieved. However, thanks to the excellent work of many investigative journalists, whistleblowers, and ultimately, the staff of the U.S. Senate Select Committee on Intelligence, the public knows quite a bit about how torture was authorized, who knew what and when they knew it, and what happened to the 119 individuals who were held incommunicado in CIA custody.

The *Washington Post* first reported about a "covert prison system" run by the CIA.[21] This initial report led to multiple other news sources investigating and reporting on the CIA rendition and detention program.[22] Three weeks later, the Parliamentary Assembly of the Council of Europe voted to appoint Senator Dick Marty, a Swiss former prosecutor, to conduct a parliamentary inquiry into "alleged secret detentions and unlawful inter-state transfers of detainees involving Council of Europe member states."[23] Over the following year, Senator Marty issued a number of reports and the Council of Europe debated and ultimately adopted the findings of the reports.

In December 2007, the SSCI "initiated a review of the destruction of videotapes related to the interrogations of CIA detainees Abu Zubaydah and Abd al-Rahim al-Nashiri."[24] Through its investigation of the destruction of the videotapes, Senate staffers realized and recognized that a deeper investigation of the program was warranted, and in March 2009, the SSCI began a review of the CIA program, "to review the program and to shape detention and interrogation policies in the future."[25] The investigation and review by the SSCI and staff members took more than three and a half years.

On December 3, 2014, the 500-page Executive Summary of the RDI Report was finally released to the public. It contains numerous redactions of information the government has asserted is classified. The full RDI Report "is a lengthy, highly detailed report exceeding 6,700 pages, including approximately 38,000 footnotes."[26] Neither a fully unredacted version of the Executive Summary nor the full RDI Report has been made available to any of the defendants or their defense attorneys in the Military Commissions, despite the fact that the defense attorneys have all obtained the security clearances for access to such classified information. Inexplicably, the government has asserted that the attorneys do not have a "need to know" and therefore can be precluded from obtaining access to the full reports.

The RDI Report is divided into the following three volumes. The first volume, entitled "History and Operation of the CIA's Detention and Interrogation Program," is divided chronologically into sections addressing the establishment, development, and evolution of the CIA's Detention and Interrogation Program. It includes an addendum entitled "CIA Clandestine Detention Sites and the Arrangements Made with Foreign Entities in Relation to the CIA's Detention and Interrogation Program." The second volume is entitled "Intelligence Acquired and CIA Representations on the Effectiveness of the CIA's Enhanced Interrogation Techniques." This volume addresses the intelligence the CIA attributed to CIA detainees and the use of the CIA's enhanced interrogation techniques, specifically focusing on CIA representations regarding the effectiveness of the CIA's enhanced interrogation techniques, as well as how the CIA's Detention and Interrogation Program was operated and managed. It includes sections on CIA representations to the media, the Department of Justice, and the Congress. Finally, the third volume, labeled "Detention and Interrogation of CIA Detainees," addresses the detention and interrogation of 119 CIA detainees, from the program's authorization on September 17, 2001, to its official end on January 22, 2009. It includes information on their capture, detention, interrogation, and conditions of confinement. It also includes extensive information on the CIA's management, oversight, and day-to-day operation of its Detention and Interrogation Program.[27]

The RDI Report documents that at least 119 people were detained by the CIA. The SSCI found documented evidence that 39 of them had been tortured. Of those 39, the SSCI found that "zero intelligence reports were disseminated based on information provided by seven [of those] 39 detainees known to have been subjected to the CIA's enhanced interrogation techniques."[28] The other 32 men who were tortured provided information that was documented, but the value of this information is disputed.[29]

It is worth discussing the language used by the CIA, and adopted by the SSCI team in drafting the RDI Report. First, the term "enhanced interrogation techniques" (EITs) was adopted to describe ten techniques that had been specifically authorized for use against the detainees. This term is the equivalent of a German phrase "Verschärfte Vernehmung" used to describe techniques used by the Nazi's during the Holocaust.[30] The term "EITs" described the techniques that were initially authorized for use against the CIA detainees included: "the attention grasp, walling, the facial hold, the facial slap (insult slap), cramped confinement, wall standing, stress positions, sleep deprivation, use of diapers, and use of insects."[31] An eleventh technique has been described often in the media using a euphemism that totally masks its true horror: "waterboarding." Waterboarding involved pouring gallons of water over the face of a detainee that had been covered by a cloth to simulate drowning. In reality, each and every one of these techniques was quite damaging.[32] And, both the Ninth Circuit Court of Appeals and one of the judges serving in the Military Commissions have described the techniques as torture.[33]

What Was Gained and What Was Lost

When the RDI Report was released, there was a new administration, and a new director of Central Intelligence. President Obama had, through Executive Order 13491,[34] banned the use of any interrogation technique not approved by the Army Field Manuel, and ordered that the CIA shut down all detention facilities as well as the interrogation program. His new director of Central Intelligence, John Brennan, fought to keep the RDI Report fully classified to ensure that the U.S. public never learned the details of the atrocities committed in their names. He was unsuccessful in suppressing the information but insisted that the CIA be allowed to simultaneously publish a response to the information contained in the RDI Report. In the opening paragraphs of the response, Director Brennan admits: "enhanced interrogation techniques are not an appropriate method to obtain intelligence" and that "their use impairs our ability to continue to play a leadership role in the world."[35] The CIA Response asserts: "In particular, the Agency disagrees with the Study's unqualified assertions that the overall detention and interrogation program did not produce unique intelligence that led terrorist plots to be disrupted, terrorists to be captured, or lives to be saved."[36] However, this statement was specifically refuted by the RDI Report which explains that in its assertion regarding the results of the RDI program: "the CIA consistently omitted the significant amount of relevant intelligence obtained from sources other than CIA detainees who had been subjected to the CIA's enhanced interrogation techniques—leaving the false impression the CIA was acquiring unique information from the use of the techniques."[37]

Although the CIA Response does not use the word torture to describe the techniques and conditions that the detainees in the CIA "Black Sites" were subjected to, it does not deny that the techniques and conditions described in the RDI Report happened. However, nobody involved in the torture program has ever been held accountable, and many of the details remain classified. Specifically, who did what to whom, where, and when remain classified, and therefore, unavailable to the general public for transparent discussion and, more importantly, accountability.

Even if one believes that the RDI program "produce[d] unique intelligence that disrupted terrorist plots, enabled terrorists to be captured, and lives to be saved,"[38] the question remains: At what cost? The damage done first to the men who suffered the torture is a huge uncompensated cost, and in the greater scheme, the damage to the reputation of the United States and its leadership role in the world has not, decades later, been repaired.

Another thing that was lost was the opportunity to try those accused of planning and participating in the attacks of September 11, 2001, in a regularly constituted court.[39] Instead, President Bush decided to rely on a fraught and antiquated military tribunal: the so-called "military commissions."[40] This decision has resulted in myriad delays, few convictions, and, as of publication date, no trial for those accused of planning and implementing the attacks of September 11.

Military Commissions

As many have written, and my personal experience has confirmed, the Military Commissions at Guantanamo are an aberration of a U.S. justice system that has, for two centuries, prided itself on transparency and accountability for both the government and the defendant. The limitations—especially on free expression—placed on the defense and the defendants by the Military Commissions Act[41] and the government's invocation of the National Security Privilege are staggering, and seem designed not to protect our freedoms but rather to hide horrific acts of torture committed with the approval of the highest echelons of the government.[42]

Since the detention center was opened in 2001, more than 750 men and children have been held at Guantanamo.[43] Of those, approximately 540 were transferred out of the prison or released during the Bush Administration, and during the Obama Administration, 201 detainees died, were transferred, repatriated, or resettled in third countries. In May 2018, one detainee was transferred to his home country to finish out his sentence. In 2020, forty men remain in detention on Guantanamo: five are charged with offenses related to the attacks of September 11; one is charged with planning the bombing of the U.S.S. Cole in Aden Harbor, Yemen; one is charged with various war crimes for his alleged involvement with Al Qaeda training camps in Afghanistan; one pled guilty and is awaiting sentencing; one was found guilty and has challenged his conviction and sentence. The remaining thirty-one men have been detained for almost two decades with no charges, including one who was only seventeen years old when he was detained.[44] Five of the men were approved for transfer out of Guantanamo at the end of the Obama Administration, but their transfers were not finalized and they remain detained.[45]

Dating back to the Revolutionary War, the United States has used military commissions to try those accused of war-related offenses. However, throughout this long history, military commissions have been used on the battlefield—or nearby—and close in time to the commission of the conduct alleged. In contrast, those accused of war crimes in the Military Commissions at Guantanamo Bay, Cuba are being tried years after the conduct, at a facility that is thousands of miles away from the site of the alleged crime. Long ago, the U.S. Supreme Court "stated, in sweeping terms, that where no military emergency prevents the civilian courts from operating, military courts are unconstitutional."[46]

In the first challenge to the Guantanamo military commissions system, the Supreme Court held that the president had exceeded his powers by failing to get Congressional approval for the use and structure of the military commissions.[47] Congress then hastily enacted the Military Commissions Act of 2006. Significant portions of that Act were later found unconstitutional as well.[48] And while Barak Obama campaigned for President on a promise that he would close down the detention facility at Guantanamo, he failed to do so during his eight years in office.[49] Instead, Congress passed the Military Commissions Act of 2009,[50] and this deeply flawed legislation is the guide for the trials of seven men: five who are charged with the attacks of September 11 (Khalid Shaikh Mohammad, Khalid bin 'Atash, Ramzi bin al Shibh, Ammar al Baluchi and Mustafa al Hawsawi); one charged with the bombing of the U.S.S. Cole (Abd Al-Nashiri). The third trial involves a man the government asserts is named Hadi al Iraqi, but who asserts he is Nashwan al Timor. None of the trials for these men has begun as of this writing.

Limitations Imposed on Freedom of Expression in the Military Commissions

Communication about Torture

From the moment they arrived on Guantanamo the first week of September 2006,[51] the men who had been held in CIA-controlled "black sites" around the world were told that they could not tell anybody about their experiences there. For weeks, they continued to be held incommunicado at the detention facility that was located on a Navy base surrounding Guantanamo Bay, Cuba. They were told that they were in U.S. military custody—even though the CIA continued to have operational control of the detention facility.[52] Finally, in October 2006, members of the International Committee of the Red Cross ("ICRC") were allowed to meet with the men who had been detained and tortured by the CIA. For the first time—for some of the men, in more than four years—they were allowed to tell the stories of their capture, torture, and rendition to various black sites across the globe. However, the ICRC was not allowed to publicly comment on the stories of torture.

The men were also given the opportunity to send letters to their families through the usual ICRC process. However, before any letters would be released to the ICRC, they were first sent to CIA and military censors who scrubbed them of any mention of torture. To this day—almost two decades later—all letters written by the men detained at Guantanamo are screened by the CIA and the military before being sent to their families. The government's justification for this is that the men were exposed to classified information as a result of their detention in the CIA's RDI program and national security interests are more important than transparency.

The problem with this justification for censorship is that it is inconsistent with the Executive Order that describes what is and is not classified information and what information can and cannot be deemed to be classified.[53] While government employees who have security clearance are obligated to protect information that has been properly deemed to be classified, those who do not have a security clearance have no obligation to the government to keep secrets that were revealed to them. That the U.S. government tortured these men and held them incommunicado for years, then denied them the right to fully discuss what happened when they were allowed to communicate, is simply unacceptable in a democracy committed to freedom of speech and expression. Of course, the men had no control over their "exposure" to the classified information, and certainly did not agree to be subject to it. Nevertheless, they are precluded from sharing their experiences with their families or the rest of the world. This is a critical limitation, not only because of the restraint on free expression but because the Convention Against Torture requires "the means for as full rehabilitation as possible."[54] Rehabilitation necessarily includes the ability for those who have been tortured to talk about it to redress its psychological impact.

The government did not stop at censoring ICRC letters. Although the U.S. Constitution protects the right to free expression, and all attorney-client communications are privileged, the government created an elaborate system to ensure that none of the men detained can share details of their torture that the government has not yet declassified. Their attorneys are first required to obtain a Top Secret security clearance, then they must sign a Memorandum of Agreement before they are allowed access to their clients or allowed to review any materials related to their client's case that prohibits them from disseminating any of the information they receive from the government. The defense attorneys are also bound by a Protective Order that restricts the dissemination of any communication from their clients beyond the defense team.[55] Disclosure—even unintentional disclosure—can (and has) result in the revocation of one's security clearance as well as potential criminal charges.

While the Executive Order that defines classified information precludes the government from classifying any information to conceal a violation of law, or merely because it is embarrassing,[56] the Military Commissions Act precludes any court—military or civilian—from even reviewing a classification decision.[57] So defense attorneys have no way to challenge the government's classification decisions no matter how clearly they violate the Executive Order. And so, many of the details regarding the torture program remain classified, even though they may conceal violations of law. Further, almost two decades after the events at issue, it is hard to fathom the national security at risk that would be caused by the revelation of the details of the RDI or torture program—it is more likely that the remaining information remains classified to protect the torturers.[58]

Dissemination of Art Created at Guantanamo

Since soon after their arrival at Guantanamo, many of the men who are detained have created art. Some created art as a way to spend time or learn a new skill. Some created art as a way to ameliorate the impact of their torture. And some created art as a way to tell the stories of the suffering they experienced. For years, the art that was created was shared with lawyers and family members through ICRC letters. However, that all changed in the spring of 2017 when the John Jay College of Criminal Justice in New York City sponsored a public exhibition of art created by Guantanamo detainees.[59] The exhibition drew significant media attention and led to a change of policy. The Department of Defense took the unusual position that all art created while at Guantanamo was deemed to be the property of the Department, thus taking away the ability of the artists to disseminate their art. Ammar al Baluchi, one of the artists whose art was displayed and received significant attention,[60] sought to have the restrictions rescinded, arguing that the creation and dissemination of his art was part of his defense strategy of mitigation of his sentence. His piece "Vertigo at Guantanamo," sought to capture the effects and impacts of his torture at the hands of the U.S. government. Unfortunately, the military judge overseeing the matter deferred to the detention facility commander, finding that regulations governing the distribution of detainee artwork fall outside the Commission's jurisdiction.[61] Thus, yet another restriction on communication by those detained has been allowed.

Threats to Defense Counsel

Another way in which the government has attempted to silence the stories about the torture inflicted during the CIA program has been to threaten defense attorneys with criminal prosecution if they seek to fully investigate what happened to their clients. In 2008, the Department of Justice investigated lead counsel for Khalid Shaikh Mohammad after he sought to call as witnesses the government agents who had been involved with the torture program.[62] No charges were ever filed, but the "shot across the bow" was just the first of many attempts by the government to limit public disclosure about the details of the torture program.[63]

Then, in 2017, the government prohibited the defense from making any efforts to identify or contact current or former CIA employees, regardless of whether they are or were overt or covert employees because those efforts might somehow disclose classified information. This directive led to substantial litigation about the impact on the defense attorneys' ability to effectively represent their clients in the case where the government is seeking the execution of the defendants.[64] The matter remained unresolved at the time of this writing, more than three years later.

Another example of the attempts to interfere with the rights of the defendants to effective representation was an attempt to strip numerous defense counsel of their security clearance after a pleading was filed which, it was later determined, inadvertently included classified information. And the efforts have gone beyond the military commissions: an attorney who was litigating to seek compensation for the harm of torture on behalf of her client in the European Court of Human Rights was stripped of the security clearance required for her to meet with her client. Those are just four examples of attempts by the government to chill the free expression of defense counsel. Many more examples of the chilling effect on both free expression and interference with the effective assistance of defense counsel have been demonstrated in the military commissions, but none has been satisfactorily resolved.[65]

Limitations on Public Trial

> Between distance, delays, and cancellations, it has been exceedingly difficult to closely follow the GTMO proceedings. We made several attempts to attend CCTV sites at military bases, got credentials, but never actually got to see anything. Very little GTMO news gets reported on, and the lack of transparency doesn't feel anything akin to justice.
>
> –Kristen Breitweiser, Lorie Van Auken, and Mindy Kleinberg.[66]

By holding the proceedings on a restricted naval base some 800 miles removed from the continental United States, the government has effectively prevented the public from witnessing proceedings in person. Although a small number of family members of those injured or killed in the attacks are allowed to attend the proceedings, they, along with members of the media and representatives from "NGOs" observe proceedings from a gallery at the back of the hearing room. A forty-second delay of the audio from the proceedings has been instituted in an effort to prevent these observers from hearing any classified information inadvertently presented by a witness or attorney. This set-up effectively precludes interaction between the public and the participants in the proceedings; no member of the public (including victims or their family members) is ever allowed to speak with any of the defendants. The prosecution team controls all communication between the family members of victims of the attacks with the media or the NGO observers, as well as controlling the communication between victim family members and the defense attorneys for those accused of involvement in the attacks. Further, the public is completely precluded from attending any proceeding where either the defense or the government seeks to discuss classified information. Those sessions are wholly closed to the public, and any transcripts of the proceedings are significantly redacted.

Since 2012, the government has been transmitting a Closed Circuit TV ("CCTV") feed to a few remote viewing locations within the northeastern corridor of the United States, all of which are on military bases which have strict restrictions regarding who can get on base to attend. These proceedings also are on a forty-second delay. However, by transmitting proceedings only to military facilities, the government has erected barriers to the public witnessing proceedings remotely—attendees must have government-issued identification, and, if they are not an American citizen, must arrange for a military escort at all times.

A recent report conducted by the Government Accountability Office[67] indicates that substantial numbers of interested persons—9/11 victims, family members of victims, the media, and the general public—are denied a reasonable opportunity to observe proceedings either in-person or remotely because (1) all the remote viewing locations are on the East Coast; (2) the locations are at secure military facilities, which are difficult to access for civilians and foreign nationals; (3) the Office of Military Commissions website is often not updated to reflect current hearing schedules; and (4) pleadings, orders, and transcripts are, as a matter of course, significantly delayed beyond the fifteen business day timeline for release to the public.

Accordingly, both the public and the defendants' rights to a transparent process and a public trial are severely limited. Few reporters make the difficult trek to Guantanamo, and those who do have very limited ability to shine a light on the proceedings because of the cloak of secrecy.

CONCLUSION

After the attacks of September 11, Americans united in our grief for the lives lost and the shattering of our sense of security. In the wake of that unity, some of our leaders made decisions on our behalf that still reverberate. Instead of upholding American ideals of freedom and democracy and respect for human rights, instead of seeking to unite the world in a peaceful response, decisions were made that the United States would resort to violence instead of seeking peace, the government would use the techniques of torture instead of seeking justice and the government would use the mechanisms of secrecy instead of transparency. These decisions led to the unending wars in Afghanistan and Iraq, the deaths of tens of thousands of innocent civilians, the detention of hundreds of innocent men and children, and a military commission proceeding that—more than nineteen years after the attacks—still has no real possibility of an open, public trial that adheres to the dictates of the Geneva Conventions or the U.S. Constitution. The delay of justice for the victims of the attack, the stain on the United States' reputation as a country that adheres to the rule of law, and the failure to respect the human rights of those accused of the attacks are collectively a tragedy that could have, and should have, been avoided.

NOTES

1. The Military Commissions on Naval Station Guantánamo Bay, Cuba will be referred to herein simply as "Guantanamo" using the Americanized spelling of the place name.

2. As an employee of the Department of Defense of the U.S. government with a security clearance at the Top Secret/Sensitive Compartmented Information (TS/SCI) level, I am obligated to include this statement on any and all public writings. *See* DoD Instruction 5230.29 Security and Policy Review of DoD Information for Public Release.

3. Barghouti, Mourid. 2000. *I Saw Ramallah*. Translated by Ahdaf Soueif. Cairo and New York: The American University of Cairo Press.

4. United States, Central Intelligence Agency, *Comments on the Senate Select Committee on Intelligence Report on the Rendition, Detention, and Interrogation Program*, June 27, 2013, 6, *hereinafter* "RDI Report, CIA Response."

5. United States. 2001. The USA PATRIOT Act: preserving life and liberty: uniting and strengthening America by providing appropriate tools required to intercept and obstruct terrorism. [Washington, D.C.]: [U.S. Dept. of Justice].http://purl.access.gpo.gov/GPO/LPS39935.

6. The full impact of the USA/Patriot Act is beyond the scope of this chapter.

7. United States Senate Select Committee on Intelligence, *Committee Study of the Central Intelligence Agency's Detention and Interrogation Program*, Approved December 13, 2012, Updated for Release April 3, 2014, Declassification Revisions December 3, 2014, *hereinafter* "RDI Report." *Forward* at 3.

8. "Protocol I" Protocol Additions to the Geneva Conventions of August 12, 1949, and Relating to the Protection of Victims of International Armed Conflicts, June 8, 1977, 1125 U.N.T.S. 3.

9. *See generally* the Military Commissions Act, 10 U.S.C. §§949a *et. seq* which contains significant omissions to generally accepted requirements, such as a speedy trial, and authorizes the use of hearsay beyond the usually accepted exceptions of federal and military courts-martial trials.

10. The case is entitled *The United States of America v. Khalid Shaikh Mohammad, Walid Muhammad Salih Mubarak Bin 'Attash, Ramzi Bin Al Shibh, Ali Abdul-Aziz Ali, Mustafa Ahmed Adam Al Hawsawi*. Walid Muhammad Salih Mubarak Bin 'Attash's preferred name is Khallad bin 'Atash, Ali Abdul-Aziz Ali's preferred name is Ammar al Baluchi. I will use the defendants' preferred name and spelling.

11. Due to the difficulty in transliterating from Arabic to English, both Usama bin Laden and Osama bin Laden have been used to spell the name of the purported leader of Al Qaeda. I will use the more common spelling: Osama bin Laden.

12. National Commission on Terrorist Attacks upon the United States. 2004. *The 9/11 Commission Report: Final Report of the National Commission On Terrorist Attacks Upon the United States*. New York: Norton at 254.

13. *Id.* at 261.

14. *Id.* at 14.

15. Selected Speeches of President George W. Bush 2001–2008. White House Archives, September 11, 2001 (https://georgewbush-whitehouse.archives.gov/infocus/bushrecord/documents/Selected_Speeches_George_W_Bush.pdf).

16. Selected Speeches of President George W. Bush 2001–2008. White House Archives. September 20, 2001.

17. *Id.*

18. Memo from Jay Bybee to Jim Haynes, DATE: January 22, 2002 SUBJECT: "Application of Treaties and Laws to Al Qaeda and Taliban Detainees" and "Standards for Conduct for Interrogation under 18 U.S.C. §§ 2340-2340A" available at https://nsarchive2.gwu.edu/torturingdemocracy/documents/.

19. *Id.*

20. For a description of the common law privilege, see *United States v. Reyn*olds, 345 U.S. 1 (1953).

21. See Priest, Dana. 2005. "CIA Holds Terror Suspects in Secret Prisons." *Washington Post*, November 2, 2005. https://www.washingtonpost.com/archive/politics/2005/11/02/cia-holds-terror-suspects-in-secret-prisons/767f0160-cde4-41f2-a691-ba989990039c/.

22. Because the U.S. government has continued to specifically assert the National Security Privilege over the locations of the detention centers, I again point out that I am in no way confirming nor denying any of the specific information contained in the news and governmental reports cited herein.

23. Council of Europe, Parliamentary Assembly, Doc. 10748, *Alleged secret detention centres in Council of Europe member states,* Motion for a resolution, November 23, 2005. Available at https://assembly.coe.int/nw/xml/XRef/Xref-DocDetails-en.asp?FileID=11071&lang=en.

24. RDI Report, 8.

25. RDI Report, Forward, 3.

26. RDI Report, 36.

27. RDI Report, p. 8.

28. SSCI RDI Report, Findings and Conclusions, fn. 1.

29. Compare SSCI RDI Report with CIA Response

30. Horton, Scott. 2007. "The German Experience with Enhanced Interrogation." *Harper's Magazine*, May 29, 2007. https://harpers.org/2007/05/the-german-experience-with-enhanced-interrogation/.

31. RDI Report, Forward, 2 at fn. 1.

32. *See e.g.* RDI Report, Introduction at p. 3 ("Sleep deprivation involved keeping detainees awake for up to 180 hours, usually standing or in stress positions, at times with their hands shackled above their heads. At least five detainees experienced disturbing hallucinations during prolonged sleep deprivation and, in at least two of those cases, the CIA nonetheless continued the sleep deprivation.").

33. *Husayn v. Mitchell*, 938 F.3d 1123, 1126 (9th Cir. 2019) and UNITED STATES OF AMERICA v. MAJID SHOUKAT KHAN, AE 033 RULING Defense Motion for Pretrial Punishment Credit and Other Related Relief, June 4, 2020, available at www.mc.mil.

34. Executive Order 13491—Ensuring Lawful Interrogations, January 22, 2009.

35. CIA Comments on the Senate Select Committee on Intelligence Report on the Rendition, Detention, and Interrogation Program, June 27, 2013.

36. CIA Comments at p. 3.

37. RDI Report, Findings and Conclusions, p. 2–3.

38. *Id.*

39. Common Article 3, Section 1(d) of the Geneva Conventions requires all trials of "[p]ersons taking no active part in the hostilities" conducted by parties to a non-international armed conflict to be held by a "regularly constituted court affording all the judicial guarantees which are recognized as indispensable by civilized peoples."

40. Executive Order dated November 13, 2001, "Military Order—Detention, Treatment and Trial of Certain Non-Citizens in the War Against Terrorism." 66 Fed. Reg. 57833 (Nov. 16, 2001).

41. 10 U.S.C. §§949a *et. seq.*

42. There is some disagreement about when President George W. Bush learned of the specific "enhanced interrogation techniques" used in the "RDI" program (compare RDI Report at Forward, 18, n. 17, with RDI Report, CIA Response at 6.) However, it is clear that Secretary of State Colin Powell and Secretary of Defense Donald Rumsfeld were consulted as the "enhanced interrogation techniques" were being developed. *See* RDI Report at 334–335. Further, while some may quibble with whether all of the "enhanced interrogation techniques" constituted torture, there is a general consensus that the euphemistically entitled "waterboarding" technique constitutes torture. *See* Dana Carver Boehm, *Waterboarding, Counter-Resistance, and the Law of Torture: Articulating the Legal Underpinnings of U.S. Interrogation Policy*, 41 U. TOL. L. REV. 1, 14–15, 19–41 (2009).

43. Human Rights First, "Guantanamo by the Numbers" October 10, 2018. Available at https://www.humanrightsfirst.org/resource/guantanamo-numbers.

44. *Id.*

45. *Id.* Abdul Latif Nasser, who was cleared for release, but remains in detention, was the subject of a radio documentary "The Other Latif," available at https://www.npr.org/podcasts/809233558/the-other-latif.

46. Michael C. Dorf, "The Orwellian Military Commissions Act of 2006," *Journal of International Criminal Justice* 5, no. 1 (2007): 10–18.

47. *Id.*, Hamdan *v. Rumsfeld*, 548 U.S. 557, 126 S. Ct. 2749 (2006).

48. *Boumediene v. Bush*, 553 U.S. 723 (2008).

49. The Obama Administration's attempts to do so were stonewalled by Congress. *See* PUBLIC LAW 111–84—OCT. 28, 2009, NATIONAL DEFENSE AUTHORIZATION ACT FOR FISCAL YEAR 2010, Sec. 1041, which prohibited any Federal funds from being used "to release into the United States, its territories, or possessions, any individual . . . who is located at United States Naval Station, Guantanamo Bay, Cuba, as of October 1, 2009, who—

(1) is not a citizen of the United States; and (2) is—

(A) in the custody or under the effective control of the Department of Defense; or

(B) otherwise under detention at the United States Naval Station, Guantanamo Bay, Cuba."

50. United States Code, Chapter 47A of title 10; 10 U.S.C. § 948a *et. sec.*

51. RDI Report at 80.

52. RDI Report at 160.

53. The President Executive Order 13526, Classified National Security Information, December 29, 2009. Available at https://www.archives.gov/isoo/policy-documents/cnsi-eo.html.

54. United Nations, Convention against Torture and Other Cruel, Inhuman or Degrading Treatment or Punishment, Article 14. Available at https://www.ohchr.org /en/professionalinterest/pages/cat.aspx.

55. *See* Military Commissions Ruling in *U.S. v. Khalid Shaikh Mohammad et. al.*, AE 018U, ORDER Privileged Written Communications, November 6, 2013, available at https://www.mc.mil/Portals/0/pdfs/KSM2/KSM%20II%20(AE018U(KS M%20et%20al)).pdf.

56. Executive Order 13526, *Supra.*

57. 10 U.S.C. §949p-1c "Trial counsel shall work with the original classification authorities for evidence that may be used at trial to ensure that such evidence is declassified to the maximum extent possible, consistent with the requirements of national security. *A decision not to declassify evidence under this section shall not be subject to review by a military commission or upon appeal.*" (emphasis supplied.)

58. *See e.g.*, the very first finding of the RDI Report: "The CIA's use of its enhanced interrogation techniques was not an effective means of acquiring intelligence or gaining cooperation from detainees." (p. 2 of 19.)

59. The exhibition can be viewed online at https://www.artfromguantanamo.com.

60. *See* Exhibit A.

61. *See U.S. v. Mohammad et. al*, AE 563D ORDER Mr. al Baluchi's Motion to Invalidate Restrictions on Public Dissemination of Mr. al Baluchi's Artwork, May 11, 2018. Available at https://www.mc.mil/Portals/0/pdfs/KSM2/KSM%20II%20(AE56 3D(ORDER)).PDF.

62. *See United States v. Kiriakou*, Case No. 1:12MJ33 (United States District Court for the Eastern District of Virginia), Affidavit in Support of Criminal Complaint and Arrest Warrant, 23 January 2012, pp. 3–5 (detailing three-year FBI investigation focusing on defense counsel, but concluding that "no laws were broken by the defense team.").

63. For a more detailed account of all the ways in which the government has interfered with, or attempted to interfere with the defense, see *U.S. v. Mohammad et. al.* AE 530S, Response to AE 530F, Government Status of Investigation and Motion for Reconsideration of the Provision of Laptops to the Accused and an Order for a Walled-Off Forensic Review of All of the Accused's Laptops, and Response to Mr. Hawsawi's, Mr. Bin 'Attash's, and Mr. Ali's Motions for Return of the Laptops and/or Other Specified Relief, November 20, 2017, p. 14–23, available at https://www.mc.mil/Portals/0/pdfs/KSM2/KSM%20II%20(AE530S(KS M)).pdf.

64. *See U.S. v. Mohammad et. al*, AE524 (AAA) Mr. al Baluchi's Motion to Dismiss, or in the Alternative, to Compel the Government to Produce Witnesses for Interview, September 25, 2017, and other pleadings in that series, available at https:// www.mc.mil/CASES.aspx.

65. U.S. v. Mohammad et. al. AE 530S, *Supra.*

66. As told to defense attorneys for Ammar al Baluchi, see U.S. v. Mohammad et. al, AE007L (AAA) Mr. al Baluchi's Response To Government Motion For Public Access To Open Proceedings of This Military Commission Via

Closed-Circuit Television Transmission, May 24, 2019, available at https://www.mc.mil/Portals/0/pdfs/KSM2/KSM%20II%20(AE007L(AAA)).pdf.

67. U.S. Gov't Accountability Office, GAO-19-283, Military Courts: DOD Should Assess the Tradeoffs Associated with Expanding Public Access to and Information About Terrorism Trials (2019) (hereinafter "GAO Report").

PART III

COUNTER-TERRORISM LAWS AND JOURNALISTIC PRACTICE

Chapter 9

Journalism on Ice—National Security Laws and the Chilling Effect in Australian Journalism

Richard Murray, Rebecca Ananian-Welsh, and Peter Greste

INTRODUCTION

On a cold winter morning in the Australian capital Canberra, the doorbell rang at the modest home of a prominent political journalist, Annika Smethurst. The seasoned reporter had been getting ready for another day at work in her parliament house office on June 4, 2019, when she opened the door to seven plain-clothed police officers brandishing a search warrant. The police entered Smethurst's house, and rifled through her personal files, her bathroom cupboards, even her underwear drawers, looking for clues that might reveal the identity of the person who gave her a story she had published over a year earlier.

Smethurst had published a series of stories based on a classified memo leaked from within the Department of Defence. Smethurst's story revealed that the departments of Home Affairs and Defence had secretly been considering expanding the powers of the national electronic eavesdropping agency to include domestic communications. The Australian Signals Directorate is primarily responsible for snooping on international communications, and any decision to turn its listening devices inward would have had important implications for civil liberties. The story of the raid exploded on traditional and social media. Rarely had Australian security agents gone after journalists; the country has a robust tradition of strong, contrary journalism, that the security services and politicians have largely respected, and the outrage from the public and the media was swift and loud. This particular incident looked uncomfortably like the more jackbooted regimes that Australian governments had criticized in the past, though the police said they were doing nothing beyond enforcing a section of the Crimes Act that prohibits the unauthorized communication or release of classified information (Karp 2019).

Then, barely twenty-four hours later, it happened again. Another police squad marched into the offices of the Australian Broadcasting Corporation in Sydney, this time searching for evidence of sources for another story, known as the Afghan Files. ABC journalists Dan Oakes and Sam Clark had exposed allegations of war crimes committed by Australian Special Forces in Afghanistan. The stories of unlawful killings of unarmed men and children were based on hundreds of pages of leaked documents and raised serious questions about the culture and conduct of the elite troops (Oakes and Clark 2017).[1] The ABC's managing director insisted to the Australian Federal Police (AFP) nothing was published that directly compromised the security of the soldiers on the ground or Australia more broadly, and he argued that the story was clearly "in the public interest" (Martin and Lyons 2019).

Either above-referenced police operation on its own would have raised serious concerns about freedom of speech in Australia and press freedom in particular, but together the two incidents were widely criticized for appearing to be a crackdown on uncomfortable journalism (Devine 2019; Keane 2019; Koch 2019). Prime Minister Scott Morrison, Home Affairs Minister Peter Dutton, and the head of the Australian Federal Police all insisted the operations were both lawful and conducted without political influence (Devine 2019; Keane 2019; Koch 2019). The two politicians went on to argue that nobody—including journalists—should be above the law.

While the raids were clearly unusual, they drew public attention to trends that academics had been monitoring for years; namely a unique enthusiasm by successive Australian governments for enacting hastily drafted and loosely framed national security legislation that either directly or indirectly intrudes on civil liberties in general and press freedom in particular. University of New South Wales professor George Williams counted more than eighty separate federal laws passed since 9/11 that deal with national security—more than any other western democracy (2013). As early as 2009, the University of Reading's Lawrence McNamara began assessing the actual and potential impact of the legislation on the work of journalists, and its broader implications for democratic debate and accountability (McNamara 2009). Early in 2019—six months before the police raids—our team from the University of Queensland began building on McNamara's work by reassessing the state of the legislation, particularly in light of a slew of new laws enacted in the decade since he published his findings. We found not only a marked shift in legal restraints on what would have been considered legitimate journalistic inquiry in the past but also a shift in the culture of the civil service toward secrecy far beyond what is considered necessary for national security. That includes the creative interpretation of the law. For example, in an unprecedented move, the warrant the police executed to search the ABC's offices cited an old provision of the Defence Act, that makes it a criminal offense to receive stolen Commonwealth property—in this case government documents.

In this article, we summarize the legal framework that has emerged in Australia since 9/11, and examine the direct and indirect effects on journalists and their sources. We then assess the impact of the legislation on the health of Australia's democracy, and concludes that if national security includes maintaining the health of our political system, laws that undermine one of the key pillars of that system—namely a robust free press—fail in their ultimate objective. To gauge the impact of Australia's national security laws on journalism and journalists, twenty prominent and senior journalists and editorial figures from across Australia's public and private news media landscape were interviewed. In keeping with the University of Queensland's ethical frameworks and guidelines in working human research subjects, the interviews and associated analysis were conducted under conditions of anonymity. The resulting data was coded around the laws that were identified as concerning and detrimental to the processes of public interest journalism.

AUSTRALIAN COUNTER-TERRORISM LAW

When Al Qaeda toppled the Twin Towers in 2001, governments around the world felt compelled to review their counter-terrorism laws, but few undertook the task from as low a base as Australia, or tackled it with quite as much enthusiasm. In 2001, the country had not a single national counter-terrorism law, and only one of the eight regional governments—the Northern Territory—had a statute that even mentioned terrorism (Williams 2011). Since then, the Australian Government has enacted more national security laws than any other liberal democracy (Blackbourn, McGarrity, and Roach 2019; Williams 2011, 2013). From 9/11 until the end of the conservative Howard government in 2007, parliament passed a total of forty-eight separate pieces of national counter-terrorism legislation into law: an average of one new statute every 6.7 weeks (Williams 2013). As Canadian legal scholar Kent Roach (Williams 2011) observed:

> [T]his degree of legislative activism is striking compared even to the United Kingdom's active agenda and much greater than the pace of legislation in the United States or Canada. Australia's hyper-legislation strained the ability of the parliamentary opposition and civil society to keep up, let alone provide effective opposition to, the relentless legislative output. (310)

Since 2007, that extraordinary enthusiasm for national security legislation has slowed somewhat, but certainly not stopped. In the five years to 2020, the government has taken aim at the threats posed by foreign terrorist fighters, espionage, foreign interference, encrypted communications, and more. In this crowded and complex counter-terrorism context, once exceptional war-time measures—such as control orders and secret evidence—have migrated to the regular criminal justice sphere and become permanent, normalized features of most Australian States and Territories.

The counter-terrorism agenda has justified the introduction of schemes for warrantless searches,[2] the banning of organizations,[3] preventive detention,[4] indefinite post-sentence detention,[5] control orders,[6] citizenship stripping, advocacy and sedition offenses, secret evidence in civil and criminal trials, and, uniquely, the secret detention and compulsory interrogation of non-suspect individuals by the domestic spy agency the Australian Security Intelligence Organization (ASIO).[7] The passage of these laws was eased by Australia's lack of a national bill or charter of rights (a factor that sets Australia apart from every other liberal democracy); and by a far from unique rhetoric of urgency, exceptionalism and fear.

The rapid expansion of Australian national security law since 9/11 has been accompanied by a pronounced emphasis on secrecy. The government has harnessed criminal and security laws to plug leaks of embarrassing information, while the powers of law enforcement and intelligence agencies have been vastly expanded. While several civil society groups have complained about the impact of those laws on human rights, much of the concern has focused on their impact on press freedom as one of the most fundamental checks on government overreach and the abuse of power. Broadly, there are four classes of law causing concern, namely those which: "gag" speech, expand surveillance powers, create secrecy offenses, and permit secret evidence in court.[8]

Gag Laws

While governments need a degree of confidentiality to operate effectively, in a democracy the media acts as a kind of whistle of last resort for those seeking to expose government wrong-doing, mismanagement, corruption, or the abuse of power. Shield laws, designed to help journalists protect their sources, are an explicit acknowledgment of the role that news organizations play in holding governments to account. In 2011, the federal attorney-general Robert McClelland successfully introduced a shield provision for journalists into the Commonwealth Evidence Act. But at the same time, successive governments have also passed a range of gag style offenses that criminalize mere communication in certain cases under Australian national security law.

Anybody who has been detained and/or questioned by ASIO under certain classes of warrant faces onerous restrictions on their communications while the warrant is in force (which may be up to twenty-eight days for interrogation and seven days for detention).[9] It is even an offense to reveal that such a warrant has been issued, the content of that warrant, or any facts relating to its execution, while the warrant is in force. The disclosure of *operational information* is also an offense, both while the warrant is in force and within two years of its expiry, and those restrictions extend to legal advisers, representatives, parents, guardians, and siblings of anybody who has been detained or questioned. The legal definition of "information" is so vast that Mark Rix from the University of Wollongong has argued, "The breadth, meaninglessness and vacuousness of the term provide the government, and ASIO, with an almost impenetrable and unfathomable legislative screen for hiding information and tightly controlling its use and disclosure" (Rix 2013). Similar restrictions apply to "preventive detention orders" ("PDOs"). PDOs allow for brief, secret incarceration for up to forty-eight hours under federal law or fourteen days under state law (Lynch, McGarrity, and Williams 2015). The orders may be issued to protect the community from an imminent terrorist attack or to protect evidence of a recent attack. Anyone disclosing even the *existence* of a PDO, including the detainee's lawyer, interpreter, or any police office, risks five years in prison.

One of the most controversial gag laws in Australia's national security framework is section 35P of the *Australian Security Intelligence Organisation Act 1979* (Cth) (ASIO Act). In 2014, the government introduced a regime that empowered the federal attorney-general to declare certain ASIO actions to be "special intelligence operations" (SIOs). The SIO designation was designed to allow ASIO officers to break the law in the course of their work, without risking prosecution. An undercover agent working under an SIO, for example, could carry drugs to break open a narcotics ring. Anybody disclosing even the existence of an SIO runs the risk of spending up to five years in prison; or ten years if the disclosure is "aggravated" (endangering the health or safety of any person, prejudicing an SIO, or if the person intends such a thing) (Rix 2013). Not only is it illegal to say anything about an SIO, the law includes "related" information, likely to include operations by regular law enforcement agencies working to support ASIO. The problem for any journalist keeping tabs on the security services is knowing when they are covering an SIO. *Any* national security or counter-terrorism-related action by law enforcement or intelligence operatives may be an SIO, and the designation exists in perpetuity. Therefore, even investigating the history of ASIO becomes a highly risky proposition. The scheme appears to rely on journalists contacting the attorney-general's department before reporting on anything that might carry an SIO designation (Rix 2013).

Few researchers seriously challenge the need for secrecy in the nation's domestic spy agency. There is clearly a need for laws to help stop information leaks that might compromise ongoing ASIO operations or place lives at risk. But the secrecy provisions and gag orders are so oppressive that they make it dangerous for any journalist or whistleblower to expose cases where the agency has abused its power or engaged in corrupt practices.

Overall, the oppressive legislation surrounding ASIO operations has lead Rix (2013) to conclude:

> The secrecy surrounding information, national security information, security, national security, international relations, and law enforcement interests is baffling, all-pervasive and largely impenetrable. Successive Australian governments have successively added to this secrecy and impenetrability. It is far less clear whether this has helped to make Australians more secure from the threat of terrorism. It is clear, however, that it has left them more vulnerable to the secret, clandestine and sometimes illegal activities of ASIO which, surrounded in secrecy founded on sloppy, all-encompassing and unfathomable legislation, is subject to few if any requirements for openness, transparency and accountability. (259)

Data Surveillance Powers

In 2015, as the world was coming to terms with the shocking attack by Islamic extremists on the offices of the satirical magazine Charlie Hebdo in Paris, the Australian Government introduced a law requiring all telecommunications service providers in Australia to retain customer metadata for at least two years (Sarre 2017). Under the law, more than twenty government agencies can access almost any Australian's metadata without a warrant.[10]

Metadata is not the content of any communications; it is the data *about* the communications. It includes who a user communicates with (via any channel such as emails, phone calls, text messages, or some other form of communication), the time and place that the communications were made and received, and so on. Civil liberties and media groups said the law undermined privacy and exposed privileged communications, including between journalists and their sources. The attorney-general at the time, George Brandis, dismissed those concerns, describing metadata as nothing more than "the outside of the envelope" and went on to say the passage of the law is an "urgent priority," and "vital to investigate terrorism and organized crime" (Brevini 2017, 80).

Metadata therefore has the potential to reveal "an enormously rich trail of information regarding users' locations, calls and networks" (Sarre 2017, 170). Reports have since suggested that many other agencies have relied on state-based powers to access retained data so that by late 2018 some 350,000 requests for access to metadata were being received by telecommunications service providers each year.[11]

For journalists and their confidential sources, the scheme was potentially disastrous. If a government agency could trawl through phone and email records at will, they could easily find who had been blowing the whistle and leaking information, fatally undermining that crucial journalist–source relationship. After loud protests from the media and civil liberties groups, the government finally agreed to introduce "Journalist Information Warrants" (JIW), required when a government agency is seeking access to journalists' or their employers' metadata to identify who they had been communicating with (Brevini 2017).

But the JIW scheme is fraught with problems. The law only covers sources of journalists "working in a professional capacity." A warrant is not required to identify a source who provided information to a "non-professional" journalist (such as a citizen journalist, blogger, or volunteer at a community radio station). Similarly, a person is only a "source" under the Act when they expect their information is going to be published. Thus, the JIW only applies to some journalist–source interactions and offers no protection to journalistic confidentiality outside what could narrowly be called "professional" journalism.

To get around the law, journalists were widely encouraged by the organizations they work for to use encrypted communications with sources (Ackland 2015; Dobbie 2015). Then, on the evening of the final parliamentary sitting day of 2018 and over strong concerns of opposition parties, government departments, industry and the public,[12] the federal government passed the *Telecommunications and Other Legislation Amendment (Assistance and Access) Act 2018* (Cth) ("*TOLAA*").

Rushed through because of the "urgency" of the situation (though the government never explained the need for haste), the *TOLAA* creates a complex set of processes giving law all government enforcement and intelligence agencies the power to ask and even force telecommunications "providers" (defined with extravagant breadth to include everyone from major ISPs to repairmen) to undertake "acts and things" to assist the agency in its law enforcement or intelligence-related work. In the assessment of lawyers, that benign phrase, "acts and things," can include embedding backdoor weaknesses and decryption technologies into target devices—an extraordinary power that completely undercuts the very concept of private secure communications. While a requesting agency doesn't need a warrant to force a "provider" to build a weakness into a target device, they do need a traditional warrant to gain access to the actual content of the information, documents, or communications.

Under these laws, there is every chance that journalists who investigate national security matters or serious crimes, or who work with government sources with access to classified information, will be subject to a legally sanctioned digital assault. They risk general metadata access, targeted metadata access to identify their sources under a JIW, orders under the *TOLAA* to place back doors in their encrypted or protected data, and warrant-based access to their (now decrypted) communications. Remember, these forms of data surveillance are all covert, so each could take place without the journalist or their employer ever being aware of them. And at no stage are their interests, or those of the industry, ever represented. But this is much less of an issue for the journalists themselves, than it is for the public for which they are reporting, and the democracy in which they operate (Ananian-Welsh 2019).

Secrecy Offences

While gag laws have closed down opportunities to expose wrong-doing inside Australia's security services, and metadata and decryption laws opened up communications between journalists and sources, the government hasn't been neglecting civil servants more broadly. Most prominently, amendments introduced in 2018 created broadly framed foreign interference and secrecy offenses, as well as twenty-seven new espionage offenses that go far beyond catching traditional cloak-and-dagger spies.

The General Secrecy Offence is particularly concerning. This offense criminalizes intentional "communication" or "dealing with" government information made or obtained by a current or former Commonwealth officer,[13] and the person is reckless as to whether:

- the information has a security classification of "secret" or "top secret";[14]
- the communication or dealing damages the security or defence of Australia;[15]
- the communication or dealing interferes with or prejudices the application of a Commonwealth criminal offence;[16] or
- the communication or dealing harms or prejudices the health or safety of the Australian public.[17]

The penalty for communicating information is imprisonment for five years,[18] while the penalty for the more loosely defined "dealing with" information is imprisonment for two years.[19]

With staggering breadth, the verb, "dealing with," includes receiving, obtaining, collecting, possessing, recording, copying, communicating, or publishing all or part of the information, including the effect or description of the information.[20] Simply receiving an unsolicited letter becomes a criminal offense, as well as mere possession, copying, or making notes of communications. The key criterion of the offense is therefore that the person is reckless as to the security classification of the material.[21]

The legislation makes some attempts to protect press freedom by providing a "journalism defence" for anyone communicating information in the business of reporting news.[22] For that defense to apply, the person must have:

- dealt with the information in their capacity as a "person engaged in the business of reporting news, presenting current affairs or expressing editorial or other content in news media."[23]
- have reasonably believed that engaging in the conduct was in the public interest.

  The defense is also available to administrative staff acting under the direction of a journalist, editor, or lawyer, who reasonably believed the conduct was in the public interest.[24]

For journalists, though, the more troubling amendments introduced in 2018 include eleven underlying espionage offenses and sixteen offenses of aggravated espionage, with penalties ranging from fifteen years to life imprisonment. Among them, is a "Core Espionage Offence," which essentially concerns dealing with national security information to be communicated to a foreign principal (Kendall 2019).[25] Where the person dealing with information intends to prejudice Australia's national security, or advantage the national security of a foreign country, the prescribed penalty is imprisonment for life.[26] If a person is merely reckless as to that prejudice or advantage, the penalty is up to twenty-five years imprisonment. National security in this context is defined with concerning breadth to include Australia's political, military, and economic relations.[27]

The definition is so broad that a journalist simply receiving an unsolicited letter from a Commonwealth civil servant wanting to expose, say, corrupt trade negotiations (which are defined as matters of economic security), becomes guilty of an offense. If they take that note to their editor to discuss what to do with it, the editor likewise faces the possibility of jail time. And if they publish the story, they could be guilty of "communicating to a foreign principal," as foreign governments and government-controlled entities could see the story along with everyone else.

Another form of espionage criminalizes dealing with security classified information to be communicated to a foreign principal, subject to a prescribed penalty of up to twenty years imprisonment. No mental element of intention or recklessness is required to make out this offense. Unlike the General Secrecy Offense, there is no journalism-based defense available under the espionage or foreign interference frameworks.[28]

IMPACT

When McNamara published his research on the impact of national security legislation on Australian journalism in 2009, he found while there was the potential for a chilling effect, no such effect was felt among Australian journalists. He said:

> The pursuit of security has seen a significant impact on the ability of the media to obtain information and convey it to the public. In large part, the potential effects of the laws remain far greater than the actual effects. However, although the resilience and robustness of the media persists for the time being, it does mean that this situation will continue. (114)

More than ten years later, Australia's news media is in a precarious state. The digital disruption of the industry has eroded its "resilience and robustness."

This part of this chapter is drawn from interviews with journalists working across the spectrum of Australia's mainstream news organizations. All interviewed journalists agreed there is a chilling effect in Australian journalism and it had become more keenly felt in the past decade. The chilling effect has been driven by a variety of factors but at its heart it the fundamental weakening and destabilizing impact of the digital disruption of the journalism that has left journalism as an industry exposed. This has resulted in an Australian Government emboldened by these changes imposing a raft of laws that do not enhance the capacity of Australian journalists to act in the interests of the fourth estate. Defamation laws, issues of suppression and open justice, and draconian freedom of information and right to information regimes all contribute to difficult conditions for journalists.

The ceaseless legislative changes analyzed in the first part of this chapter have had a devastating impact in the practice of doing journalism in the public interest. These impacts can be broadly categorized into two categories—secrecy and surveillance. The interviews with Australian journalists revealed a clear onset of a chilling effect in how journalists go about their duties and practice their craft. The chilling effect is most keenly felt in the ways journalist's relationships with sources had been stilted, a growing culture of secrecy and distrust with government, and a growing sense of uncertainty and insecurity for journalists.

Surveillance

The Data Retention Act (2015) has changed the way journalists deal with sources. This means all sources. There is a tendency when talking about the impact of mechanisms and processes of surveillance on the practice of journalism to emphasize what this means to whistleblowers (Pearson and Fernandez 2018; Ricketson 2018). The journalists interviewed in the study felt that although the situation for whistleblowers in Australia was perilous, this had always been the case and this was something they could anticipate. The real changes have come in journalist's capacity to access everyday sources—the kinds of sources needed to what has been traditionally viewed as everyday journalism. This includes covering government activities. One interviewee said:

> With the use of non-disclosure agreements, legal pressure and the general culture of bullying and intimidation has become much more sophisticated, which has, from my perspective, had a chilling effect on people's willingness to come forward and increased the amount of fear and trepidation that they feel when they do come forward, and those risks may not be real ones but they are certainly perceived risks on the part of the people that I deal with.

Across the course of the interviews, it became clear changing structural conditions within the government had stifled information flows. According to some of the interviewees, this had been exacerbated by a shift away from tenured employment to contract-based employment for Australia's bureaucrats. Contrary to stated commitments to transparency and accountability from Australian government departments and agencies, some of the interviewees claimed that government staff contracts include nondisclosure clauses making talking to journalists potentially professionally devastating. This combined with bullying tactics on the part of the Australian Government and corporate Australia and new and enhanced legal pressures served to stop the sources at all levels of their respective organizations coming forward.

In the context of national security, data retention laws were viewed as a key contributor to the chilling effect in Australian journalism. These laws have resulted in a creeping sense of insecurity for journalists. Unlike issues of secrecy and the associated criminalization of journalism, under data retention laws journalists feared for the safety and anonymity of their sources rather than themselves. A prominent news editor summed up the impact of data retention laws in no uncertain terms.

> Metadata retention laws have had a big impact. We find sources, and potential sources, are more cautious. They're scared. They're harder to find, and it's harder to protect their anonymity, which has an impact on the practical conduct of investigative journalism. That's the biggest change. The biggest change is fewer people come to us. When people do come to us, it means we have to be much more cautious and careful in the way that we protect their anonymity, if

> that's what they want. That is an impediment, if you like, to the efficiency of what we do.

When sources do come forward, the act of communicating with journalists has the potential of exposing them as a source because of the mode or delivery of information. The ability for government to access and collect metadata has become a mechanism by which people's communication can be tracked. This, in turn, has led to journalists abandoning sources and, in extreme cases, stories because of fears for the safety of sources. A prominent Australian journalist said:

> I've killed off parts—like significant parts—of a story because I know that publishing will lead to the identification of a source. This is mainly because it's the sort of privileged information that only a few people have seen or whatever and they will know that if I publish it. The government can use my metadata to quite easily link me back to whoever's spoken to me. It just puts everything that we used to be able to do with relative ease into this kind of uncertainty in terms of source protection and source communication.

In reaction to this, senior newsroom staff across Australia have become sensitive to what one interviewee euphemistically termed "unhygienic" approaches to sources. Stories are routinely killed off and journalists are self-censoring at the suggestion of sources being exposed. Australian journalists are abandoning digital communication—email, text messages, mobile, and smartphones—in favor of traditional forms of communication. Face-to-face communications have enjoyed a renaissance as have traditional letter drops. At the same time, in the interests of "hygienic" communications, journalists are making use of sophisticated encryption apps in an effort to thwart government efforts to track them and their communications. However, as one interviewee said, these apps are only as effective as the people who use them. As soon as communications become overly complex, many sources become anxious and are scared away.

Secrecy

The other category of the national security laws having an impact on Australian journalism applies to secrecy. These laws are designed to ensure the Australian Government can maintain control over the information they deem secret. These laws find expression in the ASIO Act (1979) and more recently the Espionage and Foreign Interference Act (2018). Through Section 35P of the ASIO Act, the Australian Government has been able to designate Special Intelligence Operations (SIO)—this meant government activities given SIO status could not be reported on. Transgressions are punishable with a jail sentence. Interviewees complained SIO's were poorly defined in law and this led to high levels of risk aversion around publishing stories that might be subject to an SIO. As bad as SIO's are, they are a known quantity and can be prepared for. That is not so for the Espionage Act.

Although untested, the Espionage Act (2018) has sent a chill through Australian journalism. In the wake of the AFP raids on the ABC and News Corp, what little trust Australian journalists had in their relationship with the Australian Government disappeared. Despite an awareness the Espionage Act had not been implemented with the expressed intention of targeting journalists, there emerged a sense that journalism was being criminalized and the Espionage Act only served to heighten this. One interviewee said:

> It was clearly designed to prevent the public service and people in the defence and security forces from leaking information, but the media was captured in it. The result is journalists going about their normal business would have been criminalised doing absolutely basic journalism.

Interviewees described the initial draft of the legislation as "appalling" and "destructive." After a public campaign spearheaded by media and legal organizations highlighting the draconian nature of the proposed legislation, changes were made. Despite these changes, a chilling effect persisted. The same interviewee said:

> Activity which was once normal journalism and perfectly legal in any circumstances—research, receiving documents, talking to sources—the research end of journalism, if you like, which had never ever before been criminalised in any way is now potentially criminalised.

The opaque nature of the law was a cause for anxiety. In the wake of the Australian Federal Police raids on journalists and the organizations for which they work, interviewees expressed a strong distrust in the Australian Government. There emerged a clear sense that if the Australian Government wanted to get them, they would do so with the tools at their disposal, and the Espionage Act was another weapon in the government's arsenal.

What distinguished the Espionage Act from other secrecy laws was, in the eyes of many senior editorials staff, the potential impacts of the laws on the lives and career of journalists outweighed the public interest of publishing some stories. This resulted in important but risky stories going untold. A senior editorial figure put it best saying, "Good journalism is important, but no story is worth being jailed over."

CONCLUSION

Conditions for Australian journalists reporting in the public interest are deteriorating. A relentless march of national security laws have eroded free speech, including through gag laws and onerous secrecy offenses. Extensive frameworks of covert government surveillance can, and have, been used to target journalists and identify their confidential sources. Once exposed, those sources (as well as journalists) may be vulnerable to prosecution for a wide range of overlapping, often untested, offences. Newsroom professionals face the challenge of navigating this rapidly evolving legal environment, which is characterized by staggering complexity, secrecy, and uncertainty. The AFP raids on the ABC and Smethurst in June 2019 demonstrated both the capacity and willingness of law enforcement agencies to harness national security law to target public interest reporting and, appropriately, sent shockwaves through Australian and international media. But the raids also represented a surprisingly open manifestation of the kinds of (generally covert) powers capable of being harnessed by government agencies to investigate journalists and their sources.

The AFP raids prompted two parliamentary inquiries into the impact of law and law enforcement on press freedom and, in December 2019, the Australian Law Reform Commission identified "press freedom and whistleblowers" as one of five priority areas in "the future of law reform" (Parliament of Australia 2019, 2020; Australian Law Reform Commission 2019). These steps toward possible reform are to be commended. They represent a timely acknowledgment that press freedom is a core component of Australian democracy, but is neither recognized nor protected under Australian law. At present, press freedom remains a vague notion, easily swept aside (or, more often, ignored) as fresh tranches of national security law are enacted, interpreted, and enforced. Whether law reform will eventuate, and the form it might take, remain to be seen. We submit that the scope and complexity of the legislative assault on free speech can only be addressed through robust, far-reaching reform: a Media Freedom Act would have greater potential to support press freedom than, say, technical amendments to individual statutes.

When combined with a journalism industry in change, these factors have placed Australian journalists' capacity to act as agents of the fourth estate in question. At best, these changes can be seen through the lens of an unintentional breakdown in trust between the government and the news media. At worst, the laws and their associated impacts represent a sustained attack on the kinds of journalism that work in the interests of keeping the actions and decision making of the powerful honest, accountable and transparent. Either way, the kinds of stories that sustain and maintain a healthy democracy are going untold, and will continue to go untold until law reform begins to thaw the chilling effect experienced by journalists and sources. The vivid reality of how Australian journalism has been "chilled" by successive tranches of legislation was expressed by one interviewee, who said:

> It's a real problem. There have been stories which could have been told or should have been told which haven't been told because of a combination of the ASIO Act, the Espionage Bill and metadata laws. That's the chilling effect in practice. The chilling effect is a real thing. There are real stories that don't get told because the risks are just too high, particularly for the sources. Because we take our responsibility to protect our sources very seriously, it effectively kills stories and they are stories within the public interest . . . we're not talking about trivial stories, we're talking about the important stories.

Australian public interest journalism has been put on ice with far-reaching consequences for the health of Australian democracy. Like so many other places in the world, the recent story of journalism in Australia has been doing more with less. As journalism as an industry has become less influential in Australia, Australian federal and state governments have become more emboldened in their attacks on the industry. With recent mass job losses across Australian journalism, this is a trend that is not set to change soon.

NOTES

1. The ABC's head of Investigative Journalism, John Lyons, photographed and live-tweeted throughout the nine hours the police spent trawling through their files (Lyons 2019).
2. *Crimes Act 1914* (Cth) s 3UEA.
3. Provided that the attorney-general is satisfied on reasonable grounds that the organization "is directly or indirectly engaged in, preparing, planning, assisting in or fostering the doing of a terrorist act" or "advocates the doing of a terrorist act" (discussed further below): *Criminal Code Act 1995* (Cth) sch ('*Criminal Code* (Cth)') ss 102.1(2)(a)–(b).
4. *Criminal Code* (Cth) div 105.
5. *Criminal Code* (Cth) div 105.
6. *Criminal Code* (Cth) div 105 div 104.
7. *Australian Security Intelligence Organisation Act 1979* (Cth) pt III div 3.
8. For discussion of secret evidence, see Lynch, Tulich and Welsh (2013).
9. For the 28-day limit: *Australian Security Intelligence Organisation Act 1979* (Cth) s 34E(5)(b).

   For the 7-day limit: *Australian Security Intelligence Organisation Act 1979* (Cth) s 34F.

10. *Telecommunications (Interception and Access) Act 1979* (Cth) s 110A ('*Interception and Access Act*').

11. Commonwealth, *Parliamentary Debates*, House of Representatives, 6 December 2018, 12777–12779 (Adam Bandt). See also, Communications Alliance Ltd, Submission No 87 to Parliamentary Joint Committee on Intelligence and Security, *Review of the Telecommunications and Other Legislation (Assistance and Access) Bill 2018*, concerning the specific agencies (including state agencies and local councils) that had made requests for metadata.

12. Commonwealth, *Parliamentary Debates*, House of Representatives, 6 December 2018, 12777–12779 (Adam Bandt), 12792–12794 (Andrew Wilkie).

13. *Criminal Code Act 1995* (Cth) ss 122.4A(1)(c), (2)(c).

14. Ibid s 122.4A(1)(d)(i), (2)(d)(i).

15. Ibid s 122.4A(1)(d)(ii), (2)(d)(ii).

16. Ibid s 122.4A(1)(d)(iii), (2)(d)(iii).

17. Ibid s 122.4A(1)(d)(iv), (2)(d)(iv).

18. Ibid s 122.4A(1).

19. Ibid s 122.4A(2).

20. Ibid s 90.1(1)–(2).

21. Ibid s 122.4A(1)–(2).

22. Ibid s 122.5(6)–(7).

23. Ibid s 122.5(6).

24. Ibid s 122.5(6). A person will not have reasonably believed that dealing with the information was in the public interest if the conduct was for the purpose of directly or indirectly assisting a foreign intelligence agency or military organisation: s 122.5(7).

25. *Criminal Code Act 1995* (Cth) s 91.1.

26. *Criminal Code Act 1995* (Cth) s 91.1.

27. Ibid (Cth) s 90.4.

28. Three defenses are available to a charged espionage offense. However, these defenses fail to address the potential impact of the laws on press freedom: See Australian Lawyers for Human Rights, Submission No 7 to PJCIS, Parliament of Australia, *Review of the National Security Legislation Amendment (Espionage and Foreign Interference) Bill 2017*, January 22, 2018, 6; Whistleblowers Australia, Submission No 51 to PJCIS, Parliament of Australia, *Review of the National Security Legislation Amendment (Espionage and Foreign Interference) Bill 2017*, March 26, 2018, 3–4, 7; Human Rights Watch, Submission No 10 to PJCIS, Parliament of Australia, *Review of the National Security Legislation Amendment (Espionage and Foreign Interference) Bill 2017*, January 22, 2018; Parliamentary Joint Committee on Human Rights, Parliament of Australia, *Human Rights Scrutiny Report* (2018): 246–254.

REFERENCES

Ackland, Richard. 2015. "Data Retention: 'Journalist Information Warrants' are Warrants in Name Only." *The Guardian*, March 23, 2015. https://www.theguardian

.com/commentisfree/2015/mar/23/data-retention-journalist-information-warrants-are-warrants-in-name-only.

Ananian-Welsh, Rebecca. 2019. "Journalistic Confidentiality in an Age of Data Surveillance. *Australian Journalism Review* 41 (2): 225–239.

Australian Law Reform Commission. 2019. "The Future of Law Reform: A Suggested Program of Work 2020-25." Canberra: Australian Government. https://www.alrc.gov.au/wp-content/uploads/2019/11/Future-of-Law-Reform-Final-Report_v3web.pdf.

Blackbourn, Jessie, Nicola McGarrity, and Kent Roach. 2019. Understanding and Responding to Right Wing Terrorism. *Journal of Policing, Intelligence and Counter-terrorism* 14 (3): 183–190.

Brevini, Benedetta. 2017. "Metadata Laws, Journalism and Resistance in Australia." *Media and Communication* 5 (1): 76–83.

Devine, Miranda. 2019. "AFP Raids had Nothing to Do with National Security." *The Daily Telegraph*, June 25, 2019. https://www.dailytelegraph.com.au/rendezview/afp-raids-had-nothing-to-do-with-national-security/news-story/c1ba74dc07ed4ad04a610360cdf0905a.

Dobbie, Mike. 2015. "Data Retention and Your Journalism." https://www.meaa.org/news/data-retention-and-your-journalism/.

Karp, Paul. 2019. "Law Used to Justify Annika Smethurst Raid Unconstitutional, Her Lawyers Say." *The Guardian*, September 30, 2019. https://www.theguardian.com/media/2019/sep/30/law-used-to-justify-annika-smethurst-raid-unconstitutional-her-lawyers-say.

Keane, Bernard. 2019. "How Angry Men Use Power in Australia." *Crikey*, June 11, 2019. https://www.crikey.com.au/2019/06/11/how-angry-men-use-power-in-australia/.

Kendall, Sarah. 2019. "Australia's New Espionage Laws: Another Case of Hyper-legislation and Over-criminalisation." *The University of Queensland Law Journal* 38 (1): 125–161.

Koch, Tony. 2019. "Why the AFP Media Raids are Even More Sinister than Many Thought." *Sydney Morning Herald*, June 15, 2019. https://www.smh.com.au/national/why-the-afp-media-raids-are-even-more-sinister-than-many-thought-20190614-p51xoo.html.

Lynch, Andrew, Nicola McGarrity, and George Williams. 2015. *Inside Australia's Anti-terrorism Laws and Trials*. Sydney: NewSouth.

Lynch, Andrew, Tamara Tulich, and Rebecca Welsh. 2013. "Secrecy and Control Orders: The Role and Vulnerability of Constitutional Values in the United Kingdom and Australia." In *Secrecy, National Security and the Vindication of Constitutional Law*, edited by David Cole, Federico Fabbrini, and Arianna Vedaschi, 154–172. Cheltenham, UK and Northampton, MA, US: Edward Elgar Publishing.

Lyons, John. 2019. "I Live-tweeted the AFP's Every Move as They Raided the ABC's Sydney Headquarters." *ABC News*, June 10, 2019. https://www.abc.net.au/news/about/backstory/investigative-journalism/2019-06-08/federal-police-raid-abc-office-john-lyons-live-tweeting/11192898.

Martin, Sarah, and Kate Lyons. 2019. "Peter Dutton Denies Prior Knowledge of AFP Raids on ABC and News Corp." *The Guardian*, June 5, 2019. https://www.theguardian.com/australia-news/2019/jun/05/peter-dutton-denies-prior-knowledge-of-afp-raids-on-abc-and-news-corp.

McNamara, Lawrence. 2009. "Counter-terrorism Laws: How They Affect Media Freedom and News Reporting." *Westminster Papers in Communication & Culture* 6 (1), 27–44. http://doi.org/10.16997/wpcc.103.

Oakes, Dan, and Sam Clark. 2017. The Afghan Files. *ABC News*, July 11, 2017. https://www.abc.net.au/news/2017-07-11/killings-of-unarmed-afghans-by-australian-special-forces/8466642.

Parliament of Australia. 2019. "Press Freedom – Parliament of Australia." https://www.aph.gov.au/Parliamentary_Business/Committees/Senate/Environment_and_Communications/PressFreedom.

———. "Inquiry into the Impact of the Exercise of Law Enforcement and Intelligence Powers on the Freedom of the Press," May 1, 2020. https://www.aph.gov.au/Parliamentary_Business/Committees/Joint/Intelligence_and_Security/FreedomofthePress.

Pearson, Mark, & Joseph M. Fernandez. 2018. "Surveillance and National Security 'Hyper-legislation'—Calibrating Restraints on Rights with a Freedom of Expression Threshold. In *In the Name of Security—Secrecy, Surveillance and Journalism*, edited by Denis Muller and Johan Lidberg, 51–76. London: Anthem Press.

Ricketson, Matthew. 2018. "When One Person's Noble Whisterblower Becomes Another's Poisonous Leaker." In *In the Name of Security—Secrecy, Surveillance and Journalism*, edited by Denis Muller and Johan Lidberg, 101–120. London: Anthem Press.

Rix, M. (2013). "Security without Secrecy? Counter-terrorism, ASIO and Access to Information." In *Spooked: The Truth about Intelligence in Australia*, edited by Daniel Baldino, 240–263. Sydney: New South Publishing.

Sarre, Rick. 2017. "Metadata Retention as a Means of Combatting Terrorism and Organised Crime: A Perspective from Australia." *Asian Criminology* 12: 167–179.

Williams, George. 2011. "A Decade of Australian Anti-terror Laws." *Melb. UL Rev.* 35 (3): 1136–1176.

———. 2013. "The Legal Legacy of the War on Terror." *Macquarie LJ* 12: 3–16.

Chapter 10

Anti-terrorism Regulation and Journalism Practice in Uganda

Florence Namasinga Selnes

INTRODUCTION

This chapter examines anti-terrorism regulation in Uganda and its implications for journalism practice in the East African country. It deals with how counter-terrorism legal frameworks affect journalists and media houses in the processes of gathering, reporting, and publishing news. The Anti-terrorism Act (2002) and the Anti-terrorism Act of 2015 and 2017 (amendments) make it a crime punishable by death upon conviction for abetting terrorism. The threat of terrorism in Uganda has opened the door to illegal detention, torture, and the targeting of political opponents. The counter-terrorism law also makes publishing and disseminating information that promotes terrorism a criminal offense. Therefore, in addition to a plethora of other media regulations, the anti-terror legislation has consequences for media freedom, freedom of expression, and journalism practice.

In this chapter, I interrogate the implications of the anti-terrorism regulation from journalists' point of view and address the following two questions: How does the anti-terrorism law affect journalism in Uganda? How do journalists perceive counter-terrorism laws in relation to their profession? These questions are addressed through document analysis of Uganda's counter-terrorism regulation and interviews with a purposively selected sample of practicing journalists. The deliberations of this research will contribute to global debates about anti-terror legal frameworks and their implications on individual and institutional freedoms. The chapter is organized as follows. After the introductory section, I will give a brief account of Uganda's media landscape and an overview of the regulations that relate to journalism and the media. Then, I will discuss the anti-terrorism regulation, specifically focusing on sections that relate to journalism. Next, I will discuss theoretical perspectives that underpin the study followed by an explanation of methodological procedures. Finally, I present the key findings of the study, analyses, and inferences of the findings before I offer my concluding remarks in the last two sections.

UGANDA: THE POLITICAL CONTEXT

Uganda experienced a lot of upheaval under different political regimes after gaining independence from the British in 1962 (Mutiibwa 1992 cited in Mwesige 2004, 4). The East African nation went through political and economic instability until Yoweri Museveni assumed power in 1986. Museveni, who has ruled over the country for over thirty years, is credited for bringing relative political and economic stability. International development agencies portray Uganda under Museveni as a success story due to gains in the provision of social services, sustained growth, sociopolitical stability, and relatively good governance (United Nations Development Program [UNDP] 2013).

Despite the improvements, Uganda with a population of over 40 million people is still ranked among the poorest countries in the world (Tasch 2016). Today, the country is regarded as neither democratic nor purely authoritarian. This is because the country is characterized by features such as some level of political competition after the lifting of a ban on political parties in 2005, presidential and parliamentary elections, and the operation of privately owned media (Tripp 2010). At the same time, the country exhibits authoritarian traits which include restriction of political competition in addition to abuse of civil liberties (Joseph 2011). Furthermore, security agencies use excessive force against opposition politicians and those who express alternative views or question government policies. There are reports of imprisonment, torture, and sometimes killing of political opponents, electoral fraud, and gagging of the media (Tangri and Mwenda 2010). Thus, Uganda fits Diamond's (2002) definition of a semi-democratic state in a sense that, despite freedoms guaranteed in the constitution, civil liberties are suppressed. Moreover, the holding of periodic elections does not necessarily mean that they are free because their fairness is often compromised to the extent that electoral outcomes, while competitive, deviate from popular preferences. Civil and political liberties are limited as some opposing political voices cannot organize public rallies or even appear on certain radio stations (Perrot, Makara, Lafargue, and Fouere 2014).

In 2017, the ruling party voted to amend Article 102(b) of the constitution and scrapped the constitutional presidential age limit provision. Subsequently, they succeeded in eliminating the presidential age limit to give Museveni leeway to continue contesting in elections (Reuss and Titeca 2017).

Article 102(b) of the constitution put the age limit of the president at seventy-five years, which means that Museveni would be ineligible to contest in 2021 when Uganda is expected to hold the next presidential elections since he will be seventy-seven. The legal and parliament affairs committee (dominated by National Resistance Movement [NRM] members of parliament [MPs]) voted for the anti-age limit bill and extended elective office to seven years.[1] These constitutional amendments constitute a plan to enable Museveni to contest for a sixth term or remain in power for life (Daily Monitor 2017). Earlier in 2005, the same government used patronage, political maneuvering, and bribery to get MPs to support the lifting of presidential term limits[2] so that Museveni can contest in future elections. As the government pushes for constitutional changes, there is increased impunity, intolerance, and brutality orchestrated by security forces. As a result, MPs, politicians, and activists opposing constitutional changes were arrested and tortured (Biryabarema and Akena 2017; Eyotaru and Namuloki 2017; Sserunjogi 2017; The Observer 2017).

THE UGANDAN MEDIA LANDSCAPE

The media is one of the sectors that expanded rapidly in the past thirty years after the government liberalized both print and broadcast sectors to give way for private players. At the same time, independent journalism has expanded and plays a significant role in informing and educating citizens in addition to setting the agenda for public discussion.

Article 29(1a) of the constitution of Uganda guarantees freedoms of expression and of the media as well as the rights of information and assembly. However, in practice, this constitutionally guaranteed freedom is restricted due to widespread concerns about censorship as the government targets critical voices through legislation, prosecution, and persecution of journalists. For example, proposed amendments to the Press and Journalist Act of 1995 require print media to be registered annually and be licensed by the statutory Media Council. It gives the Council power to revoke a license in case of breach of licensing conditions and the power to close a newspaper if it publishes content that endangers national security (Biryabarema 2010). Additionally, the Uganda Communications Commission (UCC), the regulator of broadcast media, lacks independence from the appointing authority as its licensing procedures are arbitrary and susceptible to manipulation and influence by the appointing authority (African Media Barometer [AMB] 2012; Freedom House 2016). Several privately owned radio stations have had their licenses suspended under this law and some have been forced into self-censorship once they reopened to avoid renewed conflict with authorities. The broadcasting regulator has also issued warnings to television stations, and, in some cases, directed them to stop hosting commentators deemed to be flouting the law. For example, in October 2016, the UCC ordered NTV-Uganda to stop featuring views of a renowned government critic or risk having its license revoked (Anena 2016). Earlier, the regulator had warned nine news organizations, directing them to stop hosting another controversial media commentator (Ibid).

There are other laws in Uganda that impact journalism practice. For example, the Public Order Management Act of 2013 stipulates that any meeting of three or more people may require police authorization. Such meetings range from private gatherings to social or work-related seminars such as press conferences (Gwayaka 2011). The law, branded by Amnesty International (2011) as a serious blow to open political debate, gives the police discretionary powers to veto and break up meetings and gatherings of as few as three people discussing political issues in public spaces (BBC 2013). The meeting could be a press conference, thereby having a bearing on journalists' work regarding access to sources and reporting issues such as activities of opposition politicians. It limits media practitioners' roles of seeking, receiving, and imparting information as it imposes indirect limitations to attending and reporting proceedings of outlawed meetings (BBC 2013). Several journalists have been injured and had their equipment destroyed at such meetings. It is under these circumstances that the anti-terrorism law puts additional weight on existing legal frameworks that already imposed restrictions on the media and journalism practice.

TERRORISM IN UGANDA

Uganda, like neighboring Kenya and a few other countries in Africa, is vulnerable to terror threats and attacks. In addition to security threats posed by rebel groups such as the Lord's Resistance Army (LRA)[3] and the Allied Democratic Forces (ADF),[4] the country has experienced terror attacks. The most pronounced ones include two suicide bombings that occurred on July 10, 2010, in Kampala—Uganda's capital. The attacks, which were carried out by Al-Shabaab, a terrorist organization based in Somalia, killed about seventy-four people and left over seventy injured (Aljazeera 2010). Reports indicated that Al-Shabaab carried out the attacks to punish Uganda for sending peace-keeping troops to Somalia. Another attack occurred in July 2014 when gunmen attacked and killed civilians, military officers, and policemen in south western Uganda (AFP 2014). Such incidents gave the government ground to pass legislation to curb terrorism and to prosecute suspected terrorists. For example, some of the suspects of the 2010 terror attacks have since been sentenced to life in prison while several others are awaiting trial (BBC 2016).

UGANDA'S ANTI-TERRORISM LAW

The growing threat of terrorism around the world has prompted many countries, including Uganda, to enact regulation to fight the vice. Passed in 2002, the Ugandan anti-terrorism law had, as of June 2020, been amended twice, bringing into being, the Anti-Terrorism (Amendment) Act 2015 and the Anti-Terrorism (Amendment) Act 2017. Section 7(1a) of the Anti-terrorism Act 2002 states that a person who "engages in or carries out any act of terrorism commits an offence and shall, on conviction be sentenced to death if the offence directly results in the death of any person" (Anti-terrorism Act 2002, 5). Initially, the law regarded a terrorist as a person who, indiscriminately and without due regard to the safety of others or property, carries out terror activities for purposes of influencing the government or intimidating the public . . . for a political, religious, social, or economic aim (Section 2 Anti-terrorism Act 2002, 6). The amendments to the law have expanded the activities that fall within the definition of terrorism. Thus, the Act defines a terrorist as a person who:

> carries out or perpetrates any act, whether occurring in Uganda or elsewhere, that constitutes a crime in accordance with agreements, protocols and treaties described in the annex to the International Convention for the Suppression of the Financing of Terrorism, 1999; or travels outside Uganda for the purpose of the perpetration, planning, or preparation of, or participation in terrorist acts or the providing or receiving of terrorist training. (Anti-terrorism [Amendment] Act 2017, 1)

The Anti-terrorism Act under Section 10 gives the Minister of Internal Affairs authority to designate anyone a terrorist suspect if they have "reasonable grounds to suspect" that person is engaged in certain activities, including membership in a terrorist organization or commission of a terrorist act (Anti-Terrorism [Amendment] Act 2017).[5] Additionally, the law criminalizes contribution to or collection of funds in any context with the knowledge that it will be used by a terrorist person or organization for the purpose of committing a terrorist act. It also sanctions expeditious freezing, seizure, and forfeiture of assets and property that is suspected to be linked to terrorist activities. According to Section 8 (Anti-terrorism Act 2002, 7):

> Any person who aids or abets or finances or harbors, or renders support to any person, knowing or having reason to believe that the support will be applied or used for or in connection with the preparation or commission or instigation of acts of terrorism, commits an offense and shall, on conviction, be liable to suffer death.

In direct relation to media operations and journalism practice, the anti-terror regulation makes it an offense to publish any information that could be connected to terrorism. Particularly, Section 9 states:

> anyone who establishes, runs or supports any institution for . . . publishing and disseminating news or materials that promote terrorism; or any person who, without establishing or running an institution for the purpose, trains any person for carrying out terrorism, publishes or disseminates materials that promote terrorism, commits an offence and shall be liable on conviction, to suffer death. (Anti-terrorism Act 2002, 7)

Moreover, sections 18 and 19 of the Act empower the state to intercept communication including letters, postal packages, telephone calls, and emails and all forms of communication involving any person, electronic surveillance of any person, monitoring meetings of any groups of persons, and searching of premises of any person.

Legislation on terror is justifiable due to the increasing threat of terrorism and the rise of terror activities all over the world (Okurut 2017). The rise of terrorist organizations such as Al-Shabaab and Boko Haram has made it permissible for African governments to step up efforts to fight against terrorism. For example, the twin bombings in Kampala in 2010 were reportedly masterminded by Al-Shabaab, a Somali-based terror organization (Al Jazeera 2010).

Under the anti-terrorism law, the government established various entities such as the Uganda Police Directorate of Counter Terrorism, the Counter Terrorism Police Unit, and the Joint Anti-Terrorism Taskforce. The law gives discretionary powers to these security agencies to counter-terrorism. While these organizations have registered several successful missions, including foiling terror plots, and arresting several suspects (Masaba 2017; Okurut 2017, 75), they are criticized for arbitrary arrests, illegal detention, and torture of subjects (Human Rights Watch 2011; Kiyonga and Lubwama 2017). The war on terrorism in Uganda has also opened the door to the practice of targeting political opponents (Gumede 2019). Critics and human rights organizations argue that governments use anti-terrorism regulation to silence critical voices and infringe on the right of access to information and freedom of expression. Whereas the fight against terrorism and enactment of legislation rests upon a valid cause, counter-terrorism laws have been used across Africa to target opponents of the ruling elite (Gumede 2019; New Vision 2001). Okurut (2017), for instance, observes that agencies charged with curbing terrorism do so in a manner that disregards human and civil rights and the rule of law.

In addition to being used to target opponents, the anti-terrorism law has a direct bearing on journalism as it criminalizes the publication and dissemination of material or news that promotes terrorism. Moreover, the Act further stipulates that journalists' material can be subjected to terrorism investigations and journalists can be charged and prosecuted under the law. This has implications for journalism practice, especially in relation to the ideals of confidentiality and fortification of sources. These sections potentially restrict freedom of expression, including journalists who attempt to contact any person that the government labels a "terrorist." Subsequently, the government uses the law to restrain journalists regarding what they cover and whom they interview as sources. Contravention of the law carries a mandatory death sentence.

The government's actions toward journalists and the media through laws such as the Anti-terrorism Act can be better understood and explained by the sociology of journalism theory. This is specifically because this theory provides a framework that appropriately demonstrates the relationship between journalism, on the one hand, and the political context within which it is practiced, on the other. Laws developed by politicians positively and negatively affect how media organizations and journalists operate.

THE SOCIOLOGY OF JOURNALISM

According to the sociology of journalism theory, journalism is determined by interactions between journalists and other actors that include sources, audiences as well as broader political and economic context. As McNair (1998) and Schudson (2003) observe, journalism does not exist in a vacuum but is influenced by factors such as organizational pressures on journalists and the politico-economic context within which media operate. According to the sociology of journalism thesis, journalism is influenced by factors such as political pressures, professional requirements, source tactics and strategies, technological possibilities, and constraints as well as economic pressures (McNair 1998, 14). This means that journalistic work is a result of traditions, economic factors, political constraints, technological developments, and social dynamics of the culture within which news media exist (Avilés and León 2002, 356). As this chapter is concerned with how anti-terrorism regulation impacts journalism practice, the theoretical propositions of sociology of journalism offer useful insights. The political context in which laws and regulations are formulated and enforced is of particular relevance to this chapter.

The political environment is a frame within which parameters of journalistic activity are drawn, and, as McNair (1998, 83) argues, "journalists are not free agents." They work in a political context comprising regulations that can either facilitate or constrain their work. Laws can restrict or promote media freedoms, freedoms of expression and assembly, and freedom of access to information. In political systems characterized by the suppression of dissenting views and control of the media using regulation and state organs, news media are subjected to direct and indirect censorship. Journalistic work is restricted as reportage perceived to be critical is met with intimidation or arrest.

McNair's description of political pressure as a determinant of journalism is consistent with the literature on journalism in semi-democratic settings. Governments in such contexts employ anti-democratic tactics against journalists in their quest to preserve political control. As such, journalists must surmount multiple draconian laws, which politicians often justify on the grounds of strengthening national security, fighting terrorism, and preserving national unity. Although expressive rights are constitutionally guaranteed in many countries in Sub-Saharan Africa, these rights are limited by regulations such as sedition, criminal defamation, publication of false news, official secrets laws, public-order-related laws, and the laws on terrorism. Some of these laws restrict who may work as a journalist and limit what can be published. As pointed out earlier, laws such as the Press and Journalist Act 2014, the UCC Act 2014, the Public Order Management Act 2013, the Computer Misuse Act, the Interception of Communication Act 2010, and Anti-terrorism Act 2002 have a deterring effect on journalism. The laws give security forces powers to use excessive force that, for example, can amount to breaking into premises of suspects which often leads to assault. Because journalists and the media are among those targeted and intimidated under such laws, they often engage in self-censorship in anticipatory obedience. As Peter G. Mwesige, the director of the African Center for Media Excellence (ACME), an organization that supports journalists in Uganda, argues, laws such as the Anti-terrorism Act infringe on the right of journalists to express themselves and the rights of citizens to access information (Natabaalo 2016).

METHODOLOGY

To examine how Uganda's anti-terror regulation affects journalism practice, I relied on document analysis of news stories and reports related to journalists, the media, and the anti-terrorism legislation. In addition, I reviewed legal documents relating to the anti-terrorism law, the Regulation of Interception of Communication Act and the Computer Misuse Act as well as reports by media development organizations such as the Human Rights Network for Journalists in Uganda (HRNJ-U) and the Collaboration on International ICT Policy in East and Southern Africa (CIPESA). These documents are publicly available online. Additional data were generated through interviews involving journalists with the aim of obtaining their views about the perceived effect of the anti-terrorism law on their work. A total of fourteen journalists were interviewed. The journalists were selected using purposive sampling. I selected journalists who were knowledgeable and had directly and indirectly been affected by the legislation in question. The data were collected between October 2019 and June 2020. The interviewees were drawn from both broadcast and print media. I will present the findings in the next section and provide examples generated from document analysis and interviews to illustrate the implications of the anti-terrorism law on journalism in Uganda. For ethical and safety reasons, all the respondents are anonymized in the text.

THE IMPACT OF THE ANTI-TERRORISM LAW ON JOURNALISM IN UGANDA

This section presents the findings related to how the anti-terrorism legislation affects journalists and media organizations in Uganda. The findings are presented and discussed in accordance with themes that I developed from the analysis. The major themes addressed in this section are: raiding and searching of premises; detention and criminal charges; and interception of communication, monitoring, and surveillance of journalists. I combine cases in which media organizations and individual journalists were affected by the anti-terror legislation and draw on journalists' views to illustrate how the law impedes journalism.

Raiding and Searching of Premises

As indicated earlier, Section 9 of the Anti-terrorism Act 2002 gives security agencies the power to search the premises of anyone. As such, journalists and media organizations have had their premises raided, broken into, and closed off by security agencies as the examples outlined below indicate. Journalist John Njoroge and his family woke up one night in 2008 to deafening noise in their home in Kampala. The noise was from the smashing glass of windows instigated by military officers who broke into their house in search of documents related to a story the journalist had been pursuing (DW 2017). The story, about the conduct of Uganda's intelligence forces, had been published in *The Independent*—a fortnight magazine. A couple of days later, the military raided the premises of *The Independent* and confiscated computers, CDs, and all gadgets that were suspected of containing the documents they were looking for. Njoroge and the magazine's publisher and editor were arrested and later charged (Kwera 2008). This case is significant because, although journalists were charged with sedition, the search of their premises was conducted based on the Anti-terrorism Act of 2002. While the journalists in this case were charged with sedition, the act of searching premises is provided under the anti-terror legislation. This shows an overlap in the law's interpretation. It demonstrates that the government can apply any existing laws to penalize perceived offenders who may include journalists and media houses.

In another case, security agencies raided and cordoned off two media houses: Monitor Publications Limited and Red Pepper Publications Limited in May 2013 (Committee to Protect Journalists 2013; Natabaalo 2013). The premises of the two media houses were declared a crime scene and remained occupied by security forces for eleven days. The security agents were searching for a letter authored by Uganda's former chief spy David Sejusa. In the letter, Sejusa made several allegations including a plan to have President Museveni's son, Muhoozi Kainerugaba, succeeding his father in what came to be known as "the Muhoozi project" and a plot to assassinate senior army commanders (Arinaitwe 2013). *Daily Monitor*, the main privately owned daily newspaper and *Red Pepper*, a tabloid magazine, were out of circulation for close to two weeks. Two radio stations, *Dembe FM* and *KFM*, which are linked to *Daily Monitor*, were also shut down.

The raid and subsequent closure alarmed the entire media fraternity countrywide. The most obvious impact of a two-week closure of the media house was business related as media houses lost revenue from both circulation and advertising during the period of shutdown. This is a common tactic deployed by the government of Uganda that evokes a plethora of laws to target independent media whose coverage is deemed unfriendly (Bichachi 2013; Rukuuka 2012; Tabaire 2007). *Daily Monitor* in particular has borne the brunt of government wrath as the newspaper fought legal battles in which its journalists were charged with defamation, sedition, and publishing false news in addition to suffering an advertising ban. For example, its founders faced enormous pressure barely a year in existence when the government stopped all its departments from advertising with the young newspaper in 1993 due to the latter's perceived support of the opposition (Balikoowa 1995). This threatened to destroy the newspaper before it could find its footing. Legal battles, coupled with the arrest and intimidation of its journalists as well as continued police raids resulting in temporary shutdown, not only dented the company's financial base but also negatively affected the way journalists do their work. This is highlighted by several journalists who were interviewed in this chapter. For instance, in particular reference to the 2013 shutdown of *Daily Monitor*, one journalist explained that the incident had "a chilling effect on editors and young journalists whose free-spirited effort to live the ideals of independent journalism was greatly damaged. Some have since left the practice" (personal communication, June 9, 2020). The anti-terrorism regulation is one of the laws used by the state to target media organizations and journalists. A respondent, for example, pointed out that the government sealed off and searched the premises of the media organization he worked for and subsequently declared it a crime scene under Section 19(5g) of the anti-terrorism law.

In addition to broad-daylight raids, some media houses have experienced covert break-ins disguised as burglary. For example, *The Observer*, another independent newspaper, lost almost all its desktop computers, laptops, cameras, hard drives, and its computer server in April 2017 (The Independent 2017). While it has never been established who was behind the burglary, the then managing editor, Richard M. Kavuma, was quoted saying that the thieves were probably looking to destroy evidence that might have incriminated those who wished to control it (The Independent 2017). This implied that the burglary could be related to stories the newspaper had been investigating. It should be noted that the media organization had suffered a similar break-in barely six months earlier in October 2016. While police investigations have not, as of June 2020, come up with a report to show who was behind the burglary or that there was no direct linkage to terrorism, it is implied that provisions in the law embolden anyone to commit such offenses against journalists.

Detention and Criminal Charges

As journalists faced arrest and media organizations cordoned off under the anti-terrorism law as demonstrated earlier, #JournalismIsNotaCrime trended widely on social media in November 2016. The hashtag was a Twitter campaign that sought the dropping of terrorism charges against journalist Joy Doreen Biira. The journalist was detained and charged with abetting terrorism after she shared information about clashes between the military and guards of a traditional monarch (Natabaalo 2016; The East African 2016b). Biira was particularly accused of circulating a video, Facebook post, and tweets with graphic images of the aftermath of a battle between security forces and the royal guard of the king of the Rwenzururu Kingdom, a traditional monarch in the Rwenzori region of western Uganda (CPJ 2016, Natabaalo 2016). The journalist was indicted for illegally filming activities of the military (Natabaalo, 2016), which the state equated to abetting terrorism. Local media reported that sixty-two people died during the battle (The East African 2016a). Several individuals and organizations reacted to Biira's detention and condemned the anti-terrorism law because abetting terrorism is a criminal offense in which the offender may face up to seven years in prison upon conviction. For example, the Committee to Protect Journalists observed in a statement on the case that journalism is not terrorism. The organization further noted: "It is bad enough that Ugandan authorities desired to censor coverage of a newsworthy event, but the use of anti-terrorism laws to intimidate a journalist is a vast overreach. . . . The state's charges against Joy Doreen Biira should be dropped without delay" (Committee to Protect Journalists 2016). Additionally, ACME's director Peter G. Mwesige, a former journalist himself, said: "It's a tragedy that they still have laws that equate telling the story about violence or insecurity or conflict to terrorism. . . . It is really absurd that a journalist can be arrested, detained and charged simply for relaying images of what is going on, unwelcome as it is" (Natabaalo 2016). At the time of writing in June 2020, it was still not clear what became of Biira's charges.

In another case, Augustine Okello, a radio journalist based in northern Uganda, went missing in early July 2011 after meeting a security official. It was established toward the end of that month that the journalist was under arrest over terrorism-related acts (HRW 2011). He was not charged for over two weeks and his whereabouts were concealed. The journalist was later produced in court and charged with treason, an offense punishable by death (Reporters Without Borders 2011). While the government dropped the charges against Okello (HRNJ-U 2018), the journalist battled a likely death sentence for seven years. Okello summarized the impact of the criminal charges as follows:

> A lot of resources were wasted, time, money and the psychological torture that I have gone through. It is a big load that has brought me down for seven years. I need to wake up and begin a new life now. If it wasn't this, I would be very far in my career. (HRNJ-U 2018)

From Okello's quote above, it is implied that charges labeled against him prevented him from doing his work and from progressing as a journalist. Criminal charges of that nature followed by long court appearances drain victims physically, psychologically, and financially. The bigger effect of such charges is that several journalists in Uganda have quit the profession for safer occupations. As noted elsewhere, news organizations such as Monitor Publications Limited (the publisher of *Daily Monitor*) have in the past ten years lost experienced journalists to other professions partly for safety reasons (Namasinga 2018). Between 2012 and 2016 alone, the media organization lost about ten senior journalists (Oluka 2016). Such departures have long-term implications for the development of the journalism profession.

Findings from the interviews further revealed that security officers use legal frameworks such as the anti-terrorism laws to threaten journalists to prevent them from covering opposition politicians. For example, a respondent explained in an interview: "I have never been directly affected by the law but when Bobi Wine returned from the Arua fracas, I was put in a car for two hours [by the security agents] with my camera person telling us that what we were doing was facilitating terrorism" (personal communication, January 15, 2020). Bobi Wine, also known as Robert Kyagulanyi Sentamu, is a member of parliament who became popular through music. He is highly critical of the current government establishment and surprised the ruling party when he won the parliamentary election in a landslide victory. The fracas referred to by the interviewee occurred in 2018 when riots broke out in Kampala, as supporters of Bobi Wine demanded his release (BBC 2018). While Bobi Wine was arrested and charged with treason, the journalist was not put in prison but only held for two hours. He was threatened and prevented from covering the riots. Although the journalist stated that he had never been affected by the anti-terrorism law, he noted: "Look, we were rounded up and the guy [security agent] had the right to do anything and perhaps no one would even know about our whereabouts." Being accused of abetting terrorism would frighten anyone in Uganda who knows what becomes of terror suspects. As another interviewee opined, the anti-terrorism regulation is applied as a tool to silence journalists. The inherent danger of the law to freedom of the media is self-censorship. The interviewee narrated his experience:

> I got an anonymous call from someone who wanted me to interview a suspected terrorist [Jamil Mukulu].[6] Obviously getting an interview with [Mukulu] sounded like a big [career] breakthrough. I had to make up my mind right away on whether I would conduct the interview or not . . . I contacted my supervisor and we weighed in on the possible implications. Upon my supervisor's advice I asked the anonymous caller for more time. The caller immediately retracted the interview. . . . Obviously, I did not know whether the caller was Mukulu's emissary or a set up by the state. (personal communication, June 1, 2020)

The above narrative can be looked at in two different ways. One is that the journalist missed an opportunity to get an exclusive interview with one of the most wanted suspected terrorists; and two, that a journalist survived being trapped and caught on the wrong side of the anti-terrorism law. Either way, the journalist will spend the rest of his life wondering whether he missed a once-in-a-lifetime opportunity or survived an orchestrated plan in which he would be implicated under the law.

Furthermore, the findings showed that the anti-terrorism law curtails investigative reportage because it makes it a criminal offense to meet with or have contact with suspected terrorists (Anti-terrorism Act 2002). According to one respondent, this provision affects investigative and balanced reporting for lack of opportunity to interview suspected terrorists. The journalist added: "This leaves me with only one option of relying on information provided by prosecutors and security which sometimes may turn out to be cooked up to achieve their goals" (personal communication, June 5, 2020). Just like the journalist who explained how he could not interview a suspected terrorist, this current excerpt points to how the law on terrorism hamstrings journalists and media organizations in regard to communication with certain sources.

Generally, journalists regard the anti-terrorism law as a legislation that curtails their work. As one interviewee noted: "How the law has been applied invites a sense of fear among journalists and media organizations whenever they think of touching sensitive security matters" (personal communication, January 22, 2020). This sentiment is also echoed by the interviewee who was temporarily detained as he covered unrest in which supporters of opposition politician Bobi Wine demonstrated against his apprehension. The journalist said that he lost interest in covering such stories that have the potential to expose him to detention and harassment. In another interview, a respondent said, "if a journalist writes a story that is interpreted as promoting terrorism, the law gives the police the leeway to arrest you." He further noted: "The result then, is that journalists censure themselves and write one-sided stories that never give a voice to the other party that has been labelled a terrorist or terror organization" (personal communication, January 25, 2020). What the respondent's view points to is that cases of harassment of journalists and the sheer existence of sections that threaten journalism in the Anti-terrorism Act induce some journalists into censorship. As one journalist noted: "I have on several occasions been shielded by security personnel not to talk to suspected terrorists facing trial. This leaves me in a panicky mood and instills fear in me that affects quality of my work" (personal communication, June 13, 2020). All in all, journalists who were interviewed perceived the anti-terrorism law as suppressive and as a weapon deployed to clamp down government opponents and the media that highlight the wrongdoings of those in power.

Interception of Communication, Surveillance, and Monitoring

Part VII of the anti-terrorism Act of 2002 provides for interception of communications and surveillance. Section 19(1) of the Act authorizes the government to intercept communications and conduct surveillance on people to track down suspected terrorist activities. Related to this section (in the anti-terror regulation) is the Interception of Communication Act of 2010 (amended in 2012). This legislation also provides for lawful interception and monitoring of certain communications during their transmission through a telecommunication, postal, or any other related service or system in Uganda (see Regulation of Interception of Communication Act 2010). The implication of this law is that journalists and news organizations are susceptible to online and offline surveillance and monitoring by government agents. The government justifies surveillance out of fear of ICTs being used in planning, coordinating, and executing terrorism activities (see Mair 2016). Moreover, the sections on surveillance in anti-terrorism and national protection laws infringe upon journalism practice, especially the ethical requirement to protect sources as a way of guaranteeing quality journalism (Posetti 2017). The Anti-terrorism Act of 2002 criminalizes being in possession of information or contacts of individuals or organizations the state considers as terrorists. Additionally, the law imposes a blackout concerning gazetted terrorists and how their activities may affect the public. Although the Data Protection and Privacy Act (2015) regulates the collection and processing of data, the law is rendered useless by the Interception of Communications Act (2012) that allows the government to monitor electronic communication and to censor all forms of communications. The government invokes all these laws to justify monitoring and surveillance as well as prosecuting private individuals and journalists.

The Computer Misuse Act of 2011 is another law related to interception of communication and anti-terror legislation. It was enacted to prevent illegal access and use of electronic systems such as the Internet, computers, and mobile phones. Several people have been prosecuted under this law since its enactment. For example, former Makerere University research-fellow-turned-activist Stella Nyanzi was sentenced under Section 25 of this law in August 2019 for offending the president through her Facebook posts (The Independent 2019). Nyanzi had been in jail since November 2018. Television journalist Gertrude Tumusiime Uwitware was abducted and assaulted in April 2017 for publishing an article on her blog in which she supported a political cause that was perceived as negative by the regime (Committee to Protect Journalists 2017). Uwitware's posts were related to a campaign for collecting sanitary towels in Kampala. She later quit her job.

In Uganda, opponents of the ruling government can easily be arrested and charged with terrorism. Such cases mean the anti-terror law can be used to settle political scores. However, because the law already hamstrings journalists and media houses, the latter often cannot call out the government over some of its excesses in the use of that law. This argument echoes sentiments that laws such as the Anti-terrorism Act target opposition politicians and anyone who criticizes the ruling government (New Vision 2001). The critics of the government could be politicians, journalists or media organizations that report what is regarded as negative coverage. This is consistent with Gumede (2019) who argues that African leaders use anti-terrorism laws to silence journalists and restrict access to information. He further notes: "Criticizing leaders and governments, questioning human rights violations by the state and reporting critically on state violence against citizens are portrayed as encouraging or participating in terrorism." Gumede's observation is not far from the views of Uganda journalists cited in this chapter. The case of Joy Doreen Biira that was cited earlier in this section is a good example of how the government treats journalists who report state violations against citizens.

CONCLUDING REMARKS

In addition to offering insights on how security legislation impedes freedom of expression and journalism practice, this study has some theoretical implications as well. More specifically, the sociology of journalism framework underscores the role of political institutions and actors in conditioning journalism practice and determining how media organizations conduct their business. The analysis of the findings showed that the Anti-terrorism Act contains sections that constrain journalists, media organizations, and their potential sources. Journalists regard the legislation as limiting them from freely gathering, sourcing information, and publishing news that may be perceived as connected to terrorism or promoting it. Furthermore, it controls journalists' interaction with certain sources that the government may at any time label as suspected terrorists. Whether the enactment of anti-terror was intended to genuinely fight terrorism or to target government opponents is beyond the scope of this chapter. But as the findings in the preceding sections demonstrate, the law has a deterring effect on journalism practice. The findings are therefore in tandem with the sociology of journalism notion that journalism is a result of interactions between journalists, media organizations, and the wider context within which journalism is practiced (McNair 1998; Schudson 2003). Furthermore, the findings confirm that the political environment is a frame within which parameters of journalistic activity are drawn, and, as McNair (1998, 83) argued, "journalists are not free agents." They work in a political context comprising laws and regulations that can either facilitate or constrain their work. In political systems such as Uganda's that are characterized by the suppression of dissenting views, news media are subjected to direct and indirect censorship through numerous laws. In the context of this chapter, the analysis indicated that anti-terror regulation limits journalism practice. Thus, the chapter confirms the view that a journalist is "a cog in a wheel over whose speed and direction he/she may have little or no control" (McNair 1998, 62). Despite the passion and desire to execute their duties, journalists and media organizations must adhere to the laws, which sometimes lead to censorship and a hindrance to the profession.

Summing up, the findings obtained through document analysis and interviews with journalists showed that the anti-terrorism legislation grants government and security agencies the power to search premises and even confiscate the property of anyone suspected of involvement in terrorism. As a result of this, journalists and media organizations have lost property and equipment during such raids in addition to revenue. The most affected media houses include *Daily Monitor* and *The Observer*. This is because these news publications often publish stories that cast a negative light on the government. The government invokes laws such as the Anti-terrorism Act to censor journalists and prevent the media from reporting on cases of corruption and gross human rights violations. Second, the analysis indicates that journalists face arrest and prosecution on charges of facilitating terrorism for exposing inhumane actions by security agencies and the government. The examples of journalists who were detained and threatened with criminal charges related to terrorism highlight how government uses terrorism as an excuse to suppress independent coverage. Third, the analysis demonstrated that government invokes legislations such as interception of communication to penalize journalists and media organizations and journalists. The same offense is stipulated in the Anti-terrorism Act 2002. This implies that the government can arbitrarily choose which provisions of the different legislations it can charge its victims. The interception of communication is an independent act, but it has its roots and a direct connection to the anti-terror law. Since interception of communication is also introduced in Part VII of the Anti-Terrorism Act, the government invokes this regulation to monitor all forms of communication under the guise of preventing terrorism. This affects journalism, especially journalists' communication with their sources. As has been said of other draconian media laws in Uganda, the anti-terrorism regulation aims at suppressing critical journalism by giving government powers to arrest and detain anyone in relation to terrorism. The law criminalizes the publication of a material that is likely to promote terrorism. This provision suppresses critical journalism because it concerns journalist's work and creates uncertainty regarding the nature of stories that may be interpreted as promoting terrorism.

One of the main effects of the anti-terrorism law on journalism is self-censorship. Journalists and media organizations must choose between coverage of stories that may land them in jail on charges of terrorism. The anti-terrorism law is suppressive because it gives the government extrajudicial powers to imprison suspects without bail and carries a maximum death sentence. Reports of vicious treatment of terror suspects in Uganda scares anyone from being caught on the wrong side of the terrorism law.

In conclusion, the enactment of the anti-terrorism law and the attendant suppressive media legislation on journalists as outlined in the foregoing paragraphs is evidence of how politics plays a powerful role in determining journalism in Uganda. The political context within which journalism is practiced, including media legislation, can facilitate or constrict journalism. In political systems characterized by suppression of dissenting views and control of the media using regulation, news media are subjected to direct and indirect censorship. Journalistic work is restricted as reportage perceived to be critical is met with intimidation, arrest, and prosecution. If the real goal of the Anti-terrorism Act is to combat terrorism, the government and the state at large would benefit by giving media organizations freedom to investigate, report, and highlight issues related to the vice than suppressing them into fear. Therefore, journalists and media organizations ought to be treated as important allies in fighting terrorism and peace building because, when they are allowed to participate in this process, they inform and educate citizens about terrorism and give voice to marginalized sections of the populace. The government ought to repeal sections in the anti-terrorism law that criminalizes the production and dissemination of material related to covering terrorism issues. More importantly, the government should remove any ambiguities in the law that limit media organizations from freely doing their work.

NOTES

1. There is a push to amend Article 105(1). The constitution provides that a person can hold elective office for five years. But this article is entrenched and cannot therefore be amended unless through a referendum.
2. There is a proposal to reintroduce term limits in the constitution.
3. The LRA began operating in Uganda in 1989 under the leadership of Joseph Kony. The rebel group destabilized the northern part of the country, southern Sudan, and the eastern region of the Democratic Republic of Congo. See GlobalSecurity.org (n.d.).
4. The rebel group started operations in 1995 in the mountainous border areas of Uganda and DR-Congo. See United Nations Security Council (n.d.).
5. See Goitom (2017).
6. He is a suspected terrorist and leader of Allied Democratic Forces. He was captured and arrested in 2015 and was as of June 2020 still under trial on terrorism charges. See The Independent (2020).

REFERENCES

ACME. 2010. “Overview of the State of Media Freedom in Uganda: A Research Report. Accessed July 6, 2020. http://acme-ug.org/wp-content/uploads/Research-Report-on-State-of-Media-Freedom-in-Uganda.pdf.

AFP. 2014. "Uganda Fighting: Dozens Killed in Clashes between Tribal Militia and Security Forces.” Accessed June 21, 2020. https://www.cbc.ca/news/world/uganda-fighting-dozens-killed-in-clashes-between-tribal-militia-and-security-forces-1.2698007.

African Media Barometer. 2012. *The First Home Grown Analysis of the Media Landscape in Africa: Uganda 2012*. Windhoek, Namibia: Friedrich-Ebert-Stiftung.

Aljazeera. 2010. “Al-Shabab Claims Uganda Bombings.: July 13. Accessed June 21, 2020. https://www.aljazeera.com/news/africa/2010/07/2010711212520826984.html.

Amnesty International. 2011. "Stifling Dissent: Restrictions on the Rights to Freedom of Expression and Peaceful Assembly in Uganda." Accessed December 15, 2020. https://www.amnesty.org/en/documents/AFR59/016/2011/en/.

Anena, Harriet. 2016. "Regulator Warns NTV on Breach of Minimum Standards." *African Centre for Media Excellence*. October 28, 2016. https://acme-ug.org/2016/10/28/regulator-warns-ntv-on-breach-of-minimum-standards/.

Arinaitwe, Solomon. 2013. "NRM Historicals Split 'on Muhoozi Project.'" *Daily Monitor*, March 8, 2017. https://www.monitor.co.ug/News/National/NRM-historicals-split-on---Muhoozi-Project-/-/688334/1855602/-/6tvpjdz/-/index.html.

Avilés, Jose A. García, and Bienvenido León. 2002. "Journalistic Practice in Digital Television Newsrooms: The Case of Spain's Tele 5 and Antena 3." *Journalism* 3 (3): 355–371. https://doi.org/10.1177/146488490200300304.

Balikowa, David Ouma. 1995. "Media Marketing: An Essential Part of a Free Press for Africa." *Media, Culture & Society* 17 (4): 603–613.

BBC. 2013. "Uganda Public Order Bill Blow to 'Political Debate.'" Accessed May 27, 2014.http://www.bbc.com/news/world-africa-23587166.

———. 2016. "Uganda 2010 Bombing: Five Given Life in Jail." Accessed June 21, 2020. https://www.bbc.com/news/world-africa-36400842.

———. 2018. Uganda's Bobi Wine: Pop Star MP Charged with Treason. https://www.bbc.com/news/world-africa-45282125 accessed January 25, 2020.

Bichachi, Odoobo Charles. 2013. "The Dark History of Uganda's Media and Past Governments." *Daily Monitor*, June 2, 2013. Accessed September 26, 2016. https://www.monitor.co.ug/Magazines/PeoplePower/The-dark-history-of-Uganda-s-media-and-past-governments/-/689844/1869456/-/11sp5nj/-/index.html.

Biryabarema, Elias and James Akena. 2017. "Lawmakers Brawl in Uganda Parliament for Second Day over Presidential Age Limit." *Reuters*, Accessed September 27, 2017. https://www.reuters.com/article/us-uganda-politics/lawmakers-brawl-in-uganda-parliament-for-second-day-over-presidential-age-limit-idUSKCN1C21VI.

Biryabarema, Elias. 2010. "Ugandan Media Says Proposed Media Law Draconian." *Reuters*, March 16, 2010. Accessed November 30, 2016. https://www.reuters.com/article/ozatp-uganda-media-20100316-idAFJOE62F0CY20100316.

CPJ. 2013. "Monitor, Red Pepper Closures Spark Protests in Uganda." Accessed June 16, 2020. https://cpj.org/2013/05/monitor-red-pepper-closures-spark-protests-in-ugan/.

———. 2016. "Ugandan Journalist Joy Doreen Biira Charged with 'Abetting Terrorism.'" Accessed November 12, 2019. https://cpj.org/2016/11/ugandan-journalist-joy-doreen-biira-charged-with-a.php.

———. 2017. "Ugandan Journalist Abducted, Kidnapped." Accessed September 3, 2019. https://cpj.org/2017/04/ugandan-journalist-abducted-assaulted.php.

Constitution of the Republic of Uganda. Accessed December 14, 2020. http://www.statehouse.go.ug/sites/default/files/attachments/Constitution_1995.pdf.

Daily Monitor. 2017. "85 Percent Ugandans Oppose Age Limit Amendment." Accessed December 11, 2017. http://www.monitor.co.ug/News/National/85-percent-Ugandans-oppose-age-limit-amendment/688334-4221200-s7hjvsz/index.html.

Diamond, Larry. 2002. "Elections Without Democracy: Thinking About Hybrid Regimes." *Journal of Democracy* 13 (2): 21–35.

DW-Academie. 2017. Protecting Sources and Contacts: Five Digital Security Tips for Journalists." Accessed January 13, 2020. https://www.dw.com/en/protecting-sources-and-contacts-five-digital-security-tips-for-journalists/a-38988993.

The East African. 2016a. "Death Toll in Western Uganda Fighting Rises to 62." Accessed January 16, 2020. https://www.theeastafrican.co.ke/news/Death-toll-in-western-Uganda-fighting-rises/2558-3467588-6ufvkaz/index.html.

———. 2016b. "Journalist Joy Doreen Biira Arrested after Attack on Palace in Uganda." January 12, 2020. https://www.theeastafrican.co.ke/news/Journalist-Joy-Doreen-Biira-arrested-Kasese/2558-3468054-format-xhtml-1o52lu/index.html.

Eyotaru, Olive, and Josephine Namuloki. 2017. "Presidential Guards Take over Parliament, Arrest 27 MPs." *The Observer*, December 11, 2017. http://observer.ug/news/headlines/55138-presidential-guards-take-over-parliament-arrest-27-mps.html.

Freedom House. 2016. "Freedom in the World 2016: Anxious Dictators, Wavering Democracies: Global Freedom under Pressure." Accessed December 22, 2017. https://freedomhouse.org/report/freedom-world/freedom-world-2016.

GlobalSecurity.org. n.d. "Lord's Resistance Army (LRA)." Accessed December 13, 2020. https://www.globalsecurity.org/military/world/para/lra.htm.

Goitom, Hanibal. 2017. "Uganda: Parliament Passes Anti-Terrorism Amendment Bill." Accessed December 21, 2020. https://www.loc.gov/law/foreign-news/article/uganda-parliament-passes-anti-terrorism-amendment-bill.

Gumede, William. 2019. African Leaders Use Anti-terror Laws to Silence Journalists." Accessed January 16, 2020. https://mg.co.za/article/2019-09-25-00-african-leaders-use-anti-terror-laws-to-silence-journalists/.

Gwayaka, Magera Peter. 2011. "Uganda's Public Order Management Bill and What it Means for Media Freedom." *African Centre for Media Excellence*. Accessed December 19, 2016. https://acme-ug.org/2011/12/19/ugandas-public-order-management-bill-and-what-it-means-for-media-freedom/.

HRNJ-U. 2018. "State Withdraws Charges against a Lira-based Journalist after Five Years." Accessed December 14, 2020. https://www.hrnjuganda.org/state-withdraws-charges-against-a-lira-based-journalist-after-five-years/.

Human Rights Watch. 2011. "Uganda: Torture, Extortion, Killings by Police Unit." Accessed March 23, 2020. https://www.hrw.org/news/2011/03/23/uganda-torture-extortion-killings-police-unit.

The Independent. 2017. "Break-in at Ugandan Newspaper Deals Blow to Media." Accessed January 13, 2020. https://www.independent.co.ug/break-ugandan-newspaper-deals-blow-media/

———. 2019. "Dr Stella Nyanzi Jailed." Accessed January 14, 2020. https://www.independent.co.ug/dr-stella-nyanzi-jailed/.

———. 2020. "Former ADF Commander Jamil Mukulu Seeks Bail," May 28, 2020, sec. NEWS. https://www.independent.co.ug/former-adf-commander-jamil-mukulu-seeks-bail/.

Joseph, Richard. 2011. "Democracy and Reconfigured Power in Africa." *Current History* 110 (739): 324–330.

Kiyonga, Derrick, and Siraje Lubwama. 2015. "Witness Reveals JATT's Ugly Torture Methods." *The Observer,* June 29, 2015. Accessed February 2, 2020. https://www.observer.ug/news-/38490-witness--reveals-jatt-s-ugly-torture-methods.

Kwera, Francis. 2008. "Ugandan Police Raid Magazine, Arrest Staff." Accessed January 13, 2020. https://www.reuters.com/article/idUSL26500311.

Mair, David. 2017. "#Westgate: A Case Study: How Al-Shabaab Used Twitter during an Ongoing Attack." *Studies in Conflict & Terrorism* 40 (1): 24–43. https://doi.org/10.1080/1057610X.2016.1157404.

Masaba, Simon. 2015. "Uganda Arrests Two Terror Suspects. *New Vision*, April 17, 2015. Accessed January 20, 2020. https://www.newvision.co.ug/new_vision/news/1323705/uganda-arrests-terror-suspects.

McNair, Brian. 1998. *The Sociology of Journalism.* New York: Bloomsbury.

Mwesige, Peter. 2004. "Can You Hear Me Now? Radio Talk Shows and Political Participation in Uganda." PhD diss., Indiana University.

Namasinga, Florence. 2018. "Sourcing in Converged Media Spheres: A Study of How Print Journalists in Uganda Use Social Media in Routine News Coverage." PhD diss., University of Oslo.

Natabaalo, Grace. 2013. "Newspapers Remain Closed as Police Ignore Court Order, Arrest Activists. *African Centre for Media Excellence*. Accessed June 14, 2020. https://acme-ug.org/2013/05/24/newspapers-remain-closed-as-police-ignore-court-order-arrest-activists/.

———. 2016. "Drop Charges against KTN Journalist-Press Freedom Advocates." *African Centre for Media Excellence*. Accessed January 16, 2020. https://acme-ug.org/2016/11/30/drop-terrorism-charges-against-ktn-journalist-press-freedom-advocates/.

New Vision. 2001. "Terrorism Bill Anti-opposition." Accessed October 23, 2020. https://www.newvision.co.ug/new_vision/news/1023930/terrorism-anti-opposition.

The Observer. 2017. "Age Limit: Mayor Lukwago, MP Bobi Wine Arrested." Accessed December 17, 2019. https://observer.ug/news/headlines/55233-age-limit-mayor-lukwago-mp-bobi-wine-arrested.html.

Oluka, Benon Herbert. 2016. "Good Journalism Doesn't Happen in a Vacuum; It needs Your Support. *African Centre for Media Excellence*, Accessed December 28, 2016. http://acme-ug.org/2016/09/28/good-journalism-doesnt-happen-in-a-vacuum-it-needs-your-support/.

Okurut, Emmanuel. 2017. Preventing Human Rights Violations by Law Enforcement during Counterterrorism Operations in Kenya and Uganda. Unpublished Thesis, University of Pretoria. Accessed January 20, 2020. https://repository.up.ac.za/handle/2263/64630. Accessed 20 Jan 2020.

Perrot, Sandrine., Sabiti Makara, Jerome Lafargue, and Marie-Aude Fouere. 2014. *Elections in a Hybrid Regime: Revisiting the 2011 Ugandan Polls*. Kampala: Fountain Publishers.

Posetti, Juliet. 2017. *Protecting Journalism Sources in the Digital Age*. Paris: UNESCO.

Rukuuka, Bareebe Solomon. 2012. *The Rise and Rise of The Monitor*. Kampala: Tutajua Limited.

Reuss, Anna, and Kristof Tetica. 2017. "Removing the Presidential Age Limit in Uganda: The Power of Cash and Coercion." *Open Democracy*, August 7, 2017. Accessed December 6, 2017. https://www.opendemocracy.net/en/removing-presidential-age-limit-in-uganda-power-of-cash-and-coercion/.

Reporters Without Borders. 2011. "Radio Presenter Facing Possibly Death Penalty on Treason Charge." Accessed December 9, 2020. https://rsf.org/en/news/radio-presenter-facing-possibly-death-penalty-treason-charge.

Sserunjogi, Mukiibi Eriasa. 2017. "Age Limit Chaos: Nambooze Tells How Her Back was Injured." *Daily Monitor*, December 11, 2017. Accessed December 30, 2018. https://www.africanewshub.com/news/7790027-age-limit-chaos-nambooze-tells-how-her-back-was-injured.

Schudson, Michael. 2003. *The Sociology of News*. New York: Contemporary Societies.

Tabaire, Bernad. 2007. "The Press and Political Repression in Uganda: Back to the Future?" *Journal of Eastern African Studies* 1 (2): 193–211. https://doi.org/10.1080/17531050701452408.

Tangri, Roger, and Andrew Mwenda. 2010. "President Museveni and the Politics of Presidential Tenure in Uganda." *Journal of Contemporary African Studies,* 28 (1): 31–49. https://doi.org/10.1080/02589000903542574.

Tasch, Barbara. 2016. The 25 Poorest Countries in the World." *Business Insider*, April 3, 2016. Accessed April 12, 2016. https://www.businessinsider.com/the-25-poorest-countries-in-the-world-2016-4.

Uganda Legal Information Institute. 2002. "The Anti-terrorism Act, 2002." Accessed December 12, 2020. https://ulii.org/system/files/legislation/act/2002/2002/Anti%20terorrism%20Act%202002.pdf.

———. 2017. "The Anti-Terrorism (Amendment) Act, 2017." Accessed December 12, 2020. https://ulii.org/system/files/legislation/act/2017/4/Anti%20Terrorism%20Amendment%204%202017.pdf.

Tripp, Aili Mari. 2010. *Museveni's Uganda: Paradoxes of Power in a Hybrid Regime*. Boulder, CO: Lynne Rienner.

UNDP. 2013. "Human Development Report." Accessed November 15, 2015. http://hdr.undp.org/en/2013-report.

United Nations Security Council. n.d. "Allied Democratic Forces (ADF)." Accessed December 13, 2020. https://www.un.org/securitycouncil/sanctions/1533/materials/summaries/entity/allied-democratic-forces-%28adf%29.

Chapter 11

Between Voice and Silence

India's Counter-terrorism Laws and Self-censorship of Journalists in the Kashmir Conflict

Mohammad Imran Parray

INTRODUCTION

The enactment and practice of counter-terrorism laws by modern democratic nation-states, by invoking catchphrases such as "national security" and "public interest," have adversely impacted forums of public discussion globally, reducing access to free information and threatening civil liberties (e.g., Cram 2006; Gomez 2004; Head 2002; Hocking 2003; Kumar 2004). A major target of such legislations are journalists who have been witnessing a disabling impact on their profession as counter-terrorism laws continue to affect them in investigating and reporting on matters of public interest (McNamara 2009; Simons and Strovsky 2006). Such laws prevent them from performing routine aspects of their profession and give birth to a culture of journalism where independent and investigative reporting is met with punishment.

In this chapter, while exploring the use of counter-terrorism laws by the Indian state against members of the journalistic community, I argue that local journalists on the nation's fringes often resort to self-censorship in the wake of widespread misuse of counter-terrorism laws against journalists. Focusing on Kashmir, a northernmost Himalayan region marred by decades of political conflict that has since gained international attention, where harassment of journalists by the state and its agencies by invoking counter-terrorism laws is very common, the chapter presents recent evidence of how democratic states hide behind the veneer of security and countering terrorism arguments while imposing severe restrictions on free speech. The region of Kashmir presents a classic case in South Asia of a situation where counter-terrorism laws have been systematically turned against members of the journalistic community. Political violence and state terror have been unleashed to a point where journalists are either coerced into silence or they themselves become a part of the legitimizing and normalizing discourse, which justifies draconian anti-terror laws and similar excesses as a necessary evil in the interest of national security and integrity.

The chapter draws on archival data, yet-to-be-translated Urdu-language monographs, and in-depth interviews with journalists in Kashmir to elucidate the range of challenges that counter-terrorism laws pose to the practice of journalism in a conflict zone. The archival data, gathered by the author during the past three years of fieldwork in the region, has been used to offer a historical background of the laws' first enactments by the state during the British colonial rule and the rationale behind their continued future invocations by the postcolonial Indian nation-state. Such clampdowns on free speech, journalists warn, exhaust both democracy and journalism in the long run.

COUNTER-TERRORISM LAWS IN INDIA: A BRIEF BACKGROUND

At the turn of the new millennium, the Indian state began to strengthen its counter-terrorism apparatus following the September 11, 2001 attacks in the United States and the December 13 attack on the Indian Parliament. A number of new anti-terror laws such as the Prevention of Terrorism Act of 2002 (POTA), Unlawful Activities (Prevention) Act (UAPA), and others were added to the existing arsenal of anti-terror laws. Scholars (e.g., Kumar 2004) have tried to trace the genealogy of these laws, which are found to have roots in colonial-era rules. The British colonial state made use of "preventive custody" to detain any person that it suspected posed danger to its settlements. Preventive custody was authorized by multiple laws such as the East India Company Act of 1784, the Defense of India Acts of 1915 and 1939, the Government of India Act of 1919, the Rowlatt Act of 1919, and the Bengal Criminal Law Amendment Act of 1925 (Kumar 2004, 199).[1] Colonial rulers used these laws for widespread abuse, often trying leaders of Indian nationalist struggle under them to safeguard "national security."

It is this colonial hangover that saw the postcolonial Indian state enact laws like the Terrorist and Disruptive Activities (Prevention) Act of 1987 (TADA), the exercise of which and other laws resulted in "widespread torture, arbitrary detention, and harassment of mostly innocent citizens" (Kumar 2004, 207). Of all laws, however, the Armed Forces (Special Powers) Act 1958 (AFSPA) is specifically seen as draconian because it gives unbridled powers to Indian armed forces in conflict regions of Kashmir and the northeast.

Counter-terrorism laws in India are enacted at both central and state levels. While laws like AFSPA, TADA, POTA, and UAPA were passed by the Indian Parliament, states have formulated their own laws like the J&K Public Safety Act, the Maharashtra Control of Organized Crime Act, the Karnataka Control of Organised Crime Act, and the Chhattisgarh Vishesh Jan Suraksha Adhiniyam (Sen et al. 2015, 8). Although recognized as vital for the security and sovereignty of the state (Garge 2019), anti-terrorism laws on the whole in India have been found to be draconian, the misuse of which have severely impacted human rights and civil liberties (Dhavan 2008; Kumar 2004; Manoharan 2009; Sen et al. 2015).

The militant struggles in parts of the northeast of India and Jammu and Kashmir state (now a Union Territory after the Indian Government revoked Article 370 and 35A of the Indian Constitution, which guaranteed a semi-autonomous status to the former princely state) are seen by the state as potential threats to its sovereignty and security. To these major fault lines are added the rebellion in Punjab, the left-leaning Maoist and the Naxalite movements in central India, and the so-called "Islamic terrorism with international linkages" (Manoharan 2009). The state logic that emphasizes these fault lines, however, does not take note of the far-right extremism (because of the intermixing of the state and the Hindutva) that many scholars refer to as the "saffron terror" (Bidwai 2008a, 2008b; Gittinger 2011) and "Hindutva fascism" (Banaji 2018), the vocal posturing of which poses a major threat to the Indian democracy.[2] In the northeast and Kashmir, armed forces have widely misused counter-terrorism laws resulting in large-scale human rights violations (Wani and Desai 2018). The Indian Government has itself revealed that human rights violations under the controversial AFSPA are the highest in Jammu and Kashmir followed by the northeastern state of Assam (Das 2017).

"IF YOU'VE GOT THEM BY THE BALLS, THEIR HEARTS AND MINDS WILL FOLLOW":[3] ARITHMETIC OF GAINING ACQUIESCENCE BY USING FORCE

It has been observed that the growing practice of murdering journalists and widespread attacks on the freedom of expression and speech in South Asia led to self-censorship by journalists (Mazzarella and Kaur 2013, 304). This pattern of gaining acquiescence from journalists by using force on them is apparent in India's fringes where the state deploys a range of methods to threaten and silence journalists who try to expose corruption in the government, cases of human rights violation, and other politico-economic malaises. The state has at its disposal multiple apparatuses to silence journalists among which counter-terrorism laws are the most used around its peripheries such as Kashmir and the northeast region. This silence naturally gets manifested in self-censorship by journalists. The assassination of three journalists—Jagendra Singh in 2015, Rajdev Ranjan in 2016, and Gauri Lankesh in 2017—in mainland India point to the crimes against journalism and disregard toward journalists and their work.

During the past three decades, thirty-one journalists have been killed in India's northeast (Sinha 2017). The threat has mainly emanated from state armed forces with special powers, unknown gunmen, and members of the United Liberation Front of Assam or ULFA, a militant outfit that seeks to carve out an independent state separate from the Union of India. The northeast, a region embroiled in perpetual conflict, is perceived by its local journalists as the "forgotten corner of the country" because of the indifference of the mainstream Indian media toward the region (Sinha 2017, para. 20). For them, not much attention is given to the killings of journalists in the northeast as compared to those in mainland India. Journalists in the northeast lack support of civil society organizations and judiciary at moments when members of their profession are killed and brutalized by government forces, militant groups, and unknown gunmen for exposing widespread wrongdoings in the region (Pisharoty 2018).

The Indian state security apparatus is seen to ferociously target journalists in these conflict-ridden regions where reporters are subjected to life threats, imprisonment, and accusations to conspire with the enemies of the state (Siddiqui 2019; Sinha 2017; Rina 2017). According to a collaborative study by the Indian media watch website Newslaundary, Committee to Protect Journalists, and International Center for Journalists, forty-six of sixty-two media workers were killed since 1992 who worked in small towns for regional language press (Siddiqui 2017, 39). Such studies expose the vulnerabilities in India's peripheries, particularly those whose territoriality is embroiled in disputes with neighboring countries.

In the context of Kashmir, journalists have been and are being targeted and suppressed to adopt silence (Murthy and Seshu 2019). Since the eruption of armed insurgency against the Indian state in the 1990s, twenty-one persons associated with various media have been killed by armed forces, militant outfits, and unidentified groups (cited in Murthy 2017, 10–11). Murthy's situation report (2017) makes apparent that the main targets of insurgents were media persons working with state broadcaster *Doordarshan Kendra* while state armed forces have shot dead local journalists and calligraphers working with local newspapers to instill fear among the indigenous journalist fraternity. However, some died while covering gun battles between insurgents and armed forces while others like Mushtaq Ali—in whose memorial Srinagar's press enclave has been named—and Asiya Jeelani became victims of landmines, car, and parcel bombings. Indeed, the fallout of these assassinations was silence. In 1990, for instance, when the director of *Doordarshan* Lassa Kaul was gunned down by insurgents, the station remained closed for three years. In 1993, when Radio Kashmir news reader Mohammad Shafi Bhat was murdered, his colleagues immediately resigned in defense of their lives. In 1991, the killing of Mohammad Shaban Vakil, the editor of Urdu-language weekly *Al-Safa*, by insurgents, served as "a warning to journalists to discipline themselves" (Gull 2010, para 7). The murder of stringer Ghulam Mohammad Lone along with his son by armed forces in 1994 had, to borrow Seshu's (2020) term, "a chilling effect" on other stringers working in hinterlands of Kashmir where human rights abuses were widespread.

The use of such force against members of the journalistic community forces us to reflect on the myriad of options available with the state and other actors to silence the press, which, in turn, takes our attention to the role of the state's armed forces, insurgents, and anonymous groups in a conflict zone in not only enforcing the policy of information control in their own ways but also forcing journalists to take sides. Maqbool (2019) succinctly observes that the "truth still remains unsaid, suppressed, and under siege" in Kashmir (para 2). Although journalist killings have lessened (the editor of English daily *Rising Kashmir* Shujaat Bukhari was assassinated on June 14, 2018, outside his office by unknown gunmen), the policy of information control has assumed more abstract contours in recent times.

The state, however, continues to detain journalists under draconian anti-terror laws, raid printing presses and newspaper offices, and seize newspaper copies. In 2016, when Kashmir was undergoing a political turmoil in the wake of a popular militant commander's death, the state police raided newspaper offices in Srinagar, the capital city, detained newspaper staff, and seized printed newspaper copies in what the local editors and journalists termed the "direct attack on freedom of press" (Bhatnagar 2016, para. 1). Furthermore, the journalists continue to live "on a razor's edge" (Maqbool 2018, para. 4). As recently as 2016, the state forces fired live ammunition on journalists when they were covering a protest in Srinagar (Wani 2016). A wounded photojournalist later recalled:

> I saw a masked policeman pointing his pellet gun[4] towards me and I abruptly stood up. As he was about to press the trigger, I displayed my two cameras shouting I am from "Press." After a few seconds, I heard a deafening sound and some hot metal objects hitting me my left eye, nose, stomach and thighs. I found myself in a pool of blood. (Wani 2016, para. 7)

The pellets hit photojournalist Zuhaib Maqbool in his eyes, blinding him partially. Though he has resolved to get back to his profession, the prospects for his return seem unlikely. Like Maqbool, another journalist, Mir Javed, too was targeted with pellets by forces. "I was punished for highlighting atrocities by forces on people," a news report quoted him (Ibid, para. 18) "I was standing on a road when forces in a [police] vehicle fired pellets on me without any provocation. Over 100 pellets hit my body including the left eye. I had to undergo two eye surgeries and still have not regained full vision. Two pellets are still in my eye" (Ibid, para. 18–19).

A 1991 report by Asia Watch notes that "[t]he arbitrary manner in which government authorities in Kashmir have threatened, harassed and limited the free movement of journalists has resulted in widespread restrictions on the press which appear to extend beyond those permitted under international law" (Asia Watch 1991, 101). The report emphasized that government forces repeatedly threaten local vernacular press and perceive journalists as pro-militant. Throughout the 1990s, the Indian Government took action against local Urdu newspapers under TADA, accusing newspaper editors of guiding the local freedom movement (Press Council of India 1991, 62). However, according to the Press Council of India, it was "totally counter-productive and wrong to write off all local newspapers, editors and correspondents as pro-militant or, worse, pro-Pakistani" (Press Council of India 1991, 72).

In view of these complexities, the Kashmir Valley during the 1990s was termed as "another Beirut" because of the constant occurrence of "shoot-outs, bombings, cordon-and-search operations, and curfew" (Press Council of India 1991, 67). In such a milieu of "low-intensity warfare," truth became in what Phillip Knightley remarks "the first casualty" (Knightley 2004) and journalists had no choice but to adopt silence or self-censor.

"PUBLIC SAFETY ACT": SILENCING LOCAL VOICES

Apart from gaining acquiescence from journalists by using force on them, a number of security-related laws, such as the draconian Public Safety Act or PSA, are systematically used by the Indian state to repress the press in Kashmir (Bukhari 2012). For instance, the editor of Urdu newspaper, *Wadi Ki Awaz*, Ghulam Nabi Shaida, became the first journalist victim of the draconian Public Safety Act in 1986 when he was arrested for "inciting communal tension" through his writings (Bukhari 2012b, para. 3). He was imprisoned for forty days and his office and printing press were sealed. The journalist was subjected to "solitary confinement in the infamous Red-16 interrogation cell" in Srinagar.[5] Shaida had to endure what Bukhari calls a "protracted legal battle" to restart his newspaper (Ibid, para. 4). During the heydays of the armed rebellion in early 1990, he was again booked under the Act along with other journalists on the orders of Governor Jagmohan; six newspapers were sealed (Bukhari 2012b). Bukhari alerted that the use of the PSA against journalists is a "continuous process." In 2005, Rehmatullah Khan, editor of English daily *Rehmat*, was arrested; he was later released after the intervention of the High Court that nullified the charges leveled by the state against him. Rouf Ahmad Khan of *Srinagar News* "languished in jail for more than a year" on charges of "aiding and abetting militancy" (Bukhari 2012b, para. 9). His employer Gulzar Ahmad told Bukhari that "[i]t was completely a fabricated case. He would be with us round the clock. It was just the government's excuse to suppress the media which reflected the people's voice" (Ibid). Mohammad Maqbool Khokhar, popularly known as Maqbool Sahil, reporter of Urdu weekly *Chattan*, was arrested in 2004 under the PSA and Official Secrets Act on charges of espionage for "passing on vital security information to Pakistan" (Ibid, para. 10). The dossier prepared against him was intense:

> The subject has developed relations under the garb of journalism with secessionists and militant organizations. The activities of the subject are directly and adversely related to the defense and security of the country and being a potent threat, it is imperative to prevent the subject from indulging in activities prejudicial to the security of the state. (Ibid)

Bukhari writes that despite the intervention of the High Court that nullified the PSA, the government agencies kept extending Maqbool's detention; he was finally released in January 2008. Prior to his release, when he was presented in the court for the first time in August 2007, Bukhari reported that Maqbool had told:

> This is a concocted case against me. I used to work as a genuine journalist and was taking photographs of Army camps as part of my professional job but they used the same against me. The Court has refused to entertain these charges and quashed my PSA. I have been treated as a political prisoner while I am a journalist. They continued to avoid presenting me before the Judge and this is for the first time in three years that they brought me here. This is a lawless society and this goes against freedom of press, expression and even the Constitution of the country. (Bukhari 2012b, para. 13)

The PSA provides legal immunity to members of the executive and constraints the authority of the judiciary to review detention orders that can authorize imprisonment of a person for years without trial. This element of the Act resembles the Vernacular (Oriental Languages) Press Act of 1878, enacted by the British colonial state against vernacular newspapers, which too eliminated judicial restraint on the government action on the press (Israel 1994, 6).[6] Yet, the major difference between the two laws is that while the latter was repealed after only three years of its enactment, the PSA has been in force in Kashmir since 1978 when it was first enacted by the Sheikh Abdullah-led National Conference government.

For Bukhari (2012a), the "repression [is] not just an aberration but illustrative of the existing restrictive framework" of various laws in practice (para. 2). Besides the PSA, he writes, the state can invoke J&K Customs Act 1901 to "ban [the] circulation of newspapers and other journals and books without assigning any reason" (Ibid, para. 12). Bukhari notes that the state can seize printing presses and publications by invoking the Jammu and Kashmir State Newspapers (Incitement and Offences) Act of 1919. A reporter is bound to disclose the source of information under Jammu and Kashmir Public Security Rules 1946; its violation can lead to three years of imprisonment with a fine. Bukhari writes that "[r]ight from 1990, the media has faced the brunt of the [state's] repressive measures during which the offices and printing presses were sealed umpteen times and journalists were harassed, intimidated and arrested several times" (Ibid, para. 6). He terms 2010 as the year of "press emergency" (Ibid, para. 1) in Kashmir state when the publication of newspapers was banned for five months and journalists covering the summer unrest were assaulted by Indian paramilitary forces on roads. Such behavior of armed forces, he argues, is not random but emanates from the laws that govern the state. In fact, he notes, the many legislations brought in the past twenty-five years to contain the movement for Azadi [freedom] concurrently target media and impinge upon their functioning. On top of this, Indian troops and police raid, detain, and interrogate journalists (Hussain and Saaliq 2020; Peerzada 2020).

As recently as September 2017, India's federal counter-terrorism bureau the National Investigation Agency or NIA arrested a young Kashmiri photojournalist Kamran Yousuf on charges of being "part of an international terrorist gang conspiring to wage war against the Indian security forces" in Kashmir (Gettleman and Kumar 2018, para. 3). The NIA reasoned that Yousuf is not a "real" journalist because he never takes pictures of the government's "developmental" activities such as the inauguration of schools, hospitals, or bridges, which is the "moral duty of a real journalist" (Angad 2018, para. 4). Journalists in Kashmir see Yousuf's arrest as a punishment for what he covered—"explosive anti-government protests and militant activity"—and an "absurd" intervention of a government agency to dictate journalists "what to report and not report" (Gettleman and Kumar 2018, para 4.). This is interesting when the state determines who is a "real" journalist. Although within journalism, there is a raging debate among groups of practitioners and academia on a problematic like this,[7] it is intriguing to see the state also joining the fray of critiques in defining who is and who is not a journalist. Within journalism, research has been undertaken that attempts to outline the boundaries of journalism vis-à-vis other social and cultural forces and institutions (e.g., Lewis 2012). Like Maqbool Sahil, Yousuf was accused of a "well-planned criminal conspiracy run by [militants] in Pakistan to wage war against India" (Gettleman and Kumar 2018, para. 14), a charge Kashmiri journalists term as "ridiculous" (Ibid, para. 15). Yet, Yousuf's arrest has sent across the message to the intended audience: young photographers who documented militant funerals and anti-government protests are learning to discipline themselves by covering more "official" events. After six months in detention, a judge in New Delhi released Yousuf on bail on March 13, 2018, for lack of "credible evidence" (Kumar and Schultz 2018, para 4). On the court judgment, the Committee to Protect Journalists remarked:

> CPJ is pleased that Kamran Yousuf has been granted bail and that the court acknowledged he was working as a journalist at the time of his arrest. Given the prosecution's failure to present any credible evidence against him, Indian authorities should immediately drop all charges. The charges against Yousuf are a clear attempt to muzzle reporting on the ongoing conflict in Kashmir and the photojournalist should never have been detained in the first place. (Committee to Protect Journalists 2018, para. 2)

Yousuf's case shows that journalists continue to be tied to militant groups and their activities. Surprisingly, he was accused of being in league with Hafiz Muhammad Saeed of Jamaat-ud-Dawah and Syed Salahuddin of United Jihad Council to "wage war against the Government of India by carrying out terrorist and secessionist activities" in Jammu and Kashmir (National Investigation Agency 2018, para. 1). The charges against Yousuf and eleven others including Saeed and Salahuddin were framed under the Indian Penal Code and Unlawful Activities (Prevention) Act 1967, and from the January 19, 2018, press release of the agency it would appear to a general reader that all the twelve persons charge-sheeted, including Yousuf, are connected.

In addition to state legislation, the Indian federal laws rooted in British colonial logic are also used against journalists to implicate them in different cases. In 2002, Iftikhar Gilani, the New Delhi bureau chief of the Jammu-based English newspaper *Kashmir Times*, was arrested from his house under the Official Secrets Act for "possessing classified documents" (Committee to Protect Journalists 2002, para. 3). Gilani was accused of "collecting data on army formulations and deployment of security forces in Jammu and Kashmir . . . which entailed a fourteen-year jail term" (Gilani 2005, 4). In his memoir, *My Days in Prison*, Gilani describes the ordeal that he had to face during his trial; he remained imprisoned for seven months in Delhi's maximum-security prison Tihar Jail. In his foreword to Gilani's first-hand account, Indian journalist Siddharth Varadarajan writes:

> The shocking story that this book tells is not just an indictment of the capriciousness and arbitrariness of power, or a grim chronicle of sheer viciousness of the Indian state. It is also a depressing account of how all the so-called estates of society—including the Fourth Estate—came face to face with an obvious injustice and were found wanting. (Gilani 2005, ix)

Gilani was released in January 2003 by an Indian judge in the wake of the government request for withdrawal of the case in the "public interest." Prior to his release, the Indian military had submitted a report to the Indian Government, noting that the documents found in the possession of Gilani were "neither secrets nor a threat to national security" (Reporters Without Borders 2003, para. 2). The case against the journalist therefore appeared weak to the government and in the wake of mounting pressure from rights organizations, Gilani was finally freed. The case against him, Varadarajan writes, "collapsed under the weight of its own inconsistencies and contradictions" (Ibid, x). In 2015, India's leading English daily *The Hindu* argued in its editorial that the state coerces "media and political opponents into adopting self-censorship and unwarranted self-restraint" (The Hindu 2015, para. 2).

GENEALOGY OF PRACTICE: BRITISH IMPERIAL ORDER, DOGRA AUTOCRACY, AND THE SPECTER OF SILENCE

Self-censorship as a voluntary practice among journalists in Kashmir dates to the British colonial rule in South Asia in the late nineteenth and early twentieth centuries. In princely vassals of the *raj* such as Jammu and Kashmir, vernacular newspapers were banned and blacklisted by the princely political order. As a consequence, to safeguard their publishing endeavors, local editors sought to adopt silence over issues that the king didn't like talking about. Newspapers, poor at finances and mostly individual endeavors, were subservient to the state for advertising revenue. The Dogra state, therefore, either banned the newspapers or blacklisted them. In certain cases, it ceased printing devices, private property, and even banished editors (Taseer 1988). The aim of banning or blacklisting the newspapers was to win, what Smith (1997) calls in a different context, "acquiescence" of editors and journalists to censor on their own the anti-state news and views. While some editors such as Abdul Salam Rafequi of the weekly *Al-Rafeeq* did not yield to the pressures of the Dogra state with the result of which he had to cease the newspaper's publication and embrace exile, others such as M. A. Saabir of *Al-Barq*, despite being equally critical of the state, had to finally adapt to the tastes of the Dogra state by "showing improvement . . . in the tone of the paper" and, therefore, internalizing self-censorship in his journalistic practice.[8] Dangerfield (1937, 341), writing in the context of England, argues that self-censorship is the "censorship of conscience." Indeed, when M. A. Saabir internalized censorship on *Al-Barq*, it was a compromise with his conscience because, as his correspondences with the state show, he was relentless in reporting the plight of Kashmiri Muslims under the Dogra administration and in no way wanted to self-censor the newspaper until the Dogra state came up with legal action against the editor and blacklisted his weekly.[9]

Blacklisting newspapers has been a key operative tool for the state to silence the press in Kashmir. When a newspaper is blacklisted, it is unable to receive advertisements from the government and no official information is provided to the newspaper in the form of official releases. It is a deterioration of the relationship between the government and the newspaper, who no more go along well. As such, to discipline the press, the government disassociates itself from the newspaper and imposes sanctions that include stopping advertising revenue and official information. For local publishers and editors, it is a major setback. Blacklisting was a tool quite often used by the Dogra autocracy against the periodical press of the 1930s because these periodicals wrote against the atrocities of the princely rule. Since revenue was a major hindrance to the functioning of newspapers, the Dogra state cut advertisements revenue and put them in the "blacklist" category. And once the newspaper was backlisted, it had only two choices: either to cease publication or acquiesce. When, in 1935, the editor of *Al-Barq* wrote to the Dogra court asking why his newspaper was blacklisted, he was informed that he should either write what he is writing on his own terms or adhere to the tastes of the government to get advertisements (Publicity Department, File No. 167/321/N-152/B, Jammu and Kashmir State Archives, Government of Jammu and Kashmir). In the context of Brazil, Smith (1997) argues that governments use such tactics along with the use of force to gain "acquiescence" of the press to government censorship. And when this acquiescence is gained, self-censorship gets exercised concurrently. In 1936, the Dogra state blacklisted Urdu-language *Wattan* because of the newspaper's independent style of reporting, and in 1943 *Hamdard*, *Al-Barq*, and *Amar* met with the same treatment (Mohiuddin 2006 [1972], 58).

Self-censorship, as an unexplored function of the human mind, has always been there, lurking inside their heads and influencing words that they utter and the decisions that they take. On the other hand, self-censorship in relation to journalistic practice was a remarkable theorization because it struck at the heart of the problem: the flow of information is scuttled not only by governments as we saw it but also by journalists and editors themselves owing to various sociopolitical, socioeconomic, or moral reasons. Dangerfield (1937) called this "invisible censorship." In fact, one of the most remarkable transformations in the patterns of imposition of censorship is that it has slowly internalized in media organizations and journalists alike who censor on their own; the state no more directly disciplines the media, but the control is telepathic. The term "self-censorship" is attributed to Graham Hutton, who was an assistant editor at *The Economist* during the 1930s. Speaking before the New York Herald Tribune Forum in the United States, Hutton had complained of "self-censorship" of the English press and attributed this phenomenon to "predatory libel laws" and "control by three millionaires of three newspapers with a total circulation of more than six million" in England (Dangerfield 1937, 334). An eminent American journalist once told Dangerfield that "English foreign correspondents—whatever the political color of the newspaper they serve—present substantially the same picture of foreign affairs; and that this is not due to any official censorship, but to some mysterious, telepathic agreement between the official mind and the editorial mind" (Dangerfield 1937, 334–335). He, however, celebrates that "no such state of affairs exists in America, where there still remains a good deal of independent newspaper ownership" (p. 334). A lot has, however, changed since 1937 when Dangerfield wrote this. The American press has shown a more telepathic understanding of their government's war policies and has exercised self-censorship on matters of enormous public importance. For Dangerfield, self-censorship is a "willingness on part of the public to blind itself to unpleasant facts" and that it is psychological than political in England (p. 338).

On the contrary, however, self-censorship of journalists in the context of Kashmir can be mainly seen as political in that the state and its allied forces curb journalists' activities with the aim to control the flow of information solely for political reasons. In 1907, when German Christian missionary J. F. Peter sought permission to start *Ladakhi Phooiyan*, a Bodhi-language newspaper, he was directed to desist from printing comments on political, social, and economic policies of the Dogra state. Thus, Peter internalized self-censorship and published missionary material in the form of human interest stories (Taseer 1988, 84). In a more recent context, Murthy (2017, 4) writes that the Indian Military Intelligence detains journalists in Kashmir without any charges and interrogates them about their stories and sources of information which finally leads to self-censorship by reporters to "minimize the harassment of families who live in fear." Furthermore, the Indian army controls information by intimidating sources of information such as victims or their kin "to the extent that common people are afraid to talk to journalists due to fear of repercussions" (Murthy 2017, 6). Apart from detention and interrogation of journalists, army and intelligence personnel make regular visits to their homes and harass their families (Murthy 2017, 4).

SELF, PROFESSION, AND STATE: INTERNALIZING THE STRUCTURE OF CONTROL

Despite the misuse of national security laws by the state, Hassan (2011, 332) reports in her survey that 68% of respondents (journalists) in Kashmir felt "laws are necessary for controlling media" in the region. In total, 30% of her respondents opined that media should be "self-regulatory." Her respondents suggested that laws should regulate the media while not restricting its freedom. She reports a respondent as saying that "laws ensure not only accountability of news organizations but it [*sic*] also ensure safety and job security of the journalists associated with it" (Hassan 2011, 332). She reports that 77% of her respondents have faced restrictions while performing their duties and 79% of journalists believed that the media in Kashmir do not enjoy freedom as guaranteed by the Indian Constitution. In total, 56% of her respondents observe that the existing legal system doesn't offer them sufficient protection.

It is in the backdrop of this milieu that self-censorship among members of the journalistic community emanates from a number of usual practices of coercion that the Indian state has been deploying in the fringes of the nation-state. After the revocation of Article 370 of its nation's Constitution, which guaranteed special status to Kashmir, the Indian Government imposed an internet shutdown for months that cut journalists from the rest of the world. In local journalist's understanding, they were "left out and cold" (Thakur 2019, para. 1). According to a Kashmiri journalist, "the state's relationship with the local press in Kashmir is similar to its relationship with the people in Kashmir: the exercise of the power over the powerless" (Maqbool 2019, para. 8). In recent times, Kashmiri journalists have been summoned by the National Investigation Agency, interrogating them about their news work and sources of information. The deployment of counter-terrorism laws and physical attacks on journalists intertwined with the logic of advertising revenue produces a complex censorship milieu in Kashmir. Thus, self-censorship as a fundamental index not only gets exercised at the level of a journalist but also at the level of editors and publishers too, which, in turn, has transformed self-censorship into a norm and is articulated from both Weberian and Durkheimian positionalities. Summing up his decades-long experience in reporting the Kashmir conflict, a journalist remarked: "What the Indian state and other actors here want is our silence and we are expressing that silence. It is a norm now and we've no choice than to internalize it" (HR, personal communication, August 7, 2018).

Journalists have become more guarded since August 2018 when journalist Asif Sultan of the English magazine *Kashmir Narrator* was arrested by Indian police under accusations of being "in contact" with indigenous rebel group Hizbul Mujahideen and "glorifying" militants in his news reports

(Masood 2018, para. 1). Since his arrest, Sultan remains in prison under the Unlawful Activities (Prevention) Act despite his family, employer, and local journalist unions in the region denying the charges and challenging his detention (Bhat 2019). While Sultan was languishing in prison, the National Press Club (NPC) awarded him with the John Aubuchon Press Freedom Award 2019 for his reporting to "disclose the truth in trying circumstances" (Donnelly 2019, para. 2). The NPC members observed that Sultan's case "reflects worsening conditions for the press and citizenry in Kashmir and that it was completely unacceptable for India to violate the basic human rights of reporters and to deny the people of Kashmir access to unfiltered information through an unfettered press" (Ibid, para. 5, 7).

For local journalists, cases like Sultan's force them to self-censor, which directly affects the quality of journalism. "If you do not self-censor your work, one has to be ready to face the reprisals. In a place where organizations are not in a position to protect themselves from the state, how can they offer support to us" (AJ, personal communication, September 7, 2018).

CONCLUSION

In this chapter, I argue that the widespread misuse of counter-terrorism laws in India—often wrapped in the rhetoric of "national security" and "public interest"—against members of journalist communities at nation's margins has resulted in a disabling impact on their profession. As a consequence of this disabling impact, self-censorship by journalists has become a new norm. Such a practice, it is proposed, adversely impacts forums of public discussion, reduces access to free information, threatens civil liberties, and exhausts democracy and journalism in the longer run even if self-censorship appears to be normalizing in journalistic circles. Taking the case of Kashmir, a northernmost Himalayan region marred by decades of political conflict, I explicate on how modern nation-states (in this case India) hide behind the cover of security and countering terrorism rhetoric while imposing severe restrictions on free speech, a legacy bequeathed to the postcolonial nation by the British colonial state. I outline a range of counter-terrorism laws used by the Indian state against journalists in Kashmir, often implicated for secessionist inclinations and their relationship with armed militants fighting the Indian state. This complex interlocking of securitization and freedom of press poses a serious challenge to the field of journalism in that journalists now more increasingly self-censor information, the publication of which would otherwise put them and their families in danger.

This chapter demonstrates how the Indian state security apparatus ferociously targets journalists in the conflict-ridden regions where journalists are subjected to assassinations, life threats, imprisonment, and accusations to conspire with the enemies of the state. This stifling cycle exposes the vulnerabilities of India's peripheries such as Kashmir and the northeast, the territoriality of which is embroiled in disputes with neighboring countries such as Pakistan and China. This growing practice of muzzling the press with draconian laws has created a culture of fear among journalists, which directly affects the quality of journalism.

NOTES

1. Similar to the British colonial laws, a number of laws authorized preventive detention in postcolonial India. Such laws include the National Security Act of 1980 (NSA), the Conservation of Foreign Exchange and Prevention of Smuggling Activities Act of 1974, the Prevention of Black-Marketing and Maintenance of Supplies of Essential Commodities Act of 1980, the Prevention of Illicit Traffic in Narcotic Drugs and Psychotropic Substances Act of 1988, the Terrorist and Disruptive Activities (Prevention) Act of 1987. See Kumar (2004, 212).
2. The word "Hindutva," coined by V. D. Savarkar in his 1923 manifesto *Essentials of Hindutva*, refers a far-right militant nationalism that seeks to create political mobilization around Hindu religious identity. See Banaji (2018).
3. The famous quote attributed to Theodore Roosevelt was a common dictum applied by counterinsurgency forces of the Indian state in Kashmir during the early 1990s when an armed insurgency against the Indian state broke out. See Levy and Scott-Clark (2012).
4. Pellet gun is a lethal weapon used by Indian armed forces on unarmed protestors and civilians alike in Kashmir. See Wani (2017). For a detailed report on the impact of pellet guns on Kashmiri youth, see Amnesty International India (2018).
5. I owe this information to Shujaat Bukhari who shared with me the original manuscript of his article "Laws that Render Media Defenseless in Kashmir," part of which appeared on the media watch website *The Hoot* in 2012. Bukhari was assassinated by unknown gunmen outside his office in Srinagar on 14 June 2018.
6. Additionally, Canning Press Act of 1857, although short-lived, removed the element of judicial review on an executive action against newspapers in colonial India while the review had been introduced in Metcalfe's 1835 Act (Israel 1994, 6).
7. See, for example, Carlson and Lewis (2015).
8. Government of Jammu and Kashmir (n.d.).
9. Ibid.

REFERENCES

Amnesty International India. 2018. "Losing Sight in Kashmir: The Impact of Pellet Firing Shotguns." Accessed December 5, 2020. https://amnesty.org.in/wp-content

/uploads/2018/01/Losing-Sight-in-Kashmir-The-Impact-of-Pellet-Firing-Shotguns.pdf.

Angad, Abhishek. 2018. “Moral Duty of a Real Journalist is to Cover Govt Development Activity: NIA.” *The Indian Express*, February 16, 2018. http://indianexpress.com/article/india/moral-duty-of-a-real-journalist-is-to-cover-govt-development-activity-nia-kamran-yusuf-arrest-5065841/.

Asia Watch. 1991. *Human Rights in India: Kashmir Under Siege*. New York: Human Rights Watch.

Banaji, Shakuntala. 2018. “Vigilante Publics: Orientalism, Modernity and Hindutva Fascism in India.” *Javnost-The Public* 25 (4): 333–350.

Bhat, Tariq. 2019. “J&K: Charge-sheet Filed against Journalist Accused of Sheltering Militants.” *The Week*, February 7, 2019. https://www.theweek.in/news/india/2019/02/07/j-k-charge-sheet-journalist-militants.html.

Bhatnagar, Gaurav Vivek. 2016. “Police Raid Newspaper Offices in Kashmir as Part of Information Flow Crackdown.” *The Wire*, July 16, 2016. https://thewire.in/politics/newspapers-fail-to-hit-stands-as-police-raid-media-offices-in-kashmir.

Bidwai, Praful. 2008a. “Saffron Terror.” *TNI*, November 13, 2008. https://www.tni.org/my/node/13763.

———. 2008b. “Confronting the Reality of Hindutva Terrorism.” *Economic and Political Weekly* 43 (47): 10–13.

Bukhari, Shujaat. 2012(a). “Laws that Render Media Defenseless in Kashmir.” *The Hoot*. Accessed December 10, 2020. http://asu.thehoot.org/free-speech/media-freedom/laws-that-render-media-defenseless-in-kashmir-part-i-8623.

———. 2012(b). “How can a Government Muzzle Peoples’ Voices? Part II.” *The Hoot*. Accessed December 10, 2020 http://asu.thehoot.org/story_popup/how-can-a-government-muzzle-peoples-voices-part-ii-8624.

Carlson, Matt, and Seth C. Lewis. 2015. *Boundaries of Journalism: Professionalism, Practices and Participation*. Abingdon and New York: Routledge.

Committee to Protect Journalists. 2002. “India: Journalist Arrested under Official Secrets Act.” Accessed May 2, 2019. https://cpj.org/2002/06/india-journalist-arrested-under-official-secrets-a.php.

———. 2018. “India Releases Photojournalist Kamran Yousuf on Bail.” Accessed December 10, 2020. https://cpj.org/2018/03/india-releases-photojournalist-kamran-yousuf-on-ba.php.

Cram, Ian. 2006. “Regulating the Media: Some Neglected Freedom of Expression Issues in the United Kingdom’s Counter-terrorism Strategy.” *Terrorism and Political Violence* 18 (2): 335–355. https://doi.org/10.1080/09546550600570184.

Dangerfield, George. 1937. “Invisible Censorship.” *The North American Review* 244 (2): 334–348.

Das, Shaswati. 2017. “Jammu & Kashmir Tops List on Rights Abuses under AFSPA, Assam Second.” *Livemint*, July 29, 2017. https://www.livemint.com/Politics/CcFJoIMR39wtQwiIoIfi3O/Jammu--Kashmir-tops-list-on-rights-abuses-under-AFSPA-Assa.html.

Dhavan, Rajeev. 2008. *Publish and be Damned: Censorship and Intolerance in India*. New Delhi: Tulika Books.

Donnelly, John M. 2019. "National Press Club Announces 2019 Press Freedom Honorees." *The National Press Club*, August 22, 2019. https://www.press.org/newsroom/national-press-club-announces-2019-press-freedom-honorees.

Garge, Ramanand. 2019. *Jurisprudence of Anti-Terrorism Laws – An Indian Perspective*. New Delhi: Vivekananda International Foundation.

Gettleman, Jeffrey, and Hari Kumar. 2018. "Journalist or Terrorist? Kashmir Photographer Is Jailed, Pending Answer." *The New York Times*, February 20, 2018. https://www.nytimes.com/2018/02/20/world/asia/kashmir-kamran-yousuf-photographer.html.

Gilani, Iftikhar. 2005. *My Days in Prison*. New Delhi: Penguin.

Gittinger, Juli. 2011. "Saffron Terror: Splinter or Symptom?" *Economic and Political Weekly* 46 (37): 22–25.

Gomez, James. 2004. "Dumbing Down Democracy: Trends in Internet Regulation, Surveillance and Control in Asia." *Pacific Journalism Review* 10 (2): 130–150.

Government of Jammu and Kashmir. n.d. "File No. 167/321/N-152/B," Publicity Department, Jammu and Kashmir State Archives.

Gull, R.S. 2010. "Silenced." *Kashmir Life*, March 13, 2010. https://kashmirlife.net/silenced-shaban-vakil-10785/.

Head, Michael. 2002. "Counter-terrorism Laws: A Threat to Political Freedom, Civil Liberties and Constitutional Rights." *Melbourne University Law Review* 26: 666–689.

Israel, Milton. 1994. *Communication and Power: Propaganda and the Press in the Indian Nationalist Struggle, 1920-1947*. Cambridge: Cambridge University Press.

Hassan, Ruheela. 2011. *Journalism in Kashmir: Law and Practice* (Unpublished doctoral dissertation). University of Kashmir, Srinagar.

Hocking, Jenny. 2003. "Counter-terrorism and the Criminalisation of Politics: Australia's New Security Powers of Detention, Proscription and Control." *Australian Journal of Politics & History* 49 (3): 355–371. https://doi.org/10.1111/1467-8497.00291.

Hussain, Aijaz and Sheikh Saaliq. 2020. "Indian Agency Raids Home of Journalist, Activists in Kashmir." Associated Press, October 8, 2020. https://apnews.com/article/india-kashmir-bukhari-pravez-ahanger-8eeb61fb0a02909893f5d1aa35101c9b.

Knightley, Phillip. 2004. *The First Casualty: The War Correspondent as Hero and Myth-maker from the Crimea to Iraq*. Baltimore: The John Hopkins University Press.

Kumar, C. Raj. 2004. "Human Rights Implications of National Security Laws in India: Combating Terrorism while Preserving Civil Liberties." *Denver Journal of International Law & Policy* 33: 195–222.

Kumar, Hari, and Kai Schultz. 2018. "Indian Court Grants Bail to Kashmiri Photographer Held on Terrorism Charge." *The New York Times*, March 14, 2018. https://www.nytimes.com/2018/03/14/world/asia/kashmir-kamran-yousuf-bail.html.

Levy, Adrian, and Cathy Scott-Clark. 2012. *The Meadow: The Kashmir Kidnapping that Changed the Face of Modern Terrorism*. London: Penguin.

Lewis, Seth C. 2012. "The Tension between Professional Control and Open Participation: Journalism and Its Boundaries." *Information, Communication & Society* 15 (6): 836–866.

Maqbool, Majid. 2018. "On razor's edge." The Hindu BusinessLine, July 13, 2018. https://www.thehindubusinessline.com/blink/know/on-razors-edge/article24407382.ece.

Maqbool, Majid. 2019. "The Government has Made Journalism Impossible in Kashmir." *The Telegraph Online*, November 4, 2019. https://www.telegraphindia.com/opinion/media-freedom-the-government-has-made-journalism-impossible-in-kashmir/cid/1715650.

Manoharan, N. 2009. "Trojan Horses: Counter-Terror Laws and Security in India." *Economic and Political Weekly* 44 (46): 20–24.

Masood, Bashaarat. 2018. "Kashmir Journalist Was 'in contact' with Hizbul Militant, Cops Tell Court." *The Indian Express*, September 9, 2018. https://indianexpress.com/article/india/kashmir-journalist-was-in-contact-with-hizbul-militant-cops-tell-court-5346809/.

Mazzarella, William, and Raminder Kaur. 2013. "Between Sedition and Seduction: Thinking Censorship in South Asia." In *Routledge Handbook of Media Law*, edited by Monroe E. Price, Stefaan G. Verhulst and Libby Morgan, 303–324. London: Routledge.

National Investigation Agency (NIH). 2018. "Charge Sheet Filed in NIA case No. RC-10/2017/NIA/dli (J&K Terror Case)." Accessed August 8, 2019. http://www.nia.gov.in/writereaddata/Portal/PressReleaseNew/489_1_PressRelease19012018.pdf.

McNamara, Lawrence. 2009. "Counter-terrorism Laws: How They Affect Media Freedom and News Reporting." *Westminster Papers in Communication & Culture* 6 (1): 27–44.

Mohiuddin, Sofi. 2006 [1972]. *Jammu wa Kashmir mein Urdu sahafat*. Srinagar: Ashraf Book Centre.

Murthy, Laxmi. 2017. "Kashmir's Media in Peril: A Situation Report." *International Federation of Journalists*. Accessed on December 10, 2020. https://samsn.ifj.org/wp-content/uploads/2017/12/Kashmir-Situation-Report-IFJ-2017.pdf.

Murthy, Laxmi and Geeta Seshu. 2019. "Silence in the Valley: Kashmiri Media After the Abrogation of Article 370." *Economic and Political Weekly*, October 11, 2019. https://www.epw.in/engage/article/silence-valley-kashmiri-media-after-abrogation.

Peerzada, Aamir. 2020. "The Kashmir Journalists 'Harassed' and 'Questioned' for Doing Their Job." BBC, October 31, 2020. https://www.bbc.com/news/world-asia-india-54655948.

Pisharoty, Sangeeta Barooah. 2018. "What it's Like to Be a Journalist in India's Northeast." *The Wire*, May 3, 2018. https://thewire.in/media/what-its-like-to-be-a-journalist-in-indias-northeast.

Press Council of India. 1991. *Crisis and Credibility: Report of the Press Council of India, January and July 1991* (Lancer Paper 4). New Delhi: Lancer International.

Reporters Without Borders. 2003. "Indian Military Says Detained Journalist Iftikhar Gilani Is Innocent." *Ifex*, January 2, 2003. https://ifex.org/indian-military-says-detained-journalist-iftikhar-gilani-is-innocent/.

Rina, Tongam. 2017. "For Journalists in the North East, Vandalism and the Threat of Physical Harm are Daily Hazards." *Scroll*, Nov 30, 2017. https://scroll.in/article/859584/for-journalists-in-the-north-east-murder-vandalism-and-threat-of-physical-harm-are-daily-hazards.

Sen, Srijoni, Rukmini Das, Raadhika Gupta, and Vrindika Bhandari. 2015. "Anti-Terror Laws in India-A Study of Statutes and Judgements, 2001-2014." *Vidhi-Centre for Legal Policy*. Accessed May 14, 2020. https://vidhilegalpolicy.in/wp-content/uploads/2020/06/150531_VidhiTerrorismReport_Final.pdf.

Seshu, Geeta. 2020. "Kashmir Media Policy: Accentuating the Curbs on the Freedom of Press." *Economic and Political Weekly*, August 19, 2020. https://www.epw.in/engage/article/kashmir-media-policy-accentuating-curbs-freedom-press.

Siddiqui, Furquan Ameen. 2017. "Threats to Journalists in India: Journalism in the Age of Intolerance and Rising Nationalism." Reuters Institute Fellowship Paper, University of Oxford.

Simons, Greg, and Dmitry Strovsky. 2006. "Censorship in Contemporary Russian Journalism in the Age of the War against Terrorism: A Historical Perspective." *European Journal of Communication* 21 (2): 189–211. https://doi.org/10.1177%2F0267323105064045.

Sinha, Chandrani. 2017. "31 Journalists Killed in 30 Years in India's North East." *Firstpost*, October 23, 2017. https://www.firstpost.com/india/journalists-fear-to-tread-in-indias-north-east-as-31-murders-in-30-years-see-little-police-action-4160467.html.

Smith, Anne-Marie. 1997. *A Forced Agreement: Press Acquiescence to Censorship in Brazil*. Pittsburgh: University of Pittsburgh Press.

Taseer, Rashid. 1988. *Naqoosh-e-sahafat: Tarikh-i-sahafat Jammu wa Kashmir, 1867 ta July 1988*. Srinagar: Mohafiz Publications.

Thakur, Sankarshan. 2019. "Diary of Srinagar Lockdown: Cut out Like Never Before." *The Telegraph*, August 8, 2019. https://www.telegraphindia.com/india/diary-of-srinagar-lockdown/cid/1696258.

The Hindu. 2015. "A pernicious law." July 16, 2015. https://www.thehindu.com/opinion/editorial/criminal-defamation-a-pernicious-law/article7426091.ece.

Wani, Arif Shafi. 2016. "While Capturing Kashmir's Pellet Plight, Photojournalists Brave Pellets and Batons." *Greater Kashmir*, October 26, 2016. http://www.greaterkashmir.com/news/front-page/while-capturing-kashmir-s-pellet-plight-photojournalists-brave-pellets-and-batons/231897.html.

Wani, Ayjaz Ahmad, and Dhaval D. Desai. 2018. *The Road to Peace in Kashmir: Public Perception of the Contentious AFSPA and PSA*. Mumbai: Observer Research Foundation.

Wani, Fayaz. 2017. "Pellet Guns Used by Cops in Jammu and Kashmir Has Injured 1725 People since July 2016: Government." *The New Indian Express*, November 18, 2017. http://www.newindianexpress.com/nation/2017/nov/18/pellet-guns-used-by-cops-in-jammu-and-kashmir-has-injured-1725-people-since-july-2016-government-1704055.html.

Chapter 12

Investigative Journalism and Counter-terrorism Law in Cameroon

Peter Tiako Ngangum

INTRODUCTION

Media freedom is grounded in the principle of freedom of expression, which is instrumental in maintaining the health and vibrancy of a democratic culture. It enables communities to be engaged in civil discourse. As such, it is central to the making of moral and political choices that are important to the way we live (Barendt 2005; McNamara 2009a). For this reason, the constitutions of many nations have provided specific guarantees for the rights to freedom of expression. This is the case with many states that have embraced democratic and multi-party political systems and others that are currently transitioning to democracy such as Cameroon.

Fundamental democratic freedoms of communication, freedom of expression, and freedom of the press are inscribed in the preamble of the Cameroonian constitution. According to Voorhoof and Cannie (2010), the primary principles underpinning freedom of expression are the discovery of truth and democracy. The former presupposes the freedom to criticize while the latter facilitates free and independent media (especially investigative journalism) to monitor and scrutinize democratically elected individuals. Citizens must therefore be free to receive and impart information relevant to their choices in the political and/or electoral process. However, the state also has a duty to restrict or regulate these freedoms to ensure that individuals are treated with respect, and that non-state actors do not corrupt public discourse. In Cameroon, the limits on freedom of expression are determined by the state, and ultimately scrutinized by domestic judicial authorities. As this freedom is not absolute, the crucial difficulty of its application has always been in balancing competing rights and interests. This tension involves determining what information needs to be part of the public debate in the interest of benefiting democracy, and what information causes harm to individuals and society and should therefore be restricted or sanctioned by national authorities (Voorhoof and Cannie 2010). However, this balancing act begs the question: At what stage can freedom of expression, say, in the context of investigative journalism, be restricted? And on what basis? Who gets to decide what type of speech is permissible and what is not? These issues are familiar terrain for legal, media, and political experts who deal with contested issues of public interest (McNamara 2009a, 2009b).

To safeguard contributions to public debate, journalists and media organizations with a message outside of mainstream discourses rely on a high level of freedom of expression. In a democracy, public authorities should be exposed to consistent scrutiny by citizens and anyone should be able to draw the public's attention to situations they consider unlawful (Voorhoof and Cannie 2010). One of the ways freedom of expression is being challenged in Cameroon, particularly in journalism practice, is related to the adoption and subsequent use of counter-terrorism legislation. There has been a growing pattern of arrests, trials, and detention of journalists under national security legislation, not just in Cameroon, but also in many countries across the globe. As securitization becomes the major priority of governments worldwide, broadly written counter-terrorism legislation is being twisted to silence investigative journalism. It is in light of this context that I examine the tensions of investigative journalism and counter-terrorism law in Cameroon.

While the discussion in this chapter is centered on issues relating to investigative journalism and the Cameroonian counter-terrorism legislation, there are other ways in which the analysis contained in this chapter may offer insightful inputs. First, the practical effect of counter-terrorism laws in Cameroon is not only on journalism practice but also on different communities that rely on the news media. Second, the globalized nature of media organizations, news reporting, and the rise of digitization also gives the law an international dimension. Furthermore, the implications and issues that arise with politics, law enforcement, and security in Cameroon might in the future be usefully compared to similar patterns in the region or elsewhere across the globe. Third, an investigation of how Cameroonian anti-terrorism law affects investigative journalism is important because it provides an opportunity for a critical study of how—both putative and real—constitutional commitments to freedom of expression and freedom of the press are operationalized in the context of national security and anti-terrorism legislation. In identifying these factors as significant, comparisons need to be made cautiously, especially as journalists in Africa, including Cameroon, operate in phenomenally different political and security contexts where freedom of expression and of the press does not rest on strong political, historical, and legal foundations.

Against this backdrop, this chapter addresses the following questions: (a) To what extent are constitutionally guaranteed rights of freedom of expression guaranteed amid the advent of anti-terrorism legislation in Cameroon? (b) What are the consequences of using counter-terrorism laws that are prone to conflate freedom of expression with terrorist acts? I will begin with a discussion of relevant historical and political contexts of Cameroon that inform the integration of the counter-terrorism legislation in the rational-legal system. Next, I will discuss the theoretical and methodological approaches that underpin the analysis. Then, I will describe the Cameroonian counter-terrorism law and its wider effect on press freedom and investigative journalism. Finally, I will unpack the law's criminalization of journalistic activities, demand for information and the duty to inform proactively, and punitive provisions on failure to denounce acts of terrorism and glorification of terrorism.

POLITICS, TERRORISM, AND COUNTER-TERRORISM IN CAMEROON: A CONTEXT

The territory in present-day Cameroon was annexed in 1884 by Germany. After the defeat of Germany in the First World War, the Germans lost Cameroon along with all their other African colonies. The League of Nations placed the western part of Cameroon under British mandate and the eastern part under French mandate, an arrangement which the United Nations confirmed in 1945 when it replaced the League of Nations. While Britain administered northern and southern Cameroon as parts of northern and eastern regions of its colony in Nigeria, France governed the remaining part of Cameroon (French Cameroon) as an autonomous part of its colonial empire. This division laid the basis for the creation of a future Anglophone minority and a Francophone majority in the country (Fonchingong 2013; Tangwa 1999).

When Nigeria gained its independence on October 1, 1960, as a federal republic, the United Nations proposed a plebiscite in Cameroon under British mandate with two options: to achieve independence by joining the independent Federal Republic of Nigeria or to achieve independence by joining the independent Republic of Cameroon. An UN-conducted plebiscite took place on February 11, 1961, and Southern Cameroonians voting overwhelmingly (70.49%) to achieve independence by joining La République du Cameroun while Northern Cameroon opted to remain a part of the Federal Republic of Nigeria. After the plebiscite, a constitutional conference was held in Foumban between Southern Cameroon and La République du Cameroun during which a federal system was adopted. Thus, the Federal Republic of Cameroon came into existence, composed of two federated states: West Cameroon with its capital at Buea and East Cameroon with its capital at Yaoundé.

Following the political liberalization in the 1990s, the political agenda in Cameroon became increasingly dominated by what came to be known as the "Anglophone problem," which poses a major challenge to the efforts of the state to forge national unity. The root of this problem may be traced back to 1961 when the political elites of two territories with different colonial legacies—one French and the other British—agreed on the formation of a federal state. Contrary to expectations, this did not provide for the equal partnership of both parties let alone for the preservation of the cultural heritage and identity of each. It turned out to be merely a transitory phase to the total integration of the Anglophone region into a strongly centralized, unitary state. This, in turn, created an Anglophone consciousness: the pent-up feeling of being "marginalized," "exploited," and "assimilated" by the Francophone-dominated state (Konings and Nyamnjoh 1997). In October 2016, Anglophone nationalism took a dramatic escalation following a series of sit-in strikes and nonviolent actions initiated by common law lawyers and teachers' trade unions. The common law lawyers and teachers' trade unions were protesting government policy of assimilation through the imposition of civil law judges to preside over cases in common law courts and French-speaking teachers to teach in Anglophone schools (Ngangum 2018).

Civil society organizations coordinating the strike and protest actions were banned on January 17, 2017. Prominent leaders of the organization including Justice Ayah Paul Abine, Dr. Felix Agbor Balla, Dr. Neba Fontem, and Mr. Mancho Bibixy were arrested and transferred to the nation's capital, Yaoundé. They are being tried in a military court on charges of terrorism, which carries the death penalty if found guilty (Ngangum 2018).

It is within this political context that Cameroon adopted the 2014 anti-terrorism legislation to counter the rising threat of terrorist attacks from Boko Haram, which was particularly active in the northern region. The conflict between Boko Haram and the government has already caused 1,500 deaths and led to 155,000 displaced persons and 73,000 refugees. The region became vulnerable to a jihadist insurrection due to geographical and cultural overlap with north-eastern Nigeria, the presence of an intolerant version of Islam, and the repercussions of the Chadian civil wars. Boko Haram exploited these vulnerabilities to make the far north a logistics base, a safe haven, and a source of recruitment (International Crisis Group 2016).

Boko Haram's violence has been manifested through kidnappings, ransom demands, and suicide bombings. The February 19, 2013 kidnapping of the Moulin-Fournier family and the November 14, 2013 kidnapping of French priest Georges Vandenbeusch at Nguetchéwe are notable examples. The Cameroonian government estimates that 1,098 civilians, 67 soldiers, and three policemen had been killed in targeted attacks by Boko Haram terrorists since 2013. In 2014, there were up to thirty-seven Boko Haram attacks against Cameroonian soldiers (Kouma 2017, 727). According to Amnesty International (2016), between July 2015 and July 2016, Boko Haram carried out at least 200 attacks, including 46 suicide bombings, in the far north region of Cameroon, killing over 500 civilians and over 67 members of the security forces since 2014 (Amnesty International 2016). Cameroon responded by putting in place defense and security mechanisms to contain Boko Haram threats. The Rapid Intervention Battalion, an elite unit of the army is fully engaged with the fight against Boko Haram. In this operation, Cameroon has benefited from French military assistance. The United States has provided military personnel and soldiers in charge of conducting airborne intelligence, surveillance, and reconnaissance in the region (Kouma 2017).

THEORETICAL FRAMEWORK

The chapter draws from the pluralist authoritarian media system theory developed by Hallin and Mancini (2004) to examine investigative journalism and counter-terrorism law in Cameroon. From the beginning of the liberalization process in the 1990s to the start of the year 2000, most African countries were seen as nations in transition, emerging democracies, or undergoing democratic consolidation. Hence, their media has been analyzed through the prism of the transition paradigm (Frère 2015). Although these regimes were deemed to be "transitionary," they hardly fulfilled a genuine democratic promise, mixing liberal features and authoritarian traits. Cameroon has a semblance of democracy in that it regularly holds elections, has opposition parties, and a media landscape that was liberalized in 1990. However, these democratic aspects are a façade. This is not unique to Cameroon because many of the regimes in Sub-Saharan Africa cannot be easily classified as either authoritarian or democratic because they display some characteristics of both (Ottaway 2004).

According to Ottaway (2004, 3), semi-authoritarian regimes are "ambitious systems that combine rhetorical acceptance of liberal democracy, the existence of some formal democratic institutions, and respect for a limited sphere of civil and political liberties with essentially illiberal or even authoritarian traits." It is important to note that in these regimes, there is a pluralist civil society, private media do operate, multiparty elections are organized, and institutions are established, supposedly representing the interests of the various categories of the population. At the same time, dictatorial rule is also prevalent: ongoing violations of human rights, a strong governmental intolerance for the expression of dissenting views, electoral manipulation, and attempts to prevent any change in the regime's control over the country are commonplace.

By allowing a certain level of political and media freedom, these regimes give the illusion of democracy while ensuring that these freedoms will not lead to any real change, often by using control or pressure mechanisms. Ottaway (2009) contends that semi-authoritarian regimes are not in transition. They are not emerging democracies evolving toward democratic consolidation but are semi-authoritarian by design, not by default. They are successful semi-authoritarian regimes rather than failed democracies. Cameroon presents the same paradoxical characteristic, mixing liberal traits with authoritarian practices.

According to Frère (2015), the concept of a pluralist authoritarian media system seems to be contradictory at first glance until a distinction is made between the façade and what lies beneath. On the façade, we see a pluralist media landscape, a free market open to private initiatives, an absence of a priori control over media content, a diversity of political parties interacting with media outlets, and journalists who have gained autonomy and professionalism through the establishment of their own codes of ethics, professional associations, and regulatory bodies. However, behind the interface, media organizations in Cameroon must maneuver around authorities who wish to control the flow of information through direct political pressure, indirect economic obstacles, manipulation of the judiciary system, and restrictive antiterrorism legislation. Thus, despite the daily rhetoric about the "democratic" character of the media landscape, Cameroon does not provide an enabling environment for the growth of investigative journalism. As Ottaway (2004, 17) emphasizes, a semi-authoritarian regime owes its existence not only to the deliberate manipulation of democratic institutions but, because the regime is accepted by a large portion of the population, to a support that cannot be achieved without the media's involvement. As Olivier de Sardan (2004) argues, such regimes are characterized by a "double speak." In this way, public norms as well as constitutional and institutional apparatuses constitute a "formal language," on one hand, and practical arrangements, unexpressed codes of daily life, and "informal language," on the other. The media are often at the center of that double speak.

METHODOLOGY

This study uses case law, questionnaires, and interviews to inform the discussion. Questionnaires were sent to twenty-five investigative journalists and human rights lawyers on October 30, 2019, for self-completion. The sample was composed of ten females and fifteen males, nine lawyers, and sixteen journalists (seven working for the broadcast media and nine worked as print journalists). The working experience of the respondents ranged from 6 to 18 years. The choice of investigative journalists was meant to get a picture of what happens when the media reports on or investigates national security and terrorism. The lawyers approached here represent journalists and/or media organizations in courts. Most of these lawyers also give journalists legal counseling and make recommendations about what can be published. Two weeks after questions were distributed, all the respondents had completed the questionnaire, yielding a response rate of 100%.

To get a deeper insight into the complexities of the 2014 anti-terrorism law, intensive interviews were used to complement self-completion questionnaires. Thus, five follow-up in-depth interviews were conducted with five respondents (three journalists, two lawyers) who provided arguments and concrete examples to questions asked. The intensive interviews each lasted approximately forty minutes. The questionnaire contained twenty-eight questions covering inter-alia background information, type of media/legal institution, job title, education and training, work experience, professional threats and concerns, investigating and reporting security and terrorism, the 2014 anti-terrorism legislation, the constitutionality of the 2014 anti-terror legislation, clarity and legality of the 2014 anti-terror legislation, access to information and sources, press–police relationship, criminalization of journalistic activities, press freedom, and issues of freedom of expression. The results of the questionnaire and intensive interviews both inform the research findings reported in this chapter. To protect the anonymity of the respondents, pseudonyms are used.

THE CAMEROON ANTI-TERRORISM LEGISLATION AND ITS RAMIFICATIONS ON FREEDOM OF EXPRESSION

Cameroon took measures to protect the fundamental rights and freedoms of everyone living within its jurisdiction in the context of rising terrorism threats discussed earlier. Key provisions of the law, particularly the articles that are relevant to expressive rights, are discussed here. According to Chapter 2, Section 2 of the 2014 anti-terror law:

> Whoever, acting alone as an accomplice or accessory, commits or threatens to commit an act likely to cause death, endanger physical integrity, cause bodily injury or material damage, destroy natural resources, the environment and cultural heritage with intent to: (a) intimidate the public, provoke a situation of terror or face the victim, the government and/or national and international

> organization to carry out or restrain from carrying out an act or renounce a particular position; (b) disrupt the national functioning of public services, the delivery of essential services to the public to create a crisis situation among the public; (c) create widespread insurrection in the country; (d) shall be punished with the death penalty. (Law No. 2014/028)

In Chapters 2–5, the law puts forward the death penalty to all those who are guilty of "financing acts of terrorism," "laundering of the proceeds of terrorism," and "recruitment and training of people" to participate in acts of terrorism. Section 8 of Chapter 2 (acclamation of acts of terrorism) of the law provides severe sanctions for all those who acclaim acts of terrorism. Section 8 states that: "Whoever publicly acclaims acts of terrorism shall be punished with imprisonment of 15–20 years or a fine of twenty-five million francs (25.000.000) FCFA to fifty million (50.000.000) FCFA or both imprisonment and fine."

All the respondents of this study strongly agreed that the anti-terrorism law was not compatible with international human rights law. According to Steve, a senior media law lawyer, Article 2 of the law is very broad on the definition of terrorism (personal communication, November 18, 2019). Evidence from Cameroon indicates many journalists and media practitioners who disseminate alternative or critical political discourse are experiencing various forms of harassment, intimidation, and even legal prosecution under broadly framed terrorism charges sanctioned by state-sponsored counter-terrorism legislation. Echu, a senior human rights lawyer contends that "the law is very broad, not well formulated and explicit to guide the society on how and when to exercise their fundamental freedoms" (personal communication, November 18, 2019). Many journalists interviewed quoted cases of constant obstruction of information access from the authorities and constant questioning of motives for stories and interviews. According to one senior investigative journalist at one private print and broadcast media organization in Douala:

> This law is complex because of its context and its application. Indeed, its application constitutes a real violation of press freedom. It falls out with the MUNICH convention, which clearly states that journalists must tell the truth and above all have access to all sources. In the case of Cameroon, the mere fact that a journalist gives the floor to an actor of the Anglophone crisis currently affecting the South West and North West provinces can expose him. In the end, it is a law put in place for a perfect muzzling of the press in Cameroon. It is a means of controlling the system in place. (Jane, personal communication, November 15, 2019)

Another senior journalist working at one private broadcast media outlet in Douala argued:

> The 2014 Cameroon anti-terrorism legislation has seriously influenced the way journalists investigate, gather, and present news stories. More than ever before journalists and newsrooms are conscious of prison, threats, and dismissals. Angles of reporting, choice of language and persons interviewed are well thought through. Everyone is on the defensive. It is very difficult for us being a private media organ. We get constant threats of license withdrawal. In order to protect our jobs and media organ, there is a lot of self-censorship to stay out of trouble. (Liz, personal communication, November 15, 2019)

Consider the following case, for example. Three students were found guilty of "non-denunciation of terrorism acts" by a military court in Cameroon on October 19, 2016 (The Guardian 2017, 1). They were handed a ten-year jail sentence for sharing a joke through text messages about Boko Haram. The students were arrested in December 2014, when one student, Fomusoh Ivo Feh, forwarded a text message he received from his friend, Afuh Nivelle Nfor. The message read: "Boko Haram recruits' young people from 14 years old and above. Conditions for recruitment: 4 subjects at GCE (General Certificate of Education), including religion." Nfor, in turn, sent the message to a third student, Azah Levis Gob. A teacher, who confiscated the phone, saw the text, and contacted police, who in turn arrested the students. In January 2015, the trio was transferred to a prison in Yaoundé. The text was intended as a comment on the difficulty of finding a good job without being highly qualified, the joke being that even Boko Haram would not recruit without good exam results (Guardian 2017, 1).

Many journalists and lawyers are concerned about the prevailing state of freedom of expression. According to Ama, a journalist at a private newspaper in Douala:

> It is difficult to talk of freedom of expression in the present context. Journalists are afraid to investigate news stories, report the facts or publish their findings. If they do, they are tagged as enemies of the state. Some journalists and media organizations, especially those of the state-owned media, have been reduced to public relations officers in order to stay out of trouble. Press freedom and freedom of expression have been killed. Practicing journalism has been made almost impossible, as every journalist is a potential terrorist. Even a balanced report can still run you into trouble. (Ama, personal communication, November 15, 2019)

Ama deplores the new context of terrorism and how the 2014 counter-terrorism law affected press freedom and investigative journalism. Asked whether the upsurge of the law has increased self-censorship and a decrease in investigative journalism, Ama responded:

> Yes, the case of Mimi Mefo who spent days in jail for her investigative reporting. The case of Meme Dominique who was almost crucified by the authorities and his hierarchy for visiting Muyuka and reporting on the 4-month-old baby who was shot and killed by purported military men. Their experiences scar others, thus increasing self-censorship. To be honest, no journalist is free so long as he/she is practicing in Cameroon. The fear of reprisal grips many. (personal communication, Ama, November 15, 2019)

Dominique Meme Nwakimo, referenced in the quote above (line 2), is an investigative journalist working for *Canal 2 International,* one of Cameroon's leading private broadcast media organizations located in the economic capital of Douala. Nwakimo visited the scene where a four-month-old baby was killed and investigated the situation by conducting interviews with residents as well as the deceased's parents and family. When the journalist aired his report, he and his media organization incurred a barrage of threats from the authorities. The journalist's media outlet issued him with a warning and temporary suspension (Ama, personal communication, November 15, 2019). Many journalists argued that since the inception of the counter-terrorism law and the intensification of the Boko Haram and the Cameroon Anglophone problems, their profession has been marked by safety concerns.

Another example of how Cameroon's anti-terrorism legislation is affecting journalism is the case of investigative journalist Denis Nkwebo of the French-language daily newspaper *Le Jour*, who had his car destroyed in an early morning explosion on April 24, 2014. According to Nkwebo, sources within the government had warned him to be careful in his investigation and coverage of Cameroonian security forces (Associated Press 2014). In an April 15 article, Nkwebo said security forces were struggling to stop a spate of kidnappings and armed attacks in the regions bordering unstable Nigeria and the strife-torn Central African Republic (Associated Press 2014).

Although the anti-terrorism legislation has affected expressive rights in Cameroon, investigative journalism is particularly hit the hardest. The ensuing subsections focus on the criminalization of journalistic activities, that is, how the law has been invoked to arrest and prosecute journalists. The existence of the anti-terrorism legislation in Cameroon presupposes that journalists ought to be subservient to the securitization priorities of the state. Also, there are ramifications for the failure to denounce acts of terrorism and the glorification of terrorism.

The Criminalization of Journalistic Activities

According to Walker (2017), the criminalization of journalistic activities emanates from an apprehension that investigative journalism might pose a serious threat to national security. By way of evidence of current attitudes, it is instructive to refer to the *Joint Services Publication 440*, United Kingdom Ministry of Defense, a restricted security manual devised in 2001 (Ministry of Defence 2001). It lists investigative journalists as nontraditional threats to security whose activities are to be monitored in the same way as foreign intelligence services as well as subversive and terrorist organizations. It is in this spirit that several prosecutions have been mounted against investigative journalists under Cameroonian anti-terrorism legislation as we are going to read below.

On July 30, 2015, Ahmed Abba, a *Radio France International* (RFI) correspondent, was arrested by security officers as he left a security briefing organized by the governor of the far north region of Cameroon. The journalist had spent most of the previous day investigating and interviewing refugees fleeing Boko Haram's insurgency in the far north region. It is therefore no surprise that the governor's security briefing came as a backdrop to three suicide bombings in July that left at least thirty-four people dead. According to the Committee to Protect Journalists (CPJ), Ahmed Abba was charged under Cameroon's anti-terrorism law, convicted by a military tribunal for "non-denunciation of terrorism" and "laundering of the proceeds of terrorist attacks" after two years in custody. He was sentenced to ten years in prison and a fine of around 85,000 euros (CPJ 2017). He was finally released in December 2017, after a military appeal court in Yaoundé reduced his jail term to twenty-four months (CPJ 2017).

According to the CPJ:

> The authorities are using the law against journalists such as Abba who report on the militants and others who have reported on unrest in Cameroon's English-speaking regions or are critical of Biya's administration. In addition to detaining journalists, authorities have banned news outlets deemed sympathetic to the Anglophone protests, shut out internet in regions experiencing unrest and prevented outside observers, including CPJ, from accessing the country by delaying the visa process. (CPJ 2017, 7)

Also, on October 31, 2018, Mimi Mefo was summoned to appear before the national gendarmerie in Douala as part of a false news/information and cybercrime investigation. The journalist, who also runs her own website and reports on social media about political unrest in Cameroon's western regions, was questioned for several hours and was charged with publishing and propagating information infringing on the territorial integrity of the Republic of Cameroon. During questioning, the police presented screenshots of the journalist's Facebook pages and accused her of cyber-crimes, arguing that most of the content she published constituted an attack on state security. The journalist was placed in preventive detention on November 7, 2018, but was released four days later following unprecedented national and international mobilization (CPJ 2018; Mefo 2019). According to Mefo:

> The regime has been using anti-terror and cybercrime laws to intimidate, threaten and silence the media. Since 2017, at least 20 journalists have been arrested and jailed in Cameroon for doing their jobs. I stopped publishing information on Facebook and my website for several months because of constant threats and intimidation. The crisis in Cameroon remains highly under-reported. Journalists are not guaranteed safety when travelling to conduct investigations, and access to information is a major problem. A government who imprisons a journalist is weak, scared of being exposed. (Mefo 2019, 1)

The above testament echoes the concerns of yet another journalist:

> How many reports or investigations have you seen or read about the Anglophone crisis? Those who wanted to take the leap like Mimi Mefo and Hanson are both exiles today. This law is creating a psychosis and has become a hindrance on practice. (Jane, personal communication, November 15, 2019)

It is in this context that I argue that while Cameroon has been and still is an especially egregious example of the cynical and political exploitation of terror offenses, the trend toward the disproportionate criminalization of journalists is unprecedented. In the recent context of terrorism, the misuse and abuse of national security legislation to identify government critics or silence critical investigative journalism is highly concerning. The dangers apply not only to journalists but also to their sources, who may face threats or violent reprisals for giving interviews. Whether the meetings are conducted face-to-face, through telephone, or over internet, they are susceptible to government surveillance (Walker 2017). Perhaps unsurprisingly, the CPJ (2018) has ranked Cameroon as the second-worst jailer of journalists in Sub-Saharan Africa after Eritrea, with seven journalists behind bars for their work as of December 1, 2018. The CPJ report notes that most of the journalists detained in Cameroon are facing charges linked to fake news, and to news that endangers state security (CPJ 2018).

The Demand for Information and the Duty to Inform Proactively

The deployment of the anti-terrorism legislation in Cameroon assumes that journalists ought to be subservient to the securitization priorities of the state. This assumption is inconsistent with the duty of the media and hence journalists' role to present information or inform the public proactively. The Cameroonian government approach would dismiss this key journalistic ethic, making journalists oblige to provide and withhold information about security and terrorism the way it sees fit, often in a way that is prone to self-serving interests of the government. This would demand the media turn themselves into self-tasking policing and security bodies (Walker 2017).

This insidious duty is contained in the 2014 Cameroon counter-terrorism legislation. Section 1 of the Cameroon 2014 anti-terrorism law, which sets out the purpose and scope of the legislation states that "the provisions of the penal code, the criminal procedure code and the military justice code that are not repugnant to this law shall remain applicable." Hence, an offense is committed when, per Section 107 of the penal code entitled "failure to report," individuals do not disclose information deemed to be against the national interest of the nation: "Any citizen who in time of peace fails to inform the defence, administrative and legal authorities, as soon as he comes to know of it, of any activity liable to injure the defence of the nation, shall be punished as under the last forgoing section" (Law No.2016/007, 41).

Thus, drawing from Section 1 of the 2014 anti-terror legislation, the penal code has been invoked to arrest and prosecute many journalists for failure to provide information to the authorities. Examples include Félix Ebolé Bola, president of the Cameroon's National Union of Journalists and a senior reporter at the French-language daily newspaper *Mutations*; Rodrigue Tongue of the opposition French-language daily newspaper *Le Messager*; and Baba Wamé, a former journalist. These journalists were charged in 2014 under Section 107 of Cameroon's Criminal Code and placed under judicial control. Under this state control, they were forced to register with the police each week and were prevented from publishing in the media. They were charged with the crime of "non-denunciation" by possessing national security information concerning an insurgent from the Central African Republic and failing to notify the authorities. In December 2015, the three appeared before a military tribunal judge and informed that the case against them would move forward, although all three journalists denied having uncovered any information that could undermine security, saying they wished to protect their sources (Dita, personal communication, November 20, 2019; Freedom House 2016). They had been investigating a story about allegations of collusion between elements of the security forces and a leader of an armed group from the Central African Republic who had been accused of previously attacking a town in eastern Cameroon. According to Freedom House (2016), if convicted, the three journalists could be sentenced to jail terms between one and five years and/or a fine between 50,000 to 5 million CFA (approximately US$832–US$8,325).

Paul, a junior human rights lawyer, expressed serious concerns over the use of military courts to try civilians (personal communication, November 18, 2019).

Chapter 1, Section 1 of the 2014 anti-terrorism law stipulates that "the offences provided for in this law shall fall exclusively under the jurisdiction of military tribunals." According to Ben, a senior media law lawyer, "military courts should not in any circumstances have jurisdiction over civilians" (personal communication, November 16, 2019). The case law of the African Commission is noticeably clear on the fact that military tribunals lack authority to try civilians. In the *Kevin Mgwanga Gunme et al. vs. Cameroon*, the African Commission stated that:

> Trial by military courts does not per se constitute a violation of the right to be tried by a competent organ. What poses a problem is the fact that, very often, the military tribunals are an extension of the executive, rather than the judiciary. Military tribunals are not intended to try civilians. They are established to try military personnel under laws and regulations which govern the military. The accused persons were not military personnel. The offences alleged to have been committed were quite capable of being tried by normal courts, within the jurisdictional areas the offences were allegedly committed. The Commission finds that trying civilians by the Yaoundé and the Bafoussam Military Tribunals was a violation of Article 7(1) (b) of the Charter.

According to investigative journalist Denis Nkwebo of the French-language daily newspaper *Le Jour*, "if you fail to denounce to the authorities those planning a public demonstration, you could face charges" under the counter-terrorism law (Hansrod 2019, 1). Another investigative journalist expressed similar concerns:

> For upholding information which authorities deem a threat to the state is punishable under the 2014 anti-terrorism legislation. How then do we protect our sources? To be honest, I am scared reporting some hard news for fear of reprisal not only from the authorities but also from the terrorists. (Ama, personal communication, November 15, 2019)

The question is: Do journalists have a legal or legitimate excuse to disregard this obligation or duty to inform proactively or is there any justification for journalists failing to report? Walker (2017) argues that a reporter may discover information about terrorism by interviewing a terrorist leader or terrorism operatives, or by witnessing a paramilitary display. A journalist's act may also include arranging, attending, or reporting such events, which, in turn, may implicate the reporter in various offenses. First, the offense of "failure to report," as discussed above, contributes to a dangerous chilling effect on the investigation and reporting of terrorism. Journalists can expect close attention from the police and security services as well as hostility and special restrictions from their superiors in their workplaces.

The second effect is the direct threat of prosecution in a military tribunal, imprisonment, and suspension of operating licenses (Ama, personal communication, November 15, 2019; Dita, personal communication, November 20, 2019). Such a threat occurred in the cases of Ahmed Abba, Mimi Mefo, and Meme Dominique, as indicated earlier in this chapter. A string of prosecutions and the chilling effects of the post-Abba-Bibixy-Mefo era have plunged relations between security agents, the judiciary, and investigative journalists into a deep freeze. This is very disturbing considering the supposed watchdog role of the media in society and its involvement in exposing crimes at national and local levels. One journalist's remark was very instructive over the climate of fear underpinning investigative journalism across the country:

> Nobody wants to risk spending the rest of their life in prison. I still remember when I was a columnist on a talk show on *Equinoxe Télévision,* management decided that we should never discuss the Anglophone crisis again without guidance from those in charge. This situation explained this fear of reprisals felt by people now working as journalists in Cameroon. Cameroon has been going through a crisis in the English-speaking part of the country for more than 3 years now. Has any Cameroonian media already had the courage to deal with this news, by making a real raid on the field, presenting the situation as it is? I think not. And this is the reality. (Jane, personal communication, November 15, 2019).

A junior journalist of one private newspaper, Ian, noted: "There is a general atmosphere of fear and mutual suspicion. You don't investigate and report on the issue of federalism, secession, the violence and human rights abuses committed by security forces" (personal communication, November 16, 2019). When asked how news organizations were coping with the counter-terrorism law, Jane, previously referenced, maintained:

> The media, like my own, just like journalists, distance themselves from certain information. Just as the journalist is afraid of being locked up, the press boss does not want his business to be shut down. Thus, you may have the good faith and courage to do a job, but it is simply not published or broadcast. (personal communication, November 15, 2019)

One junior human rights lawyer added: "To many journalists, self-censorship saves them the risk of arrest and imprisonment or from the dragnet of those who seek to silence the media" (Piet, personal communication, November 18, 2019). Since the passage of the 2014 counter-terrorism law in Cameroon, the perception of terrorism has exerted a new kind of pressure on the media, and, specifically, on investigative reporting. This shows that as people find new ways to express themselves, semi-authoritarian regimes are developing many roundabouts to silence freedom of expression and investigative journalism. When counter-terrorism legislation intrudes into journalistic activities, not only does it undermine journalists' ability to report accurately and to hold those in power to account, it also puts their sources at risk.

Failure to Denounce Acts of Terrorism and Glorification of Terrorism

The 2014 counter-terrorism law prohibits the acclamation, encouragement, and glorification of terrorism. Chapter 2, Section 8 (acclamation of acts of terrorism) of the law imposes heavy charges for those who acclaim acts of terrorism. This provision, I argue, may violate the right to press freedom and freedom of expression, as a vast latitude of expression and acts could be misconstrued as the glorification, acclamation, or encouragement of acts of terrorism or its non-denunciation. The use of an expression such as "non-denunciation" of terrorism, "acclamation" or "glorification of acts of terrorism" is of particular concern in the context of the highly subjective interpretation of these terms.

For example, on February 9, 2017, security forces arrested Mofor Ndong, the publisher of the independent bi-monthly Bamenda newspaper *Voice of the Voiceless*. Two other journalists, the *Guardian Post's* bureau chief Amos Fofung and Atia Tilarious Azohnwi, political editor of *The Sun Newspaper*, were arrested a few hours after Ndong. Ndong was charged on July 14, 2017, with propagating terrorism, false information, and rebellion. Under Cameroon's anti-terror law, Chapter 2, Section 2, the charges carry the death penalty. The journalist had come under the surveillance of the security forces at the time of his arrest, following intelligence reports that alleged he planned to distribute pamphlets for the *Southern Cameroons National Council* (SCNC), a separatist movement advocating Anglophone interest (CPJ 2017). Its activists, who had been banned after the government, claimed these were contrary to the constitution and liable to jeopardize national peace and security. Mofor Ndong argued that the pamphlets contained no incitement to violence but only stipulated that there was no treaty between Southern Cameroons and La République du Cameroon to be in a union (CPJ 2017). Similarly, journalist Michel Biem Tong, who reported on the crisis in the Anglophone regions of Cameroon, was arrested and charged with "glorifying terrorism" (CPJ 2017; African Freedom of Expression Exchange 2019). On August 30, 2017, the office of President Paul Biya announced that Cameroon was ending criminal proceedings against fifty-five individuals detained during unrest in the country's two English-speaking regions, including Ndong. At the time of his release, Ndong had spent more than eight months in jail (African Freedom of Expression Exchange 2019).

Also, the senior divisional officer for Mezam in the North West Province of Bamenda, Songa Pierre, shut down the popular radio station *Hot Cocoa FM 94.0*. The authorities cited unethical practices in the morning program called *Biggest Breakfast Show* (BBS) anchored by Kevin Brenda. The show provided a platform for the public to call and give their opinion about the crisis unfolding in the Anglophone regions of Cameroon. The action of the radio station made the authorities angry. According to them, the radio station and the journalist ran programs advocating terrorism and separatist tendencies as well as posing threats to national peace and security (African Freedom of Expression Exchange 2019). On February 8, 2017, the judicial police raided the journalist's home with no warrant, searched the entire premise, and, after finding nothing, confiscated the journalist's laptop, which contained significant documents and articles on the Anglophone crisis (Musa 2017; African Freedom of Expression Exchange 2019).

Radio Hot Cocoa, through its interactive program BBS, which started in 2016, acted as a forum for discussion of the Cameroon Anglophone crisis. Such radio programs fall within the ideal of the media serving the public interest. What seems to establish and give credibility to the work of these journalists and their media organizations in the eyes of the public is their ability to criticize and denounce, to contradict official information, and provide a forum for the people to express themselves through participatory radio programs. Thus, in a context where the authorities provide limited space for alternative views, journalists and their media organizations are perceived as voices for the voiceless and are appreciated when they serve public interests rather than act as public relations officers for the state and other interests.

Furthermore, the police raids at Kevin Brenda's home without a warrant as well as the attendant searches and acts of confiscation pose a serious threat to the protection of journalistic sources, a key ethical value of investigative journalism. There is growing concern about the chilling effect that raids and searches have on journalists, their sources, and news outlets. In addition, searches of newsrooms and journalists' homes to obtain documents, video, files, and other information collected by the journalist raise additional concerns over orders to testify or disclose information (Banisar 2007). Raids and searches of journalists' homes and workplaces are significant obstacles to the media's ability to fulfill their vital role of a public watchdog that is inherently connected to the freedom to receive and impart information.

CONCLUSION

According to Walker (2017), the modes of treating journalists akin to terrorists or police officers are not a new phenomenon. This history of demands, threats, and prosecution extends over several decades. However, the adverse stances seem to be growing more prevalent and more insistent. Factors that might explain this trend have been broadly identified as reflecting two vectors. One relates to the perceived nature of terrorism. Terrorism is seen as more threatening, and, therefore, demands greater societal mobilization and tolerance to risks. As a result, counter-terrorism is allowed to transcend other values, including freedom of expression, press freedom, and investigative journalism.

The other factor relates to the perceived nature of journalism and the media. The official and general perception seems to be that the media have grown immensely powerful in recent years and should be viewed as more threatening to the interests and needs of counter-terrorism legislation. In Cameroon, changes in technology have altered the media landscape, which was long controlled by the state and biased toward the ruling political party. However, with a growing percentage of the population now online, primarily through social media and mobile phones, it has become easier to bypass state-controlled media, and social media are becoming a critical method of information consumption and political messaging. The media have been at the forefront in sensitizing the public on the virtues of a democratic system, promoting development, and acting as watchdogs of society, sometimes against the wishes of the government.

As this chapter has indicated using the Cameroonian experiment with counter-terrorism legislation, many journalists and media practitioners who disseminate alternative or critical political discourse are experiencing various forms of harassment, persecution, intimidation, and even legal prosecution under broadly framed terrorism charges sanctioned by state-sponsored counter-terrorism legislation. Thus, the law remains a serious threat to freedom of expression.

To move forward with enhancing security and fight terrorism without compromising expressive rights, it is important to reform the anti-terrorism law to make it comply with the Cameroonian constitution and international human rights standards by revoking the death penalty, granting civilian courts jurisdiction to adjudicate crimes of terrorism, and providing a clear definition of terrorism. Also, the law should ensure that all detainees are charged with a recognizable criminal offense and tried in accordance with international standards.

REFERENCES

African Freedom of Expression Exchange. 2019. "Analytical Report on the Safety of Journalists in Cameroon 2017-2019." https://www.africafex.org/afex/wp-content/

uploads/2019/09/Analytical-Report-on-the-Safety-of-Journalists-in-Cameroon-Jan.-2017-and-July-2019.pdf.

Amnesty International Reports. 2016. "Human Rights Under Fire: Attacks and Violations in Cameroon's Struggle with Boko-Haram." Dakar: Amnesty International Publications.

Associated Press. 2014. "Explosion Targets Journalist's Car in Cameroon, Press Group Says." *New Europe*, April 25, 2014. https://www.neweurope.eu/article/explosion-targets-journalists-car-cameroon-press-group-says/.

Banisar, David, 2007. "Silencing Sources: An International Survey of Protections and Threats to Journalists' Sources." Privacy International Global Survey Series. http://dx.doi.org/10.2139/ssrn.1706688.

Barendt, Eric. 2005. *Freedom of Speech*, 2nd ed. Oxford: Oxford University Press.

Committee to Protect Journalists. 2017. "Journalists Not Terrorists: In Cameroon, Anti-terror Legislation is Used to Silence Critics and Suppress Dissent." Accessed September 13, 2020. https://cpj.org/reports/2017/09/journalists-not-terrorists-cameroon-ahmed-abba-anti-terror-imprisoned.php.

———. 2018. "CPJ Calls on Cameroon to Release and Drop Charges against Mimi Mefo." Accessed October 2, 2020. https://cpj.org/2018/11/cpj-calls-on-cameroon-to-drop-charges-against-mimi.php.

Fonchingong, Tangie. 2013. "The Quest for Autonomy: The Case of Anglophone Cameroon." *African Journal of Political Science and International Relations* 7 (5): 224–236.

Freedom House. 2016. "Cameroon." Accessed April 14, 2020. https://freedomhouse.org/report/freedom-press/ 27 April 2016/Cameroon.

Frère, Marie-Soleil. 2015. "Francophone Africa: The Rise of 'Pluralist Authoritarian' Media Systems?" *African Journalism Studies* 36 (1): 103–112. https://doi.org/10.1080/23743670.2015.1008176.

Hallin, Daniel, and Paolo Mancini. 2004. *Comparing Media Systems: Three Models of Media and Politics*. New York: Cambridge University Press.

Hansrod, Zeenat. 2019. "When Anti-Terrorism Laws are Used to Sacrifice Free Speech." *RFI*, March 10, 2017. http://en.rfi.fr/Africa/20171001-media.

International Crisis Group. 2016. "Cameroon: Confronting Boko-Haram." Crisis Group Africa. https://www.crisisgroup.org/africa/central-africa/cameroon/cameroon-confronting-boko-haram.

Kevin Mgwanga Gunme v. Cameroon, Communication/decisions/266/2003, 26th ACHPR AAR Annex (Dec 2008 – May 2009).

Konings, Piet, and Francis B. Nyamnjoh. 1997. "The Anglophone Problem in Cameroon." *Journal of Modern African Studies* 35 (2): 207–229.

Kouma, Jean Cottin G. 2017. "Cameroon Fighting Boko-Haram." *International Relations* 1 (4): 727–737.

Law No. 2014/028 (Law on the Suppression of Acts of Terrorism in Cameroon). 2014. https://www.assnat.cm/gestionLoisLegislatures/libraries/files_upload/uploads/Lois/2014-028fr.pdf.

Law No. 2016/007 (Law Relating to the Penal Code). 2016. https://www.wipo.int/edocs/lexdocs/laws/en/cm/cm014en.pdf.

Mefo, Mimi T. 2019. "Index Awards 2019." https://www.indexoncensorship.org/2019/04/awards-mimi-mefo-speech/.
McNamara, Lawrence. 2009a. "Counter-terrorism Laws and the Media: National Security and the Control of Information." *Security Challenges* 5 (3): 95–115.
———. 2009b. "Counter-terrorism Laws: How They Affect Media Freedom and News Reporting." *Westminster Papers in Communication and Culture* 6 (1): 27–45.
Ministry of Defence. 2001. "The Defence Manual of Security Volumes 1, 2 and 3 Issue 2." Accessed October 12, 2020. http://wla.1-s.es/uk-mod-jsp-440-2001.pdf.
Musa, Wilson. 2017. "Cameroon - Crisis in Bamenda: Doors of Radio Hot Cocoa FM 94.0 Sealed." *Cameroon-Info.net*, January 11, 2017. http://www.cameroon-info.net/article/cameroon-crisis-in-bamenda-doors-of-radio-hot-cocoa-fm-940-sealed-278946.html.
Ngangum, Peter. 2018. "Peaceful Protests Against Government Policy of Assimilation-A Human Rights Based Approach." Paper presented at the International Association for Media and Communication Research Annual International Conference, Law Section, June 20 - 24, 2018 University of Oregon, Eugene, Oregon, USA.
Olivier de Sardan, Jean-Pierre. 2004. "État, bureaucratie et gouvernance en Afrique de l'Ouest francophone: Un diagnostic empirique, une perspective historique." *Politique Africaine* 96: 139–162.
Ottaway, Marina. 2004. "Democracy Challenged: The Rise of Semi-authoritarian State." Washington: Carnegie Endowment for International Peace.
———. 2009. "Ideological Challenges to Democracy: Do They Exist?" In *New Challenges to Democratization*, edited by Peter Burnell and Richard Youngs. London and New York: Routledge.
McVeigh, Karen. 2017. "No Laughing Matter: Cameroon Students Face 10 Years in Jail for Boko-Haram Joke." *The Guardian*, September 21, 2017. https://www.theguardian.com/global-development/2017/sep/21/no-laughing-matter-cameroon-students-face-10-years-in-jail-for-boko-haram-joke.
Tangwa, Godfrey.1999. "Colonialism and Linguistic Dilemmas in Africa: Cameroon as a Paradigm." *Quest* 13 (1–2): 2–17.
Voorhoof, Dirk, and Hannes Cannie. 2010. "Freedom of Expression and Information in a Democratic Society." *International Communication Gazette* 72 (4–5): 407–423. https://doi.org/10.1177/1748048510362711.
Walker, Clive. 2017. "Investigative Journalism and Counter-terrorism Laws." *Notre Dame Journal of Law, Ethics and Public Policy* 31(1): 129–174.

PART IV

COUNTER-TERRORISM LAWS AND CITIZEN EXPRESSION

Chapter 13

Peru's Counter-terrorism Law in Post-conflict Times

Gabriela Martínez

INTRODUCTION

The twentieth century has been one of political and social turmoil throughout Latin America. The triumph of the Cuban Revolution in 1959 along with the widespread and deep structural social and economic inequalities across countries in Central and South America inspired several political revolutions in the latter part of the twentieth century. Peru was not immune to this, having some insurgent attempts in the 1960s even though they were rapidly shut down (CVR 2003, 379). Later, however, it would suffer a twenty-year internal armed conflict between 1980 and 2000, in which subversive groups, unlike in previous political uprisings, were immediately labeled as terrorist organizations.

The insurgency in Peru constituted a serious menace to democratic life in the latter years of the twentieth century, and each government in turn set in place or expanded legislative sanctions for terrorism. However, the misuse of anti-terrorism legislation was and continues to be one of the most widespread threats to freedom of expression, particularly artistic and media expressions. In Peru, since early on, anti-terrorism laws have included the sanction for apology of terrorism, which has been loosely defined and is generally open to interpretation. Using the political economy of communications as an analytical framework, I will analyze how freedom of expression is deterred, questioned, and penalized under the law typifying apology of terrorism in post-conflict times in Peru.

I am interested in probing how apology of terrorism is used, and in some cases abused, to attempt to silence citizens' dissent, as well as gag artists, activists, and institutions whose work is related to Peru's historical memory of the internal armed conflict. I will draw attention to Article 316 and

Article 316-A of the Peruvian Penal Code that deal with terrorism and apology of terrorism, respectively. The notion of apology of terrorism was introduced in the penal code in 1981 under the Presidency of Fernando Belaúnde Terry (1980–1985), although the act itself was not defined. Subsequently, the article of apology of terrorism was reaffirmed under different governments, first in 1992, then revised and amended in 2003, 2007, and 2017, when five legislative projects from 2016 were passed, and the new law creating Article 316-A was approved (Calderón 2018, 19).

This chapter will focus primarily on the impact of the norm since 2017 when Article 316 was last amended, and Article 316-A was introduced typifying apology of terrorism with concrete language indicating what constitutes the act of apology of terrorism, which previously had been vaguely defined. I will argue that the tension between freedom of expression and the state's desire to restrict the range of that freedom signals an ongoing conflict between citizens and the state (MacNamara 2009, 27). This tension has existed for at least three decades or more, and the specter of terrorism exacerbates such tension to the detriment of common citizens, artists, media professionals, and institutions working toward reconciling Peruvian society. The specter of terrorism is accompanied by the lasting legacy of a culture and politics of fear ingrained in the collective psyche (Burt 2006, 40) despite the fact that the terrorist threat has been eradicated for the most part.

THE FIRST COUNTER-TERRORISM LAW

The first counter-terrorism law, Legislative Decree 46, includes an article referring to apology of terrorism. This decree goes back to 1981, when the government of Belaúnde Terry (1980–1985) was confronting the beginnings of what developed into an armed internal conflict that lasted two decades, from 1980 to 2000. The internal conflict unfolded primarily in the highlands of the country, particularly in the department of Ayacucho. Over time, the conflict spread out including in urban areas across the country, particularly the capital, Lima. One of the main actors in this conflict was the Partido Comunista del Perú-Sendero Luminoso (PCP-SL),[1] a Maoist branch of the PCP, that declared war against the Peruvian State. A few years later, in 1984, a socialist group, the Movimiento Revolucionario Tupac Amaru (MRTA),[2] also took up arms against the State. Both groups saw themselves as revolutionary guerrilla movements aiming to change the course of the nation toward communist or socialist rule. However, their military tactics evolved in such a manner that soon the State labeled them as terrorist organizations and considered their actions terrorist acts.[3]

In 1981, Belaúnde Terry's government, facing the challenge of Sendero Luminoso, introduced Decree 46 containing eleven articles that typified terrorism.[4] This legislative decree provided the initial framework, which would later be revised and expanded under the governments of Alan García Perez (1985–1990) and Alberto Fujimori (1990–2000) (Rivera Paz 2007, 2). The Legislative Decree 46 essentially contained criminal regulations defining and sanctioning terrorism, and it typified belonging to a terrorist organization, acts of collaboration with terrorism, instigation, and apology for terrorism, among others as terrorism crimes. However, the legislation lacked a clear, precise, and concrete definition of exactly what act could be considered as terrorism or as apology of terrorism (Rivera Paz 2007, 3).

Rivera Paz (2007, 1–5) explains that the anti-terrorist legislation has been one of the busiest regulatory bodies in Peru's recent history, and he points out that between the presidencies of Belaúnde Terry and Fujimori there had been over forty normatives, although most of them promulgated during the Fujimori regime. In the past twenty years, after the Fujimori regime, several new norms, amendments, and expansions of the counter-terrorist laws have continued to be added to the penal code.

President Alberto Fujimori, elected in 1990, mounted a self-coup in April 1992, dissolving the Congress. He then ordered the revision of the Constitution as well as of the penal code. In May 1992, Fujimori signed Decree 25475, heralding the advent of the new counter-terrorism law (Rivera Paz 2007, 3). Decree 25475, and other decrees that came after it, have been used to amend the language in Article 316 of the penal code, addressing terrorism and apology of terrorism. However, it is important to note that despite the various amendments over the years, the current counter-terrorism laws still use the framework of Fujimori's Decree 25475 (Calderón 2018, 52; Pastrana Sánchez 2019, 52).

BRIEF HISTORICAL CONTEXT FOR THE DEVELOPMENT OF COUNTER-TERRORISM LAWS

In May 1980, when Peru transitioned back to democratic life after twelve years of military dictatorship, Sendero Luminoso, led by philosophy professor Abimael Guzmán, declared war against the State. Sendero Luminoso, a Maoist group that broke off from Peru's Communist Party, carried out its first attack in May of 1980. The attack was a day before the long-awaited national elections, and it took place in the remote Andean village of Chuschi in Ayacucho, a predominately peasant indigenous area of the country. Sendero Luminoso's attack killed a few policemen and destroyed ballot boxes (CVR 2004, 97; Gorriti 2009, 43). This event was barely covered by the press, and it appears as a small criminal note on the back pages of a few newspapers. At that moment, no one gave Sendero Luminoso or the attack enough attention.

However, by 1981, attacks from this group against state forces and civilians became more noticeable for their frequency and increasing brutality. Sendero Luminoso's main objective was to overthrow the government through an armed struggle. It is within this framework of unfolding conflict in which Decree 46 came into existence in 1981. From that moment on the State's strategy was that of "war against terrorism" (Siles Vallejo 2015, 77; De la Jara 2008, 235).

Decree 46 typified terrorism, including the crimes of belonging to a terrorist organization, collaborating with terrorists, instigating terrorism, and apology of terrorism, among others (Rivera Paz 2007, 2). Since this first counter-terrorist law typifying terrorism and apology of terrorism, the media are considered as a tool that potentially could serve terrorists. Articles six and seven in this decree address the media and apology of terrorism in general terms. The articles state the following:

> Artículo 6: El que mediante la imprenta, la radio, la televisión u otro medio de comunicación social incitare a un número indeterminado de personas para que comentan cualquiera de los actos que conforman el delito de terrorismo, será reprimido con penitenciaría no menor de cuatro años, ni mayor de ocho años.
>
> Article 6: Anyone who incites any number of people to comment on any of the acts that make up the crime of terrorism through the press, radio, television, or other means of social communication will be punished with a penitentiary of no less than four years and no longer than eight years (translation by author).
>
> Artículo 7: El que públicamente hiciere la apología de un acto de terrorismo ya cometido o de la persona que hubiera sido condenada como su autor o cómplice será reprimido con penitenciaría no menor de tres años, ni mayor de cinco años.
>
> Article 7: Anyone who publicly condones an act of terrorism already committed or for the person who has been convicted as its author or accomplice will be punished with a penitentiary of no less than three years and no more than five years (translation by author).

Rivera Paz (2007, 2–3) suggests that the definitions of what it means exactly to engage in the diverse actions typified as terrorism, and in particular apology of terrorism, have never been explicit. Thus, many times, this has been open to interpretation and in consequence, innocent people have been unjustly punished.

Ten years after Decree 46, the most important changes in the counter-terrorism legislation were under the Fujimori regime that introduced two counter-terrorist laws: Law 25475 for counter-terrorism and Law 25659 for treason to the nation. These have served as the framework for several norms that came after, modifying and expanding the penal code to fight Sendero Luminoso and the MRTA. The MRTA, similar to Sendero Luminoso, declared war against the State and engaged in terrorist acts as part of their tactics for an armed struggle (Siles Vallejo 2015, 76). As mentioned before, Law 25475 continues to serve as the framework for the current counter-terrorist laws. However, Law 25659 was highly controversial because it allowed for military trials of civilians as well as military and civilian "tribunales sin rostro" or "faceless courts"[5] (Rivera Paz and Alvarez Yrala 2003, 1; Degregori and Rivera Paz 1993, 25). However, in April 1995, Law 26447 signals the end of "faceless courts" due to internal and external political pressure for the growing human rights abuses. But, in October of the same year, Law 26537 established a new validity time for the same courts which were dismantled a few years after.

Later, during the transitional period after the fall of the Fujimori regime and the return to a more democratic environment and times of peace, the elected governments of Alejandro Toledo (2001–2006) and Alan García (2006–2011) passed Decree 924 in 2003 and Decree 982 in 2007, respectively. These two decrees modified Article 316 of the penal code and typified apology of terrorism as a special crime although the language was still somewhat vague in relation to what exactly constitutes apology of terrorism. One important aspect of Law 982, decreed in 2007, is that this included, as one of the aggravating circumstances of terrorism, the act of praising or publicizing a terrorist act or the person who committed a terrorist act through communication or media technologies, including social media platforms (Calderón 2018, 19). We must not forget that both Facebook and YouTube came to life a few years earlier; the first one in 2004, and the second in 2005. Peruvians adopted these social platforms fairly fast, circulating a variety of content, prompting the power elites to consider social media potential tools for apology of terrorism, just like radio or television.

In 2017, during the brief government of Pedro Pablo Kuczynski (2016–2018), Article 316 was modified again by Law 30610. In addition to the more general description of terrorism in Article 316, Article 316-A was created, exclusively defining apology of terrorism this time with more specific language. Article 316-A establishes that anyone who *justifies* or *exalts* a terrorist act or a person who has been convicted of a terrorist act would be detained and prosecuted for apology of terrorism. It also specifies that if the justifying or exaltation is "a) exercising the status of authority, teacher, or administrative staff of an educational institution, or b) using or facilitating the presence of minors, the penalty of prison shall not be less than six years or more than 10 years in prison" (Law 30610 and 316-A 2017, Peru) (translation by author). Furthermore, the new article 316-A specifies that if anyone justifies or exalts terrorist acts or a person who has been convicted of terrorism through *objects, books, writings, audio, visuals, and audiovisuals, or any media or communication technology*, they will receive a minimum of eight years and a maximum of fifteen years in prison. This specificity covers a lot of ground in terms of the possible mediated nature of apology of terrorism, but what it doesn't do is clarify what exactly constitutes a justification or exaltation of terrorist acts or what a person has to do to be convicted of such actions. Is publishing a picture of a person who is convicted of terrorism punishable with apology of terrorism? Is writing the history of Sendero Luminoso apology of terrorism? Could creating a piece of art commemorating victims of both state repression and non-state actors be considered apology of terrorism? Can a personal opinion contextualizing the reasons for insurgency or other political opinion be considered a justification of terrorism, and, therefore, apology of terrorism? The fact that there is no specific explanation of what could be deemed a justification or exaltation leaves the door open to interpretation, creating a dangerous environment for freedom of expression.

The social context in which Article 316 was revised and amended, and Article 316-A was introduced took place during a long teachers' strike between June and September of 2017. This strike was controversial because some leaders of the Comité Nacional de Reorientación y Reconstrucción (Conare), which is a part of the teacher's union, Sindicato Unico de Trabajadores de la Educación or SUTEP, were identified as having ties to the Movimiento por Amnistia y Derechos Fundamentales or MOVADEF. MOVADEF, an organization linked to Sendero Luminoso, has been advocating since its foundation in 2009 for the liberation of Sendero Luminoso's top leader Abimael Guzmán and several others who either were intellectual authors or carried out terrorist acts during the internal conflict. MOVADEF argues that those people are political prisoners who should be liberated (Valle Riestra 2013, Ideele Revista online). MOVADEF militants have organized public meetings and have marched carrying banners with the picture of Abimael Guzmán. In addition, MOVADEF has been active in the blogosphere campaigning for Guzmán's release from prison.

Article 316-A was introduced at a moment in which MOVADEF was getting public attention and infiltrating legitimate workers union organizations, like SUTEP. The language in Article 316-A targets directly MOVADEF's attempts to infiltrate the teachers' union and schools. In addition, it serves to deter any teacher or any person from critically discussing the recent history of the country. Subsection 4 from bill 30610 introducing 316-A states:

> Si el agente lo realiza en su condición de director, subdirector, personal docente o administrativo de una institución educativa, mediante objetos, textos escolares, escritos, imágenes visuales o auditivas destinadas a la enseñanza, la pena

privativa de libertad será no menor de quince ni mayor de dieciocho años, imponiéndose quinientos días multa e inhabilitación del ejercicio del cargo, conforme al numeral 9) del articulo 36 del Código Penal.

If the agent performs in their capacity as director, associate director, teacher, or administrative staff of an educational institution, through objects, textbooks, written, audio or visual imagery intended for teaching; imprisonment will be no less than fifteen and no more than eighteen years of imprisonment, imposing five hundred days fine and disqualification from the exercise of the position, according to numeral 9) of article 36 of the penal code. (translation by author)

It is clear that Article 316-A is not used only to combat MOVADEF and likeminded groups or people. Such measures were also used to restrain and silence political enemies, the media, artists, activist, as well as institutions working with topics related to the internal conflict period. The amendments to Article 316 and the passing of Article 316-A did not resolve the conflict between the prohibition of apology and the respect that must be afforded to the right to freedom of expression. The latest amendments actually further what Jo-Marie Burt termed "the instrumentalization of fear" (2006, 33) as the current political elites and others continue to harness the existing culture of fear instilled in society due to the collective trauma caused by the internal conflict.

LASTING POLITICS OF FEAR

The knowledge about the internal conflict as it was unfolding in the 1980s and 1990s was primarily mediated by a rather sensationalistic press that published shocking images of violence again and again (Bourque and Warren 1989, 19–20). There was not a day without newspaper reports or television news where gruesome imagery was portrayed displaying bodies in mass graves, tortured people, buildings and public assets destroyed by bombings, and so on. What this cultural imagery did was instill fear in the larger population, in addition to the first-hand experience of thousands of people directly exposed to the various actors perpetrating violence: Sendero Luminoso and the MRTA, State forces, paramilitary forces, and civil patrols known as rondas campesinas.

Both Sendero Luminoso and State forces used widespread violence as a means to exert their control and send a powerful message to the rest of the social fabric, each with different goals: one to defeat the terrorist movement, and the other to defeat the State. In this highly violent and polarized context, activists and common citizens became afraid. Young people constantly feared the police and the military because the latter tended to suspect youngsters, and in particular, university students. Human rights and social activists lived in fear for their lives since many times they were labeled as terrorists or sympathizers of Sendero Luminoso. Sendero Luminoso also distrusted and viciously attacked young people and activists who did not join their cause (Burt 2006, 40–41). But fear did not come only due to State and terrorist violence; the economic erosion and ultimately the collapse of the economy due to hyper-inflation contributed to a sense of complete uncertainty which was frightening to most. During the decades of the 1980s, 1990s, and 2000s, a large percentage of Peruvians could not meet their basic needs. The middle-class shrank noticeably. Highly educated people and professionals were doing menial jobs or working two or more jobs to make ends meet.

In this environment of multidirectional violence created by political, social, and economic deterioration, a "culture of fear" developed. Thus the common citizen willingly surrendered their rights in exchange for order and stability (Burt 2006, 35). Throughout the 1990s, the Fujimori regime capitalized on such a culture of fear converting it into an important instrument to demobilize the larger society and silence political opposition. The fearful environment allowed Fujimori to mount a self-coup. In 1992, he closed down the Congress without much resistance from the citizenry. Then, his government expanded the counter-insurgency laws 25475 and 26659 granting the military extra powers, not only to combat terrorism but also to set in place military courts to judge civilians. Similarly, his government expanded powers for civilian courts, authorizing both the military and civilian courts to have "faceless courts." Detainees who were tried by the "faceless courts" were not provided with minimal opportunities to prove their innocence, and usually were found guilty. In addition to amendments to the counter-insurgency legal framework, the decade of the 1990s was marked by extrajudicial executions, enforced disappearances, and the institutionalization of corruption within state institutions that can be felt even today.

The defeat of Sendero Luminoso and the MRTA, the fall of the Fujimori regime in 2000 due to corruption and human rights abuses, and the transition to a more democratic and peaceful time in 2001 did not completely eliminate the culture of fear. All democratic governments that came after Fujimori, members of the Congress, and followers of party ideologies have continued using the specter of terrorism to control and punish opposition or dissent. Mainstream television continued to warn against Sendero Luminoso by producing programming representing landmark cases in which Sendero Luminoso exerted violence against civilian populations. On one hand, this helps build historical collective memory; and on the other, it solidifies the existing fear while warning newer generations against the evils of political conflict and terrorism. In this manner, the culture and instrumentalization of fear remains alive and well into the twenty-first century, permeating a society that remains politically and socially unreconciled in its totality.

THE LUM'S CASE

The Lugar de la Memoria, la Tolerancia y la Inclusión Social, more commonly known as LUM, is a museum devoted to the historical collective memory of the internal armed conflict. Currently, the Minister of Culture oversees the museum's operations as a State museum. The LUM, which was officially opened in 2015, is a place surrounded by controversy since long before its opening. Once it was described to me by poet José Carlos Aguero (personal communication) as a "hot potato that no one wants to have in their hands" because for some the museum tells the "official story" responding to a neutral and uncritical vision of the internal conflict. For others, the LUM's permanent exhibition and some of its temporary exhibitions unfairly demonize the role of the State and the military. Despite the careful curation of the museum to present a balanced story of the conflict based on years of research, data acquired, and the report by the Truth and Reconciliation Commission, there are still people who deem the museum biased supporting leftist ideologies and even terrorism.

The LUM has the permanent exhibition that directly addresses the years of the internal conflict, and it also hosts temporary exhibitions, theater presentations, and film exhibitions. In August of 2017, the LUM inaugurated a temporary exhibition "Resistencia visual 1992. Carpeta colaborativa" ("Visual Resistance 1992. Collaborative Dossier"). The exhibition showcased the art work of thirty-six graphic artists. Each artist contributed one mono-color silkscreen of poster size. To provide context, the exhibition was accompanied by audiovisuals, newspaper clips, magazines, and other artifacts related to the year 1992 and the larger historical memory of the internal conflict. Karen Bernedo was the curator for the temporary exhibition at the LUM; she is an activist and curator of the Museo Itinerante Arte por la Memoria (Itinerant Museum Art for Memory), which also focuses on Peru's historical memory of the internal conflict.

When Bernedo was interviewed by LaMula.pe (August 16, 2017) and was asked about the focus on 1992, she explained that in 1992 many significant events took place becoming emblematic of that moment in the history of the internal conflict. Bernedo and the participating artists used this year as an inspiration and point of departure for their artistic work. Bernedo further explained that the year 1992 was a moment that "marked a before and after" due to the nature of the events. The exhibit makes an important connection between past and present embracing collective memories of terrorist acts as well as abuses of counter-terrorism efforts on the part of the government. The exhibit serves to engage and understand Peru's contemporary realities under the shadow of its past.

Bernedo listed as examples the dissolution of the Congress by the then-president Fujimori; the capture of Sendero Luminoso's leader Abimael Guzmán; the extrajudicial assassination of eight students and a professor from Universidad La Cantuta by the paramilitary group Colina, later linked to President Fujimori and his right-hand man Vladimiro Montesinos; the assassination by paramilitary forces of Pedro Huilca, leader of Peru's workers' union CGTP; the sterilization of low-income women without their knowledge or consent under the Fujimori regime; Sendero Luminoso's massive bomb attack in Tarata street located in the middle-class neighborhood of Miraflores; Sendero Luminoso's assassination of popular leader and activist Maria Elena Moyano in the shantytown of Villa El Salvador; among others.

The exhibition and Bernedo's declarations stirred up reaction from some politicians in Fujimori's party and his followers. Similarly, people siding with the military and conservative factions of the country accused the curator, the participant artists, and the LUM of promoting an ideology of discord, revenge, and ultimately of apology of terrorism. In the online opinion blog Politico.pe (August 28, 2017) Karina Calmet writes an article entitled Lugar de la Memoria con Amnesia (The Place of Memory with Amnesia) where she states that the exhibition is made of a "selective memory" and that the LUM is wasting tax monies to "reventar cuetes" (slang for "celebrate") the bias of the left. Calmet questions why the LUM does not host art exhibitions celebrating the military who fought against Sendero Luminoso to save the country from terrorist acts. She further asks before closing, why there are no exhibitions to praise the special forces that liberated the hostages held in the Japanese Embassy in Lima by the MRTA.

The controversy around "Resistencia visual 1992: Carpeta colaborativa" forced LUM's director, sociologist Guillermo Nugent, to resign from his position. However, the Minister of Culture at that time, Salvador del Solar, denied that Nugent's resignation was censoring the LUM or the exhibition. According to del Solar, Nugents resignation happened because he did not make good use of judgment when accepting to host at the LUM the controversial temporary exhibition. The office of Minister del Solar issued a press release stating that the exhibition was damaging the image of the LUM, and the spirit in which the museum was founded to neutrally tell Peru's history without ideological slants.

Although LUM's director had to vacate his position, the Minister ordered the exhibition to remain open until the agreed closing date in an effort to counter the press and others who were raising concerns about censorship as well as pointing out the influence or control of Fujimori's political party over government institutions. Fujimori's party members and their allies were prone to resort and use apology of terrorism law in their attempts to silence people whenever there was a legitimate art exhibition, report, or criticism that covers the disgraced government of Alberto Fujimori. Former president Fujimori remains in prison for various charges including human rights abuses, willful embezzlement, appropriation of public funds, and ideological falsehood in detriment of the State.

Ironically, the controversy generated around "Resistencia Visual 1992" and all the press coverage the exhibition received fueled public interest in the exhibition, making it an absolute success. The attempt to shut down free expression backfired against the Minister of Culture, the government, and in particular against Fujimori's party and its allies. This shows the ongoing struggles between political elites seeking to control narratives of past and present and citizens who demand a truly democratic society in which freedom of expression and political critique are not void of their meaning.

In April 2018, a year after the controversy of "Resistencia Visual 1992" that forced LUM's director to resign, Gabriela Eguren, art historian and LUM's specialist in charge of the museum's educational area was accused of apology of terrorism. This time the accusation came from retired army general and congressman, Edwin Donayre, from the political party Alianza para el Progreso (APP). Congressman Donayre also accused the LUM of fostering elements of apology of terrorism. This came about after the congressman visited the permanent exhibition of the LUM disguised and posing as a Colombian citizen, a victim of Colombia's internal conflict. Donayre was accompanied by a couple of friends, one of which posed as a displaced person from Peru's internal conflict. One has to question the ethical stance of this visit, which was no less than an attempt to bring false charges against the museum.

Donayre himself, tells in an interview with RPP (RPP 2018) that he disguised himself with a wig, a hat, jeans, and posed as a mild deaf-mute person because he didn't want to give away his voice or accent not to be recognized. Gabriela Eguren, in an interview with journalist Rosa Maria Palacios (Palacios 2018), confirms that Congressman Donayre indeed pretended to be deaf-mute and that she was told that his condition was due to having been tortured in Colombia. Donayre's friend asked Eguren to speak louder for Donayre to hear her better; however, what they wanted was to get a better recording of what she was saying.

Donayre's friends did the talking and asked Gabriela Eguren questions while she led a three-hour museum tour for Donayre, his friends, and other LUM visitors not connected to the congressman. The impostors recorded a video of the guided visit to later edit a six-minute clip that Donayre circulated in social media denouncing the LUM, and in particular Eguren, of apology of terrorism. Donayre, in his interview with RPP on May 17, 2018, contends that Eguren presented information diminishing the important role of State forces in the fight against terrorist groups. According to him, Eguren talked about the military and the State as perpetrators of human rights abuses while presenting Sendero Luminoso and the MRTA as victims (RPP Noticias May 17).

Donayre's friends, while having a conversation with Eguren, asked the latter's opinion regarding the controversial presidential pardon granted by President Kuczinsky to former president Fujimori to free him from prison,[6] to which Ms. Eguren responded that given Fujimori's old age and fragile health it seemed understandable. However, she added that, under the premise of old age and poor health, the lawyers who represent Sendero Lumino's leader Abimael Guzmán could also request similar treatment for their elderly and ill client. According to Donayre's accusation, Eguren's response to his friends is apology of terrorism for suggesting that Guzmán could have similar treatment to Fujimori. Eguren's defense was that Donayre took what she said out of context during three hours of information, condensing everything into a brief video clip for social media. She explained in an interview with well-known journalist and lawyer Rosa María Palacios, that the impostors have distorted the guided tour and conversation to fit Donayre's stance to attack the LUM and its employees. Congressman Donayre and his political bench, along with politicians from other parties including Fujimori's, demanded Ms. Eguren's removal from her position at the LUM. The political mounting pressure from the Congress forced the Minister of Culture to remove Eguren from the LUM.

The LUM's case through the examples of "Resistencia Visual 1992" and Gabriela Eguren illustrate the impact of Article 316-A. Although the artists who participated in the exhibition or employees of the museum were not prosecuted for apology of terrorism, these cases show how the political class and some followers of certain parties misuse the concept of apology of terrorism and the law to restrict freedom of expression and instill fear in people. There has not been many prosecutions for apology of terrorism, but since Article 316-A was approved, the number of accusations is increasing. This new framing of what constitutes apology of terrorism is lending itself to monitor any expression that may question the current political status quo, the official story of the internal conflict, or the lack of awareness of Peru's recent historical past.

THE CASE OF DANIELA CHACÓN

In September 2017, Daniela Chacón and Maria Sedano, both former photography students of the institute Centro de la Imágen, designed a class art project based on two iconic photographs that the students made into posters.

One was Sendero Luminoso's leader Abimael Guzmán and the other former president General Juan Velasco Alvarado, a nationalist/populist army general who became president through a coup in 1968, governing until 1975. Velasco Alvarado implemented a series of reforms that transformed Peruvian society: agrarian reform, educational reform, media reform, and nationalized all natural resources in the hands of foreign companies, among others.

On top of each poster, the students placed text that read "Héroe Nacional" ("National Hero"), and below an electronic address where people could send feedback reacting to the poster(s). In Chacón's declarations to the press, she explained that the idea behind this was to probe how many people, especially young people of their generation, knew who these two men were and what their role in Peruvian society had been (ATV Noticias March 7, 2018). Are they indeed heroes? The average person with less than twenty-five years of age is not familiar with either Abimael Guzmán or General Juan Velasco Alvarado. The artistic and provocative idea to measure knowledge and generate reactions to stimulate dialogue about the impact of these two men landed them in jail, accused for apology of terrorism. Although the image of General Velasco Alvarado is not linked to terrorism, the one of Guzmán, leader of Sendero Luminoso is, and this is why the students were denounced before the authorities.

The prosecutor asked for fifteen years of prison for Daniela Chacón as intellectual author, and 500 thousand Peruvian soles (roughly US $70,000) in civil reparations in favor of the state (IPYS 2019). Hector Bendezú, Chacón's lawyer, argued against the prosecution using freedom of expression as the basis for her artistic, intellectual, and sociological school exercise through photography. Several witnesses corroborated that this was a school assignment with no political motives or intention of apology of terrorism (*La República,* August 31, 2019). Furthermore, the accused did not have an affiliation or even a minimal connection to any political organization, much less sympathy for Sendero Luminoso. In fact, Daniela Chacón explained that during the years of the internal conflict her father, Victor Ch. Vargas, a well-known photojournalist, was kidnapped and tortured by members of Sendero Luminoso for photographing and publishing photos of their terrorist acts. Also, when her mother was pregnant with Daniela, members of the MRTA threatened her mother, with a gun to her stomach. Thus, for Daniela, there was nothing heroic about those people or their ideologies. Her intellectual and artistic work was far from praising the leader of Sendero Luminoso or any subversive ideologies (ATV Noticias, March 7, 2018).

According to Daniela's declarations to newspaper *La República* (August 31, 2019), once her case started circulating in social media and mainstream media, she suffered harassment from people who began deeming her as "terruca" (slang for terrorist); however, people defended her and the right to freedom of expression in social media and some of the press. Her case is iconic because it brought to center stage the controversial law of apology of terrorism in addition to shedding light on the open wound and fear that the internal conflict has left where bypassers or neighbors are vigilant and willing to denounce what they may deem terrorism or apology of terrorism.

The well-respected magazine *Caretas* (July 4, 2019) published an article with the headline “Apologia al Absurdo” (Apology of the Absurd) discussing the absurdity of putting through this legal battle experience to a young and upcoming photographer. In the online blog *Punto Seguido* from Universidad del Pacifico, Danitza Saavedra (September 27, 2019), a journalism student, offers some insights about what is considered by local terrorism experts apology of terrorism (i.e., political motives, exaltation of terrorist acts and terrorists). Saavedra’s article headline warns that one should be careful with what one says. This idea of exerting self-censorship is in contradiction with the values of a democratic and open society, and it only reinforces the culture of fear.

In 2019, the prosecutor Luis Landa had to drop the charges against Chacón because beyond the school assignment he could not prove Chacón’s intention of apology of terrorism. On one hand, by dropping the charges, the Public Ministry and the Judicial Branch have succeeded in showing that it is possible for the State to investigate and determine whether or not an individual is responsible and whether or not such an individual deserves sanctions for acts of apology of terrorism, in harmony with the Constitution and the fundamental rights. On the other hand, Chacón’s two years legal ordeal sent a threatening message to teachers and students, and the population in general. This case, along with those from the LUM, show how the politics of fear have carved a deep scar in Peru’s society, and how the anti-terrorism law in post-conflict Peru is deployed to continue intimidating and controlling the production of knowledge and critical artistic expression.

CONCLUSION

Peru’s democracy remains fragile, and as a consequence, the specter of terrorism lingers. The ambiguity of apology of terrorism is utilized by power elites, easily casting a shadow over legitimate social pleas for change, critiques of rampant corruption, and protests for economic and political stability in the country. Furthermore, any revisiting of the historical memory of the past internal conflict is immediately scrutinized under the shadow of terrorism, impeding an open and healthy engagement with a traumatic chapter of Peru’s recent history.

In the past decade, aside from valid accusations against MOVADEF, the public arm of Sendero Luminoso, some other accusations of apology of terrorism to individuals, institutions, and labor unions have been politically motivated, and not for valid concerns indeed connected to apology of terrorism, like the LUM examples. Oftentimes, focusing on potential cases of apology of terrorism serves as a distraction to more substantial problems not being addressed.

Terrorism and apology of terrorism should be fought, but the fight must be within the framework of democratic legitimacy. The laws for apology of terrorism need to be more explicit to avoid open interpretations. The expansionary trend of behaviors that can be considered criminal in the matter of apology of terrorism calls for a need to rethink the legitimacy of accusations and punishment; all the more when modified Article 316 and the creation of Article 316-A are in contradiction with the fundamental right to freedom of expression. The problem generated by the open classification of these crimes has an example in Peru where art exhibitions, guided museum tours, school assignments, photographic and media creations are being used as damning evidence to accuse and even legally prosecute people who have no actual connection to terrorist organizations or terrorist acts, and are not engaging in *justification* or *exaltation* of terrorists or their actions.

It is worth considering the role of the bodies whose actions have an impact on freedom of expression and the right to democratically critique, question, and dissent. The Public Ministry and the Judiciary system alone are not responsible, but also the Congress, the Executive Power, and the Constitutional Court, bodies that support the expansion of anti-terrorists laws, particularly apology of terrorism as we saw it in 2017. In Peru's post-conflict times, domestic terrorist acts are no longer common. Thus, for those wanting to silence people and those aiming to control certain narratives from past and present, apology of terrorism is a good recourse to damage opponents, silence dissent or people who question, and ultimately maintain a culture of fear where freedom of expression is suppressed. This is, of course, not unique to Peru. We see the trend in other Latin American countries (i.e., Chile, Argentina, Colombia) where different governments confronting contemporary social struggles due to structural inequalities paint labor unions, youth social movements, and people who dissent as a threat to society. Hence, it is the responsibility of the State in each country to help strengthen democracies, create pluralistic and inclusive environments where different voices are heard, experiences of the past and the present are shared, and where democratic and open dialogue is fostered while structural social conditions are improved.

NOTES

1. Partido Comunista del Perú-Sendero Luminoso (PCP-SL) is led by Abimael Guzmán who was a philosophy professor at the University of Huamanga in Ayacucho

where he founded this Maoist group, recruiting first many of his students. Most Peruvians refer to the PCP-SL simply as Sendero Luminoso, which is how I am referring to it in this chapter. Abimael Guzmán is serving life in prison for terrorism charges since September of 1992 when he was captured.

2. The Movimiento Revolucionario Tupac Amaru (MRTA) led by Victor Polay started in 1984 primarily as an urban guerrilla group, but it also spread out to different areas of the country with major places of action being parts of the low-lands of Huánuco and the Alto Huallaga. The MRTA fairly soon became a narco-terrorist group controlling coca-growing areas where farmers pay them "cupos" or "taxes" toward the "revolution."

3. There is extensive literature on Peru's internal armed conflict and the evolution of Sendero Luminoso and the MRTA. Some recommended authors are Carlos Iván Degregori, Gustavo Gorriti, Victor Peralta, Deborah Poole, Cynthia McClintock, among others.

4. Decreto Legislativo No.046 including its eleven articles can be found at http://www.pagina-libre.org/asociacion-peru/Textos/Fondo/Legislacion/DL_046_texto.html Last accessed August 20, 2020. This legislative decree was signed by President Fernando Belaúnde Terry in March 1981.

5. Faceless Tribunals denied detainees the right to know who the judge in their cases were; judges performed their duties wearing hoods to conceal their identity and speaking through voice-distorters.

6. In December 2017, then-president Pedro Pablo Kuczynski (PPK), signed a presidential pardon granting former president Alberto Fujimori his liberty. This stirred massive protests, the resignation of members of PPK's own party, and ultimately it was one of the various reasons for PPK's fall from power that led to his resignation. Currently, PPK is serving house arrest in Lima, Peru.

REFERENCES

ATV Noticias, March 7, 2018. Interview with Daniela Chacón https://www.youtube.com/watch?v=oL2B4Wa8kRE.

Bourque, Susan C. and Warren Kay B. 1989. "Democracy without Peace: The Cultural Politics of Terror in Peru." *Latin American Research Review* 24 (1): 7–34.

Burt, Jo-Marie. "'Quien habla es terrorista': The Political Use of Fear in Fujimori's Peru." *Latin American Research Review* 41 (3): 32–62.

Calmet, Karina. 2017. "Place of Memory with Amnesia." *Politico.pe*, August 28, 2017. https://www.politico.pe/lugar-de-la-memoria-con-amnesia/.

Calderón, Andres. 2018. *Tendencias en libertad de expresión en el Perú*. Palermo, Spain: Centro de Estudios en Libertad de Expresión y Acceso a la Información, Universidad de Palermo.

Chipana, Juan. 2019. "Apología al absurdo." *Caretas*. July 4, 2019. https://caretas.pe/nacional/apologia-al-absurdo/.

Comisión de la Verdad y la Reconciliación (CVR). 2004. *Informe Final. Tomo I*. Lima:UNSM/PUCP.

———. 2003. *General Conclusions. II-Responsibilities for the Conflict.* Decreto Legislativo No.046. 1981. Accessed January 25, 2020. http://www.paginalibre.org/asociacionperu/Textos/Fondo/Legislacion/DL_046_texto.htl.

Decreto Legislativo No. 25475. Accessed October 25, 2020. http://www.oas.org/juridico/pdfs/mesicic5_per_6_dec_ley_25475.pdf.

Decreto Legislativo No. 924. 2003. Accessed October 25, 2020. http://www2.congreso.gob.pe/sicr/cendocbib/con4_uibd.nsf/D1128B075B578C6F05257A6E005C328B/$FILE/DL_924.pdf.

Decreto Legislativo No. 982. 2007. Accessed October 25, 2020. http://www2.congreso.gob.pe/sicr/cendocbib/con4_uibd.nsf/448FEBA50C50F63B05257A6E005C3C8C/$FILE/DL_982.pdf.

Degregori, Carlos Iván and Carlos Rivera Paz. 1993. *Perú 1980-1993: Fuerzas Armadas, Subversión y Democracia. Redefinición del papel militar en un contexto de violencia subversiva y colapso del régimen democrático.* Documento de Trabajo No.53. Serie: Documentos de Política No.5. Lima: IEP Ediciones.

De la Jara, Ernesto. 2008. "El papel de la sociedad política frente a la violencia política." In *Perú en el siglo XXI*, edited by Luis Pásara. Lima: PUCP.

Gorriti, Gustavo. 2009. *Sendero: Historia de la guerra milenaria en el Perú.* (second edition). Lima: Planeta.

Instituto Prensa y Sociedad (IPYS). 2019. "Perú: Fiscalía pide 15 años de prisión contra estudiante de fotografía por apología al terrorismo." Accessed November 10, 2020. https://ipys.org/libertad-de-expresion/alertas/peru-fiscalia-pide-15-anos-de-prision-contra-estudiante-de-fotografia-por-apologia-al-terrorismo.

LaMula.pe. 2017. "Karen Bernedo: 'Los hechos de 1992 han marcado un antes y un después en la historia del Perú'" Accessed October 20, 2020. https://redaccion.lamula.pe/2017/08/16/los-hechos-de-1992-han-marcado-un-antes-y-un-despues-en-la-historia-del-peru-video/victorliza/?platform=hootsuite.

Law No. 25659. 1992. Traición a la patria.

Law No. 26447.1995. Anula los "tribunales sin rostro."

Law No. 26537. 1995. Establece nuevo plazo de vigencia de "tribunales sin rostro."

Ley No. 30610. 2017. Modifica Articulo 316 e incorpora Articulo 316-A al Código Penal, Tipificando el delito de apologia del terrorismo.

MacNamara, Lawrence. 2009. "Counter-Terrorism Law: How they Affect Media Freedom and News Reporting." *Westminster Papers in Communication and Culture* 6 (1): 27–44. http://doi.org/10.16997/wpcc.103.

Palacios, Pamela. 2019. "Daniela Chacón: 'Para mi la cárcel ya comenzó hace rato.'" *La República*, August 31, 2019. https://larepublica.pe/politica/2019/08/31/terrorismo-apologia-sendero-luminoso-abimael-guzman-fiscalia-daniela-chacon-para-mi-la-carcel-ya-comenzo-hace-rato/.

Palacios, Rosa Maria. 2018. Interview with Gabriela Eguren. May 18, 2018. https://www.youtube.com/watch?v=aOfuuJBAdyI.

Pastrana Sánchez, Maria Alejandra. 2019. Apología del terrorismo y otros delitos afines: Evolución y tendencias en España y en el Perú. *Revista Derecho & Sociedad*, 52.

Rivera Paz, Carlos. 2007. "Ley penal, terrorismo y estado de derecho." *Revista Quehacer*, 167. http://www2.congreso.gob.pe/sicr/cendocbib/con4_uibd.nsf/33A

82E9BDC1BD47F05257BF600190E1A/$FILE/Ley_Penal_Terrorismo_y_Estado_de_Derecho.pdf.

Rivera Paz, Carlos, and Edgar Alvarez Yrala. 2003. "La nueva legislación antiterrorista: Avances y límites." Accessed October 24, 2020. http://hrlibrary.umn.edu/research/Peru-La%20nueva%20legislacion%20antiterrorista.pdf.

RPP. 2018. Interview with Congressman Donayre. May 17, 2018. https://www.youtube.com/watch?v=7Jj7hKIxH5k.

Saavedra, Danitza. 2019. "Terrorismo: Cuidado con lo que se dice." *Punto Seguido*, September 27, 2019. https://puntoseguido.upc.edu.pe/terrorismo-cuidado-con-lo-que-se-dice/.

Siles Vallejo, Abraham. 2015. *La lucha antiterrorista en el Perú: agujeros negros legales, agüeros grises y el arduo camino constitucional. Lecciones peruanas para la guerra contra el terrorismo global. Revista de la Facultad de Derecho*. Lima: PUCP.

Valle Riestra, Esteban. 2013. "El Sendero del MOVADEF: de la lucha armada a la participación política." Accessed October 18, 2020. https://revistaideele.com/ideele/revista/227.

Chapter 14

Extremism

Russia's Crackdown on Free Speech and Religious Freedom in the Name of National Security

Daniel Ortner

INTRODUCTION

In 2002, the Russian Federation enacted a law entitled "On Fighting Extremist Activity." This law was initially developed as a national security tool for combating the rise of Islamic Fundamentalism or other extremist ideologies (Fagan 2009). But in the hands of zealous prosecutors, the law has become a tool for banning religious literature, suppressing political dissent, confiscating property, and even jailing dozens of Jehovah's Witnesses merely for continuing to belong to their faith. Despite being rebuked by the European Court of Human Rights on several occasions, Russia has continued to use the Extremism Law to suppress individual liberty in the guise of national security.

In 2016, yet another invasive incursion on free expression and religious liberty was adopted in the name of national security. When Russia adopted a package of anti-terrorism, cybersecurity, and data storage measures, a provision dramatically curtailing missionary work was surreptitiously snuck into the package. Despite reassurances that this Yarovaya Law would not restrict religious worship, in practice, this law has criminalized routine expressions of faith such as discussing God in one's own home. Russians have even been jailed for the unauthorized teaching of yoga.

With both the Extremism Law[1] and the Yarovaya Law,[2] national security motives have given way to the suppression of minority faiths and unpopular expression. This chapter explores Russia's use of these laws in a continued attack on freedom of expression and freedom of religion in the name of national security.

THE EXTREMISM LAW

Russia's Extremism Law was adopted in June 2002 (Ortner 2015). Extremism was defined in four ways: (1) incitement of religious hatred; (2) committing a crime motivated by religious hatred; (3) obstruction of the lawful activity of religious associations accompanied by violence or the threat of violence; and (4) propaganda of the exclusivity, superiority or inferiority of citizens according to their attitude toward religion or religious affiliation (Fagan 2009).

The first and last provisions have proven to be the most controversial because of their broad language and open-ended scope (Kravchenko 2018). The first provision was used to prosecute members of the punk rock band, Pussy Riot, after their infamous "punk prayer" performance inside of the Cathedral of Christ the Savior in Moscow (Reuters 2014). It was also used to ban episodes of the cartoon *South Park*, a painting depicting Mickey Mouse preaching the Sermon on the Mount in the place of Jesus Christ, and the controversial "Innocence of Muslims" video (Ortner 2016). In July 2013, Russia further criminalized "insulting the religious feelings of believers" as a direct response to the actions of Pussy Riot (Russian Criminal Code Section 148).[3] That law, which is closely related to the Extremism Ban, has been used to threaten theatrical productions that are opposed by the Russian Orthodox Church (Arnold 2017).

The last provision of the Extremism Law, on the other hand, is the source of efforts to target religious literature and religious organizations, allowing religious literature to be placed on a list of extremist material to be banned. Many of these attempts sparked massive public outcry. Notoriously, a prosecutor in the Siberian town of Tomsk unsuccessfully brought a suit to place a translation of the book, *Bhagavad Gita*, onto the list after a Federal Security Service commissioned study found that the book "contains signs of incitement of religious hatred and humiliation of an individual based on gender, race, ethnicity, language, origin, or attitude to religion" (Ortner 2015, 2). Fortunately, international outrage ultimately led to the dismissal of that suit (Ibid). A subsequent 2015 amendment bars certain sacred texts such as the Bible or the Koran from being labeled as extremist (Arnold 2015). However, other religious texts have not been spared. In particular, texts by Islamic leaders Said Nursi and Tablighi Jamaat remain banned (United States Commission on International Religious Freedom, n.d.) Most dramatically, the extremist law has led to the banning of the Jehovah's Witness faith in Russia and the criminalization of its membership.

RUSSIAN CONSTITUTIONAL COURT'S NARROWING CONSTRUCTIONS

The Russian Constitutional Court has refused to review the constitutionality of the Extremism Law but has issued several narrowing constructions which in theory should help reduce the risk of abuse. In 2013, the Court explained that the law did not permit texts to be restricted solely because the texts "did not conform to common views, established traditions and beliefs, or moral and religious preferences" (*Ibragim Ibragimov v. Russia* 2018, para. 44, quoting Russian Constitutional Court Decision No. 1053-0/2013, 10–11).[4] In 2017, the court explained that lower courts had to take into account not just the text itself but also "its potential ability, in modern society and in combination with beliefs widespread in society, to acquire characteristics that were inadmissible from the standpoint of constitutionally protected values" (Ibid, para. 46, quoting Russian Constitutional Court Decisions 463-O/2017, 4).[5] Again in 2017, the Court explained that works could not be banned based solely on the "subjective perception" of the material (Ibid, para. 47, quoting Russian Constitutional Court Decisions 906-O/2017, 6).[6] Further, "classic literary works which were part of the history and culture of a people, had been widely distributed in some historical period, had been subject to voluminous scientific research and widely quoted, and which had never before been banned for calling on its followers to commit extremist activities or for being a source of extremist ideology, could not be declared extremist" (Ibid, para. 47, quoting Russian Constitutional Court Decisions 906-O/2017 p. 6–7). These narrowing constructions meaningfully limit the scope of the Extremism Law and will hopefully bring to an end the effort to ban classic religious works or the works of unpopular religious minorities.

EUROPEAN COURT OF HUMAN RIGHTS PRECEDENT

In 2018, the European Court of Human Rights finally issued long-awaited decisions in several cases challenging the application of the Extremism Law and other related laws. Even though these decisions are imperfect, they represent a source of hope that some of the worst excesses of the Extremism Law may be curtailed.

Ibragim Ibragmiov v. Russia

This lawsuit involves the writings of Said Nursi, a Turkish scholar who lived in the first half of the twentieth century (*Ibragimov v. Russia* 2018, para. 6–7). Two prosecutors in different parts of Russia successfully moved to have writings by Nursi banned because, in the opinion of some expert psychologists and psychiatrists, his writings "led the reader to form a negative opinion about adherents of other faiths and thus encouraged hatred and enmity towards them" and toward nonbelievers (Ibid, para. 9). On the other hand, a variety of experts in religious philosophy pointed out that the texts were espousing a classical version of Islam which encouraged peaceful coexistence of religions (Ibid, para. 11–13). The courts effectively ignored the religious scholars and relied solely on psychological experts. An appeal of the first decision from the trial court of the City of Koptevskiy was brought by the publisher of one of Nursi's books (Ibid para. 5–6). A separate appeal was also brought from the decision of the trial court of the City of Krasnoyark by a religious organization that distributed Nursi's writings (Ibid para. 27). Both appeals were unsuccessful in the Russian court system and so appeals were pursued before the European Court of Human Rights where the two appeals were consolidated and heard together.

The European Court of Human Rights (ECtHR) concluded that Russia's decision to ban the writings was contrary to Article 10's[7] protection of freedom of expression (European Convention on Human Rights 2013). The ECtHR began its analysis by noting some concerns with the vague scope of the Russian Extremism Law (*Ibragimov v. Russia* 2018, para. 84–86). However, the ECtHR did not determine whether the law was overly vague as the Appellants had requested, leaving that question open for a future day (Ibid, para. 84–86).

Instead, the ECtHR determined that the application of the law to Nursi's writings was disproportionate and therefore in violation of Article 10. The ECtHR first considered the degree of deference that it owed to Russia's judgment regarding what religious speech was likely to offend believers. The ECtHR agreed with Russia that a "certain margin of appreciation is generally available to the Contracting States when regulating freedom of expression in relation to matters liable to offend intimate personal convictions within the sphere of religion or to incite religious hatred or intolerance" (Ibid, para. 95). However, the ECtHR found that the "margin of appreciation . . . is not unlimited" and that judicial supervision may be "all the more necessary given the rather open-ended notion of respect for the religious beliefs of others and the risks of excessive interference with freedom of expression under the guise of action taken against allegedly offensive material" (Ibid, para. 96).

The ECtHR accepted Russia's professed interest in "helping to maintain public order, religious harmony and tolerance in a democratic society" (Ibid, para. 90), as well as its ability to prohibit speech which is "gratuitously offensive" and "do[es] not contribute to any form of public debate capable of furthering progress in human affairs" (Ibid, para.92). This would include speech "insulting, holding up to ridicule or slandering specific groups of the population" (Ibid, para.94). However, the ECtHR narrowly construed the kind of speech that could be prohibited. It explained that religious writings could only be forbidden if they could "when read as a whole and in their context, be seen as a call for violence, hatred, or intolerance" (Ibid, para. 115).

The ECtHR noted that these particular religious texts had been "widely available in many countries for decades, including in Russia for at least seven years," but the government had failed to "submit any evidence that they have caused interreligious tensions or led to any harmful consequences, let alone violence, in Russia or elsewhere" (Ibid, para.102). Without such concrete evidence, the margin of appreciation could not "justify the denial of access to a universally available important religious text to the population of a single country" (Ibid, para. 98).

The ECtHR also found that the Russian courts had improperly relied too heavily on expert opinion and failed to engage the actual text to identify which passages were "extremist" in nature. The Russian courts also failed to balance the need for the ban on "the effect of the ban on the applicants' rights under Aritcles 9 and 10 of the convention" (Ibid, para. 107). Moreover, the Russian courts stacked the decks by leaving the applicants[8] "unable to contest the findings of the expert reports or to effectively put forward arguments in defense of their position" (Ibid, para. 108).

With regard to the few passages that one of the Russian courts had identified as "extremist," the ECtHR was quite forceful in its rejection of Russia's claims. It emphasized that even if "some people might be offended" by religious statements that "does not mean that it constitutes 'hate speech'" (Ibid, para. 115). Rather, "religious groups cannot reasonably expect to be exempt from all criticism; they must tolerate and accept the denial by others of their religious beliefs and even the propagation by others of doctrines hostile to their faith" (Ibid, para. 117). Further, speech could not be restricted just because it encouraged readers to "adopt the author's religious ideology," as "freedom to manifest one's religion includes the right to try to convince one's neighbor" (Ibid, para. 122).

The ECtHR decision in *Ibragimov* is imperfect. In particular, it is regrettable that the Court did not simply invalidate the whole prohibition as irredeemably vague. And in light of Russia's well-documented misuse of the "extremism" law to punish religious minorities, the ECtHR is still too quick to give legitimacy to Russia's purported interest in preventing religious offense (Ortner 2016).

An even better opinion would have thoroughly critiqued the notion that religious truth claims by themselves can be prohibited as offensive. Last year, the ECtHR displayed admirable moral clarity when it dismantled Russia's attempt to justify its prohibition on "homosexual propaganda" (*Bayev v. Russia* 2017). There, the ECtHR explained that it would review Russia's actions skeptically in light of the "clear European consensus about the recognition of individuals' right to openly identity themselves as gay, lesbian or any other sexual minority" (para. 66). The ECtHR, therefore, utterly rejected each of Russia's purported justifications such as defending "traditional families," protecting public health, and preventing against the "promotion" of homosexuality, concluding that the law either did not advance the goal or was actively counterproductive (para. 65–83). One does not see the same moral clarity in *Ibragimov*, where the ECtHR gave far too much credence to Russia's stated goals.

Nevertheless, there is much to celebrate in the *Ibragimov* decision, which was a better decision than I predicted several years ago (Ortner 2016). In particular, the ECtHR determined that a narrower margin of appreciation is appropriate when dealing with "the rather open-ended notion of respect for the religious beliefs of others" in light of the serious "risks of excessive interference with freedom of expression under the guise of action taken against allegedly offensive material" (*Ibragimov v. Russia* 2018, para. 96). As I have argued previously, the margin of appreciation is increasingly inappropriate in freedom of expression cases in light of the increasing power of states like Russia to abuse this margin to suppress not only unpopular speech but also vital political debate (Ortner 2016). If the ECtHR applies a narrower margin of appreciation to freedom of expression cases going forward, then this decision will be a major victory for free speech in the member states.

The *Ibragimov* decision will also advance freedom of expression in several other respects. The ECtHR suggests that only true "hate speech" may be restricted and defines this category narrowly to include only speech that "when read as a whole and in [its] context" may be "seen as a call for violence, hatred, or intolerance" (*Ibragimov v. Russia* 2018, para. 98). In contrast, in past decisions, the ECtHR seemed much more willing to allow for the restriction of speech merely because it might cause offense (*Kokkinakis v. Greece* 1993, Valticos J. dissenting describing missionary work as the "rape of the beliefs of others and arguing that Article 9 of the European Convention did not protect missionary work") (Ortner 2016, 178–180). This requirement will, if consistently applied going forward, seriously limit the ability of member states to restrict speech. The requirement that state authorities identify specific passages or language rather than merely dismissing a work on a broad categorical basis, and the reminder that local courts must balance the need for a restriction against "the effect of the ban on the applicants' rights under Articles 9[9] and 10 of the convention" will also, hopefully lead to more speech protective decisions in the future.

Finally, this decision is valuable for its reaffirmation that "freedom to manifest one's religion includes the right to try to convince one's neighbor" (*Ibragimov v. Russia* 2018, para. 122). This principle will likely come before the ECtHR in the next few years as challenges to the Yarovaya Law wind their way up to the Court.

Overall, *Ibraghimov* is an encouraging decision. If Russian authorities were to heed the decision, then it would put an end to Russia's efforts to ban religious texts on the pretense that the texts assert the superiority of a faith or can be read as proselytizing to others.

Alekhina v. Russia

This case arose out of the imprisonment of members of the punk rock band, Pussy Riot, for performing their song "*Punk Prayer–Virgin Mary, Drive Putin Away*" in Moscow's Christ the Savior Cathedral (*Alekhina v. Russia* 2018, para. 13–16). Band members were convicted of "hooliganism motivated by religious hatred" (Ibid, para. 52). The Russian District Court in Khamovnicheskiy concluded that Pussy Riot's performance evidenced "religious hatred and enmity or hatred against" adherents of the Russian Orthodox Church (Ibid, para. 52).[10] Video-recordings of the performance and a variety of other Pussy Riot videos were then placed on the extremist list and outlawed throughout Russia (Ibid, para. 70–80).

The ECtHR examined two free-expression-related questions. The first was whether Russia was justified in criminally prosecuting Pussy Riot. The Court agreed with Pussy Riot that the performance was "a form of artistic and political expression covered by Article 10" (Ibid, para. 206). The Court agreed with Russia that the disruption of the performance was done in pursuit of "the legitimate aim of protecting the rights of others" to worship in the Cathedral (Ibid, para. 210). However, the decision to arrest band members and impose extensive jail time was very "severe" and disproportionate to the nature of the conduct. The Court also found that the Russian court had failed to adequately consider the content of Pussy Riot's speech or the context of their performance and had failed to provide "relevant and sufficient reason to justify the criminal conviction" (Ibid, para. 228).

Second, the Court considered whether Russia was justified in banning videos of the performance under the Extremism Law. Just as with the *Ibraghimov* decision, the Court demurred on the question of whether the Extremism Law was so vague that its prohibitions could not be said to be "prescribed by law" (Ibid, para. 258). The Court also accepted the Russian government's assertion "that the interference could be considered as having pursued the legitimate aims of protecting the morals and rights of others" (Ibid, para. 259).[11] The Court then rejected the decision to place the video on the extremist list primarily on procedural rather than substantive grounds (Ibid, para. 261–268). The Court found that the Russian District Court had failed to examine the content of the video in sufficient detail and that "[t]he virtual absence of reasoning by the domestic court makes it impossible for the Court to grasp the rationale behind the interference" (Ibid, para. 261–268). Moreover, the Russian District Court had failed to allow concerned parties to participate in the proceeding and provide a defense (Ibid, para. 265–267). Therefore, the ban was not "necessary in a democratic society" (Ibid, para. 260–269).

While *Ibraghimov* was a flawed but valuable decision, the Pussy Riot decision is simply disappointing. The Court accepted Russia's aim of "protecting the morals and rights of others" as legitimate. In addition, because the EHtCR decision focused almost exclusively on procedural defects it failed to narrow or clarify its acceptance of this aim in any meaningful fashion. The Court also once again refused to consider whether the law itself was defective. In effect, this decision by the ECtHR reads more like an invitation for Russia to try again to prohibit this kind of speech, but next time to develop a more detailed factual record and to have the trial court conduct a more thorough analysis. Despite the loss at the ECtHR, this decision could actually embolden Russia to continue to outlaw controversial or offensive material such as Pussy Riot's punk prayer.

Terentyev v. Russia

This case did not arise directly from the "extremism" ban, but involved a prosecution for speech "inciting hatred and enmity" toward a social group (Criminal Code of the Russian Federal Article 282: Incitement of Hatred or Enmity, as Well as Abasement of Human Dignity).[12] A journalist and blogger made a comment that was highly critical of the police on a social media website. The blogger called the police "pigs" and stated that "[i]t would be great if in the centre [*sic*] of every Russian city, on the main square . . . there was an oven, like at Auschwitz, in which ceremonially every day, and better yet, twice a day (say, at noon and midnight) infidel cops would be burnt" (*Terentyev v. Russia* 2018, para. 13). The ECtHR once again questioned whether the Russia law was "formulated with sufficient precision to enable the persons concerned." (Ibid, para. 54). However, the court assumed that the conduct was "prescribed by law." And since the law was applied to protect "the reputation or rights of others," it served a legitimate aim (Ibid, para. 60). However, the Court emphasized that the use of a "provocative metaphor" could not be said to be "promoting violence, hatred, or intolerance" (Ibid, para. 69–70). Moreover, since the speech in question did not target "an unprotected minority or group that has a history of oppression or inequality," the government would be required to put forward a heightened showing before it could prohibit offensive speech (Ibid, para. 76).

Terentyev is another well-intentioned freedom of expression decision that may have unintended negative consequences in Russia. In particular, by suggesting that policies targeting speech that offends minority groups is not subject to heightened scrutiny, the Court's decision opens the door for Russia to continue to go after speech that offends the sentiments of discreet minorities. The Court once again failed to clearly condemn Russia's abuse of vague and nebulous language to give prosecutors extreme discretion to go after disfavored speech.

IMPACT OF THE ECTHR DECISIONS

Russia has routinely ignored ECtHR decisions and has repeatedly threatened that it will leave the Council of Europe (Mälksoo 2018) At the moment, however, it appears that Russia's relationship with the Council of Europe is on the mend (Bushuev and Barysheva 2019; Mounier 2019). Against this background, it is worth asking whether the decisions of the ECtHR are actually having an impact on how the Extremism Law is being enforced.

The results are quite mixed. As of June 25, 2020, there are 5041 items on the Russian Extremist List. Scanning through the list reveals a wide variety of items. Some of the material on the list likely can be restricted without concern. For instance, there are quite a few items that clearly are white supremacist or Neo-Nazi propaganda. On the other hand, there remain a wide variety of religious writings, including those of Said Nursi, notwithstanding the EctHR decision (see Ministry of Justice 2020). There are, as of June 25, 2020, for instance around 200 entries in the database with the word "Islam" in the title (Ibid). There is also a variety of political content, including seventy-two entries with the word "Putin," in them (Ibid).

The Sova Center, a pro-democracy NGO, maintains a list of Russia's continued misuses of the anti-Extremism legislation (Sova Center n.d.). The Sova center identified a couple of positive trends that suggest that Russia may be slowing its assault on religious expression. The rate of growth of the Extremism List continues to slow. Now, individuals are more likely to be prosecuted for distributing materials critical of the Russian authorities than for distributing religious literature. This might suggest that the ECtHR's stronger *Ibragimov* decision regarding religious literature is having a positive impact while the Court's far weaker *Alekhina* decision regarding political speech has not had a significant impact on Russia's actions. For instance, in December 2019, a student was prosecuted for incitement to extremist activity for calling for nonviolent resistance to Putin's regime and for comparing the current government to the Third Reich (SOVA Center 2019c). Prosecutions for speech critical of religion (from a secular or nonreligious perspective) has also continued seemingly unabated, which suggests that such speech has not been seen as protected under *Ibraghimov*. For example, SOVA reported that in October 2019, an individual was fined for sharing a video of a Polish black metal band that contained anti-religious imagery (Sova Center 2019b).

But even if the *Ibraghimov* decision is having an impact, prosecutions have not completely ceased even though they are continuing at a slightly slower pace (Sova Center 2019a). There also is no indication that Russia has taken any action to compensate those previously prosecuted or remedy any of its past actions under the Extremism Law, such as restoring citizenship to an individual who was convicted and lost his citizenship for studying the works of Said Nursi (Arnold 2019a). On the contrary, Russia may be expanding its crackdown on extremism through multilateral agreements with entities such as the Shanghai Cooperation Organization[13] (Human Rights in China 2011; Mission Eurasia 2006). Russia also appears to be expanding the consequences of prosecution for possessing extremist material such as prohibiting individuals that have been convicted from membership in nonprofit organizations (Kravchenko 2019).

The results have been decidedly mixed, but on balance, it appears that the ECtHR and Russian Supreme Court decisions may be having a positive impact in reducing the rate at which religious literature is being placed on the Extremist list. However, Russia's assault on political speech and secular speech critical of religion does not appear to be slowing.

PERSECUTION OF JEHOVAH'S WITNESSES UNDER THE EXTREMISM BAN

Unfortunately, these positive trends have not been extended to the extremist ban's most high-profile victims, members of the Jehovah's Witness faith. Unquestionably the most egregious consequence of the Extremism Law has been Russia's treatment of the Jehovah's Witness faith.

Jehovah's Witnesses have been the subject of intense religious persecution throughout the world and have for this reason been called "the canary in the coal mine" of religious liberty. (Barringer Gordon 2011; Engardio 2009). If that is the case, then how Jehovah's Witnesses are being actively persecuted in Russia should be a glaring warning regarding the Russian government's hostility to freedom of religion and freedom of speech.

Pre-Extremism Law Ban and ECtHR Appeal

Jehovah's Witnesses have long been persecuted in Russia. In the mid-1990s, the local religious organization was targeted by prosecutors in Moscow and shut down on allegations of inciting religious discord and destroying family units. In 2010, the ECtHR found that the dissolution of the organization was not justified and that Russia had insufficient evidence against the organization (*Jehovah's Witnesses of Moscow v. Russia* 2010).

Application of Extremism Law

The Extremism Law was first turned against the Jehovah's Witnesses in 2007. In that year, the Rostov Regional Prosecutor's office moved to liquidate the Witnesses' Local Religious Organization in Taganrog (Jehovah's Witnesses 2017). An expert study found that the Witnesses' literature had "the potential to undermine respect" for other faiths and, accordingly, thirty-four publications were placed on the extremist list (Ibid). The local organization was also banned, its literature confiscated, and its property seized. Soon, more Witnesses' publications were placed on the list by prosecutors in other parts of Russia. About ninety-five pieces of Jehovah's Witnesses' literature were placed on the federal registry by 2017 (Human Rights Watch 2017).

Once literature was placed on the extremist list, local prosecutors used the list as a pretext for a broader crack down of Jehovah's Witnesses congregations. Local authorities have conducted raids of congregations and have been credibly accused of planting extremist literature on the premises. Based on the allegedly falsified evidence, eight local congregations were shut down for "failing to comply" with the extremist ban by 2017 (Ibid).

In 2017, the Justice Ministry began an inspection of the Jehovah's Witnesses Administrative Center in St. Petersburg. The Justice Ministry found that the central organization had continued to fund branches that had been closed and had not adequately taken steps to prevent the distribution of "extremist" literature (Ministry of Justice 2017). Accordingly, the Justice Minister declared that the whole organization was "extremist" and should be shut down. This decision was quickly upheld by the Russian Supreme Court (Human Rights Watch 2017).

As of the publication of this chapter, more than 350 members of the Jehovah's Witnesses face potential criminal prosecution and 175 have spent some time in prison (Arnold 2017). More than thirty-five remain in detention, and about two dozen are currently on trial (Arnold 2019b). Those arrested under the ban range from age 19 to 89. Eighteen members have thus far been convicted (Arnold 2017). The associated penalties have been quite severe. For instance, in November 2019, a Jehovah's Witness member from the Siberian town of Tomsk was sentenced to six years in prison for being a practicing member of the faith. A Danish citizen was also sentenced to six years in prison, drawing international attention (Jehovah's Witnesses in Russia n.d.).[14] Members of the organization also allegedly been beaten and even tortured (Luxmoore 2019; Reuters 2020).

As of June 2020, the situation remains dire for members of the Jehovah's Witness faith in Russia. There are dozens of pending appeals to the European Court of Human Rights (as of June 2020, thirty-three have been communicated to the Court and twenty-five have not yet been communicated), but that process may take several more years (Arnold 2019d; Jehovah's Witnesses Office of Public Information, E-mail to author, June 25, 2020). The outright assault on the Jehovah's Witness faith has been a terrifying but predictable consequence of a vague and easily abusable Extremism Law. While the law was enacted to target terrorism, it was easily weaponized against unpopular minority faiths such as the Jehovah's Witnesses.

YAROVAYA LAW

Origin

In 2015, the Islamic State shot down a Russian passenger jet over Egypt. In response, Russia adopted a number of provisions aimed at stopping terrorism and cybercrime the following year (Luhn 2016). This package is known as the Yarovaya Law after Russian politician Irina Yarovaya who was one of the law's chief sponsors. While it was debated in the Duma, this law received a considerable amount of attention and criticism. The law outraged civil libertarians because it imposed strict data retention requirements on telecommunications companies and permitted warrantless government access to this data (Korelina 2019; Muratov 2018; O'Brien and Galperin 2016). Indeed, the package was nicknamed the "Big Brother Law" because of the surveillance power it granted to government agencies (The Economist 2016). Many of the provisions were also criticized as costly and almost impossible to comply with, such as the requirement that all data about Russian users of Internet services be retained in Russia (Medvedev 2018). Changes to the criminal code allowing prosecutions of children as young as fourteen and punishing those who fail to report suspected crimes of terrorism also received international criticism (Sottek 2016).

But perhaps the most controversial provisions of the Yarovaya Law were not even in the bill initially but slipped into the package at the last minute and without any consultation with the Duma Committee on Affairs of Public Associations and on Religious Organizations (Masiuk 2016). These anti-missionary provisions (which I describe in detail in the following section) did not receive significant attention in the Russian media. Russian news sources celebrated the law as a valuable tool for battling terrorism and preserving data privacy, without even mentioning the missionary provisions (First Channel [ПЕРВЫЙ КАНАЛ] 2016). Even international media sources did not pay close attention to the missionary provisions. For instance, an article in *The Economist* entitled “Why Russia’s Anti-terrorism Laws are Controversial,” which was written shortly after the law was enacted, did not even mention the missionary provisions (The Economist 2016).

The Anti-Missionary Provisions

Missionary activity is defined in Article 24-1 of the Yarovaya Law as activity of a religious association or persons involving the dissemination of information about the organization’s beliefs among nonmembers of the association (Russian Federation 2016). This is obviously a very open-ended and broad definition that may encompass much of the activities of religious organizations. Pursuant to Article 24-1 of the Yarovaya Law, religious organizations have the right to engage in missionary activities in Church buildings as well as church-owned institutions like cemeteries and places where religious ordinances are carried out (Russian Federation 2016). However, missionary activities in residential premises, and buildings belonging to another religious association are forbidden.

Formal missionary activity is strictly regulated. Under the law, only religious organizations have the right to invite foreign missionaries into the country. In addition, missionaries must be issued a formal legal document from the religious organization authorizing missionary activity. Foreign missionaries are singled out for additional restrictions (Ibid).

The Law restricts any missionary work that is in violation of public safety and order, which is defined broadly and vaguely to include, for instance, any activities that “destroy the family” (Ibid). It also holds religious associations liable for any improper missionary work carried out on its behalf. The Law also declares that an organization liquidated under the Extremism Law cannot engage in missionary work (Ibid).

The fines are quite harsh. Russian citizens may be fined between 5,000 and 50,000 Roubles while organizations may be fined from 100,000 to 1 million Roubles (Zubacheba 2019).[15] According to reports from one religious organization engaged in missionary activity in Russia, property used in contravention of the law has also been confiscated, including private homes used for home churches or private religious worship (Filina 2018).

Application

Given the broad and uncertain scope of the law, it is unsurprising that it has been applied at times in an illogical and arbitrary fashion that is particularly likely to chill religious expression. For instance, one Baptist pastor was found guilty for hanging a sign with the full name of his church on it (Shellnutt

2019), even though using the full name is also required by Russian law (Filina 2018). In another instance, pastors were fined for building a playground near their house of worship because religious literature could be found in the church building and the playground might attract children to the Church building (Ibid). Church leaders even have been fined for engaging in "illegal missionary activity" for petitioning their government officials (Ibid).

The law has not only been applied to formal missionary activity, but also to individuals discussing faith in their own home or at bus stops (Arnold 2019e). One couple was even fined for praying at a dinner out with friends (Filina 2018). A group of yoga teachers were fined for unlawful proselytizing even though they had no connection with a particular religion (Ibid). For the average religious believer, it would be difficult or impossible to know what kinds of religious expression would be permitted under this law.

Enforcement of the Yarovaya Law has further chilled religious expression. Russian authorities have demanded that certain congregations release summaries of sermons preached over the pulpit and turn over attendance records (Luxmoore 2019). Russian officials have also conducted undercover operations by pretending to be investigators interested in learning more about a Church (Filina 2018). Religious leaders under such a regime will be afraid to freely preach, and religious worshipers will be reluctant to attend worship services for fear of government surveillance and persecution.

The Yarovaya Law was justified in part because of a concern of foreign religious activity, but the overwhelming number of those fined under the law have been Russian citizens. Of 159 prosecutions in 2018, only fourteen were foreigners (Filina 2018). However, many of those foreign missionaries have been deported as a consequence of the law (Ibid).

Narrowing Construction

A Baptist pastor appealed his conviction for proselytizing under the Yarovaya Law to the Russian Constitutional Court. In March 2018, the Court refused to hear his appeal, but nevertheless issued a clarification of the Yarovaya Law which has provided at least some helpful limiting principles for application of the law. Before this decision, it was unclear what exactly constituted "missionary activity." The Constitutional Court clarified that missionary activity must have three elements (Arnold 2018).[16] First, it must be carried out by a particular group of individuals. Second, it must be directed at nonmembers. Third, it must be aimed at involving those individuals in the membership of the group. Activity that is not focused on proselytizing nonmembers would therefore not qualify. Forum 18, an international organization focused on religious freedom, estimates that this decision has meaningfully curtailed some excesses of the Yarovaya Law (Arnold 2019c). For example, at least some of the prosecutions discussed above (such as prosecution of the yoga teachers referenced above) would likely not have happened in light of this narrowing construction.

Pending Appeals at the ECtHR

Indian Protestant pastor Victor-Immanuel Mani was arrested in late 2016 for advertising religious gatherings on social media and passing out religious literature. He was fined 30,000 rubles and ordered to be deported. His deportation order was overturned by the Russian Supreme Court in light of his strong ties to Russia. However, his conviction and fine were both upheld. Mani appealed to the European Court of Human Rights in July 2017. An American Baptist pastor who was convicted of holding services in his home and advertising them also appealed to the European Court in April 2017 (World Watch Monitor 2017). In both instances, the ECtHR has asked the Russian government to respond to the allegations and to distinguish between "missionary activity" and the individual sharing of beliefs, which is protected under the European Convention (Ossewaarde 2018). Even though some members of the European Court of Human Rights have expressed sympathy for proselytism restrictions intended to protect "religious peace and tolerance" (Ortner 2015, 17), it is extremely difficult to imagine the Yarovaya Law surviving review if it is applied to ordinary sharing of belief in light of the ECtHR's recent declaration that "freedom to manifest one's religion includes the right to try to convince one's neighbor" (*Ibragimov v. Russia* 2018, para. 122). As such, relief for religious believers in Russia may be on the horizon, if Russia heeds such an ECtHR decision.

CONCLUSION

Religious freedom in Russia has been decimated as part of a crusade against extremism. The extremist ban and the Yarovaya missionary law were both justified in the name of national security but have been weaponized against minority faiths and greatly suppressed the free exercise of religion. The law as applied has departed completely from any national security justification, as there is no plausible security reason for placing innocent Jehovah's Witnesses in prison merely for attending religious worship services.

Despite the horrific history of recent persecutions, there may be some guarded causes for optimism. The ECtHR and the Russian Supreme Court have provided some limits on the application of the Extremism Law that will hopefully restrain zealous local prosecutors. More liberty favoring decisions are likely forthcoming from the ECtHR in the next few years. Also, prominent Russian politicians and leaders including Vladimir Putin have expressed their concern over how "pacifist believers" have been treated like terrorists under the recent wave of laws (Lunkin 2019). Indeed, in February 2019, President Putin urged the Russian Supreme Court to establish judicial standards with regard to prosecutions concerning freedom of conscience, freedom of religion, and the right of religious association, and he signaled greater willingness to give space for minority religious faiths to practice their beliefs (RIA Novosti 2019). Perhaps, Putin's request will result in a meaningful change in how these laws are enforced. And perhaps the next round of ECtHR decisions will result in the liberation of prisoners of conscience jailed merely for sharing their faith. But for the many believers who have been targeted in the name of extremism, this may all come too late and be a hope against hope.

NOTES

1. An unofficial translation of the Extremism Law has been created by the Council of Europe and I am relying on their translation which is consistent with my assessment of the original text of the law. See Federal Law on Combating Extremist Activity of the Russian Federation (2012).

2. The Yarovaya Law was made up of several separate laws. I have not been able to find an official English translation. The portion containing the anti-missionary provisions is О внесении изменений в Федеральный закон "О противодействии терроризму" и отдельные законодательные акты Российской Федерации в части установления дополнительных мер противодействия терроризму и обеспечения общественной безопасности (Amending the federal law on anti-terrorism measures and individual legislative acts of the Russian Federal including establishing additional counter-terrorism measures and securing public safety) (enacted July 29, 2016). See Russian Federation (2016).

3. I have not found an official English translation of this law, but I have verified the translation from the original Russian ("Публичные действия, выражающие явное неуважение к обществу и совершенные в целях оскорбления религиозн ых чувств верующих").

4. With each of these cites to decisions by the Russian Constitutional Court, I am relying on a translation supplied by the European Court of Human Rights in its Ibragimov decision. The text of the Russian Constitutional Courts' decisions is in Russian and there is no official English translation. I have looked at each of the decisions myself to verify the translation employed by the ECtHR. The Russian text of this decision is available at http://doc.ksrf.ru/decision/KSRFDecision135585.pdf.

5. The Russian text of this decision is available at http://doc.ksrf.ru/decision/KSRFDecision266580.pdf.

6. The Russian text of this decision is available at http://doc.ksrf.ru/decision/KSRFDecision272322.pdf.

7. Article 10 of the European Convention on Human Rights protects freedom of expression and guarantees that: "Everyone has the right to freedom of expression. This right shall include freedom to hold opinions and to receive and impart information and ideas without interference by public authority and regardless of frontier."

8. Those seeking review from the ECtHR are referred to as "applicants."

9. Article 9 of the European Convention on Human Rights protects freedom of thought, conscience, and religion, and guarantees that: "Everyone has the right to freedom of thought, conscience and religion; this right includes freedom to change his religion or belief and freedom, either alone or in community with others and in public or private, to manifest his religion or belief, in worship, teaching, practice and observance."

10. Here, I am quoting from the European Court of Human Rights decision which quoted portions of the Russian District Court decision. I have not been able to independently read and verify the Russian District Court Decision.

11. The European Court of Human Rights's analysis of laws that allegedly violate the European Convention proceeds in two parts. It first determines whether a restriction is enacted pursuant to law and in furtherance of legitimate aims. It then considers whether the restriction is "necessary in a Democratic society" (Ortner 2015, 19).

12. A credible and reliable translation is found at https://www.legislationline.org/documents/id/4028.

13. The Shanghai Cooperation Organization is a Eurasian alliance of nations including Russia and China. Because this alliance includes several regimes that are not particularly protective of free speech, there is a danger that multilateral agreements such as those against terrorism may be used to suppress speech.

14. In June 2020, after Dennis Christensen had already spent over three years in prison, the Lgovskiy District Court in the Kursk Region granted him early release and mitigated the rest of sentence to a fine.

15. An average Russian worker earns between 17,000 and 44,000 rubles a month, with a quarter earning even less than that (Zubacheva 2019).

16. I have been able to personally verify the interpretation offered by Forum 18 of this Russian Constitutional Court decision. The Russian text of this decision is available at http://doc.ksrf.ru/decision/KSRFDecision323481.pdf.

REFERENCES

Alekhina v. Russia, ECtHR No. 38004/12 (July 17, 2018).

Arnold, Victoria. 2015. "Russia: Some but Not All Sacred Texts Exempted from Banning." *Forum 18*, November 30, 2015. http://www.forum18.org/archive.php?article_id=2126.

———. 2017. "Russia: Religious Freedom Survey." *Forum 18,* January13, 2017. http://www.forum18.org/archive.php?article_id=2246.

———. 2018. "Russia: Will Constitutional Court Reduce 'Anti-Missionary' Prosecutions." *Forum 18*, May 16, 2018. http://www.forum18.org/archive.php?article_id=2377.

———. 2019a. "Russia: Jehovah's Witness Criminal Cases – List." *Forum 18*, October 11, 2019. http://www.forum18.org/archive.php?article_id=2512.

———. 2019b. "Russia: Imprisonment Completed, Citizenship Stripped, Awaiting Deportation." *Forum 18*, May 22, 2019 https://www.forum18.org/archive.php?article_id=2478.

———. 2019c. "Russia: Jehovah's Witness Appeal Fails, Appeal to Strasbourg." *Forum 18*, May 24, 2019. https://www.forum18.org/archive.php?article_id=2479.

———. 2019d. "Russia: Second Oryol Jehovah's Witness Appeal." *Forum 18*, May 27, 2019. https://www.forum18.org/archive.php?article_id=2480.

———. 2019e. "Russia: 159 Known "Anti-Missionary Prosecutions in 2018." *Forum 18*, May 6, 2019. http://www.forum18.org/archive.php?article_id=2474.

Criminal Code of the Russian Federation. "Article 282: Incitement of Hatred or Enmity, as Well as Abasement of Human Dignity." Accessed December 12, 2020. https://www.legislationline.org/documents/id/4028.

Barringer Gordon, Sarah. 2001. "What We Owe Jehovah's Witnesses." *History Net*, January 27, 2011. https://www.historynet.com/what-we-owe-jehovahs-witnesses.htm.

Bayev v. Russia, ECtHR No. 67667/09. 2017. Accessed November 3, 2020. http://hudoc.echr.coe.int/eng?i=001-174422.

Bush, Jason. 2014. "Pussy Riot Protestors Cleared of Religious Hatred Charge." *Reuters*, April 4, 2014. https://www.reuters.com/article/us-russia-pussyriot/pussy-riot-protesters-cleared-of-religious-hatred-charge-idUSBREA330O320140404.

Bushuev, Mikhail and Elena Barysheva. 2019. "Russia in the Council of Europe: What Does It Mean for Human Rights?" *Deutsche Welle*, June 26, 2019. https://www.dw.com/en/russia-in-the-council-of-europe-what-does-it-mean-for-human-rights/a-49368822.

The Economist. 2016. "Why Russia's Anti-Terrorism Laws are Controversial." July 20, 2016. https://www.economist.com/the-economist-explains/2016/07/20/why-russias-anti-terrorism-laws-are-controversial.

Engardio, Joel. 2009. "Russia's Bans on Jehovah's Witnesses." *ACLU*, December 10, 2009. https://www.aclu.org/blog/russias-bans-jehovahs-witnesses.

Council of Europe. n.d. "European Convention on Human Rights." Accessed November 11, 2020. https://www.echr.coe.int/Documents/Convention_ENG.pdf.

First Channel [Первый канал]. 2016. "President Vladimir Putin Signs Anti-terrorism Law." July 7, 2016. https://www.1tv.ru/news/2016-07-07/305551-prezident_vladimir_putin_podpisal_paket_popravok_v_antiterroristicheskoe_zakonodatelstvo.

Fagan, Geraldine. 2009. "Russia: How the Battle with 'Religious Extremism' Began." *Forum 18*, April 27, 2009. http://www.forum18.org/archive.php?article_id=1287.

Federal Law on Combating Extremist Activity of the Russian Federation. 2012. Accessed October 21, 2020. https://www.legislationline.org/download/id/3707/file/RF_law_combating_extremist_activity_2002_am2008_en.pdf.

Filina, Olga. 2018. "Mission Unacceptable: How the Yarovaya Law is Taking Effect in Russia." Accessed October 12, 2020. https://missioneurasia.ca/articles/mission-unacceptable-how-the-yarovaya-law-is-taking-effect-in-russia/.

Medvedev, Sergey. 2018. "Yarovaya Law and New Telecoms Data Storage Requirements." *Gorodissky and Partners*. Accessed December 15, 2020. http://www.gorodissky.com/publications/articles/yarovaya-law-and-new-telecoms-data-storage-requirements/.

Human Rights in China. 2011. "Counter-Terrorism and Human Rights: The Impact of the Shanghai Cooperation Organization." Accessed December 10, 2020. https://www.hrichina.org/sites/default/files/publication_pdfs/2011-hric-sco-whitepaper-full.pdf.

Human Rights Watch. 2017. "Russia: Court Bans Jehovah's Witnesses." Accessed May 17, 2020. https://www.hrw.org/news/2017/04/20/russia-court-bans-jehovahs-witnesses.

Ibragim Ibragimov and Others v. Russia, No. 1413/08, 28621/11. 2018. Accessed November 2, 2020. http://www.bailii.org/eu/cases/ECHR/2018/684.html.

Jehovah's Witnesses of Moscow and Others v. Russia, No. 302/02. 2010. Accessed December 14, 2020. http://hudoc.echr.coe.int/eng?i=001-99221.

Jehovah's Witnesses. 2017. "Russia's Decade-Long Attack on Religious Freedom Intensifies." https://www.jw.org/en/news/legal/by-region/russia/decade-long-attack-religious-freedom-intensifies/.

———. 2020. "Imprisoned for Their Faith Infographic." Accessed November 15, 2020. https://www.jw.org/en/news/legal/by-region/russia/imprisoned-infographic-20200110/.

Jehovah's Witnesses in Russia. n.d. "Dennis Christensen." Accessed November 15, 2020. https://jw-russia.org/en/prisoners/christensen.html.

Kokkinakas v. Greece, No. 14307/88. 1993. "Accessed May 12, 2020. http://hudoc.echr.coe.int/eng?i=001-57827.

Korelina, Olga. 2019. "Russia's New 'Anti-terrorism' Restrictions on Telecoms Lead to Skyrocketing Profits for Interception-technology Companies." *Meduza,* August 7, 2019. https://meduza.io/en/feature/2019/08/07/russia-s-new-anti-terrorism-restrictions-on-telecoms-lead-to-skyrocketing-profits-for-interception-technology-companies.

Kravchenko, Maria. 2018. "Inventing Extremists: The Impact of Russian Anti-Extremism Policies on Freedom of Religion or Belief." United States Commission on International Religious Freedom. Accessed December 13, 2019. https://www.uscirf.gov/publications/inventing-extremists-impact-russian-anti-extremism-policies-freedom-religion-or-belief.

———. 2019. "Brief Report on Misuse of Anti-Extremist Legislation in January-August 2019." SOVA Center. Accessed December 11, 2020. https://www.sova-center.ru/en/misuse/reports-analyses/2019/10/d41547/.

Luhn, Alec. 2016. "Russia Passes 'Big Brother' Anti-Terror Laws." *The Guardian*, June 26, 2016. https://www.theguardian.com/world/2016/jun/26/russia-passes-big-brother-anti-terror-laws.

Lunkin, Roman. "Russia's Crackdown on Jehovah's Witnesses Hits Critical Milestone." *Moscow Times,* February 7, 2019. https://www.themoscowtimes.com/2019/02/07/russias-crackdown-on-jehovahs-witnesses-hits-critical-milestone-op-ed-a64427.

Luxmoore, Matthew. 2019. "Russia Charges Baptist Pastor in a Sign that Its Religious Clampdown Could be Spreading." *Radio Free Europe*, April 24, 2019. https://www.rferl.org/a/russia-charges-baptist-pastor-in-a-sign-that-its-religious-clampdown-could-be-spreading/29901315.html.

Mälksoo, Lauri. 2018. "The European Court of Human Rights and Russia: Quo Vadis?" *Fifteen Eightyfour: Academic Perspectives from Cambridge University Press*, November 22, 2018. http://www.cambridgeblog.org/2018/11/the-european-court-of-human-rights-and-russia-quo-vadis/.

Masiuk, Elena. 2016. "Mission Forbidden." *Novaia Gazeta,* August 21, 2016. https://www2.stetson.edu/religious-news/160821a.html.

Ministry of Justice. 2017. "On the Suspension of Activities of the Religious Organization Headquarters of the Jehovah's Witnesses in Russia." Accessed on January 1, 2020. https://minjust.ru/ru/novosti/o-priostanovlenii-deyatelnosti-religioznoy-organizacii-upravlencheskiy-centr-svideteley.

———. n.d. "Federal List of Extremist Material." Accessed June 25, 2020. https://minjust.ru/ru/extremist-materials?field_extremist_content_value=%D0%B8%D1%81%D0%BB%D0%B0%D0%BC.

Mounier, Jean-Luc. 2019. "Russia's Undiplomatic Return to the Council of Europe." *France 24*, June 28, 2019. https://www.france24.com/en/20190628-russia-undiplomatic-return-council-europe-ukraine.

Muratov, Anton. 2018. "Russia's 'Big Brother' Law Enters into Force." *Moscow Times*, July 1, 2018. https://www.themoscowtimes.com/2018/07/01/russias-big-brother-law-enters-into-force-a62066.

O'Brien, Danny and Eva Galperin. 2016. "Russia Asks for the Impossible with its New Surveillance Laws." Electronic Frontier Foundation. Accessed May 13, 2019. https://www.eff.org/deeplinks/2016/07/russia-asks-impossible-its-new-surveillance-laws.

Ortner, Daniel. 2015. "Conscientious Offenders: Russia's Ban on 'Extremist' Religious Literature, and the European Court of Human Rights." *Virginia Journal of International Law* 55 (3): 1–39.

———. 2016. "The Terrorist's Veto: Why the First Amendment Must Protect Provocative Portrayals of the Prophet Muhammad." *Northwestern Journal of Law & Social Policy* 12 (1): 1.

Ossewaarde, Don. 2018. "European Court Questions Russia over Deportations under Religious Law." *World Watch Monitor*, February 1, 2018. https://www.worldwatchmonitor.org/coe/european-court-questions-russia-over-deportations-under-religion-law/.

Reuters 2020. "Russian Jehovah's Witness Adherent was Tortured in Custody, Says Lawyer." February 14, 2020. https://www.reuters.com/article/us-russia-politics-religion/russian-jehovahs-witness-adherent-was-tortured-in-custody-says-lawyer-idUSKBN2081VP.

RIA Novosti. 2019. "Putin Recommends Issuing Guidance on Religious Association Cases." Accessed November 12, 2019. https://ria.ru/20190221/1551187340.html.

Russian Federation. 2016. "Yarovaya Law." Accessed December 22, 2020. https://tinyurl.com/vpu36eh.

Savva Terentyev v. Russia, ECtHR, No. 10692/09. 2018. Accessed May 21, 2020. http://hudoc.echr.coe.int/eng?i=001-185307.

Shellnutt, Kate. 2019. "Russian Evangelicals Penalized Most Under Anti-Evangelism Law." *Christianity Today*, May 7, 2019. https://www.christianitytoday.com/news/2019/may/russian-evangelicals-anti-missionary-fined-yarovaya-law.html.

Sottek, T. C. 2016. "Russia Moves Towards Alarming New Counter-Terrorism Law, International Center for Not for Profit Law." *The Verge,* June 26, 2016. https://www.theverge.com/2016/6/26/12033480/russia-counter-terrorism-bill-yarovaya-law.

SOVA Center. n.d. "Misuse of Anti-Extremism." Accessed December 2, 2020. https://www.sova-center.ru/en/misuse/.

———. 2019a. "Misuse of Anti-Extremism in September 2019." Accessed January 1, 2020. https://www.sova-center.ru/en/misuse/news-releases/2019/10/d41559/.

———. 2019b. "Misuse of Extremism in October 2019." Accessed January1, 2020. https://www.sova-center.ru/en/misuse/news-releases/2019/11/d41694/.

———. 2019c. "Misuse of Anti-Extremism in December 2019." Accessed January 1 2020. https://www.sova-center.ru/en/misuse/news-releases/2020/01/d41943/.

United States Commission on International Religious Freedom. n.d. "Bagir Kazikhanov (Released)." Accessed February 3, 2020. https://www.uscirf.gov/bagir-kazikhanov-released.

World Watch Monitor. 2017. "US Missionary Appeals to European Court of Human Rights Over Russian Law." https://www.worldwatchmonitor.org/2017/03/us-missionary-appeals-european-court-justice-russian-law/.

Zubacheva, Ksenia. 2019. "How Much Money Does an Average Russian Make?" *Russia Beyond,* June 3, 2019. https://www.rbth.com/business/330451-average-salary.

Chapter 15

Confronting "the Other"

Internal Constraints on Freedom of Speech to Combat Perceived External Threats

Paul Haridakis

INTRODUCTION

Even in a democracy with a strong Constitutional foundation for protecting freedom of speech, such as the United States, those protections tend to be compromised when the government is confronted with a threat like terrorism. Throughout U.S. history, various groups have challenged governance and/or aspects of the then-current social order. Their activities have ranged from simple protest to broader social movements, and, at times, even violence. Local, State, and federal governmental entities have reacted to such challenges to the social order with laws and other actions to negate the respective challenge. There are so many instances of such threats and government responses to them that they all cannot be covered in a single chapter. Here, I highlight and discuss briefly just a few examples. Each of these instances has been covered extensively elsewhere. Thus, the intent here is not to provide a comprehensive historical account of these events. Rather, the attempt here is merely to try to contextualize them and some of their effects within the theme of this book, and perhaps to remind us that threats such as terrorism are not new and governmental attempts to confront such threats have a long history in the United States. At times, the threat confronted was real. At other times, U.S. policies and actions were driven by fears that were exaggerated and are remembered more for the adverse effects they had on freedom of speech and other civil liberties than for the purpose for which they were designed.

For almost twenty years (since 9/11), policymakers in the United States have devoted considerable attention to counter-terrorism efforts in a proclaimed war on terrorism. However, this is not a recent phenomenon. Government attempts to quash social unrest, insurgency, and sedition date to the early days of the U.S. republic. For example, in 1794, after an excise tax was placed on distilled whiskey, farmers in Pennsylvania rebelled. When they failed to cease their disobedience and disperse, the first president of the United States, George Washington, led troops into Pennsylvania to put down the so-called "Whiskey rebellion." This is just one of many instances in which the government used federal troops to put down domestic disorder.[1] In 1807, Congress passed the Insurrection Act.[2] This Act granted the president specific authority to mobilize military troops and employ them domestically to quell insurrection and other civil disorder.

In addition to the use of force, the government has from its beginning relied on legislation to combat external and domestic threats to the government or domestic tranquility that impacted freedom of speech and the rights of foreigners. During the administration of our second president, John Adams, the United States passed the Alien and Sedition Acts in 1798 to foreclose seditious activity, and more. These four Acts, in combination, restricted immigration; increased the amount of time an immigrant had to reside in the United States before being eligible for citizenship; gave the president the authority to deport aliens he felt endangered "the peace and safety of the United States" or engaged in "treasonable or secret machinations" against the United States, and during wartime, the power to capture and remove an alien associated with the enemy; and provided for punishment of expression deemed seditious.[3] The Sedition Act, in particular, was used to prosecute newspaper editors who did little more than criticize the president or his administration.

Despite the long history of such actions, in the interest of space and to emphasize relatively more contemporary examples of government efforts to confront sedition, insurrection, sabotage, terrorism, and episodes of social unrest, the remainder of the discussion will focus largely on government initiatives in the twentieth and twenty-first centuries. Even that more recent history is so rife with government action to confront such threats, real and perceived, that space permits a discussion of only a few illustrative examples.

Many government initiatives that have been used in ways that repressed individual freedoms and civil liberties in the United States emerged in the guise of fighting violence and terrorism. At times, such efforts were designed to target specific identifiable groups engaged in various acts of protest, disruption, and, at times, violence. Often, those groups were comprised of foreigners or alleged to be influenced by or associated with foreign ideological groups.

ANARCHISTS

For example, in the late nineteenth and early twentieth centuries, the government was concerned with an active and growing anarchist movement. According to Barton (2015) anarchism in the late nineteenth century represents the first phase of modern terrorism. Several world leaders were assassinated, and innocent civilians were killed in anarchist attacks. There even was a brazen meeting of the International Congress of Anarchists in 1881 during which the use of violence and insurrection was endorsed (Kassel 2009, 242). Of course, there was not a monolithic body of anarchists. There were numerous different anarchist groups. Some focused on political change, some focused more on labor and worker rights, and some focused on social change and inequality in America. Some advocated change through deliberative communication and protest, rather than through illegal violence. Some anarchists did engage in terrorist acts of violence.

Prior to the late nineteenth century, U.S. government leaders tended to view anarchy as a largely European problem and a dangerous foreign ideology. However, instances of labor unrest allegedly involving anarchists, some of which included violence—such as the Haymarket bombing that occurred during a labor demonstration[4]—stirred government and public concern. U.S. States reacted, passing criminal anarchy laws targeting radicals for prosecution for their acts and ideas. After President William McKinley was assassinated by an anarchist, Leon Czolgosz, reaction to such social-political ideologies antithetical to the U.S. political system were criminalized by even more U.S. States.

By the 1920s, many of the States had passed criminal anarchy laws (or criminal syndicalism) laws. The language used in these laws tended to criminalize behavior such as advocating sabotage, violence, terrorism, and other unlawful means to achieve political or industrial change; or to organize or become a member of any group that advocated such force or violence, particularly in furtherance of overthrowing the government. What was particularly problematic with such laws is that they did not always differentiate well between the advancement of anarchism as a political ideology and anarchist acts of violence and terrorism. Thus, they often were used not to prosecute people engaged in violence, but to prosecute people based on their ideology—because they advocated anarchy or socialism as ideologies. When challenged by individuals convicted due to their expressive activities, and in the absence of any violence, the U.S. Supreme Court upheld the convictions and ruled that they did not violate the First Amendment rights of free speech (e.g., *Gitlow v. New York* 1925; *Whitney v. California* 1927).[5] It was not until the late 1960s that courts began to rule that these statutes were unconstitutional. In *Brandenburg v. Ohio* (1969), for example, the U.S. Supreme Court ruled that Ohio's statute violated the First Amendment because "constitutional guarantees of free speech and free press do not permit a State to forbid or proscribe advocacy of the use of force or of law violation except where such advocacy is directed to inciting or producing imminent lawless action and is likely to incite or produce such action" (447).

Immigration legislation also was used to confront the external threat of anarchy. For example, the Immigration Act of 1903, sometimes called the "Anarchist Exclusion Act" (Barton 2015, 304–305), authorized immigration officials to "exclude, arrest, and deport foreign born residents if they held or espoused political beliefs deemed subversive, dangerous, or undesirable by Congress" (Barton 2015, 305). Large numbers of people were affected merely because of their political views and expressive activities, and sometimes, their national origin (for more discussion see Wiecek 2001, 383; also see Kassel 2009). When it was challenged on First Amendment grounds, the Immigration Act was upheld by the U.S. Supreme Court (*Turner v. United States* 1904).

The fact is that anarchy is not inherently violent. Anarchist theorists advocate no particular class distinctions in society, and no particular governmental power structure (capitalist, socialist, or other kinds) (see Kassel 2009, 239). Consequently, many of these laws that were used to prosecute, deport, or otherwise adversely affect the liberties of anarchists were imposed on individuals who were not directly involved in violent terrorist activity, but rather adherents of a non-conformist political ideology, or worse, not even anarchists, but members of other groups, such as socialist groups and labor organizations the government also viewed as "radical."

LABOR

Labor organizations and their members often were targeted by the government for their activities. This was particularly the case when there was concern with anarchist, socialist, and/or other "foreign" influence in labor unions. Early labor unions did tend to attract some socialists, anarchists, and other "anti-establishment" radicals (Tedford and Herbeck 2017, 32). Therefore, governmental concern with labor groups often was intermixed with concerns about the rise and influence of socialist and communist ideology perceived to undermine democratic ideals and institutions in the United States. In fact, a nationwide labor strike involving unions representing workers in a variety of occupations in private and public sectors in 1919 was a major event in the Red Scare of 1919.[6]

During strikes, in particular, confrontations between demonstrators and police sometimes occurred. At times, the federal government got involved.

For example, President Grover Cleveland deployed federal troops to put down riots surrounding a nationwide railroad strike in 1894 (e.g., Congressional Research Service 2018, 39). But government efforts often went beyond attempts to thwart violence in labor unrest or to curtail socialist influence in the labor movement. Sometimes expressive activities of labor groups and their members were restricted in less egregious ways, such as government officials refusing to issue permits to labor groups to hold rallies and parades granted to other groups (*Hague v. CIO* 1939).

In all, concerns with anarchists, labor organizations, and socialists were comingled in governmental response to the perceived threats posed by each. Similarly, socialism and communism, though different, have been analogized, and concerns with perceived threats posed by both socialists and communists have led to both groups being targeted by the U.S. government.

SOCIALISTS AND COMMUNISTS

The intensity of government reaction to socialism and communism emerged and waned at different times during the twentieth century. As referenced above, the 1919 Red Scare heightened scrutiny. According to Wiecek (2001, 389), twenty-six states passed red flag laws in 1919. These laws forbade the display of red flags (a well-recognized symbol of communism) as a symbol in opposition to the government.[7]

Also in late 1919 and early 1920, U.S. attorney general A. Mitchell Palmer engaged in a campaign to round up foreign radicals (e.g., communists, socialists, and other foreign nationals). The so-called Palmer raids were triggered by terrorist use of bombs and bombings directed at public officials. In these raids, large numbers of socialists and persons of Eastern European ancestry were detained, jailed, and/or deported (see Cole 2003, 16–17 for a discussion). In response to such government actions, the American Civil Liberties Union was formed to protect First Amendment rights and denounced the violations of civil liberties by the Justice Department in its fight against communism (see Wiecek 2001, 390–391).

During times of war, wartime initiatives also were used to prosecute and subvert alleged socialist and communist activity. During the First World War, for example, the United States passed the Espionage Act of 1917[8] and a 1918 sedition amendment[9] to it. Together, this legislation outlawed both actual and verbal acts that were disloyal, treasonous, or interfered with military recruitment, and the like. Some of the first people prosecuted were socialists. These included the general secretary of the Socialist Party, Charles T. Schenck (prosecuted after circulating and mailing an anti-draft leaflet), Eugene Debs, the head of the Socialist Party (prosecuted after making an anti-war speech), and Jacob

Abrams and co-defendant immigrant residents from Russia (prosecuted after distributing leaflets criticizing the United States for aiding Czarist Russia during the Bolshevik revolution). All of these defendants were convicted for their expression (speech; writings, assembly). In each instance, on appeal, the U.S. Supreme Court affirmed the convictions of the defendants (*Abrams v. United States* 1919; *Debs v. United States* 1919; *Schenck v. United States* 1919).

The Second World War and its aftermath also provided a wartime atmosphere that led to the targeting of socialists and communists by the U.S. government. In 1940, after the start of the war, but just prior to the United States' entry, Congress passed the Alien Registration Act (commonly referred to as the Smith Act).[10] Its anti-sedition provisions outlawed speech that advocated the use of force or violence to overthrow the government in the United States. After the war it was used to prosecute socialists and communists in the United States. In perhaps, the most famous case, the Department of Justice brought charges under the Act against members of the Central Committee of the Communist Party in New York for conspiracy to form the Communist Party of the United States (see Tedford and Herbeck 2017, 57–58). They were tried and convicted, and in *Dennis v. U. S.* (1951) the U.S. Supreme Court upheld their convictions, despite the fact that they did little more than simply attempt to organize the Communist Party in the United States. There was no overt attempt to overthrow the government or take any form of violent action on their part.

Fortunately, in later cases, after some of the hysteria surrounding socialism and communism had subsided, the Supreme Court differentiated advocacy of abstract doctrine from advocacy of illegal action. The latter, according to the Court, could be proscribed pursuant to the Smith Act without violating the First Amendment. However, criminalizing the former was a violation of the First Amendment (see *Yates v. U.S.* 1957).

In addition to the Smith Act, other Cold War–era initiatives were employed to target socialists and communists. For example, pursuant to the Labor Management Relations Act that regulates labor unions, to participate in NLRB proceedings, union officers were required to file affidavits with the Department of Labor affirming that they were not members of the Communist Party.[11] The Internal Security Act of 1950 permitted targeting those for their communist political views and associations.[12] Whereas the Immigration Act of 1903 prohibited anarchists from immigration, the Internal Security Act excluded communists (see Sbardellati and Shaw, 2003 p. 510). It also required communist organizations to register with the attorney general, permitted investigation of those suspected of engaging in subversive activities, and provided for denaturalization of naturalized immigrants who joined a communist organization (see Wiecek 2001, 424–426 for discussion of these Acts).

These types of targeting of those suspected of communist activity found their way into employment and other associational decisions, as well. Pursuant to Executive Orders issued by Presidents Truman and Eisenhower, federal employees could be fired for disloyalty (Wiecek 2001, 421–422). Loyalty review applied to federal employees. But, some states, cities and private employers also required loyalty affirmations—or documents indicating employees had not been members of a party that advocated the overthrow of the United States.

THE SPECIAL CASE OF INTERNMENT DURING THE SECOND WORLD WAR

Whenever there is a perceived external threat, the focus on members of the specific groups of concern always occurs. This was the case with the Alien and Sedition Acts, the use of the Immigration Act of 1909 targeting anarchists, and the Internal Security Act of 1950 targeting communists, discussed above. The Alien Registration Act also required many non-citizen aliens staying in the United States for more than thirty days to register with the Immigration and Naturalization Service.

However, perhaps, the most infamous pre-twenty-first-century U.S. policy was the internment of Japanese Americans and others of Japanese ancestry during the Second World War. The government's largely exaggerated fear of Japanese sabotage in the United States led to this policy. To curtail espionage and sabotage, President Roosevelt issued Executive Order 9066. Persons of Japanese origin (including Japanese Americans) were required to report to relocation centers, and many were relocated to internment camps. In all, over 110,000 were interned, the vast majority of whom were U.S. citizens. Even prior to internment, the government resorted to establishing a curfew on Japanese Americans. Both the curfew (*Hirabayashi v. United States* 1943), and the internment program (*Korematsu v. United States* 1944) were upheld as Constitutional by the U.S. Supreme Court.[13]

Following the war, Congress passed the anti-communist oriented Internal Security Act of 1950, referenced earlier.[14] Title II of the Act (known as the Emergency Detention Act) empowered the president to detain those the president felt were a threat to engaging in sabotage or espionage, if the president declared an "internal security emergency." While it ultimately was not used for internment of communists, clearly the specter of internment seen during the Second World War was reinforced by the Act, as was the power of the government to invoke it (see Vladeck 2004, 176–178 for discussion).

1960'S DOMESTIC UNREST

Although the United States used immigration laws to foreclose entry of foreign anarchists, socialists, and communists into the United States, and fought wars overseas against axis powers in the Second World War and communists in Korea and Vietnam, the counter-measures and strategies discussed above were largely employed domestically. Domestic enforcement of laws targeting those deemed to advocate and/or carry out actions deemed by government actors to be radical, subversive, or terroristic continued in later decades. The 1960s, in particular, provided a volatile cocktail of activities, groups, and individuals on which the government focused.

The 1960s was a tumultuous decade of internal strife in the United States. The civil rights movement, the anti-war movement, student unrest on university campuses, and political upheaval over various social justice issues led to various groups making demands for government change. These included student groups such as Students for a Democratic Society, and a more radical offshoot, the Weather Underground; political groups such as the Black Panther Party and the Youth International Party (Yippies); and religious groups such as the Southern Christian Leadership Conference, led by Dr. Martin Luther King, and the Black Muslims. These and many other groups and outspoken dissidents attracted government scrutiny.

The government's concern with violence and disorder, in particular, led to various investigations and reports produced by government commissions. These included reports by the National Commission on the Causes and Prevention of Violence (1969), which President Lyndon Johnson established in 1968 after the assassinations of Martin Luther King and Robert Kennedy; and the President's Commission on Campus Unrest (1970), established by President Richard Nixon shortly after the shootings of students at Kent State University by National Guardsmen and shootings at Jackson State college by police.

Government actions often were taken in the name of maintaining domestic security and to prevent individual and group acts of violence. To be sure, there was some violence associated with 1960s unrest, such as large-scale riots in the Watts neighborhood of Los Angeles in 1965, and in cities across the nation in the aftermath of the assassination of Martin Luther King in 1968. However, as some of the above government reports indicate, often even nonviolent peaceful protests and marches were met with strident force and violence from government actors such as the military and law enforcement agencies. Media coverage of the era are rife with images of police force—such as the use of police dogs and fire hoses on civil rights protesters, police beatings of protesters on college campuses, and beatings of protesters during the 1968 Democratic National Convention in Chicago.

Civil Rights advocates had long faced violent threats. This included NAACP leaders and the Reverend Martin Luther King, whose home was bombed (Bermanzohn 2000, 40). At times that violence or force was perpetrated by law enforcement. In one well-known example, in Birmingham Alabama in 1963, local officials specifically tried to stop a demonstration to desegregate department stores, and obtained an injunction to forbid large demonstrations. When the demonstration went on, police beat nonviolent demonstrators with billy clubs, and used high-powered hoses and police dogs on them. After the U.S. Supreme Court ruled that racial segregation of Schools was unconstitutional, and a federal court in Arkansas ordered desegregation of a high school in the State capital of Little Rock, the governor of Arkansas employed the National Guard to prevent the first Black students from entering school (see Bermanzohn 2000, 39).

At times, government reaction was more passively aggressive to social change, such as when agencies in some southern States maintained segregation or failed to arrest perpetrators of violence against African-Americans. When "Freedom Riders" rode public buses into the southern states to register voters in the early 1960s, they were confronted with violence by members of the public. Local police as well as federal law enforcement entities simply failed to intervene and protect them. When student civil rights activists ran an ad in the *New York Times* alleging they were being met by a "wave of terror" in the South, a former public official of Montgomery Alabama sued them for defamation (see Tedford and Herbeck 2017, 86).

On college campuses, students began to assert rights and display visible political awareness in the 1960s. The growth of the student free speech movement arguably began at Berkeley in 1964, when students protested campus restrictions on their political activities and other free speech rights. Ultimately, actions became more direct and confrontational. In some instances, law enforcement personnel resorted to the use of force to quash student protest or other civil disobedience. In one example of confrontation, students at Columbia University occupied university administration buildings. Ultimately, police, perhaps a thousand or more, stormed in, expelling and arresting occupiers, and beating many with billy clubs (Gitlin 1993, 306–309).

The most notorious example of armed force against students occurred at Kent State University on May 4, 1970. This time it was not local police, but military forces (Ohio National Guard troops) that perpetrated the violence—which in this case included mass shootings and deadly force used against students. After vandalism in the city of Kent occurred on Friday, May 1, subsequent to President Nixon's announced expansion of the War in Vietnam into Cambodia, armed National Guard military troops were deployed at the order of the governor of Ohio. Troops occupied the university campus that weekend. On Monday, May 4, troops marched on students holding a rally to protest the escalation of the war in Vietnam. After dispersing students, troops abruptly turned on the students and opened fire, killing four students and wounding nine others. Less than two weeks later, police opened fire on demonstrators at Jackson State college, killing two students (one a high school student) and injuring twelve others. In the investigative report on campus unrest subsequently ordered by President Nixon, the Commission determined that the shootings at Kent State "and the deaths that followed were unnecessary, unwarranted, and inexcusable" (President's Commission on Campus Unrest 1970, 289).[15]

Another well-known example of the use of government force against protesters occurred during the 1968 Democratic National Convention in Chicago. Several counterculture and anti-establishment groups, including anti-Vietnam War activists, planned to demonstrate during the convention. The city denied permits to groups to hold rallies that week, and protected the convention site with barbed wire. The Chicago police force and National Guard troops were mobilized, resulting in far more law enforcement personnel than demonstrators (see Gitlin 1993, 319–340). Ultimately, on August 28, during the week of the convention, the police instigated what would be later described as a "police riot" (quoted in Gitlin 1993, 326). Using weapons such as billy clubs and tear gas, they descended on protesters and others who got in the way.

In addition to such overt government action, there were more covert governmental operations to address concern with domestic unrest or disorder in the decade. For example, Risen (2009, 50) noted the work of the Army Intelligence Command in the 1960s that engaged in surveillance and "monitoring anyone even remotely connected to dissent or radicalism," including religious leaders, politicians, and anti-war and civil rights activists. There appears to have been some belief in the Army that some rioting in the United States and the anti-war movement were influenced by "instigators who must have received training in insurgency tactics from overseas" (Risen 2009, 54). Groups organizing protests were sometimes infiltrated by agents posing as participants. According to Risen (2009), with the growth of campus unrest and the anti-war movement "under-cover agents were sent into classrooms, local anti-war organizations, and even, in one case, a fraternity at North Dakota college" (57). Greenberg (2011) noted that a Senate Intelligence Committee found that the use of undercover agents by the FBI to spy on even peaceful protests had become routine by the 1980s.

As the discussion to this point suggests, U.S. government entities have always been concerned with groups and/or individuals involved in what the government views as threats to civil order and national security. Whether called criminal anarchy, espionage, sedition, terrorism, or other terminology reflecting the jargon of the era, there are more similarities than differences in government responses to "counter" such threats, regardless of labels used.

Since the 1970s, there has been growth in the use of the term "terrorism" as the jargon often used to categorize the types of threats referenced above. In addition, Greenberg (2011, 35) explained that the FBI in the 1970s "developed a new paradigm of 'terrorism' to characterize most domestic security investigations." This terrorism frame has been maintained and used since the 1970s to target various groups as advancing terrorism including, according to Greenberg (2011, 38), "environmental activists, the anti-nuclear and peace movement surrounding the nuclear freeze, animal rights advocates, gay organizations, anti-apartheid groups, and Arab-Americans."

The terrorism and counter-terrorism narrative has intensified and has become more explicit in recent years. More importantly, counter-terrorism efforts have stepped up considerably, particularly after the bombings of the World Trade Center in 1993, the federal building in Oklahoma City in 1995, the U.S. embassies in Kenya and Tanzania in 1998, and, of course, the Al Qaeda attacks on September 11, 2001.

POST 9/11

In the twenty-first century, U.S. counter-terrorism efforts have focused on groups specifically identified by the government as terrorist organizations. After September 11, 2001 (9/11) attacks on the World Trade Center and the Pentagon by members of Al Qaeda, government response began immediately. The U.S. passed the USA PATRIOT Act ("Uniting and Strengthening America by Providing Appropriate Tools Required to Intercept and Obstruct Terrorism"),[16] and the Homeland Security Act;[17] established the Department of Homeland Security; authorized the use of military tribunals to try alleged terrorists;[18] and authorized the closure of special interest deportation proceedings pertaining to those suspected of having links to terrorism.[19] The president deployed military forces to Afghanistan and Iraq, and U.S. troops are still deployed in these countries. Enemy combatants have been detained in Guantanamo Bay, and the government has been very reticent to disclose information about the identities of people detained or the criteria used to classify enemy combatants. The Executive Branch also has asserted the authority to close the military trials of enemy combatants from the press and public.

Clearly, the 9/11 terrorist attacks justified a strong governmental counter-terrorism response to protect national security. But, not all of the counter-terrorism initiatives taken have affected only non-citizen enemy combatants. Some counter-terrorism laws, practices, policies, and procedures have targeted domestic communication and affected the rights of U.S.

citizens, rather directly. For example, during the administration of President George W. Bush, there were changes to the government's approach to handling requests for information under the Freedom of Information Act (FOIA). The Homeland Security Act exempted information obtained by the Department of Homeland Security from disclosure otherwise mandated by FOIA. Executive Order 13292 encouraged reclassification of material previously unclassified and to classify information in agency hands, excluding it from general disclosure (see Haridakis 2006, 14–15). The government also used a more restrictive interpretation of FOIA to refuse to disclose the number of people detained in the War on Terrorism (Haridakis 2005, 442–443).

The USA PATRIOT Act expanded the ability of the government to monitor and obtain information from U.S. citizens and residents, in addition to those identified as "enemy combatants." It authorized the acquisition of medical records from medical providers, library records of patrons from libraries, and records from corporations. It also prohibited these organizations from disclosing the requests for such records. It permitted increased and easier surveillance and monitoring of electronic communications (e.g., Internet, telephone). In addition, the Executive Branch assumed authority to monitor attorney–client communications between detainees and their attorneys.[20]

The Executive Branch issued orders establishing the use of military tribunals to try alleged terrorists. Procedures established for these tribunals also permitted their closure to the press and public. Closure arguably poses a threat to everyday U.S. citizens' First Amendment rights—particularly the right to see and hear what their government is doing. Since 1980, the U.S. Supreme Court has taken the position that a public trial is not just a Sixth Amendment right of a defendant, it also is a First Amendment right of the public to see its judicial branch at work (*Richmond Newspapers v. Virginia* 1980). Although *Richmond* occurred outside of a military setting, it has been extended to some military settings such as those dealing with military courts martial (see Haridakis 2004).

In addition to military tribunals, the government put in place procedures to close "special interest" deportation hearings—those dealing with the deportation of persons suspected of being connected to terrorist groups or terrorism. Shortly after 9/11, immigration judges were instructed by Chief Immigration Judge Michael Creppy to close these hearings. In two early cases, media organizations challenged this practice in federal courts. Each federal district court ruled that the closure of the hearings violated the First Amendment. However, on appeal, Federal Courts of Appeal split on the constitutionality of closure. In *North Jersey Media Group v. Ashcroft* (2002), the Appellate Court ruled that the government's interest in national security outweighed the right of the public and media and justified closure. In *Detroit v. Press v. Ashcroft*

(2002), the Appellate Court affirmed the lower court ruling and ruled that closure did indeed violate the First Amendment.

The tradition of government surveillance of groups assumed to pose threats, such as examples referenced earlier, has continued in the twenty-first-century war on terrorism. This practice has been being carried out by various agencies. Risen (2009) noted, for example, some post-9/11 surveillance occurred through agencies such as "the National Security Agency, the Defense Counterintelligence and Human Intelligence Center, and the domestic intelligence operations of the U.S. Northern Command, which was established after 9/11" (51). Even earlier, Friedman (2005) also speculated that the types of government-directed domestic surveillance activities that have occurred in the past were returning after 9/11 in a "coordinated federal effort through the National Guard as well as the Joint Terrorism Task Forces (JTTFs), teams of state and local police, and federal agents, led by the FBI" (4). Perhaps one of the broadest surveillance programs instituted was the global surveillance program run by the NSA. The program involved collecting metadata records of phone calls (including those of ordinary U.S. citizens not suspected of terrorism), e-mails and Internet searches, and cell phone data (see Mondale, Stein, and Fisher 2016, 2268–2279).

This sort of clandestine insidious surveillance through the power to use roving wiretaps and monitor various types of electronic and non-electronic communication affects the rights of privacy of those subjected to secret intrusion. In addition to intruding on privacy, the design and practices employed capture expressive activities such as what is said and what is read by people. This flies in the face of Constitutional individual rights the U.S. Supreme Court has protected in the past. As former Supreme Justice Thurgood Marshall wrote in one case, "If the First Amendment means anything, it means that a State has no business telling a man, sitting alone in his own house, what books he may read or what films he may watch. Our whole constitutional heritage rebels at the thought of giving the government the power to control men's minds" (*Stanley v. Georgia* 1969, 565).

The sheer volume of laws and practices implemented after 9/11 that expanded the power of the government to gather intelligence and investigate those suspected of terrorism, to collect records and intercept communications from everyday citizens, and to withhold information obtained from disclosure makes it problematic to ascertain with certainty the number of times long-standing traditions of civil liberties may have been circumvented. What is clear is that the United States implemented counter-terrorism laws and practices to confront twenty-first-century terrorism with at least as much vigor and vigilance as it did when confronting prior perceived threats to homeland security. The rhetoric after 9/11 reflected that. For example, Bowden (2007) referenced a speech to Congress delivered by President Bush shortly after the

9/11 attacks in which the president described the attackers as "the heirs of all murderous ideologies of the twentieth century . . . they follow in the path of fascism, and Nazism, and totalitarianism" (quoted on 544). This rhetorical and practical Executive Branch position provided justification for treating the attackers as such, and implementing wartime laws and initiatives to protect homeland security from them.

This brief review of government efforts to combat threats tells us much about the tenuousness of our long-standing principles and our commitment to freedom of speech and other civil liberties when butted up against perceived threats to homeland security and domestic order. When a new threat emerges, government efforts and tactics similar to those used to confront past threats are re-employed to confront the new threat. Often, these counter-terrorism actions become engrained in policy and practice—and remain available for later administrations to draw on.

We continued to see this playbook in actions taken by President Donald Trump and his administration in recent years. Shortly after taking office, President Trump implemented a travel ban on seven countries with largely Muslim populations. He claimed terrorists were among refugees seeking to enter the country at its southern border, and detention centers were created to corral refugees. In response to demonstrations and protests that occurred in the aftermath of deaths of African American citizens by police in 2020, the president referred to demonstrators as anarchists, Marxists, and radicals. He deployed law enforcement personnel from the Department of Homeland Security (created in response to the 9/11terrorist attack) to Portland, OR during demonstrations there. This was done over the objection of both the State governor and Mayor of Portland. He also threatened to invoke the Insurrection Act.

The point here is not to challenge the authority of the president to protect national security and social order. Rather, the point is that the rhetoric of "otherness" and using it to justify targeting groups deemed to be a threat to national security and social order remains a part of governmental response to those alleged to be engaging in disorder. Immigration laws, the power of detention, surveillance, and the use of military force also remain tried and true methods to which the government has turned over and over again—even when the targets of those methods are not directly involved in terrorism.

CONCLUSION

The above discussion of just some of the government efforts to respond to real and perceived threats and challenges posed by various groups in the United States indicates that they had consequences beyond thwarting the threats.

Many of the laws passed during these periods were (and some still are) used in ways that adversely affected freedom of speech and other civil liberties. Even a brief review of some of these initiatives shows similar patterns of the use of laws and practices. When threats are attributed to foreigners or foreign influence, immigration laws often are mustered to target people on the basis of their national origin. Controls on communication often involve restrictions on various types of expression (e.g., content deemed seditious), expressive activities (e.g., demonstrations, assembly), modes of expression (e.g., media), and places for expressive activities (e.g., public forums). As such, they affect access to information, regulate communication content, target specific types of speakers and groups because of their associations, and subject many to government surveillance.

There will always be ongoing threats to the existing social order by various groups. In some instances, violence sometimes has been associated with such challenges. Violence justifies legitimate government action to negate the illegal activity, and punish those who perpetrate it. However, U.S. history tells us that in the past, the government has responded in ways that limit the rights of those unconnected to the violence. Therefore, we must remain vigilant in recognizing when government action legitimately targets those involved in terrorism and other violent activities, and when it is overbroad and sweeps within its prohibitions Constitutionally protected expressive activities and liberties to get at the illegal activity it was designed to address. What we often remember about overbroad government action is its overreach in application. We must learn from history and consider past abuses when assessing new initiatives as they are adopted and employed. We don't want government response to terrorism to be as damaging to our democracy as the terrorism and illegal violence confronted.

NOTES

1. For a review, see Congressional Research Service, *The Posse Comitatus Act and Related Matters: The Use of the Military to Execute Civilian Law* (Congressional Research Service, 2018). Available at https://fas.org/sgp/crs/natsec/R42659.pdf.

2. 10 U.S.C. §§ 331–335.

3. For a discussion of these four Acts, see Thomas L. Tedford and David A. Herbeck. 2017. *Freedom of Speech in the United States* (8th ed.). State College PA: Strata.

4. Discussed in Mary S. Barton. 2015. "The Global War on Anarchism: The United States and International Anarchist Terrorism, 1898–1904." *Diplomatic History* 39 (2): 303–330, on 307. See also Whitney Kassel. 2009. "Terrorism and the International Anarchist Movement of the Late Nineteenth and Early Twentieth Centuries." *Studies in Conflict & Terrorism* 32: 237–252, on 244. In the Haymarket

incident, unionists had a confrontation with police. It was during a protest that had followed violence. Someone threw a bomb into a crowd and several police and picketers were killed and several others seriously hurt.

5. Upholding New York's law and California's law, respectively.

6. For a study of press coverage of the strikes, see Mathew Pressman, "Black and White and Red All Over?" *Journalism History* 39, no. 1 (2013): 29–39.

7. In Stromberg v. California (1931), the U.S. Supreme Court ruled that California's red flag law was unconstitutional and violated the First Amendment right to engage in free political discussion.

8. 40 Statutes at Large 219 (1917).

9. 40 Statutes at Large 553–554 (1918).

10. 54 Statutes at Large 670–671 (1940).

11. 61 Statutes at Large 136 (1947).

12. 64 Statues at Large 987 (1950).

13. Although not as widespread, persons of German and Italian ancestry also were interned in the United States during the Second World War. Treated as enemy aliens German and Italian nationals were particularly vulnerable under this policy. Unlike the case with Japanese Americans, far more often most German and Italian detainees were foreign nationals (though some U.S. citizens were detained).

14. *Supra* note 12.

15. For a review and summary of events of the weekend leading up to the May 4, 1970 shootings, and its immediate aftermath, see Carole A. Barbato, Laura L. Davis, and Mark F. Seeman, *This We Know: A Chronology of the Shootings at Kent State, May 1970* (Kent, OH: Kent State University Press, 2012).

16. Pub. L. No. 107–56, 115 Stat. 272 (2001).

17. Pub. L. No. 107–296, 116 Stat. 2135 (2002).

18. Military Order: Detention, Treatment, and Trial of Certain Non-citizens in the War Against Terrorism, 66 Fed. Reg. 57,833 (Nov 13, 2001).

19. See North Jersey Media Group v. Ashcroft, 308 F.3d 198 (3d Cir. 2002) and Detroit Free Press v. Ashcroft, 303 F.3d 681 (6th Cir. 2002); for two federal courts of appeal decisions pertaining to challenges by media organizations on grounds that closure of proceedings violated the First Amendment.

20. For more extensive discussion and analysis of these and other initiatives, see Whitehead, John W., and Steven H. Aden. 2002. "Forfeiting 'Enduring Freedom' for 'Homeland Security': A Constitutional Analysis of the USA Patriot Act and the Justice Department's Anti-Terrorism Initiatives." *American University Law Review* 51: 1081–1133.

REFERENCES

Abrams v. United States, 250 U.S. 616 (1919).

Barbato, Carole A., Laura L. Davis, and Mark F. Seeman. 2012. *This We Know: A Chronology of the Shootings at Kent State, May 1970*. Kent, OH: Kent University Press.

Barton, Mary S. 2015. "The Global War on Anarchism: The United States and International Anarchist Terrorism, 1898–1904." *Diplomatic History* 39 (2): 303–330.

Bermanzohn, Sally Avery. 2000. "Violence, Nonviolence, and the Civil Rights Movement." *New Political Science* 22 (1): 31–48.

Bowden, Brett. 2007. "The Terror(s) of our Time(s)." *Social Identities* 13 (4): 541–554.

Brandenburg v. Ohio, 395 U.S. 444 (1969).

Cole, David. 2003. "The New McCarthyism: Repeating History in the War on Terrorism." *Harvard Civil Rights-Civil Liberties Law Review* 38 (Winter): 1–30.

Congressional Research Service. 2018. The Possee Comittaus Act and Related Matters: The Use of the Military to Execute Civilian Law. Available at https://fas.org/sgp/crs/natsec/R42659.pdf.

Debs v. United States, 249 U.S. 211 (1919).

Dennis v. United States, 341 U.S. 494 (1951).

Detroit Free Press v. Ashcroft, 303 F.3d 681 (6th Cir. 2002).

Friedman, John S. 2005. "Spying on the Protesters." *The Nation*, September 19, 2005.

Gitlin, Todd. 1993. *The Sixties: Years of Hope Days of Rage*. New York: Bantam Books.

Gitlow v. New York, 268 U.S. 652 (1925).

Greenberg, Ivan. 2011. "The FBI and the Making of the Terrorist Threat." *Radical History Review* 111 (Fall): 35–50.

Hague v. CIO, 307 U.S. 496 (1939).

Haridakis, Paul. 2004. "The War on Terrorism: Military Tribunals and the First Amendment." *Communication Law and Policy* 9 (3): 317–349.

———. 2005. "The Tension Between National/Homeland Security and the First Amendment in the New Century." *Temple Political & Civil Rights Law Review* 14 (2) (Spring): 433–454.

———. 2006. "Citizen Access and Government Secrecy." *St. Louis University Public Law Review* 25 (1): 3–32.

Hirabayashi v. United States, 320 U.S. 81 (1943).

Kassel, Whitney. 2009. "Terrorism and the International Anarchist Movement of the Late Nineteenth and Early Twentieth Centuries." *Studies in Conflict and Terrorism* 32: 237–252.

Korematsu v. United States, 323 U.S. 214 (1944).

Mondale, Walter F., Robert A. Stein, and Caitlinrose Fisher. 2016. "No Longer a Neutral Magistrate: The Foreign Intelligence Surveillance Court in the Wake of the War on Terror." *Minnesota Law Review* 100: 2251–2311.

National Commission on the Causes and Prevention of Violence. 1969. *Final Report* (Washington, D.C.: U.S. Government Printing Office).

North Jersey Media Group v. Ashcroft, 308 F.3d 198 (3rd Cir. 2002).

President's Commission on Campus Unrest. 1970. *Campus Unrest* (Washington, DC: U.S. Government Printing Office).

Pressman, Mathew. 2013. "Black and White and Red All Over?" *Journalism History* 39 (1): 29–39.

Richmond Newspapers v. Virginia, 448 U.S. 555 (1980).
Risen, Clay. 2009. "Spies Among Us." *The American Scholar* 78 (1): 49–60.
Sbardellati, John, and Tony Shaw. 2003. "Booting a Tramp: Charlie Chaplin, the FBI, and the Construction of the Subversive Image in Red Scare America." *Pacific Historical Review* 72, no. 4: 495–530.
Schenck v. United States, 249 U.S. 47 (1919).
Stanley v. Georgia, 394 U.S. 557 (1969).
Stromberg v. California, 283 U.S. 359 (1931).
Tedford, Thomas L., and Dale A. Herbeck. 2017. *Freedom of Speech in the United Sates* (8th ed). State College PA: Strata.
Turner v. United States, 194 U.S. 279 (1904).
Wiecek, William M. 2001. "The Legal Foundations of Domestic Anticommunism: The Background of Dennis v. United States." *The Supreme Court Review* 2001: 375–434.
Vladeck, Stephen I. 2004. "The Detention Power." *Yale Law & Policy Review* 22: 153–195.
Whitehead, John W., and Steven H. Aden. 2002. "Forfeiting 'Enduring Freedom' for 'Homeland Security': A Constitutional Analysis of the USA Patriot Act and the Justice Department's Anti-Terrorism Initiatives." *American University Law Review* 51 (August): 1081–1133.
Whitney v. California, 274 U.S. 357 (1927).
Yates v. United States, 354 U.S. 298 (1957).

Chapter 16

The Counter-terrorism Law System in Algeria

To Serve and Protect or to Control and Oppress?

Francesco Tamburini

INTRODUCTION

Algeria witnessed a decade of brutal conflict between security forces and radical Islamist militias in the 1990s, which plunged the country into a civil war that came to be known as the "national tragedy" (Nassar 2015, 61). This war stopped the democratic process, which had begun in 1989 and gave way to a network of opaque military and political elite that have influenced and drove all major political decisions to the present day. Part of the tools used to curb terrorism was based on counter-terrorism laws that, in the long run, were also used by the Algerian regime to prolong its power. Algeria can be considered a relevant case study that can help to better understand how the critical distinction between political dissidence and terrorism makes the difference in a democratic transition. Moreover, the Algerian legislation is an example of how a regime can exploit the fears of terrorism to keep authoritarianism alive.

In this chapter, I will examine, through an historical analysis, the long and complex evolution of Algerian anti-terrorism laws and strategy. The first section will briefly introduce the Algerian historical context and discuss the cornerstone of the counter-terrorism legislation formed by Law 92-03 and other laws that shaped the regime's action to neutralize violent radical Islamism. The second section deals with the "soft strategy" that the regime used to fight terrorist groups who waged a *ǧiḥād*[1] to create an Islamic state. However, this strategy was also used, in some cases, to limit civil and political rights and curb the establishment of a real democracy. The third section deals with post-civil war legislations and the attitude of the government that exploited fear and psychological scars of the Algerian people to justify anti-terrorism measures. Anti-terrorism legislation was employed to curb protests during the 2011 riots of the Algerian Arab Spring, which failed because of the redistributive patronage based on the rentier economy. The fourth section deals with the 2016 constitutional amendments that the government used to legitimize its power and manipulate history, especially the war of independence and the national tragedy of the civil war of the 1990s. The constitutional reform, in the framework of a pseudo-democratic system, aimed to convince people that not only terrorism but also political dissent could lead to the abyss of a new internecine war. The chapter ends with a section devoted to the freedom of press and expression in Algeria, seen through the several laws enacted by the government to control information from the 1990s to the present days. The analysis of the Algerian legislation will focus on the systematic supervision operated by the government on information flows even though the 2016 constitution guarantees freedom of expression and press cannot be restricted by any form of prior censorship.

THE HISTORICAL CONTEXT AND THE BEGINNING OF ALGERIAN COUNTER-TERRORISM LEGISLATION

Since its independence in 1962, Algeria rested on three interdependent and connected elements: the state, the army, and the single-party National Liberation Front (Front de Libération National or FLN), which ruled the country with a combination of military force and repression. President Chadli Benjedid, connected to the FLN and the military, allowed the end of the one-party rule, as a part of an effort to cope with public discontent and revive a sluggish economy in 1989, which allowed Algeria to hold its first free municipal elections with more than fifty political parties involved. The Islamic Salvation Front (al-*ǧabhah al-Islāmiyah lil-Inqāḏ*, Front Islamique de Salvation or FIS), a radical Islamist party, trounced the former ruling party, winning majorities in 55% of local council. FIS also won 47% of the vote in the first round of legislative elections in December 1991, raising the concern in the FLN majority and the military that Algeria could soon be transformed into a theocratic state. The military, acting independently with the support of part of the FLN, forced president Benjedid, who seemed willing to find an agreement with the Islamists, to resign. The High State Council (HSC), composed of top senior military leaders, assumed the control of almost every aspect of Algerian governance to preserve national unity and public order.[2] HSC intervened by canceling the second round of the elections on January 12, 1992. Two days later, it appointed an interim collegial presidency, the High Council of State (HCS), which outlawed the FIS after terrorist attacks were linked to the party. With this incident, the democratic experiment in Algeria had ended. This was the beginning of the civil war that ensued between the HCS, essentially run by the military, and militants of the disbanded FIS who, together with other radical Islamists, formed various terrorist groups that unleashed a full-scale war against the Algerian state. The conflict soon escalated with terrorists targeting innocent civilians, particularly journalists and intellectuals who were deemed to be not aligned with the Islamists' vision (Quandt 1998).[3] An estimated 200,000 people lost their lives in the civil war while an unidentified number disappeared (Mundy 2015, 185).

One of the first measures taken by the HCS was the proclamation of the *ḥalat al-ṭawary* (حالة الطوارى), the state of emergency, by presidential decree 92/44 on February 9, 1992. This measure gave extra powers to the Ministry of the Interior and local communities to clamp down on Islamist movements. It also strongly limited civil and political rights, placing the power in a permanent legal black hole uncontrolled by law.[4] The state of emergency was completed by the September 30, 1992, legislative decree *Marsūm tašrī'ī* (مرسوم تشريعي), No. 92/03 *Bumukāfaḥat al-taḵrīb wa al-irhāb* (Against Subversion and Terrorism, hereafter referred as 92/03). It is important to note that the noun *al-taḵrīb* (التخريب) has a wide range of meanings such as vandalism and sabotage. However, in the French translation of the law in the Journal Officiel de la République Algérienne Démocratique et Populaire (JORADP),[5] the French word "subversive" is used as if the legislator wanted to underline the political character of the act. The 92/03 was mainly based on the 1992 Egyptian anti-terrorism law 97/1992 (Kent 2011, 84; Tamburini 2018).[6] In fact, the 92/03 contained, like the Egyptian 97/1992, a very broad concept of terrorism. Article 1 of the 92/03 considers terrorism as any offense targeting state security, territorial integrity, or the normal functioning of institutions through any action seeking to spread panic among the public and create a climate of insecurity by causing emotional or physical harm to people, jeopardizing the public's lives or freedom or attacking their property; disrupt traffic or freedom of movement on roads and obstruct public areas with gatherings; damage republican symbols and profane graves; harm the environment, means of communication or means of transport; impede the activities of public authorities and bodies serving the public, or the free exercise of religion and public freedoms; impede the functioning of public institutions; endanger the lives or damage the property of their staff; or obstruct the implementation of laws and regulations (JORADP 1992). For all these acts, penalties range from death penalty to life imprisonment (Article 8).[7]

In light of the Algerian law, the government could prosecute actions not directly linked to terrorism. For example, the government was able to stop the expression of political dissidence such as the hindering of traffic during a manifestation against the regime because disrupting traffic through roadblocks was a *modus operandi* widely used by some terrorist militias during the civil war. The general purpose remained to broaden the target of infringements that could be related to terrorism. In Western democracies, some breaches, such as blocking traffic, are not deemed as terrorist actions, nor are they considered felonies to be inserted in a penal code. As a matter of fact, according to Amnesty International, "these broadly framed provisions have been interpreted by the authorities or by the courts to include the peaceful exercise of civil and political rights."[8] Moreover, the U.N. Committee against Torture also expressed deep concern about the rather vague definition of terrorism that "could extend to acts which may be unrelated to terrorism and lay the persons thereby arrested open to actions which could violate the Convention against Torture."[9]

Trying to face the dangers coming from several terrorist groups, the 92/03 focused on the criminalization of the formation of associations, corps, groups, or organizations whose activities could be linked to the acts envisaged by Article 1.[10] Those who founded or ran such organizations were penalized with a life sentence (Article 3) whereas mere membership was punished with imprisonment from ten to twenty years. The law also created a sort of parallel justice to the formal judicial system that envisaged three special courts responsible for the fight against terrorism. The members of these courts were appointed by a secret presidential decree (Article 11). Thousands of people were sentenced between 1992 and 1995 by special courts, which restricted defense rights (Mickolus and Simmons 1997, 493). Even after the courts were abolished in 1995, terrorism-related trials continued to be far away from international standards, with judges who could not investigate allegations of torture and other ill-treatment. Hundreds of terrorism suspects were held in secret custody for years, outside any form of judicial oversight where courts tried some of them "in absentia." The judiciary called this practice "house arrest" (*assignation à résidence*), which was legal according to Article 5 of the state of emergency.[11]

On the other hand, the 92/03 also introduced non-repressive policies such as measures of amnesty and impunity for members of any armed group who surrendered. Such individuals received pardon from any crimes if it does not involve murder (Article 41). These provisions anticipated the so-called *ar-Raḥma* (clemency in Arabic) law issued on February 25, 1995, by President Liamine Zeroual, whose election was favored by the military after the dissolution of the HCS in January 1994. The *ar-Raḥma* offered repentant terrorists the opportunity to benefit from reduced sentences and reintegrate into society (Derradji 2000; JORADP 1995a).

Even though the military regime applied a security strategy that relied on the slogan "making fear change side" and waged total war against armed groups between 1993 and 1994, terrorism was not stamped out (Martinez 2000, 117).

In the long run, the 92/03 was a failure in preventing and fighting the wave of terrorist attacks, even though it was implemented by ordinances 95/10 and 95/11 (February 25, 1995) that reformed the June 8, 1966, Algerian penal code and the code of criminal procedure. These new ordinances provided a wide latitude for the government and the judiciary to arbitrarily interpret any form of opposition as being dangerously subversive. The 95/10 allowed the military to act as judiciary police officers, incorporated regulations that restricted constitutional freedoms,[12] lowered the age of criminal responsibility to sixteen, extended the infamous *muda al-tawqif* (مدة التوقيف), the term of custody, to twelve days[13] with counsel excluded, and legalized day and night searches (JORADP 1995b). The 95/11 broadened the interpretation of terrorist act by incorporating language that criminalized undermining of Algerian state's symbols, endangering environment, animals, or public health with poisonous substances, and hindering the exercise of worship. The law also reflected new realities and the development of terrorism at transnational levels. More specifically, the 95/11 redefined a terrorist as any Algerian citizen who participates or enrolls abroad in a "seditious" association, even if its activities were not directed against Algeria. Furthermore, on January 4, 1997, the Décret éxecutif 97/04 *Fixant les conditions d'exercice de l'action de légitime défense dans un cadre organisé* created the Legitimate Defense Groups, self-defense militias composed by armed civilians, whose task was to fight terrorism and protect villages from jihadist incursions (JORADP 1997). The 97/04 recognized the right to legitimate self-defense but blurred the distinction between national defense and domestic public order. The law, which essentially ended the purported state monopoly of violence, resulted in indiscriminate large-scale massacres in villages and smaller guerrilla-style bomb attacks in urban spaces. Adding to the horror, the Algerian state-sponsored security forces, namely the secret services of the *Département du Renseignement et de la Sécurité* (DRS), who infiltrated the terrorist groups believed to have been involved in rampant killings and assassinations (Gèze and Mellah 2008; Keenan 2009). Between 1994 and 1995, a combined 20,000 people disappeared from both security forces and Islamist militias (Moréas 2016). In those years, many systematic human rights abuses took place: tortures, extrajudicial executions, arbitrary arrests and detentions, and killings while in custody.[14] This led to an elusive and contradictory conflict, described by the French historian Benjamin Stora as "*guerre gigogne*" or "nested war" (Stora 2001, 234), an internal war where it was difficult to see the real enemy. In this chaotic atmosphere, the issue of the deep involvement of the government, the army, and intelligence services in the war still represents something that is very difficult to talk about openly in the Algerian society. Furthermore, due to the secrecy surrounding the counter-terrorism actions, which fall inside the jurisdiction of the regular army and the DRS, it is very hard to obtain exhaustive evidence. In addition, the lack of information was the result of several factors, such as the terror that made many citizens fearful of speaking out and restrictive government policies that limited access to international observers or journalists. The widespread violence decreased only after the election of President Bouteflika in 1999, although it did not disappear completely.

The state of emergency and the anti-terrorism law 92/03 showed, as Finn (1991, 30) rightly pointed out, that a crisis government seldom remains a limited government. A crisis government, like the HSC and those which followed, tends to be a victim of the threat of terrorism and violence that brings a normal constitutional government into conflict with the basic tenets of constitutionalism. The search for survival always requires the exercise of emergency powers that naturally shrinks personal rights and liberties recognized under normal conditions. In Algeria, the situation was worse because when a state emergency was proclaimed in addition to the 92-03, the country had just suffered a military coup, had not developed a real democracy, and constitutional checks and balances were almost non-existent (Warenfels 2007). In this sense, it is sensible to understand how the effects of counter-terrorism measures were magnified by the peculiar Algerian political situation discussed thus far.

THE SOFT STRATEGY FOR THE RESILIENCE OF POWER

The Algerian government relied on both merciless military operations and the action of the DRS to fight terrorism. As such, one could argue that Algiers's counter-terrorism approach was excessively repressive and military centric. Nevertheless, all this was also intertwined with a "soft strategy," marked by a policy of national reconciliation to curb terrorism and restore normalcy (Le Sueur 2010, 90–95). In April 1999, Bouteflika put forth the Civil Concord Law, and, in September 2005, the Charter for Peace and National Reconciliation. These new laws were based on a national reconciliation strategy, which, aside from a similar strategy in South Africa, represented a unique case in the African continent (Boumghar 2015). The Civil Concord Law granted wide-ranging impunity to members of armed groups, if they had not caused death, used explosives or committed rape. On the contrary, the Charter also included amnesty for military and state agents, regardless of the severity of the crimes they may have committed, barring any future judicial investigations into actions committed by security forces. In other words, the Charter absolved security forces from responsibility in committing human rights abuses by stating that they had acted in the supreme interest of the country (Tlemcani 2007). This deprived the victims and their families of any remedy or justice for their loss. In addition, Article 26 of the Charter banned anyone from political life who manipulated Islam for political purposes by legally excluding former FIS members from practicing any form of political activities. This measure of course benefited the regime and pro-government parties.

Thousands of Islamists surrendered, accepting the Concord Law and the Charter for Peace and National Reconciliation. Nevertheless, members of hardline groups, such as the *Groupe Islamique Armé* (GIA) and the *Groupe Salafiste pour la Prédication et le Combat* (GSPC), preferred to keep fighting. Therefore, violence, although markedly confined compared to previous years, continued.

The Civil Concord Law and the Charter were complemented by other laws as part of the same strategy. For example, the law 01/08 of June 2001 modified the time of pre-arraignment detention by the police, reducing it to forty-eight hours (JORADP 2001). The Algerian government tried to divert the attention of the people from the iron fist used to crush terrorism, and, at the same time, to gain credibility in the international community, aligning the legislation to Western standards of democracy and rule of law (Welchman 2005).

The soft legislative approach was also intertwined with an ideological counter-terrorism campaign based on a completely new attitude to religion: the state, through the Ministry of Religious Affairs, promoted the peaceful and tolerant character of Islam; the Ministry of Interior carefully monitored sermons in the mosques, trying to detect extremism at the early stage; and the government promoted nonviolent or nonpolitical forms of Salafism, such as the so-called Scientific Salafism, which seeks to Islamize society rather than create an Islamic state. Sponsoring Scientific Salafism was a strategic move because Scientific Salafists, although they recognize *ǧiḥād* as an important part of Islam, did not interpret it in a physical way but rather through a spiritual approach (Moussaoui 2015). At the same time, substantial support was given to religious Sufi orders or the *zawāyā* (Islamic monasteries or schools), which traditionally did not have any interest in political issues, rather concentrating on philosophical or theological problems. Nonetheless, the armed response to terrorist activities never faded out and the Army (and secret services) kept using all their means to curb religious extremism as well as all activities that could jeopardize the regime.

The duality of the soft and hard approaches can also be seen in the Algerian political and military power structure: the eradicators (*les éradicateurs*), the hard-liners who favored a total war and suppression of the Islamist groups; and the conciliators (*les conciliateurs*), who, on the other hand, thought that a dialogue with the political Islam was necessary. This polarization was mirrored in the Algerian society and deepened the spiral of violence, resulting in a protracted peace process.

NEW LAWS AND THE FAILURE OF THE ALGERIAN ARAB SPRING

Presenting terrorism as a continuous and systemic menace to the political and social system, the regime convinced Algerian citizens that anti-terrorism measures were a necessary evil and that the state had been the savior of the country from chaos. People had accepted the enforcement of anti-terrorist practices and the attendant loss of freedom because they did not want a return to the civil war (Addi 2011). Civil war of the 1990s is also one of the main causes for the failure of any Algerian democratization, which has prevented the country from consolidating its democratic and pluralistic transition. In this way, the "past is present" in Algeria. The war left social and psychological wounds that were particularly deep and difficult to heal. The regime has always exploited these wounds and used fear and anti-terrorism legislation as tools to delay or stop a transition to democracy. As a result, counter-terrorism law measures have hardly decreased. On the contrary, new restrictive counter-terrorism laws have been put in place. For example, Bouteflika introduced the law 05/01 on the "Prevention and Fight against Money Laundering and Financing of Terrorism" in February 2005 (JORADP 2005). This law finally filled the legal vacuum that existed in Algeria as far as the laundering of capital and financing terrorism was concerned. It criminalized any act by which any person, directly or indirectly, provided or raised funds with the intention of committing offenses classified as subversive or terrorist acts.

The Bouteflika presidencies were marked by this last anti-terrorism law, which was created to face the new dangers coming from the formation in 2006 of the Organization of Al Qaeda in the Country of the Islamic Maghreb (*Tanẓīm al-Qā'idah fī Bilād al-Maghrib al-Islāmī*) (Keenan 2012; Tawil 2010; Tazaghart 2012), a transnational terrorist group with bases outside the Algerian borders. Furthermore, Bouteflika issued amendments to the 1996 constitution that could be seen as part of the fight against terrorism. In November 2008, law 8/19 amended Article 76 of the constitution stating that "the State shall guarantee the respect for the symbols of the Revolution, the memory of the *šuhadā'* (the martyrs) and the dignity of their dependents and that of the *muǧāhidīn*" (the Arabic term for individuals engaged in *ǧiḥād*). The modification of this article was required by the will to reiterate the continuity between the FLN, the army, and the 1954 revolution that gained independence from France. This was done to prevent radical Islamism from usurping the inheritance of the traditions and values of the war of independence, as the FIS did in the 1990s. In other words, the real *muǧāhidīn* were only those veterans who fought from 1954 to 1962, the ones who founded the Algerian nation (Brandt 2014), and not the radical Islamists of the civil war. The revision was not only an attempt to stop a historical revisionism by radicalism, but it was also the reaffirmation of political supremacy and dominance of the elite. Being part of the "real *muǧāhidīn*" meant being part of the inner circle of power as well as belonging to the clan of the *aāylāt ṯawrīyya* (عائلة ثورية), the revolutionary family, and enjoying the privileges of the political caste (Tamburini 2016, 95).

During the so-called Arab Spring that shook the Middle East and North Africa (MENA) region, more than 3,000 demonstrations took place in Algeria (Belkaid 2012; Bennadji 2011). In response to these demonstrations, the regime introduced subsidies on basic foodstuff and commodities, increased employment in the public sector, and promised political reforms (Zoubir and Aghrout 2012). This explains, in part, why Algerians did not follow the example of the Tunisians, Libyans, Egyptians, or Syrians and overthrow the government despite the latter being citizens of one of the most repressive regimes in the MENA region. The regime succeeded in buying the social discontent through the oil and gas revenues in the framework of the "rentier state." As a rentier state, Algerian citizens trust the state institutions to progressively provide public goods and they tend to be more allegiant and less antagonistic to the regime (Beblawi 1987; Cavatorta 2009, 50). However, this did not stop the regime crackdown on agitators and journalists accused of posing a threat to national security. Media were often used as a platform for the regime, curtailed by informal and formal pressure. Independent journalism has been shrunk by the legal normative obligations of the 92-03, 95/10, and 95/11, and, in some cases, forced to play a national role supporting the state.

It is important to note that during the 2010–2011 riots, anti-terrorism laws were employed to treat public gatherings as "unarmed mobs." The laws were used to clamp down *taḵrīb* (subversion), which signifies vandalism and sabotage, even if the people's demands such as calls for better living conditions, higher salaries, and lower taxes were non-subversive. Nevertheless, charges of terrorism were not issued by authorities in response to these demonstrations. The laws 92/03, 95/10, and 95/11 were just a "legal key" to control or repress dissidence during the upheavals and in months that followed. However, it is crucial to underline that authorities adopted a selective strategy. Political opposition leaders were not targeted by these measures. Instead, using a preemptive strategy, security forces arrested young activists long before scheduled protests, physically preventing them from gathering in the streets. On February 24, 2011, the government decided to rescind the state of emergency decreed in February 1992. However, authorities continued to restrict such basic rights as freedom of assembly on the basis of national security even though these rights are enshrined in Algeria's constitution. This strategy did not work to restore calm in the country. Algeria continued to experience low-level popular unrest, demonstrations, and general strikes. As usual, the government reacted with a combination of short-term subsidies in addition to suppressing and intimidating activists.

THE AMENDMENT TO THE CONSTITUTION AS AN ANTI-TERRORISM TOOL

The preamble of the Algerian constitution was revised in March 2016 by the *Loi portant révision constitutionnelle* 16/01. The law 16/01 inserted in the first paragraph of the constitution referred to the civil war of the 1990s as "a real national tragedy (*māsat waṭanīyya* مأساة وطنية) that endangered the survival of the Fatherland" (JORADP 2016). It emphasized the importance of the "unshakable attachment to national unity," and the implementation by the Algerian people of a "policy of peace and national reconciliation policy, which has borne fruits and which needs to be preserved" (JORADP 2016). The preamble is a sort of manifesto of political propaganda presented as a declaration of war against terrorism and aiming to celebrate the political strategy of the government. Moreover, the preamble included the following reference to the concept of *fitna* (فتنة): "The Algerian people shall be determined to keep Algeria immune from *fitna* (violence) and all forms of extremism by establishing their spiritual and values of civilization, which call for dialogue, reconciliation and fraternity within the framework of respect for the constitution and the laws of the Republic."

Fitna is a polysemic Arabic word that signifies sedition, trial, probation, affliction, distress or hardship, intrigue, riot, discord, dissension, and civil war. In this context, civil war connotes schism and the jeopardizing of believers' purity of faith (Djait 1991).[15] In the Holy Quran, the *Sūra* II *al-Baqara* 191 states that "*fitna* is worse than killing." According to the *ḥadīth*,[16] "Sixty years of injustice are better than *fitna*" (Martinez-Gross and Du Mesnil 2011, 67). Classical Islam teaches that the duty of a Muslim is to abstain from participating or supporting civil turmoil to preserve the unity of Ummah because *fitna* is associated with *ḥarāj* (حراج), chaos, and *fasād* (فساد) or corruption. For this reason, it was condemned in the strongest terms by many authors who wrote a large quantity of "anti-*fitna* literature" (El-Fadl 2001, 197).

Although the use of *fitna* in the preamble of the constitution has been a clear reference to the national tragedy of the civil war that took place in the 1990s, it also has served as a sort of warning for all would-be street rioters and protesters asking for changes in the country. The regime tried to convince

Algerians that such changes could jeopardize the unsteady balance of the state, giving way to a dangerous jump in the dark, possibly leading to an uncontrollable *fitna*. Even sudden democratic openings that were not mediated by the government could be a danger to the order. The scare of a possible *fitna* spread even more after the Arab Spring. The image of the political black hole of Libya represented an admonishment of what could happen if central power is destabilized or challenged, not necessarily by terrorism but by untrustworthy forces or popular unrest. In his presidential rhetoric, Bouteflika focused on the stability achieved before the uprisings, trying to frame that time period as positive and significant. Using the fears of past anguishes, the Algerian government succeeded in keeping the population on a constant alert, effectively delaying once again any democratic transition (Gilbert and Moshemi 2011).

The new preamble also mentioned the Algerian army, the National Popular Army, that gave an "essential contribution to the protection of citizens, institutions, and properties against the scourge of terrorism" (JORADP 2016). These celebratory lines aimed at constitutionalizing the Algerian army and endorsing its anti-terrorist actions. The role of the army is protected by the constitution and the preamble provides a Manichaeistic representation of the reality, where the good (the army and the government) faces and prevails over the bad (terrorism). Nevertheless, the Algerian situation is complex because the Army has been used as an instrument of repression of dissidence and was involved in many episodes of violence and human right abuses against civilians during the civil war in the 1990s. Here, it is important to note that the Algerian army enjoyed substantial leverage over the government by becoming an indisputable guarantor of the continuity of the regime and the protector of order and stability (Shahin 1997). The 2016 amendment enhanced this leading role, increasing not only its historical mission for the Algerian nation but also its impunity in front of possible breaches of the rule of law.

FREEDOM OF EXPRESSION AND MEDIA: COLLATERAL VICTIMS OF ANTI-TERRORISM

Between 1993 and 1996, fifty-eight editors and reporters were assassinated by religious extremists belonging to various terrorist organizations (Campagna 1999). Tahar Djaout, murdered by a commando of the Armed Islamic Group in June 1993, wrote: "Silence is death. And you, if you speak, you die. If you remain silent, you die. So, speak out and die" (Sukys 2007, 119). Algeria was one of the most dangerous countries in the world for journalists, and those who decided to stay in the country to continue their job worked under siege-like conditions. It is difficult for journalists to remain independent where the regime controls press coverage and enforces blanket censorship.

The fight against terrorism has always affected the relationship between the government and the media (Ferchiche 2011; Gataifi 1999). National security soon became the benchmark that influenced the policy on this issue. In its war against radical Islamists, the government relied on the media to influence public opinion. The Algerian state imposed a stern control and censorship over information, arresting and prosecuting journalists who tried to attempt independent reporting. It was almost impossible to contradict official news. Accordingly, in the 1990s, the Algerian media was used as a patriotic platform by the government. Its political communication campaign aimed to legitimize its anti-terrorist strategy and discredit the Islamist guerrilla.

The situation did not improve after the civil war. Algerian government issued the January 2012 law 12/05, *yataʿllaq bālāʿalām* (يتعلق بالاعلام), or "On Information," which introduced new guidance on the publication of ideas by any written, sound, television or electronic support. The law was hailed by its proponents as an important reform that would enhance media freedom by opening the key media sectors to private ownership and ending state monopoly over broadcast media. However, it was used to place substantial limits on the ability to publish and disseminate information, which is no longer described as a right but an "activity," *našāṭ* (نشاط). The activity of information can be practiced freely with the condition that it adheres to principles related to "national identity and cultural values of society," "Islamic religion," "security and national defence," "missions and obligations of national public service," "judiciary secrets," and "economic interests of the country" (Article 2). Moreover, professional journalists must observe eleven principles contained in Article 92, such as "respecting the state's attributes and symbols," "refraining from undermining national history" and "apology of colonialism," and "refraining from disseminating or publishing immoral images or statements that hurt citizens' sensitivity." All these principles and obligations are very vague and imprecise and can lead to state censorship or even self-censorship by journalists and media practitioners, especially when news reports involve terrorism activities or opposition campaigns. Writing about the past civil war, without breaching the principles imposed by the 12/05, could also be difficult. Questioning the official national history could lead to the infringement of "national identity" or "security and national defence" principles.

The law also imposes very expensive fines of up to 500,000 dinars for press-related offenses, and journalists who fail to pay the fines can be imprisoned (JORADP 2012). The 12/05 and its restrictions are extremely ambiguous and leave the door open to unpredictable future bans. The restriction posed by the law 12/05 "On Information" and the Article 144 of the Penal Code impose prison sentences against anyone who infringes upon the honor and dignity of a magistrate, civil servant, public officer, or law enforcement officer. Predictably, this has become a powerful deterrent against dissent and has delegitimized the critical press. This happened even though the 2016 constitution, specifically Article 50, abolished prison sentences for journalists and clearly acknowledged freedom of expression.[17] The control over information flow was enhanced with the *Loi rélative à l'activité audiovisuelle* 14/04 that was adopted on February 24, 2014. According to this law, the broadcasting private media were strictly limited to programs that disseminated official statements aiming to maintain public order. Moreover, the 14/04 created the *Autorité de Régulation de l'Audiovisuel* (ARAV), or *Ṣulṭat Ḍabṭ as-Sam'ī al-Baṣarī,* which supervises all broadcasting platforms (satellite, cable, and terrestrial). The main problem with the ARAV is that it lacks independence and freedom from governmental oversight since it consists of nine members appointed by presidential decree.[18]

The security services created a network of government data information, which disseminated news to newspapers to defend the strategy of the political and military authorities. Typically, this involved a two-sided approach (Josua and Edel 2015). Rather than suppress and punish, the Algerian authorities excluded and marginalized nonconformity, on the one hand, and advanced a strategy of cooptation, on the other, by promoting journalism loyal to the regime. The opening of the broadcasting sector to private entities was just a façade of pluralism because private media were allowed to operate to the extent that they disseminated positive reporting and adhered to "national obligations." However, the political pressure could not entirely censor and stonewall dissidence in a globalized and interconnected world. As such, the government subtly relaxed its control over certain areas of freedom of expression such as refraining from interrupting internet access and allowing public debates (Driss 2012). This creates a jarring dichotomy: freedom of expression without freedom of the press.

CONCLUSION

In security terms, Algeria still remains in a difficult situation. Due to the fall of the Qadhafi regime, a huge quantity of arms belonging to the former Libyan army has been dispersed across the Sahel area, which has created deep instability along Algeria's borders (Cook and Sanderson 2016). As a result, Algeria is still heavily committed in its fight against national and transnational terrorism,[19] increasing its defense budget to over 10 billion Euros annually (one of the largest in Africa). This is also a rationale for the regime to keep its guard against subversive activities and maintain all counter-terrorism measures.

It is unpredictable for how long the Algerian regime, the so-called "Le Pouvoir" (the power) will resist popular pressure that is characterized by frequent manifestations of anger against injustices, humiliations, and lack of regard to the people (Ben Said and Rani 2015). In the Algerian dialect, there is a word to indicate the feeling of frustration against the regime: *Ḥogra*. Without any doubt, part of the frustration is the secrecy still wrapped around the actions by Algerian counter-terrorism structures, which often reports only to the Ministry of Defense, rather than the Ministry of Justice. The result is that no civilian institution or authority monitors the conduct of the secret service or the army.

Despite this lack of oversight, the regime's longevity is based on the ability to adapt itself to changing circumstances as well as its economic capacity to buy time and avoid implementing any promised changes. This general resilience is a key part of authoritarianism in the Arab world both before and after the uprisings. This strategy of implementing only low-level changes is referred to as "authoritarian upgrading" or "upgrading 2.0" in which authoritarian regimes can adapt to new circumstances without ceding to democratic reforms (Heydemann 2007).

Algerian society is stalled in an ever-lasting nightmare of fear and uncertainty that are skillfully fostered by the elite. Despite the strong will to overthrow the *niẓām* (نظام) or the system by younger generations, the past of the "black decade" of the 1990s war (Martinez 2000, 2) and the death of countless civilians is constantly haunting Algerian civil society. This is not to say that protests are non-existent. The so-called *Ḥirak* movement against Bouteflika's fifth presidential term in February–April 2019 is evidence of rising tensions between the regime and the Algerian people (Caruso 2019). The *Ḥirak* movement set up demonstrations that took place since 16 February 2019 in major Algerian towns protesting not only Bouteflika's re-election but also the whole *niẓām*. Protests led Bouteflika not to seek re-election in March 2019, but the following presidential electoral campaign in November was marked by a crackdown on peaceful anti-election protests. At least 300 people were arrested, and while most of them were later released, some were charged with harming national security and inciting an unarmed gathering, and remained in pretrial detention pursuant to provisions of the 92/03 (Zoubir 2020). The 1992 *Marsūm tašrī'ī* is once again the keystone to preserving power and stability.

The Algerian model of counter-terrorism was technically a success, but the price in terms of civil and political liberties has been high. Paradoxically, the legacy of the means used to defeat terrorism is haunting contemporary Algeria as demonstrated by the repressions on the waves of demonstrations that led to the resignation of Bouteflika in March 2019. The Algerian government can hold off popular unrest using the juridical tools of the penal code. Besides, the weak and sometimes powerless judiciary is unable to assert its independence against the executive to secure the protection of human rights (Udogu 2020). Therefore, this system tips the balance in favor of security issues compared to freedoms.

In the end, the government controls dissidence without the use of violence or hard repression. There is no need, for most of the population, despite yearning for a profound change, is scared of triggering a new civil war. When Algerians are asked about the wave of political uprisings that crossed the Arab world from 2010, the common answer is that "Algerians already had their Spring." The collective memory of the Civil War formed a psychological barrier, preventing major dissidence and revolts. This psychological attitude led Algerians to accept stern counter-terrorist legislative measures, unborn democratic reforms, and the resilience of the elite to relinquish power.

In 1955, Albert Camus wrote:

> In Algeria, as elsewhere, terrorism occurs where there is lack of hope. In fact, it always grows out of a sense of isolation where there is no last resort or future possibility, as if the windowless walls are too thick and that in order to breathe or to move about, the walls have to be blown up. (Camus 1955, para. 2, translation by author)

Even though endemic terrorism cannot be considered a national plague in current-day Algeria, Camus's words still ring. The atmosphere of suppressed freedom, censorship, and economic difficulties could at any moment give rise to new terrorism or boost violent forms of Islamic radicalism. The Algerian government cannot effectively rely on the fears of the past to justify their counter-terrorism measures to control society. These same measures, which in the past have been the invisible shield of the regime, could be the ruin of the *niẓām*.

NOTES

1. The term *ǧiḥād* comes from the root ǧ-ḥ-D and literally means "effort," and to exert oneself for the sake of God. This exertion can be realized through an inward spiritual struggle to attain perfect faith but also through a political or military struggle to further the Islamic cause.

2. The HCS was a constitutional institution introduced by the 1976 and 1989 constitutions. The purpose was the coordination of national defense with the President of the republic.

3. In opposition to Islamic, the term Islamist refers to those whose main aim is the political creation or restoration of an Islamic order.

4. The twelve-month-long presidential decree (renewed indefinitely in 1993) that enacted the State of emergency was the toughest in terms of the power given to the government to suppress dissent. See JORADP (1992, 222–223).

5. Arabic is the only official language in the Algerian Republic. Although there is an official French version of the JORADP, it is the Arabic texts that are only deemed to be authentic and have legal force.

6. The law modified Article 86 of the penal code, which provided a definition of terrorism in such vague terms that jeopardized political and civil freedoms as well as human rights in the country. Offenses include all use of force, violence, threatening, or frightening to which a felon resorts in execution of an individual or collective criminal scheme, with the aim of disturbing public order, exposing the safety and security of society, or inseminating fear among people. Additionally, per the article, it is a terrorism offense to expose people's life, freedom or security to danger; damage the environment, cause detriments to communications transport, property, funds, buildings, public or private properties; prevent or obstruct the work of public authorities, worship houses, or education institutions; or interrupt the application of the constitution, laws or statutes.

7. Crimes defined as terrorist acts are punishable "by death where ordinary law provides life imprisonment; life imprisonment where ordinary law provides imprisonment from 10 to 20 years; imprisonment from 10 to 20 years where ordinary law provides imprisonment from 5 to 10 years."

8. Amnesty International (2008, 16).

9. See United Nations (2008, 2).

10. It is important to note that the HSC decided not to mention any reference to religious factors in the 92/03, despite the main reason for the 1991 coup was the dangerous victory of a political party (the FIS) that wanted to build up an Islamic state and generated a form of terrorism that was deeply linked to radical Islam and violent forms of Salafi jihadism.

11. Article 5 of Presidential Decree No. 92-44 reads: "The minister of interior and local government may decide to place in a security facility, in a specified place, any adult individual whose activity is determined to be dangerous for the public order, public security, or the proper operation of public services" (JORADP 1992).

12. The 1989 Algerian constitution guaranteed fundamental individual and collective liberties and the rights of individuals (Article 31 and Article 32). Moreover, it stipulates the state shall guarantee the inviolability of the human person. Article 34 prohibited any form of physical or moral violence or infringement on the dignity of individuals.

13. The twelve-day limit was an excessive period of detention being in violation not only of international law but also of Article 45 of the 1989 Algerian constitution.

14. See Human Right Watch (1998).

15. In the history of Islām, *fitna* is related to the loss of unity and the fragmentation of the Muslim world, being associated with four civil wars in the Islamic Caliphate from the seventh to ninth centuries.

16. *Ḥadīth* (pl. *'Aḥādīth*) is the Arabic word for speech, report, account, or narrative. A collection of reports of the words, actions, and the silences approved of the Prophet Muhammad, it represents a source of Islamic law.

17. Article 50 consecrates the freedom of the press, but it also adds that freedom should be exercised under the law and with the respect of the religious, moral, and cultural values of the nation. Moreover, Article 51 states that the right to access information excludes private life, person's rights, legitimate interests of enterprises, and the requirements of national security.

18. The same problem affects the Regulatory Authority of Print Media (*Autorité de Régulation de la Presse*), created by the law 12/05 (articles 40–57). All its fourteen members are appointed by presidential decree (three of them directly by the President of the republic).

19. Algeria's commitment to the fight against international terrorism has a long tradition and it is witnessed by the ratification of several international conventions. These include the Arab convention for the suppression of terrorism in 1998; the Organization of African Unity (OAU) Convention on the Prevention and Combating of Terrorism in 1999; the OAU Protocol to the OAU Convention on the Prevention and Combating of Terrorism in 2007; the International Convention for the Suppression of Acts of Nuclear Terrorism in 2011; and the Arab Convention on Combating Money-laundering and the Financing of Terrorism 2014. The ratification of these conventions aimed to give Algeria regional leadership on counter-terrorism issues.

REFERENCES

Addi, Lahouari 2011. "Le régime algérien après les révoltes arabes" *Mouvements* 66 (2): 89–97.

Amnesty International. 2008. "Algeria: Briefing to the Committee Against Torture." 2008. Accessed November 13, 2020. https://www.amnesty.org/en/documents/document/?indexNumber=MDE28%2f001%2f2008&language=en.

Beblawi, Hazem. 1987. "The Rentier State in the Arab World" *Arab Studies Quarterly* 9 (4): 383–398.

Belkaid, Akran. 2012. "L'Algérie, une exception au marge du Printemps arabe?" *Les Cahiers d'Orient* 3 (107): 141–150.

Bennadji, Chérif. 2011. "Algérie 2010: L'année des mille et une émeutes." *L'Année du Maghreb* 7: 263–269.

Boumghar, Mouloud. 2015. "Concorde civile et réconciliation nationale sous le sceau de l'impunité. Le traitement par le droit algérien des violations graves des droits de l'homme commises durant la guerre civile des années 1990." *Revue Internationale de Droit Comparé* 67 (2): 349–407.

Brand, Laurie. 2014. *Official Stories. Politics and National Narratives in Egypt and Algeria.* Stanford: Stanford University Press.

Campagna, Joel. 1999. "Siege Mentality: Press Freedom and the Algerian Conflict." Committee to Protect Journalists. Accessed April 7, 2020. https://www.refworld.org/docid/47c567c232.html.

Camus, Albert. 1955. "Terrorisme et repression." *L'Express*. Accessed December 12, 2020. https://tipaza.typepad.fr/mon_weblog/2010/01/terrorisme-et-r%C3%A9pression-albert-camus.html.

Caruso, Francesca. 2019. "Bouteflika's Uncertain Fifth Term." IAI Istituto Affari Internazionali. Accessed September 2, 2020. https://www.iai.it/en/pubblicazioni/bouteflikas-uncertain-fifth-term.

Cavatorta, Francesco. 2009. *The International Dimension of the Failed Algerian Transition*. Manchester: Manchester University Press.

Cook, Jennifer and Thomas Sanderson. 2016. *Militancy and the Arc of Instability. Violent Extremism in the Sahel*. Lanham: CSIS.

Derradji, Abder-Rahmane. 2000. *A Concise History of Political Violence in Algeria, 1954-2000: Brothers in Faith, Enemies in Arms*. New York: Edwin Mellen Press.

Djait, Hichem. 1991. *La grande discorde*. Paris: Gallimard.

Dris, Cherif. 2012. "La nouvelle loi organique sur l'information de 2012 en Algérie: Vers un ordre médiatique néo-autoritaire." *L'Année du Maghreb* 7: 303–320.

El-Fadl, Khaled Abou. 2001. *Rebellion and Violence in Islamic Law*. New York: Cambridge University Press.

Ferchiche, Nessrine. 2011. *La liberté de la presse écrite dans l'ordre juridique algérien*. Paris: LGDJ.

Finn, John. 1991. *Constitutions in Crisis: Political Violence and the Rule of Law*. New York: Oxford University Press.

Gataifi, Hafid. 1999. "Power, Censorship and the Press: The Case of Post-colonial Algeria" *Research in African Literatures* 30 (3): 51–61.

Gèze, François, and Salima Mellah. 2008. "Algérie: L'impossible justice pour les victimes des années de sang." *Mouvements* 53 (1): 150–157.

Gilbert, Leah and Payam Moshemi. 2011. "Beyond authoritarianism. The Conceptualization of Hybrid Regimes." *Studies in Comparative International Development* 46 (3): 270–297.

Heydemann, Steven. 2007. *Upgrading Authoritarianism in the Arab World*. Washington, DC: Saban Center for Middle East Policy at the Brookings Institution.

Human Rights Watch. 1998. "Algeria's Human Rights Crisis." Human Rights Watch. Accessed August 3, 2020. https://www.hrw.org/report/1998/08/01/algerias-human-rights-crisis.

JORADP. 1992. "Décret Législatif n. 92-03 du 30 Septembre 1992 Relatif à la Lutte Contre la Subversion et le Terrorisme." *Journal Officiel de la République Algérienne Démocratique et Populaire* 70: 1490–1493.

———. 1995a "Ordonnance n. 95-12 du 25 Février 1995 portant mesures de clémence." *Journal Officiel de la République Algérienne Démocratique et Populaire* 11: 9–10.

———. 1995b. "Ordonnance n. 95-10 du 25 Février 1995 modifiant et complétant l'ordonnance n. 66-155 du 8 Juin 1966 portant code de procédure pénale." *Journal Officiel de la République Algérienne Démocratique et Populaire* 11: 3–5.

———. 1997. "Décret exécutif n. 97-04 du 4 janvier 1997 fixant les conditions d'exercice de l'action de légitime défense dans un cadre organisé." *Journal Officiel de la République Algérienne Démocratique et Populaire* 1: 7–8.

———. 2001. "Loi n. 01-08 du 26 juin 2001 modifiant et complétant l'ordonnance n. 66-155 du 8 juin 1966 portant code de procédure pénale." *Journal Officiel de la République Algérienne Démocratique et Populaire* 34: 13–14.

———. 2005. "Loi n. 05-01 du 6 février 2005 relative à la lutte contre le blanchiment d'argent et le financement du terrorisme." *Journal Officiel de la République Algérienne Démocratique et Populaire* 11: 3–5.

———. 2012. "Loi organique n. 12-05 du 12 janvier 2012 relative à l'information." *Journal Officiel de la République Algérienne Démocratique et Populaire* 2: 6–7.

———. 2016 "Loi n. 16-01 relatif au projet de loi portant révision de la Constitution." *Journal Officiel de la République Algérienne Démocratique et Populaire* 14: 3–36.

Josua, Maria and Mirjan Edel. 2015. "To Repress or Not to Repress. Regime Survival Strategies in the Arab Spring." *Terrorism and Political Violence* 27 (2): 289–309.

Keenan, Jeremy. 2012. "Politique étrangère et guerre mondiale contre le terrorisme dans la reproduction du pouvoir algérien." *Revue du Tiers Monde* 210: 31–50.

———. 2009. *The Dark Sahara: America's War on Terror in Africa*. London: Pluto.

Le Sueur, James. 2010. *Algeria since 1989: Between Terror and Democracy*. London and New York: Fernwood Publishing.

Martinez, Luis. 2000. *The Algerian Civil War. 1990-1998*. New York: Columbia University Press.

Martinez-Gros, Gabriel and Emmanuelle Tixier Du Mesnil. 2010. "La fitna: le désordre politique dans l'Islam medieval." *Médiévales* 60: 5–6.

Mickolus, Edward, and Susan Simmons. 1997. *Terrorism 1992–1995. A Chronology of Events and a Selectively Annotated Bibliography*. Westport: Greenwood Press.

Moréas, George. 2016. *Dans les coulisses de la lutte antiterroriste*. Paris: Editions First.

Moussaoui, Abderrahmane. 2015. "La Salafiya au Maghreb: courants, dynamiques et enjeux." *Confluences Internationales* 3: 3–46.

Mundy, Jacob. 2015. *Imaginative Geographies of Algerian Violence. Conflict Science, Conflict Management, Antipolitics*. Stanford: Stanford University Press.

Nassar, Habib. 2015. "Transitional Justice in the Wake of the Arab Uprising." In *Transitional Justice and the Arab Spring*, edited by Kirsten Fisher and Robert Stewart, 54–75. London: Routledge.

Quandt, William. 1998. *Between Ballots and Bullets: Algeria's Transition from Authoritarianism*. Washington: Brooking Institution Press.

Roach, Kent. 2011. *The 9/11 Effect: Comparative Counter Terrorism*. Cambridge: Cambridge University Press.

Rubdy, Rani, and Selim Ben Said, eds. 2015. *Conflict, Exclusion and Dissent in the Linguistic Landscape*. Language and Globalization. Palgrave Macmillan UK. https://doi.org/10.1057/9781137426284.

Shahin, Emad Eldin.1997. *Political Ascent: Contemporary Islamic Movements in North Africa*. Boulder: Westview Press.

Stora, Benjamin. 2001. *Algeria 1830–2000. A Short History*. Ithaca: Cornell University Press.

Sukys, Julija. 2007. *Silence is Death. The Life and Work of Tahar Djaout*. Lincoln: University of Nebraska.

Tamburini, Francesco. 2016. *Il Maghreb dalle indipendenze alle rivolte arabe: storia e istituzioni*. Pisa: Pisa University Press.

———. 2018. "Anti-Terrorism Law in the Maghreb Countries: The Mirror of a Democratic Transition that Never was." *Journal of Asian and African Studies* 53 (8): 1235–1250.

Tawil, Camille. 2010. *The Al-Qaeda Organization in the Islamic Maghreb: Expansion in the Sahel and Challenges from Within Jihadist Circles*. Washington, DC: Jamestown Foundation.

Tazaghart, Atmane. 2012. *AQMI, enquête sur les héritiers de Ben Laden au Maghreb et en Europe*. Paris: Picollec.

Tlemcani Rachid. 2007. *Algeria Under Bouteflika: Civil Strife and National Reconciliation*. Washington, DC: Carnegie Endowment for International Peace.

Udogu, Ike. 2020. *Human Rights in Islamic North Africa. Between Constitutional Laws and Penal Codes*. Jefferson: McFarland & Co.

United Nations. 2009. "Consideration of Reports Submitted by States Parties under Article 19 of the Convention." Accessed September 23, 2020. http://digitallibrary.un.org/record/651068.

Warenfels, Isabelle. 2007. *Managing Instability in Algeria. Elites and Political Change since 1995*. New York: Routledge.

Welchman, Lynn. 2005. "Rocks, Hard Places and Human Rights: Anti-terrorism Law and Policy in Arab States." In *Global Anti-Terrorism Law*, edited by Victor Ramraj, Michael Hor, and Kent Roach, 581–608. Cambridge: Cambridge University Press.

Zoubir, Yahia. 2020. *The Politics of Algeria. Domestic Issues and International Relations*. New York: Routledge.

Zoubir, Yahia and Ahmed Aghrout. 2012. "Algeria's Path to Reform: Authentic Change?" *Middle East Policy* 19 (2): 66–83.

Chapter 17

Counter-terrorism and Freedom of Speech in Ethiopia

The EPRDF Years

Téwodros Workneh

INTRODUCTION

The Federal Democratic Republic of Ethiopia (FDRE) adopted a comprehensive counter-terrorism legal framework in 2009. The adoption of the Anti-terrorism Proclamation (ATP) was not surprising given Ethiopia's key role in the "war on terrorism" bloc led by the United States and its allies. Specifically, Ethiopia was an active participant in military campaigns against Islamist fundamentalist groups such as the Al Qaeda-affiliated militant organization Al-Shabaab in neighboring Somalia. Although there were concerns over ATP's provisions externally at the early days of the law's inception mainly from international rights groups (e.g., Amnesty International 2009; Human Rights Watch 2009; Oakland Institute 2015), there was not a perceptible outcry internally given the government's rationalization of the law as a key securitization intervention against an imminent threat posed by external terrorists. In the years after the adoption of the ATP, however, Ethiopians would learn the law was disproportionately used to criminalize domestic political dissent against the ruling party, the Ethiopian People's Revolutionary Democratic Front (EPRDF).

Before its dissolution in 2019, EPRDF ruled Ethiopia for nearly three decades. A coalition of four ethnically organized parties, namely the Tigrayan People's Liberation Front (TPLF), Oromo Peoples' Democratic Organization, the Amhara National Democratic Movement, and the Southern Ethiopian People's Democratic Movement (Milkias 2011), EPRDF evolved from a former rebel group that toppled the military *Derg*.[1] EPRDF consolidated its power by aggressively cracking down on opposition groups and other dissidents, and, at the height of its political dominance, infamously declared a 100% victory in Ethiopia's parliamentary elections in 2015 (Arriola and Lyons 2015). Although all party members play equally important roles in the coalition, at least in principle, many see TPLF as the most decisive and influential organ, especially during the premiership of the late Meles Zenawi (Kendie 2003).

Perceptions on the legacy of EPRDF, archetypal to modern Ethiopian political history, are controversial, if not polarized. Supporters claim that Ethiopia took some progressive steps in the right path under the leadership of EPRDF. They argue equitable state building and electoral democratization were slowly implemented with elections taking place in every five years. They contend long-standing group identity questions were constitutionally addressed and ethnic groups were empowered through self-governance and cultural and linguistic autonomy, replacing unitary authoritarianism with a multiethnic egalitarian nation-state. Economically, EPRDF introduced a mixed economy with large-scale privatization that abandoned the *Derg*'s sterile command economy (Aalen 2006; Hammond 1999; Henze 1998; Maes, Closser, Vorel, and Tesfaye 2015; Mengesha and Common 2007; Oqubay 2015; Young 1996).

On the other hand, dissidents point out that the EPRDF ethnic coalition does not truly reflect a legitimate representation of the Ethiopian populace but is rather an organization set up to sustain TPLF's minority hegemony. They accuse TPLF of deliberately amplifying ethnic tensions that aimed to create insecurity amongst groups, which, in turn, affords TPLF uncontested power. They argue constitutionally guaranteed human rights have been violated routinely. The press, though free to operate constitutionally, has been harassed, with editors being regularly incarcerated or exiled. In addition, political parties that EPRDF considered threatening to its hegemony were outlawed, and those that chose to compete have been systematically marginalized. Furthermore, critics contend elections have been marred by irregularities, harassment, intimidation, ballot rigging, and even outright murders by supporters of the government. Opposition groups charge EPRDF of favoritism and nepotism by demonstrating how unaudited TPLF-owned mega-business empires and parastatals monopolize key sectors of the Ethiopian economy. Other commonly cited criticisms over EPRDF include intimidation of the rural masses through confiscation of farmlands and denial of fertilizers as retribution to opposition party support; widespread jamming, content filtering, blocking, online surveillance over information communication technologies targeting dissidents; and diversion of international aid as a tool to maximize control and submission (Abbink 2006; Arriola and Lyons 2016; Bach 2011; Berhanu and Poulton 2014; Chanie 2007; Di Nunzio 2014; Gebregziabher 2019; Gudina 2011; Hassan 2013; McCracken 2004).

While perceptions on EPRDF remain contested, it is difficult to dispute the ruling party's abysmal track record on freedom of expression. The Ethiopian press during EPRDF's tenure had been characterized by extensive instability where private newspapers and other periodicals had a very short lifespan due to state-sponsored intimidation that oftentimes culminates to the imprisonment or exile of journalists, editors, and publishers (Mengistu 2014; Teshome 2009; Workneh 2020). In the second-most populous country in Africa, broadcasting remained a state-controlled enterprise for most of the years during EPRDF's rule with the nationwide Ethiopian Radio and Television Agency and eight regional state-owned broadcasters dominating the airwaves. Internet service, which was commonly shut down in times of protests, was only accessible through the sole state-owned telecommunications provider, Ethio-Telecom. For many critical observers, this represented EPRDF's hegemonic construct that aimed to limit the accessibility of mediated communication which the party considered to be disruptive to its rule.

EPRDF's response to this criticism has usually been to create a blanket caricature of the media as "enemies" of the state's development agenda. This perception has created a widespread self-censorship culture in several state-owned media organizations (e.g., Skjerdal 2008). The party has historically defended its hegemonic rule by branding itself as a vanguard elite of economic development, a priority that relegates other social concerns, including freedom of expression (Bach 2011; Weis 2016). The "developmentalism" rhetoric of EPRDF funneled through the various state-owned media is so strong that criticism of the party became to be framed as an attack on economic development (Gebresenbet 2014). It was common practice for state media in Ethiopia to characterize opposition groups and private press *as tsere limat* (anti-development) and/or *ashebari* (terrorist), implicitly stating that "EPRDF" and "development" are one and the same: Criticism of one is invariably an attack on the other. The danger here is that, under pretense of developmentalism, EPRDF can justify the suppression of what it deems as a non-permissible, *tsere limat*, *ashebari*, speech (Workneh 2015).

It is in this context that the EPRDF-controlled House of Representatives adopted a counter-terrorism legal framework in 2009, which arguably became the most lethal legal instrument deployed by the government against opposition parties, media practitioners, and political activists. This chapter outlines how, in the context of a semi-authoritarian context like EPRDF's Ethiopia, a counter-terrorism legislation had been circumvented to leverage political control. I will start by providing some context about terrorism and counter-terrorism in Ethiopia, especially as it pertains to FDRE's involvement in the war in Somalia and its repercussions in the homeland. Then, I will discuss the ATP by focusing on its rationales, provisions, and controversies. Finally, I will critically engage with how the ATP had been deployed in the courts by arguing the Ethiopian government had weaponized the law to disproportionately target journalists, activists, and opposition figures.

TERRORISM AND COUNTER-TERRORISM IN ETHIOPIA: A CONTEXT

Ethiopia is located in the Horn of Africa region that has often been characterized by political instability, border conflicts, and guerilla fighting (De Waal 2015; Vidino, Pantucci and Kohlmann 2010). Furthermore, the Horn has witnessed some of the most consequential terrorism and counter-terrorism activities, especially as it relates to the rise of Harakat al-Shabaab al-Mujahideen, commonly known as Al-Shabaab, in Somalia (Maruf and Joseph 2018). Designated as a terrorist organization by the United States, Canada, Norway, New Zealand, United Kingdom, United Arab Emirates, and Singapore, Al-Shabaab pledged allegiance to Al Qaeda in 2012; detonated twin bombs that killed more than 500 people in Somalia's capital city Mogadishu in 2017; and claimed responsibility for the 2013 attacks on Kenya's Westgate shopping mall, among other atrocities. Despite continued reports of its deteriorating capabilities, Al-Shabab continued its attacks in Somalia and Kenya. As recently as January 15, 2019, the group carried out an attack on a Nairobi hotel complex that killed twenty-one civilians.[2] Al-Shabaab controls sizable portions in rural areas of Somalia and routinely conducts offensive that targets the Somali state and African Union Mission in Somalia (AMISOM) forces.[3]

As part of its counter-terrorism campaign in the post 9/11 era, the United States has targeted Al-Shabab and carried many airstrikes in Somalia that killed several militants including the group's leader Ahmed Abdi Godane in September 2014 (Whitlock 2014). In addition to conducting drone strikes and deploying special operations forces raids against suspected Al-Shabaab militants, the United States Africa Command (AFRICOM) trains and participates in African Union forces capacity-building programs aimed at combating the terrorism designated organization.[4]

Since 2006, Ethiopia has been a major actor in the coalition of forces that battled Al-Shabab including the United States, the Somali government, Kenya, and AMISOM (Jackson 2018). More notably, in December 2006, it has invaded Somalia to drive the Islamic Courts Union (ICU), Al-Shabab's predecessor, out of the capital city of Mogadishu (Hansen 2013). Until 2008, Ethiopian forces continued to fight with Al-Shabab in Somalia, where the latter vowed to establish sharia law in Somalia and the Horn of Africa as well as prescribing to a strand of Salafism and Wahhabism that embraces the excommunication of apostates or unbelievers amounting to stoning, amputations, and beheadings (Ibid.). Although Al-Shabab has identified Ethiopia as a historical enemy, labeled Ethiopians "infidels," and declared jihad on Ethiopia, it has hardly managed to cause the sort of far-reaching terrorist attacks it conducted in Kenya and Somalia (see Torbjörnsson 2017 for more on Al-Shabaab's limited success in Ethiopia). This is in spite of explicit support from Al Qaeda that claimed the group would "engage in Jihad against the American-made government [in Somalia] in the same way they engaged in Jihad against the Ethiopians and the warlords before them" (Hanson 2009, para. 10).

Although Al-Shabaab's actual terrorism operations in Ethiopia were not substantial, EPRDF's escalation of terrorism threats in Ethiopia as well as its proactive actions to combat this perceived threat changed the role of domestic actors of state securitization dramatically. This started with the FDRE posturing itself as a key ally to the United States in combating terrorism and terrorist groups in the Horn of Africa including Al-Shabaab (e.g., Whitlock 2011). In spite of a poor human rights record, Ethiopia positioned itself as a reliable partner in an otherwise unstable region. For EPRDF, however, this partnership served a more strategic purpose in strengthening its grip on power internally despite its unpopularity (Fraser 2017). The party has repurposed counter-terrorism apparatuses including intelligence and surveillance systems, military equipment, and technical knowhow, largely financed and set up by its Western allies, to quell critical expression, organization, and assembly domestically (e.g., Ayalew 2018). In particular, the U.S. government adopted a policy of appeasement toward the Ethiopian government's misappropriation of counter-terrorism resources that were deployed to crack down on different forms of dissent including expressive rights. As Workneh (2015) notes, EPRDF's Western partners became "oblivious to or even ignorant of Ethiopia's worsening political exclusivity" (103), allowing the former to, without meaningful accountability, undermine basic human rights under the guise of counter-terrorism efforts.

THE ETHIOPIAN ATP: RATIONALES, PROVISIONS, AND CONTROVERSY

Although Ethiopia participated in combating terrorism in the Horn of Africa extensively, it did not adopt a legislative framework of counter-terrorism until 2009. Enacted by the EPRDF-dominated Ethiopian parliament, the ATP defines terrorism and terrorist acts; designates institutional and judicial jurisdiction over terrorism crimes; modifies trial procedures and evidentiary rules; expands police powers, including powers of arrest and detention; and designates terrorist organizations and freezing assets (Federal Democratic

Republic of Ethiopia 2009). In justifying the adoption of the law, the Ethiopian government argued “the laws presently in force in the country are not sufficient to prevent and control terrorism,” and that a comprehensive counter-terrorism legislation to prosecute crimes associated with terrorist activity is necessary (Federal Democratic Republic of Ethiopia 2009, 4827). Although the ATP has been used occasionally to prosecute individuals with alleged ties to Al-Shabaab and Al Qaeda, the overwhelming majority of the cases involving the legislation targeted domestic dissidents, journalists, opposition political parties and their members, and civil society organizations (Kibret 2017). Given EPRDF’s track record of extensive human rights violations, there were sustained expressions of concern over the implications of the proposed counter-terrorism law on dissidents.

Soon after its adoption, it became clear that fears of EPRDF’s repurposing of the ATP to undermine civil liberties enshrined in the Ethiopian Constitution were legitimate. The proclamation’s extremely broad and vaguely worded language was especially prone to arbitrary interpretation. In defining what constitutes “terrorist activity,” for example, a section of Article 3 of the proclamation stipulates:

> Whosoever or a group intending to advance a political, religious or ideological cause by coercing the government, intimidating the public or section of the public, or destabilizing or destroying the fundamental political, constitutional or, economic or social institutions of the country . . . endangers, seizes or puts under control, cause serious interference or disruption of any public service . . . is punishable with rigorous imprisonment from 15 years to life or with death. (Federal Democratic Republic of Ethiopia 2009, 4829–4830)

The characterization of “interference or disruption of any public service” as a potential act of terrorism directly conflates with citizens’ rights to free assembly as well as nonviolent forms of dissonance including public demonstrations. Per this provision, a road closure caused by a peaceful demonstration may be deemed as an act of terrorism. Students protesting in university campuses may also be prosecuted with terrorism charges for disrupting a “public service.” Because it is dissidents who are likely to participate in protests and other forms of public disapproval of state actors, broad and vague language such as this disproportionately targets them.

Arguably the most consequential provision of the ATP on freedom of expression is pronounced by Article 4 that states: “Whosoever publishes or causes the publication of a statement that is *likely to be understood by some or all of the members of the public* to whom it is published as a direct or indirect encouragement or other inducement to them to the commission or preparation or instigation of an act of terrorism . . . is punishable with rigorous imprisonment from 10 to 20 years" (Federal Democratic Republic of Ethiopia 2009, 4831, emphasis added). Not only does this provision make the press directly liable for journalistic expression deemed "terrorist" by the government, it also puts anyone publishing critical content on any public platform such as social media at risk. Given how the said publication can be designated as terrorist content by virtue of the "likely" understanding of "some" members of the public leaves a substantial latitude of interpretive abuse, which, again, puts journalists, dissidents, and political opposition groups in precarious conditions of self-censorship or retribution. Consequently, it is no surprise that the ATP has probably been put into retributive effect more than any other legal framework related to communication involving electronic media.

The proclamations' "Evidentiary and Procedural Rules" is yet another provision that grants extremely broad powers to executive branches of the government. The list of admissible evidence listed in the ATP for terrorism charges surfaces privacy concerns for anyone who produces, exchanges, or stores information under the broad provisions of what constitutes "terrorist acts":

> Without prejudice to the admissibility of evidences to be presented in accordance with the Criminal Procedure Code and other relevant legislations, the following shall be admissible in court for terrorism cases: (1) intelligence report prepared in relation to terrorism, even if the report does not disclose the source or the method it was gathered; (2) hearsay or indirect evidences; (3) digital or electronic evidences; (4) evidences gathered through interception or surveillance or information obtained through interception conducted by foreign law enforcement bodies; and (5) confession of a suspect of terrorism in writing, voice recording, video cassette or recorded in any mechanical or electronic device. (Federal Democratic Republic of Ethiopia 2009, 4836–4837)

The admissibility of hearsay in charges of terrorism elevates personal opinion, partisan views, as well as fraudulent testimonies as credible evidences. This opens up an extremely corrosive due process where critical speech, individuals, or organizations can be wrongfully charged, prosecuted, and sentenced.

HOW THE ATP BECAME AN INSTRUMENT OF STIFLING DISSENT: A LOOK AT THE STATE OF FREEDOM OF EXPRESSION IN EPRDF'S ETHIOPIA

The fatal consequences of Ethiopia's adoption of a counter-terrorism framework to freedom of speech were mostly predictable because of the Ethiopian government's abysmal track record on human rights violations. Most nations' rush to adopting counter-terrorism laws is motivated by the idea of creating a lawful means to bypass existing criminal jurisprudence that may not be speedy or effective enough to respond to national security threats. In this sense, anti-terrorism laws empower governments to exercise a "state of exception" where, under perceived or real terrorism threats, normal procedures of jurisprudence in criminal law may be circumvented in the spirit of upholding "the greater good." As Ramraj, Hor, Roach, and Williams (2012, 10) succinctly summarized, the intent here is "accommodating terrorism and emergencies within the rule of law without producing permanent states of emergency and exception." It is plausible to perceive, without overlooking critical loopholes, how countries with established democratic traditions will have better institutional mechanisms to combat corrosive uses of counter-terrorism laws. In a democratically fragile country like Ethiopia where all branches of government including the judiciary are set up to buttress the self-proclaimed hegemonic project of the ruling party, the ATP has become the rule and not the exception.

Although the various charges carried out under the premises of the ATP by the Ethiopian government differ in their scope and nature, a sizable number of the cases have serious implications to the state of freedom of expression, especially mediated critical speech. Since the law came into effect, it has disproportionately targeted community members who are involved in the dissemination of information through traditional and digital media platforms, most notably bloggers, journalists, and freelance writers. For example, in *Soliana Shimeles et al v the Federal Public Prosecutor*, the state charged 10 bloggers and journalists by claiming that the defendants have ties with Ginbot 7 Movement for Justice, Freedom and Democracy (Ginbot 7) and the Oromo Liberation Front (OLF), foreign-based opposition parties that were designated as terrorist groups by the EPRDF-controlled Ethiopian parliament.[5] In *Ethiopian Satellite Television and Oromia Media Network v The Federal Public Prosecutor*, U.S.-based television stations Ethiopian Satellite Television (ESAT) and Oromia Media Network (OMN) were accused of disseminating information deemed to be in the interest of Ethiopian government-designated terrorist groups Ginbot 7 and OLF. The underlying argument of the Federal Prosecutor was based on the assumption that disseminators of information involving terrorist-designated groups act as accessories of terrorism. The ATP renders a very broad and ambiguous language that criminalizes speech deemed to be an "encouragement" of terrorism, whatever the latter is through the interpretive lens of the Ethiopian government. Consider Article 6 of the Proclamation:

> Whosoever publishes or causes the publication of a statement that is *likely to be understood by some or all of the members of the public* to whom it is published

> as a direct or indirect encouragement or other inducement to them to the commission or preparation or instigation of an act of terrorism . . . is punishable with rigorous imprisonment from 10 to 20 years. (Federal Democratic Republic of Ethiopia 2009, 4831, emphasis added)

When the determination of what encompasses an encouragement of a terrorism act is made based on the "likely" understanding of "members of the public," the outcome warrants a scenario of arbitrary interpretation, jurisprudence, and execution of the law. In other words, by keeping the law as vague and broad as possible, the government can choose to use it haphazardly to stamp out legitimate acts of political expression and dissent. Consider the case of Reeyot Alemu Gobebo, former contributor of the weekly newspaper *Feteh*. She was convicted on three counts under the terrorism law for her writings that were highly critical of the ruling party and the former Prime Minister of Ethiopia, Meles Zenawi, who was persistent in his characterization of members of the free press as "messengers" of terrorist groups. Although Reeyot Alemu was formally convicted of having ties with terrorist groups—a common blanket accusation the Ethiopian government infers to arrest journalists and freelance writers—it is important to note that Alemu and other journalists that were imprisoned with terrorism charges were targeted by the government for their continued journalistic practices that were viewed by EPRDF as divergent to its hegemonic rule.

Some context is important here. When the EPRDF-controlled parliament designated opposition political parties such as Ginbot 7 and OLF as terrorist groups, for example, its underlying premise was that they aspired to overthrow the government through armed struggle. Ginbot 7, OLF and their supporters characterize their approach as an act of resistance performed in a form of a liberation movement. They defend their armed struggle by arguing EPRDF has clamped down any possibility of democratic transition of power throughout its nearly three decades of authoritarian rule that has been marred by protests, human rights abuses, and disregard to the rule of law. Ironically, when EPRDF ascended to power in 1991 after years of armed struggle in 1991, it defended its actions by citing the former military regime left them no choice but to pursue the military route. In this sense, it is plausible to conceive how Ginbot 7, OLF, and other groups that waged an armed struggle against the Ethiopian government see their movement as one motivated by liberation.

The appropriation of counter-terrorism laws to frame domestic political dissent as acts of terrorism is not unique to Ethiopia, which brings us back to normative debates surrounding the definition of terrorism, especially as it relates to the importance of delineating acts of terrorism from national liberation struggles. As Ramraj, Hor, Roach, and Williams (2012) remind us, a good chunk of the challenge of formulating a comprehensive definition of terrorism is "stymied by long-standing concerns over the legitimate use of political violence by national liberation movements" (6). Many state-sponsored counter-terrorism legal frameworks today suffer from "under-inclusion" because of their narrow—and usually self-serving—conceptualization of terrorist acts that disregards state terrorism or disproportionately targets liberation movements (Ramraj, Hor, Roach, and Williams 2012, 114). Some countries, such as South Africa, have incorporated language that broadly addresses the tension between counter-terrorism efforts and liberation movements in their counter-terrorism laws. As Roach (2015, 23) highlights, South Africa has made a "freedom fighter exemption" in its 2004 counter-terrorism law[6] which gives recognition to ANC's history of evolving from being "a proscribed terrorist organization to South Africa's governing party." In explaining this dilemma, Harry Roque cites this lengthy—but very illuminating—commentary by the Supreme Court of Philippines in *David v. Macapagal-Arroyo*:

> Remarkable confusion persists in regard to the legal categorization of acts of violence either by states, by armed groups such as liberation movements, or by individuals.
>
> The dilemma can be summarized in the saying "One country's terrorist is another country's freedom fighter." The apparent contradiction or lack of consistency in the use of the term terrorism may further be demonstrated by the historical fact that leaders of national liberation movements such as Nelson Mandela in South Africa, Habib Bourgouiba in Tunisia, or Ahmed Ben Bella in Algeria, to mention only a few, were originally labeled as terrorists by those who controlled the territory at the time, but later became internationally respected statesmen.
>
> The dilemma facing the international community can best be illustrated by reference to the contradicting categorization of organizations and movements such as Palestine Liberation Organization—which is a terrorist group for Israel and a liberation movement for Arabs and Muslims—the Kashmiri resistance groups—who are terrorists in the perception of India, liberation fighters in that of Pakistan—the earlier Contras in Nicaragua—freedom fighters for the United States, terrorists for the Socialist camp—or, most drastically, the Afghani Mujahedeen (later to become the Taliban movement): during the Cold War period they were a group of freedom fighters for the West, nurtured by the United States, and a terrorist gang for the Soviet Union. One could go on and on in enumerating examples of conflicting categorizations that cannot be reconciled in any way—because of opposing political interests that are at the roots of those perceptions. How, then, can those contradicting definitions and conflicting perceptions and evaluations of one and the same group and its actions be explained?

> In our analysis, the basic reason for these striking inconsistencies lies in the divergent interest of states. Depending on whether a state is in the position of an occupying power or in that of a rival, or adversary, of an occupying power in a given territory, the definition of terrorism will "fluctuate" accordingly. A state may eventually see itself as protector of the rights of a certain ethnic group outside its territory and will therefore speak of a "liberation struggle," not of "terrorism" when acts of violence by this group are concerned, and vice-versa.[7]

Although EPRDF assumed political power through armed struggle, Ethiopia has not made any exceptions with regard to national liberation struggles, which, in turn, has dire consequences for media professionals doing their public mandated watchdog role. In other words, when journalists such as Reeyot Alemu report about groups such as Ginbot 7 and OLF, their actions are justified because of the enormous public interest imperative that is at stake. If and when a journalist, per the provisions of the ATP, publishes or causes the publication of groups or individuals designated as terrorists by the Ethiopian government, they will run the very likely risk of being imprisoned. Everyday journalist routines of establishing a source, conducting an interview, or simply relaying a press release involving designated "terrorist organizations" can easily be prosecutable acts. Consequently, the law has been used to convict other prominent Ethiopian journalists including Eskinder Nega Fenta, a journalist and blogger who received the 2012 PEN Freedom to Write Award, was sentenced to eighteen years of imprisonment. Another convicted journalist is 2012 Hellman-Hammett Award winner Woubshet Taye Abebe, who was sentenced to fourteen years imprisonment under the provisions of the ATP.

While the appropriation of Ethiopia's ATP to target media professionals by tying them to controversially terrorist-designated political groups is by itself an attack on the freedom of expression enshrined in the Ethiopian Constitution,[8] the more dangerous consequence is probably the chilling effect this "example" set to ordinary citizens. The indiscriminate use of "terrorist" to refer to journalists reporting on opposition groups has now evolved to include individuals whose political, economic, social, or human rights opinions differ from EPRDF's narrative. Legal frameworks such as the ATP adopted by the government have created a cloud of insecurity and fear in Ethiopian social media users when it comes to political opinions. The thin line between "dissent" and "terrorism" leads users to unwittingly undergo through different forms of self-censorship, a scenario that enables the government to create a subdued public that is reluctant in participating in a counter-hegemonic narrative.

This "fear factor" born out of the government's criminalization of critical speech is compounded by the ATP's empowerment of the state with the authority to intercept communication that endows the National Intelligence and Security Service (NISS), upon getting court warrant, to: intercept or conduct surveillance on the telephone, fax, radio, internet, electronic, postal, and similar communications of a person suspected of terrorism; enter into any premise in secret to enforce the interception; or install or remove instruments enabling the interception. As Endalkachew Chala, member of the online blogging collective Zone 9 recounts, the public prosecutor has presented transcripts of phone conversations obtained through wiretapping by the government as evidence in a court of law.[9] The frequency in which the government infiltrates into the private communication of Ethiopian citizens—especially activists and journalists with critical opinions—has become a common practice since the ATP was put in place in 2009.

While the vast power bestowed upon NISS by the ATP in soliciting information from private Ethiopian citizens reinforced the Ethiopian government's trajectory as a police state, there are important implications to be drawn from another provision of the law that requires communication service providers to "cooperate" with intelligence units. Article 14(3) of the ATP states that any communication service provider "shall cooperate when requested by the National Intelligence and Security Service to conduct the interception." The significance of this provision, especially to digital freedoms, or lack thereof, in Ethiopia is that all internet services can only be accessed through the sole internet service provider, the state-owned Ethio-Telecom. It should be recalled the telecommunications sector in Ethiopia is characterized by a vertically integrated market run by a state-owned enterprise. Although the Ethiopian government has defended its state monopoly model of the telecommunications sector by citing economic rationales, several critiques have argued the monopoly model has got little to do with economic imperatives but rather is set in place to exert control over *de facto* users (Workneh 2018). Several instances corroborate these collusion fears. During the 2005 general elections, for example, the Ethiopian government ordered the sole telecommunication provider to shut down the SMS system after opposition groups successfully deployed text-based campaigns (Stremlau and Price 2009). A 2014 Human Rights Report entitled *"They Know Everything We do": Telecom and Internet Surveillance in Ethiopia*, provides a detailed account of how the Ethiopian government acquires surveillance technologies from several countries that oftentimes are integrated with Ethio-Telecom operations, resulting in unrestricted access to call records, internet browsing logs, and instant messaging platforms (Horne and Wong 2014). In 2015, a massive online data dump involving the Italian commercial surveillance company, Hacking Team, showed numerous evidences including email transcripts, invoices, and technical manuals that directly implicated the Ethiopian government (Marczak et al. 2017). The Hacking Team's surveillance products were used by Ethiopia's Information Network Security Agency to acquire communication involving journalists affiliated with ESAT, an U.S.- and Europe-based network known for its critical views on EPRDF's rule (Peterson 2015). In this sense, the ATP's directive for communication providers in Ethiopia—Ethio-Telecom by default—to cede private information of users only formalizes what many considered to be a long-standing exercise of institutional control of the public. It should be noted, however, that the induction of language enabling NISS to solicit communication of private citizens in the ATP gave broad protections to those in the position of power at the expense of citizens' basic rights of expression.

CONCLUDING REMARKS

The adoption of the ATP by the EPRDF-led government which has led to the criminalization of a great deal of critical speech cannot be seen separately from the long-standing intimidation, imprisonment, and exile of media practitioners, opposition groups, and political activists. The proclamation, which stipulates broad and vague definitions of terrorism, created a legal-rationale bureaucracy that is subject to arbitrary interpretation and execution at the will of the state. The result was the making of a public that is unsure of what could be considered as a "terrorist" message as opposed to "normal" speech. In an attempt to not take a risk, the public in turn sought to avoid participating in political discourse altogether. Consequently, it can be argued that the ATP's enduring legacy is not only stifling the views of dissenting individuals and organizations to EPRDF's rule but also creating fear among the general public that struggles to distinguish between outlawed vs. permissible forms of expression.

Consequently, even after EPRDF's dissolution in 2019, there are fears that the ATP might continue to be used to advance political control at the expense of basic citizen rights in Ethiopia. This is not to disregard the positive steps taken by the administration of Prime Minister Abiy Ahmed in repealing some of the most problematic provisions of the ATP (see Gebre 2020). In 2020, the Ethiopian House of Representatives removed language from the ATP that was used by the EPRDF-led government to prosecute several journalists and politicians. Vaguely worded language discussed earlier in this chapter such as "encouraging terrorism" was replaced by "incitement," which offers a more tangible and commonly understood concept. Furthermore, the 2009 proclamation's stipulation of "obstruct[ing] public services" as an act of terrorism is now amended to exempt legitimate expressions of protest or dissent such as workers' right to strike (Voice of America 2020). While these moves indicate a step in the right direction, the risk of existing and future political leaders turning a page from EPRDF's circumvention of the ATP to attack opponents and consolidate power remain in the absence of a free and fair judicial system. The Ethiopian experiment with the ATP, therefore, represents a scenario of how counter-terrorism legislation and practice may often lose sight of their intended purpose of curbing acts of terrorism only to bolster state-sponsored violence against citizens.[10]

NOTES

1. EPRDF's predecessor, the *Derg*, came to power on September 1974 by ousting the last king of Ethiopia's centuries-old Solomonic dynasty, Haile Selassie I. The *Derg* was a committee of communist military officers led by former dictator Mengistu Haile-Mariam.

2. For a timeline of Al-Shabab's terrorist activities, see Council on Foreign Relations (2019).

3. Founded by the African Union's Peace and Security Council on January 19, 2007, with an initial six-month mandate, the African Union Mission in Somalia (AMISOM) is a regional peacekeeping mission under the auspices of the African Union. Supported by the United Nations Security Council, AMISOM works in concert with the Somali government to enhance national security, train Somali security forces, and foster better conditions for humanitarian aid. For more on AMISOM, see Williams (2018).

4. See United States Africa Command (2019) for AFRICOM's mission in the Horn of Africa.

5. The Oromo Liberation Front (OLF) and Ginbot 7 Movement for Justice, Freedom, and Democracy (Ginbot 7), the latter now defunct, were, until 2018, armed opposition groups designated as terrorist organizations by the Ethiopian government. Despite the government's designation of OLF and Ginbot 7 as "terrorist" organizations, both parties have large supporters.

6. Section 1(4) of the Protection of Constitutional Democracy Act exempts: any act committed during a struggle waged by peoples, including any action during an armed struggle, in the exercise or furtherance of their legitimate right to national liberation, self-determination, and independence against colonialism, or occupation or aggression or domination by alien or foreign forces, in accordance with the principles of international law.

7. G.R. No. 171396, May 3, 2006, quoted in Roque (2012, 315–316).

8. Article 29 (2) of the Ethiopian Constitution states: "Everyone shall have the right to freedom of expression without interference. This right shall include freedom to seek, receive and impart information and ideas of all kinds, regardless of frontiers, either orally, in writing or in print, in the form of art, or through other media of his choice" (FDRE House of Representatives 1995).

9. Personal correspondence, October 15, 2017.

10. A portion of this chapter was previously published on "Internet Governance in the Global South. History, Theory, and Contemporary Debates" (Ed. Daniel Oppermann 2018).

REFERENCES

Aalen, Lovise. 2006. "Ethnic Federalism and Self-Determination for Nationalities in a Semi-Authoritarian State: The Case of Ethiopia." *International Journal on Minority and Group Rights* 13 (2–3): 243–261. https://doi.org/10.1163/157181106777909849.

Abbink, J. 2006. "Discomfiture of Democracy? The 2005 Election Crisis in Ethiopia and Its Aftermath." *African Affairs* 105 (419): 173–199. https://doi.org/10.1093/afraf/adi122.

Amnesty International. 2009. "Ethiopia: New Anti-Terrorism Proclamation Jeopardizes Freedom of Expression." https://www.amnesty.org/en/press-releases/2009/07/ethiopia-new-anti-terrorism-proclamation-jeopardizes-freedom-expression/.

Arriola, Leonardo, and Terrence Lyons. 2016. "Ethiopia: The 100% Election." *Journal of Democracy* 27 (1): 76–88.

Ayalew, Seife. 2018. "The Security and Human Rights Dilemma: An Inquiry into U.S.-Ethiopia Diplomatic Relations 1991-2012." *Northwestern Journal of Human Rights* 16: 65.

Bach, Jean-Nicolas. 2011. "Abyotawi Democracy: Neither Revolutionary nor Democratic, a Critical Review of EPRDF's Conception of Revolutionary Democracy in Post-1991 Ethiopia." *Journal of Eastern African Studies* 5 (4): 641–663. https://doi.org/10.1080/17531055.2011.642522.

Berhanu, Kassahun, and Colin Poulton. 2014. "The Political Economy of Agricultural Extension Policy in Ethiopia: Economic Growth and Political Control." *Development Policy Review* 32 (s2): s197–s213. https://doi.org/10.1111/dpr.12082.

Chanie, Paulos. 2007. "Clientelism and Ethiopia's Post-1991 Decentralisation." *The Journal of Modern African Studies* 45 (3): 355–384. https://doi.org/10.1017/S0022278X07002662.

Council on Foreign Relations. 2019. "Al-Shabaab: 2004-2019." 2019. https://www.cfr.org/timeline/al-shabab.

De Waal, Alex. 2015. *The Real Politics of the Horn of Africa: Money, War and the Business of Power*. Maleden, MA: Polity Press.

Di Nunzio, Marco. 2014. "'Do Not Cross the Red Line': The 2010 General Elections, Dissent, and Political Mobilization in Urban Ethiopia." *African Affairs* 113 (452): 409–430. https://doi.org/10.1093/afraf/adu029.

FDRE House of Representatives. 1995. *Constitution of the Federal Democratic Republic of Ethiopia*. https://www.abyssinialaw.com/online-resources/state-constitutions?download=1214:the-1995-ethiopian-constitution-english-and-amharic-version.

Federal Democratic Republic of Ethiopia. 2009. "A Proclamation on Anti-Terrorism." Federal Negarit Gazeta. http://www.refworld.org/docid/4ba799d32.html.

Fraser, Elizabeth. 2017. "Ethiopia Silences the United States on Human Rights Abuses." *Oakland Institute: Blog* (blog). October 19, 2017. https://www.oaklandinstitute.org/blog/ethiopia-silences-united-states-human-rights-abuses.

Gebre, Samuel. 2020. "Ethiopia Loosens Anti-Terrorism Law Used to Subdue Opposition." *Bloomberg.Com*, January 3, 2020. https://www.bloomberg.com/news/articles/2020-01-03/ethiopia-loosens-anti-terrorism-law-used-to-subdue-opposition.

Gebregziabher, Tefera Negash. 2019. "Ideology and Power in TPLF's Ethiopia: A Historic Reversal in the Making?" *African Affairs* 118 (472): 463–484. https://doi.org/10.1093/afraf/adz005.

Gebresenbet, Fana. 2014. "Securitisation of Development in Ethiopia: The Discourse and Politics of Developmentalism." *Review of African Political Economy* 41 (sup1): S64–S74. https://doi.org/10.1080/03056244.2014.976191.

Gudina, Merera. 2011. "Elections and Democratization in Ethiopia, 1991–2010." *Journal of Eastern African Studies* 5 (4): 664–680. https://doi.org/10.1080/17531055.2011.642524.

Hammond, Jenny. 1999. *Fire from the Ashes: A Chronicle of the Revolution in Tigray, Ethiopia, 1975-1991*. Red Sea Press.

Hansen, Stig Jarle. 2013. *Al-Shabaab in Somalia: The History and Ideology of a Militant Islamist Group, 2005-2012*. Oxford/New York: Oxford University Press.

Hanson, Stephanie. 2009. "Backgrounder: Al-Shabaab." *The New York Times*, March 2, 2009. https://archive.nytimes.com/www.nytimes.com/cfr/world/slot2_20090227.html?_r=0.

Hassan, Seid Y. 2013. "The State Capture Onset in Ethiopia: Humanitarian Aid and Corruption." SSRN Scholarly Paper ID 2303692. Rochester, NY: Social Science Research Network. https://doi.org/10.2139/ssrn.2303692.

Henze, Paul B. 1998. "Is Ethiopia Democratic? A Political Success Story." *Journal of Democracy* 9 (4): 40–54. https://doi.org/10.1353/jod.1998.0062.

Horne, Felix, and Cynthia Wong. 2014. "'They Know Everything We Do': Telecom and Internet Surveillance in Ethiopia." Human Rights Watch. https://www.hrw.org/report/2014/03/25/they-know-everything-we-do/telecom-and-internet-surveillance-ethiopia.

Human Rights Watch. 2009. "Analysis of Ethiopia's Draft Anti-Terrorism Law." Human Rights Watch. June 30, 2009. https://www.hrw.org/news/2009/06/30/analysis-ethiopias-draft-anti-terrorism-law.

Jackson, Donna Rose. 2017. *US Foreign Policy in The Horn of Africa From Colonialism to Terrorism*. London: Routledge.

Kendie, Daniel. 2003. "The Causes of the Failure of the Present Regime in Ethiopia." *International Journal of Ethiopian Studies* 1 (1): 177–213.

Kibret, Zelalem. 2017. "The Terrorism of 'Counterterrorism': The Use and Abuse of Anti-Terrorism Law, The Case of Ethiopia." *European Scientific Journal* 13 (13): 1857–7881. https://doi.org/10.19044/esj.2017.v13n13p504.

Maes, Kenneth, Svea Closser, Ethan Vorel, and Yihenew Tesfaye. 2015. “A Women’s Development Army: Narratives of Community Health Worker Investment and Empowerment in Rural Ethiopia.” *Studies in Comparative International Development* 50 (4): 455–478. https://doi.org/10.1007/s12116-015-9197-z.

Marczak, Bill, Geoffrey Alexander, Sarah McKune, John Scott-Railton, and Ron Deibert. 2017. “Champing at the Cyberbit: Ethiopian Dissidents Targeted with New Commercial Spyware.” Research. Totonto: The Citizen Lab, Munk School of Global Affairs, University of Toronto. https://citizenlab.ca/2017/12/champing-cyberbit-ethiopian-dissidents-targeted-commercial-spyware/.

Maruf, Harun, and Dan Joseph. 2018. *Inside Al-Shabaab: The Secret History of Al-Qaeda’s Most Powerful Ally*. Bloomington, IN: Indiana University Press.

McCracken, Matthew J. 2004. “Abusing Self-Determination and Democracy: How the TPLF Is Looting Ethiopia.” *Case Western Reserve Journal of International Law* 36: 183.

Mengesha, Getachew Hailemariam, and Richard Common. 2007. “Public Sector Capacity Reform in Ethiopia: A Tale of Success in Two Ministries?” *Public Administration and Development* 27 (5): 367–380. https://doi.org/10.1002/pad.456.

Mengistu, Yared Legesse. 2014. “Freedom of Expression in Ferment: A Cursory Look at the Ethiopian Media Regime.” In *Free Speech and Censorship Around the Globe*, edited by Peter Molnár, 317–336. New York: Central European University Press. https://muse.jhu.edu/book/38787.

Milkias, Paulos. 2011. *Ethiopia*. Santa Barbara, CA: ABC-CLIO.

Oakland Institute. 2015. “Ethiopia’s Anti-Terrorism Law: A Tool to Stifle Dissent.” The Oakland Institute and Environmental Defender Law Center. https://www.oaklandinstitute.org/sites/oaklandinstitute.org/files/OI_Ethiopia_Legal_Brief_final_web.pdf.

Oqubay, Arkebe. 2015. *Made in Africa: Industrial Policy in Ethiopia*. Oxford University Press.

Peterson, Andrea. 2015. “Spyware Vendor May Have Helped Ethiopia Target Journalists – Even after It Was Aware of Abuses, Researchers Say.” *Washington Post*, March 9, 2015. https://www.washingtonpost.com/news/the-switch/wp/2015/03/09/spyware-vendor-may-have-helped-ethiopia-spy-on-journalists-even-after-it-was-aware-of-abuses-researchers-say/.

Ramraj, Victor V., Michael Hor, Kent Roach, and George Williams. 2012. *Global Anti-Terrorism Law and Policy*. 2nd ed. Cambridge: Cambridge University Press.

Roach, Kent. 2015. *Comparative Counter-Terrorism Law*. Cambridge University Press.

Roque, Harry L. 2012. “The Human Security Act and the IHL LAw of the Philippines: Of Security and Insecurity.” In *Global Anti-Terrorism Law and Policy*, edited by Victor V. Ramraj, Michael Hor, Kent Roach, and George Williams, 2nd ed., 310–333. Cambridge: Cambridge University Press.

Skjerdal, Terje. 2008. “Self-Censorship Among News Journalists in the Ethiopian State Media.” *African Communication Research* 1 (2): 185–206.

Stremlau, Nicole, and Monroe E. Price. 2009. "Media, Elections and Political Violence in Eastern Africa: Towards a Comparative Framework." London: The Programme in Comparative Media Law and Policy, Centre for Socio-Legal Studies, University of Oxford Center for Global Communication Studies, Annenberg School for Communication, University of Pennsylvania Stanhope Centre for Communications Policy Research. https://repository.upenn.edu/cgi/viewcontent.cgi?article=1760&context=asc_papers.

Teshome, Wondwosen. 2009. "Media and Multi-Party Elections in Africa: The Case of Ethiopia." *Journal of Human Sciences* 6 (1): 94–122.

Torbjörnsson, Daniel. 2017. "Explaining the Differences in Al-Shabaab Expansion into Ethiopia and Kenya." Swedish Defence Research Agency. https://www.foi.se/download/18.7fd35d7f166c56ebe0bb3b4/1542369060378/Explaining-the-differences-in_al-Shabaab-expansion-into-Ethiopia-and-Kenya_FOI-Memo-6061.pdf.

United States Africa Command. 2019. "About the Command." 2019. https://www.africom.mil/about-the-command.

Vidino, Lorenzo, Raffaello Pantucci, and Evan Kohlmann. 2010. "Bringing Global Jihad to the Horn of Africa: Al Shabaab, Western Fighters, and the Sacralization of the Somali Conflict." *African Security* 3 (4): 216–238. https://doi.org/10.1080/19392206.2010.533071.

Voice of America. 2020. "Ethiopia Adopts New Version of Much-Criticized Terrorism Law." January 3, 2020. https://www.voanews.com/africa/ethiopia-adopts-new-version-much-criticized-terrorism-law.

Weis, Toni. 2016. "Vanguard Capitalism: Party, State, and Market in the EPRDF's Ethiopia." PhD Thesis, University of Oxford.

Whitlock, Craig. 2011. "U.S. Drone Base in Ethiopia Is Operational." *The Washington Post*, 2011. https://www.washingtonpost.com/world/national-security/us-drone-base-in-ethiopia-is-operational/2011/10/27/gIQAznKwMM_story.html.

———. 2014. "White House Confirms Al-Shabab Leader Killed in Airstrike in Somalia." *The Washington Post*, September 5, 2014. https://www.washingtonpost.com/world/national-security/pentagon-confirms-al-shabab-leader-killed-in-airstrike-in-somalia/2014/09/05/fc9fee06-3512-11e4-9e92-0899b306bbea_story.html.

Williams, Paul D. 2018. "Joining AMISOM: Why Six African States Contributed Troops to the African Union Mission in Somalia." *Journal of Eastern African Studies* 12 (1): 172–192. https://doi.org/10.1080/17531055.2018.1418159.

Workneh, Téwodros W. 2015. "Digital Cleansing? A Look into State-Sponsored Policing of Ethiopian Networked Communities." *African Journalism Studies* 36 (4): 102–124. https://doi.org/10.1080/23743670.2015.1119493.

———. 2018. "State Monopoly of Telecommunications in Ethiopia: Origins, Debates, and the Way Forward." *Review of African Political Economy* 45 (158): 592–608. https://doi.org/10.1080/03056244.2018.1531390.

———. 2020. "Journalistic Autonomy in Voice of America's Amharic Service: Actors, Deterrents, and Safeguards." *Journalism Studies* 21 (2): 217–235. https://doi.org/10.1080/1461670X.2019.1634484.

Young, John. 1996. "Ethnicity and Power in Ethiopia." *Review of African Political Economy* 23 (70): 531–542. https://doi.org/10.1080/03056249608704221.

Chapter 18

Instrument to Rule?

Examining the Impact of Bangladesh's Counter-terrorism Laws on Freedom of Expression

Shudipta Sharma

INTRODUCTION

Freedom of expression is often considered the root of all rights since it reinforces most other rights (Ahmad 2015). Accordingly, ensuring the right for everyone to speak freely is not only important for the healthy development of societies but also for establishing democratic norms. However, this fundamental right is often violated across the world. By utilizing some crises which create an environment of fear[1] and justifying their actions by ascribing it to citizens' safety and wellbeing of the society, governments often enact laws that are used to limit peoples' right to freedom of expression (Human Rights Watch 2018). A recurrent theme that is increasingly used by governments to adopt such laws is terrorism. Terrorism is a global crisis that has led to the enactment of laws with the aim of subverting security and safety threats by many states across the world, especially after the September 11, 2001, terrorist attack in the United States. Following the event, the UN Security Council passed resolutions, which urged nations around the world to adopt legislative measures to counter terrorist acts.[2] Many countries adopted laws that give law enforcement agencies broad authority to prohibit and punish expressions that are considered to have links with acts of terror (Boyne 2010).

In Bangladesh, the impact of these counter-terrorism laws on freedom of expression is a widely discussed topic in the discourse of human rights. Like other parts of the world, the threat of terrorism is present in the country, home to one of the world's largest Muslim population of more than 150 million people. Although Islamist militant groups have been present in the country since the 1990s, Bangladesh has faced a new wave of violent extremism in recent years. Militant groups perpetrated some 147 attacks in Bangladesh between 2001 and 2016 (Fair and Abdallah 2017). Various transnational terrorist groups, such as the Islamic State of Iraq and Syria (ISIS) and Al Qaeda in the Indian Subcontinent, claimed responsibility for these brutal attacks on secular bloggers, writers, publishers, religious, and ethnic minorities, foreigners, and liberal activists (Riaz 2016). However, the attack on July 11, 2016, by a group of five youths claiming to be affiliated with ISIS on a café in the upscale neighborhood of the capital Dhaka drew the most international attention. Twenty-nine people were killed, including twenty hostages (eighteen foreigners and two locals), two police officers, five gunmen, and two café staffs (New Age 2019).

As part of the counter-terrorism strategy, the government has enacted several laws. In response to how new information and communication technologies (ICTs) have been widely used by militant individuals and groups to propagate their ideology, recruit new members, and, in several instances, provide training to their members (Hoskins, Awan, and O'Loughlin 2011), the government adopted the Anti-Terrorism Act (ATA) and introduced a clause on cyber terrorism in the Digital Security Act (DSA). Both laws have faced criticism for restricting freedom of expression (FORUM-ASIA 2018). The laws have been used to harass people since several terms in these laws are vague and broadly applicable. Human rights activists describe the laws as tools for repression on those who oppose the government (The Daily Star 2018b).

This chapter explores the use of counter-terrorism laws and their impacts on freedom of expression in Bangladesh. The chapter examines secondary sources such as news reports and articles to offer a comprehensive review of journalists', experts', and human rights activists' views on these laws. The chapter is divided into six sections. Section one discusses the significance, objectives, and methodology of the study. Section two describes the related literature and theoretical framework of the study. Section three addresses international and national human rights standards on freedom of expression. Section four discusses counter-terrorism laws in tandem with the right to freedom of expression. Section five presents the impact of counter-terrorism laws on freedom of expression.

STUDYING COUNTER-TERRORISM LAWS AND FREEDOM OF EXPRESSION: DEBATES AND THEORIES

Since freedom of expression is considered the lifeblood of democracy, it is recognized as one of the basic human rights under democratic norms of domestic, regional, and international human rights legislations. Many theories have been developed on freedom of expression and freedom of media. The theories range from the so-called constitutive theories of ancient Greeks and Immanuel Kant to the instrumental justifications of John Stuart Mill, Oliver Wendell Holmes, Alexander Meiklejohn, and others (Tsegaye 2016). Instrumental justifications focus on grounding the need for freedom of expression based on its purpose in attaining a particular goal such as the pursuit of the truth and the promotion of democracy and self-governance (Mill 1864; Dworkin 2002; Tsegaye 2016). On the other hand, constitutive approaches emphasize that freedom of expression is intrinsically good in furthering individual self-fulfillment and autonomy. This approach endorses self-expression, self-realization, and self-fulfillment which are themselves attached to human dignity (Tsegaye 2016; Dworkin 2002).

The freedom of association, expression, and media that characterize most democratic states are sources of both strength and vulnerability (Bozinovic 2018). Terming the changed nature of terrorism as "new terrorism,"[3] Bruce Hoffman (1998) observes terrorists can exploit these freedoms to spread pro-terror propaganda and incite self-radicalization. Hoffman argues this new condition has pushed different states into developing a similar response. When states in the Western hemisphere face terrorist threat that is of significant lethality, is growing in terms of material capability, and is underpinned by "hostile and unrestrained" anti-West sentiment, they are likely to draw the "same broad implications" about the threat, leading them to respond in potentially similar ways (Bozinovic 2018, 4). However, Bozinovic (2018) argues the degree to which democratic states have flexibility to regulate virulent expression is not uniform and is set in a particular sociopolitical context.

Following the 9/11 terrorist attacks in the United States, the relationship between freedom of expression and national security has been discussed widely across the world. Ignoring civil societies' concerns on the right to freedom of expression, many countries such as Iraq, Russia, and the Philippines enacted counter-terrorism laws to ensure "citizens' safety" (PoKempner 2007). There are many studies (e.g., Bozinovic 2018; Tsegaye 2016; Tura 2017) that explored the surge of securitization of legislation in response to terrorism. However, there are debates on making a balance between freedom of expression and state security, given the mainstreaming of legislative measures as necessary instruments to curb terrorism (Michaelsen 2006).

Mendel (2010) noted counter-terrorism laws are necessary since there are extreme social views, religious views, and racist attitudes that have a potential to harm national security and public peace. On the other hand, Cram (2009) offers a critical argument by highlighting how these laws limit citizens' right to freedom of expression. He cautions such intrusion could create a feeling of alienation among people. Cram also argues that restriction on freedom of expression will diminish the very existence of a democratic value to influence the outcome of public discourses through ideas and arguments. Meiklejohn (1948) also made similar observations. Instead of limiting expressive freedom, he suggested the state to use its means to promote democratic values. For him, such measures are productive and are less likely to produce a sense of alienation among dissidents.

One of the major limitations of most counter-terrorism laws lies in the vague and broad definitions of different terms. Crenshaw (2011) observes that some definitions of terrorism often end up restricting freedom of expression through counter-terrorism laws. Such definitions, Crenshaw argues, are usually expansive to encroach on constitutionally protected rights. On the other hand, Hellmuth (2015) states that the response of states to "new terrorism" often leads to more sweeping surveillance and preventive state intervention since these processes increasingly tend to target those who do not have a violent history.

In his comparative study between counter-terrorism laws of the United States and France, Bozinovic (2018) finds that, while France restricts terror-related expressions to a greater degree than the United States, the United States possesses more tools to counter terror-related expressions than its constitution suggests. The primary explanation for less forceful U.S. action stems not from constitutional limits but from a proclivity for military counter-terrorism abroad, which takes focus away from domestic measures to disrupt terrorist propaganda.

In the Ethiopian context, Tsegaye (2016) found that since the adoption of the counter-terrorism law in the country, the media in general, and the private press in particular experienced difficulties. The law was being used to stifle critical voices against the government, which, in turn, led to a heightened form of self-censorship among journalists. In another, Tura (2017) found the government of Ethiopia had abused the anti-terrorism law to stifle dissent and crack down on members of legal opposition parties, human rights activists, journalists, bloggers, and the civil society groups who criticized the ruling party and its policies.

However, there is a dearth of academic study focusing on the impacts of counter-terrorism laws on freedom of expression in the Bangladeshi context. A report titled "Shrinking Democratic Space and Freedom of Expression in Bangladesh" published by Forum-Asia in 2018 shows the right to freedom of expression has been violated by the government by abusing different legal frameworks including counter-terrorism laws. It notes: "The Government allegedly uses the ATA selectively against the opposition activists to intervene in peaceful protests and political rallies" (FORUM-ASIA 2018).

In addition, in a study of privacy and counter-terrorism laws in Bangladesh, Siddique and Akter (2016) found the right to privacy is not adequately mainstreamed due to a lack of equal compensatory provisions in the law. From these examples, it is evident that counter-terrorism laws shrink the peoples' right to freedom of expression. Moreover, governments across the world use the fear of terrorism to enact new laws for strengthening their power by establishing a surveillance society (Siapera 2012).

INTERNATIONAL AND NATIONAL HUMAN RIGHTS STANDARDS ON FREEDOM OF EXPRESSION

The right to freedom of expression is cited as one of the basic rights in the Universal Declaration of Human Rights (UDHR) adopted by the United Nations General Assembly in 1948. Article 19 of the UDHR states:

> Everyone has the right to freedom of opinion and expression; this right includes freedom to hold opinions without interference and to seek, receive and impart information and ideas through any media regardless of frontiers. (United Nations n.d.)

The International Covenant on Civil and Political Rights (ICCPR) also recognizes the right to hold opinions without interference. Article 19(2) of the ICCPR states:

> Everyone shall have the right to freedom of expression; this right shall include freedom to seek, receive and impart information and ideas of all kinds, regardless of frontiers, either orally, in writing or in print, in the form of art, or through any other media of his choice. (Office of the United Nations High Commissioner for Human Rights n.d.)

Both of these provisions recognize the right to freedom of expression in almost a similar manner. However, unlike the UDHR, the ICCPR clearly provides for the appropriate grounds for some limitations. Governments may impose some restrictions or limitations on the right to freedom of expression, per Article 19(3) of the ICCPR, "if such restrictions are provided by law and are necessary: (a) for respect of the rights or reputations of others; or (b) for the protection of national security, public order, public health, or morals." However, the UN Human Rights Committee, in its General Comment No. 34 argues that the limitations provided under Article 19(3) of the ICCPR "should be interpreted narrowly and that the restrictions may not put in jeopardy the right itself."[4]

Following the events of 9/11, the "war on terror" has influenced many countries to enact laws to counter terrorism. Those legislative measures are criticized since they have affected the notion and scope of freedom of expression. To create balance between liberty and security, the UN Security Council, in its Resolution 1456 of 2003, stipulates that "states must ensure that any measures taken to combat terrorism must comply with all their obligations under international law, in particular international human rights, refugee and humanitarian law."[5] In this regard, Paul Hoffman, the chair of the International Executive Committee of Amnesty International, contends that:

> A "war on terrorism" waged without respect for the rule of law undermines the very values that it presumes to protect. We must restore the balance between liberty and security by reasserting the human rights framework, which provides for legitimate and effective efforts to respond to terrorist attacks. (Hoffman 2004)

In 2012, the UN Human Rights Council recognized that the "same rights that people have offline must also be protected online."[6] The HR committee has also made clear that limitations of electronic forms of communication or expression disseminated over the Internet must be justified according to the same criteria as non-electronic or "offline" communications, as set out above.[7]

Furthermore, Article 39 of the Constitution of People's Republic of Bangladesh guarantees the right to freedom of expression as follows:

> (1) Freedom of thought and conscience is guaranteed. (2) Subject to any reasonable restrictions imposed by law in the interests of the security of the State, friendly relations with foreign states, public order, decency or morality, or in relation to contempt of court, defamation or incitement to an offence—(a) the right of every citizen to freedom of speech and expression; and (b) freedom of the press are guaranteed.

The scope of the right to freedom of expression and its legal limits in Bangladesh must also conform to the ICCPR since it is ratified by the former.[8] Both the Bangladeshi Constitution and the ICCPR state that this right is subject to certain restrictions. However, the Constitution says that "friendly relations with foreign States" may be a reason for restriction. This is not mentioned in Articles 18 and 19 of the ICCPR. Moreover, Article 19 of the ICCPR guarantees the "right to seek, receive, and impart information," as well as the freedom of expression. This may ensure that citizens have access to important information from government agencies or otherwise. It also guarantees that citizens or groups are allowed to circulate important information (Shahabuddin 2013).

COUNTER-TERRORISM LAWS IN BANGLADESH AND THEIR LIMITATIONS

Following the United Nations Security Council (UNSC) Resolution 1624 (2005),[9] along with many other countries, Bangladesh enacted several laws to combat terrorism. However, two are especially criticized for limiting citizens' right to freedom of expression when such expression is believed to support terrorism, terrorist acts, and terrorist organizations.

Anti-Terrorism Act 2009

The 2009 ATA was originally adopted on February 24, 2009, by the Bangladesh Parliament. The same government that adopted the law amended it twice. The latest amendment, passed by the Parliament on June 11, 2013, allows courts to accept videos, still photographs, and audio clips used in Facebook, Twitter, Skype, and other social media for trial cases. Under this amendment, the police officer concerned will immediately inform district magistrates about the occurrence of a crime that comes under the purview of this Act and files cases against the persons, entity, or foreign national. Earlier in 2012, through another amendment, the death penalty was introduced as the maximum penalty for financing "terrorist" activities (International Federation of Human Rights 2013).

The definition of a "crime" in the Act is extremely broad and vague in comparison to the customary definition of "terrorism,"[10] which does not cover "property crimes." Moreover, the vague definitions of "terrorist activities" (Laws of Bangladesh 2009) under the Act open the legislation to potential abuse and are incompatible with the principles of legality requiring that criminal liability and punishment be limited to clear and precise provisions.

In addition, according to Section 24, the investigation officer must complete the investigation of any case under this Act within maximum 120 days, beginning on the date on which information was received or recorded. Failure to do so will cause the officer to be accused of negligence in performing his/her duties. According to Section 33, the trial of a case must conclude within one year from the date on which the charge was made. On the other hand, according to Section 40(2) of the Act, the investigation officer must take approval from the government before submitting charge sheet against any case filed under the law. However, there is no time limit for the government to give the approval. This allows the government to use this Act whenever they wish. Along with local and international human rights activists, people from different sectors criticized the government for adopting the Act. For example, Ain o Salish Kendra (ASK), a local human rights organization, noted:

> Some of the provisions of this law are contrary to the human rights principles and democratic values. The provisions also undermine the essence of the personal liberty of the citizens, freedom of speech and expression and the freedom of the media. These provisions might be used as an official tool to subjugate the opposition or dissent and to curtail the fundamental rights of the people. (ASK 2013, para. 2)

Different international human rights organizations (such as the International Federation for Human Rights) also expressed their concerns over the adoption of the Act. They cautioned the Act could be applied arbitrarily since the definition of "terrorism" it contained is vague. They also described opinions expressed online should not be criminalized since it is not only a violation of freedom of expression and the right to privacy; it also represents a new pattern of persecution of any voice of dissent, as well as human rights defenders (International Federation of Human Rights 2013).

Terming the law as a "black law," former law minister of Bangladesh Moudud Ahmed argued that this law is adopted to subdue the opposition:

> The law has been formulated not to curb terrorism, but to subdue the opposition. It will be used to snatch people's human rights, basic rights, and constitutional rights as the law enforcers are given all necessary power to subdue the opposition. . . . The horrible aspect of the law is that there's no scope for giving bail to the accused as the offences will be considered as cognizable under it. (Dhaka Tribune 2013, para. 4, 6)

Since the adoption of the law, activists and politicians have expressed their concerns over citizens' human rights. By publishing statements and organizing different programs, opponents not only specifically mentioned how this law contradicts citizens' fundamental right to freedom of expression but also demanded to amend the law. However, the government did not take any action yet to consider their demands.

Digital Security Act 2018

Ignoring opposition from journalists and human rights watchdogs, the Bangladeshi Parliament passed the DSA on September 19, 2018. This legislation includes severe penalties for cyber terrorism and other crimes committed online. Justifying the adoption of the Act, the government said the law aims to curb rise in cybercrime and violent extremism in recent years (Rozario and Uttom 2018). The law, which replaced the much-criticized ICT Act of 2013, retained the most problematic provisions of the latter and added more provisions criminalizing peaceful speech (Human Rights Watch 2018).

Under Section 43, this Act grants law enforcement authorities wide-ranging powers to remove or block online information that "harms the unity of the country or any part of it, economic activities, security, defense, religious value or public order or spreads communal hostility and hatred," and conduct warrantless searches and seizures if they believe that an offense under the law has been or is being committed or there is a possibility of committing crimes or destroying evidence. Section 25(a) authorizes sentences of up to three years for publishing information that is "aggressive or frightening." However, the broad terms are not defined in the law that creates the possibility of violating freedom of expression. Section 31 imposes sentences of up to ten years for posting information that "ruins communal harmony or creates instability or disorder or disturbs or is about to disturb the law and order situation." With no clear definition of what speech would be considered a violation of the law, the provision leaves for the government-wide margins to prosecute the speech it does not like.

People from different sectors have been opposing the law since its adoption. Responding to the adoption of the law, Brad Adams, Asia director of Human Rights Watch, remarked:

> The new Digital Security Act is a tool ripe for abuse and a clear violation of the country's obligations under international law to protect free speech. With at least five provisions criminalizing vaguely defined types of speech, the law is a license for wide-ranging suppression of critical voices. (Human Rights Watch 2018, para. 2)

Along with others, journalists have been demanding amendments to the law since there are some sections that could be used to control the media. Mahfuz Anam, general secretary of the Bangladesh Editors' Council, stated: "We think the Digital Security Act is an obstruction to press freedom. If the law remains in force, none of us—the press media, television [channels], and the online media—will be able to do our professional duty independently" (The Daily Star 2018a, para. 6).

In line with the development of Internet infrastructures, a vibrant online community has developed in Bangladesh. Although there are many limitations, the online community has many success stories (Sharma 2014). For example, bloggers and online activists have been criticizing the Act, describing it as horrendous as it relates to the gag it puts on free speech (UCA News 2018).

ABUSES OF COUNTER-TERRORISM LAWS

Counter-terrorism laws, in addition to being deploying to combat terrorism, are being used to stifle political dissent in several cases in Bangladesh.

This trend especially affects human rights activists, members and leaders of opposition political parties, and bloggers. The vague and broadly applicable definitions of several terms of the laws help the government to repress dissenting voices. However, since ATA requires time-consuming procedure to be maintained, the DSA is widely used to limit the right to freedom of expression in the country.

According to a report of Article 19, a human rights organization, at least sixty cases have been filed under the DSA as of May 2020 (Article19 2020). At least 108 people have been affected under the cases for expressing their opinion on different contemporary issues, especially on social media. The number of DSA-affiliated cases was seventy-one and sixty-three in 2018 and 2019, respectively.[11] The numbers show that the cases under the DSA have increased significantly in 2020 when the country as well as the world is suffering from coronavirus crisis. Several cases have been filed against those people who criticized the government for managing the crisis on social media (Wahiduzzaman 2020).

HARASSING OPPOSITION POLITICAL PARTY MEMBERS AND LEADERS

Since the adoption of the ATA and DSA, political leaders and rights activists have been claiming that the laws could be used to harass opposition party leaders. Their assumption was found to be true since several cases have been filed against top opposition leaders under these laws (The Daily Star 2016). On April 29, 2015, police filed charges against leaders of the main opposition party, Bangladesh Nationalist Party (BNP), including its secretary general Mirza Fakhrul Islam Alamgir, under the ATA for allegedly throwing a petrol bomb on passenger bus that killed a passenger on the spot while several others were seriously injured. However, the court relieved them from the charge the following year since their involvement in the incident was not proven (The Daily Star 2016). In another instance, ahead of the 2019 general election, a case was filed against a BNP candidate under the DSA over their reported audio clip instigating violence. Meanwhile, the BNP leader alleged that the case was filed out of vengeance to keep him away from the election race (The Financial Express 2018). Since the present government came to the power in 2009, hundreds of opposition party leaders and members have been sent to jail after being arrested under different laws, although it was evident that the counter-terrorism laws have made it easier to harass them (TRT World 2018).

REPRESSING DISSENTING VOICES

Counter-terrorism laws, especially the DSA, are being widely used to repress dissenting voices. A report prepared by Article 19 says the number of cases under the DSA have rapidly increased during the coronavirus crisis. In seventy-one days (from March 1 to May 10, 2020), forty-three cases were filed under the law (Zaif 2020). Of these, eleven cases were filed for writings related to the coronavirus on social media; six cases were filed against defendants for writing against a minister, a parliamentarian, and a mayor; five charges were made against defendants for writing against relief stealing; three charges were made for writing against the prime minister; and four cases were filed for writing against police (Zaif 2020).

On May 6, 2020, eleven people, including a cartoonist, Ahmed Kabir Kishore, two journalists, Sweden-based Tasneem Khalil and U.S.-based Shahed Alam, and a writer, Mushtaq Ahmed, were charged under the DSA. Four of them including Ahmed Kabir Kishore and Mushtaq Ahmed were arrested on the same day (Islam and Saad 2020). In the charges, police said:

> These people have been knowingly posting rumors against the Father of the Nation, the Liberation War and the coronavirus pandemic to negatively affect the nation's image and to create confusion among the public through the social media and cause the law and order situation to deteriorate. (Islam and Saad 2020, para. 6)

In this statement, like other terrorism acts, police described that the arrestees' write-ups in social media could deteriorate law and order situation in Bangladesh (Islam and Saad 2020). However, their Facebook posts show that they criticized the government on different issues of managing the coronavirus crisis and asked the government to take effective steps. The actions and explanations of the law enforcement agencies show the law could be used in many ways including repressing dissenting voices, an outcome critics have warned against since the adoption of the law.

CONTROLLING JOURNALISM

Since the preparation of DSA, there was widespread concern among journalists and rights activists about potential implications for freedom of speech. In 2018, Article 19, previously referenced, recorded a total of seventy-one cases filed under the then Section 57 of the ICT Act, and, later, the newly enacted DSA which came into effect in October of the same year. In 2019, the number of recorded cases initiated under the DSA amounted to sixty-three. From January to April 2020, forty-five cases have been recorded, most of which have been filed against journalists and media editors (Article 19 2020). On May 1, 2020, three local journalists were arrested and sent to jail in a case filed under the Act by the police in Narsingdi, a city located 50 kilometers north-east of Dhaka, capital city of Bangladesh (The Daily Star 2020).

In another instance, a Dhaka-based journalist, Shafiqul Islam Kajol, turned up fifty-three days after he disappeared on May 3, 2020. He was held in police custody at a border town 150 miles from where he had last been seen. Later, he was jailed for trespassing and for Facebook posts he wrote criticizing an alleged sex-trafficking ring run by an official in the ruling party (Jago News 2020). Along with promoting self-censorship, right activists consider these kinds of harassments of journalists in these cases to be a pathway to institutionalizing arbitrariness and violating the commitment to establish rule of law (Abrar 2019, Dhaka Tribune 2020).

INSTRUMENT TO PRACTICE ABSOLUTE POWER

Section 40(2) of the ATA states the investigation officers must take approval from the government before submitting charge a sheet.[12] As a result, under this section, the government can approve a case in one day while keeping others pending. For example, per a newspaper report, on July 23, 2016, trial proceedings of twenty-seven cases involving terror and militant activities were halted in different courts of Chattogram, a port city located 250 kilometers south-east of Dhaka, which have been waiting for years for government's approval as required by the law. The cases were filed between 2010 and 2015 (Chakraborty 2016).

The DSA, in addition to other aspects discussed earlier, is criticized since it gives unlimited power to the police to arrest anybody on suspicion without warrant and without needing any approval of any authority (Human Rights Watch 2018). There are several incidents where law enforcement used this law to arrest people. For example, on May 6, 2020, records show Minhaj Mannan Emon, a businessman, was arrested by police in a case under the DSA although he had been allegedly in police custody since May 5, 2020 (Islam and Saad 2020).

DISCUSSION AND CONCLUDING REMARKS

Given the new traits of terrorism which heavily depend on communication tools, there is little doubt that states must respond to curb the threat.

Adoption of counter-terrorism laws is one of the major measures to combat terrorism. Following international bodies' calls to do so, many countries have enacted laws as a part of their counter-terrorism strategy. However, most of these laws did not follow the international standards in drafting the laws which are often used to violate the fundamental right to freedom of expression.

In the Bangladesh context, in line with the growing usage of ICTs, terrorist activities have been taking new shapes and the number of deadly attacks has increased. Along with enacting counter-terrorism laws, the government has taken different steps in de-radicalization processes. However, politicians use citizens' fears to increase their power and control over society (Curtis 2004). Like many other countries, this assumption is found to be true in Bangladesh. By utilizing peoples' fear, the government adopted several laws stating that it would help to curb terrorism and to ensure national security. Despite criticism from opposition parties, journalists, and rights activists regarding several clauses which limit civil liberties, the government adopted the laws in the name of countering terrorism. Several evidences discussed in this chapter demonstrate how the government ignored its legal obligations to the Constitution and international agreements that guarantee peoples' right to freedom of expression.

Broad and vague definition of several terms (such as "crime" and "terrorist activities") creates opportunity for the state to abuse the laws and to stifle dissent and political opposition under the guise of protecting national security. Like other countries (such as Ethiopia), the Bangladeshi government has been utilizing these laws to control both traditional journalism and citizen journalism. Along with journalists, bloggers and online activists have been harassed by the extensive use of the laws. Utilizing Section 40(2) of the ATA, the government has been practicing power to implement the law arbitrarily and conveniently.

Ensuring freedom of expression is not only a prerequisite to establish democracy in a society but also a basic requirement for individual development. Views expressed by a citizen or group ought to be countered, challenged, and contested by advanced logic, reason, and explanation—not by control, threat, or coercion. Although it is expected that every law should be adopted respecting citizens' fundamental rights, the counter-terrorism laws in Bangladesh fall short of this promise.

NOTES

1. Culture of fear (or climate of fear) denotes the notion that people may incite fear in the general public to achieve political or workplace goals through emotional bias.

2. United Nations (UN) Security Council Resolutions 1368, 1373 and 1377 of 2001, 1390 of 2002, 1455 and 1456 of 2003, and 1526 of 2004.

3. "New terrorism" is a concept introduced by Bruce Hoffman in 1998 and further developed by other scholars. According to this concept, terrorism has transformed from a form of violent *political communication* to a perceived *duty* to kill as many people as possible, which pushes states to respond more forcefully since the cost of mistakes is higher (Hoffman 1998).

4. UN Human Rights Committee, General Comment No. 34, "Article 19, Freedoms of Opinion and Expression," CCPR/C/GC/34(2011).

5. See United Nations Security Council Resolution (2003).

6. HRC Resolution 20/8on the Internet and Human Rights, A/HRC/RES/20/8, June 2012.

7. General Comment No. 34, *op cit.*, para 43.

8. International Covenant on Civil and Political Rights (ICCPR) adopted December 16, entered into force March 23, 1976. Bangladesh ratified the ICCPR in 2000.

9. See United Nations Security Council Resolution (2005, para. 1).

10. Since the act of terrorism is a debatable issue there is no current agreement regarding of a universal legal definition of the term. Scholars and practitioners have been proposing different customary definitions of terrorism. For instance, United Nations General Assembly Resolution 1566 (2004) refers to terrorism as:

"criminal acts, including against civilians, committed with intent to cause death or serious bodily injury, or taking of hostages, with the purpose to provoke a state of terror in the general public or in a group of persons or particular persons, intimidate a population or compel a government or an international organization to do or to abstain from doing any act, which constitute offences within the scope of and as defined in the international conventions and protocols relating to terrorism, are under no circumstances justifiable by considerations of a political, philosophical, ideological, racial, ethnic, religious or other similar nature, and calls upon all States to prevent such acts and, if not prevented, to ensure that such acts are punished by penalties consistent with their grave nature" (para. 3).

11. 37 cases filed under the Section 57 of ICT Act and 34 under the DSA enacted in October 2018.

12. A record made in a police station of the charges against a person.

REFERENCES

Abrar, C R. 2019. "Defending the Mother of All Rights." *The Daily Star*, November 10, 2019. https://www.thedailystar.net/opinion/human-rights/news/defending-the-mother-all-rights-1825189.

Ahmad, Fayazuddin. 2015. "Restrictions on Freedom of Expression." *The Daily Star*, October 6, 2015. https://assetsds.cdnedge.bluemix.net/law-our-rights/restrictions-freedom-expression-152341.

ASK. 2013. "ASK Condemn the Overnight Bill: Anti-Terrorism Act 2013." Accessed June 30, 2020. http://www.askbd.org/ask/2013/06/20/condemn-overnight-bill-anti-terrorism-act-2013/.

Article 19. 2020. "Bangladesh: Increase in Charges under DSA as Government Seeks to Silence Criticism." Accessed July 4, 2020 https://www.article19.org/resources/bangladesh-increase-in-charges-under-dsa-as-government-seeks-to-silence-criticism/.

Boyne, Shawn Marie. 2010. "Free Speech, Terrorism, and European Security: Defining and Defending the Political Community." *Pace Law Review* 30 (2): 417–483. https://digitalcommons.pace.edu/plr/vol30/iss2/17.

Bozinovic, Filip. 2018. "Restrictions on Expression as a Counter-Terror Policy in the United States and France: Divergence by Design or Curious Convergence?" *Claremont-UC Undergraduate Research Conference on the European Union* 2018 (1). https://scholarship.claremont.edu/urceu/vol2018/iss1/3.

Chakraborty, Pranabesh. 2018. "27 Anti-terror Cases Stuck." *The Daily Star*, July 23, 2016. https://www.thedailystar.net/frontpage/27-anti-terror-cases-stuck-1258096.

Cram, Ian. 2009. *Terror and the War on Dissent: Freedom of Expression in the Age of Al-Qaeda*. Berlin Heidelberg: Springer.

Crenshaw, Martha. 2011. *Explaining Terrorism: Causes, Processes and Consequences*. Abingdon: Routledge.

Curtis, Adam. 2004. *The Power of Nightmares: The Rise of the Politics of Fear*.

Desk, Jago News 2020. "Bangladeshi Journalist Jailed after Mysterious 53-day Disappearance." *Jago News 24*. May 8, 2020. https://www.jagonews24.com/en/national/news/49612.

Dhaka Tribune. 2013. "BNP Castigates Government for Passing Anti-terrorism Bill." June 12, 2013. https://www.dhakatribune.com/uncategorized/2013/06/12/bnp-castigates-government-for-passing-anti-terrorism-bill.

———. 2020. "TIB: Digital Security Act Curtailing Freedom of Expression." June 20, 2020. https://www.dhakatribune.com/bangladesh/2020/06/20/tib-digital-security-act-curtailing-freedom-of-expression.

Dworkin, Ronald. 2002. *Sovereign Virtue: The Theory and Practice of Equality*. London: Harvard University Press.

Fair, C. Christine, and Wahid Abdallah. 2017. "Islamist Militancy in Bangladesh: Public Awareness and Attitudes." Accessed December 10, 2020. https://resolvenet.org/system/files/2017-09/RSVE_04BangladeshBrief_MilitantSupport2017.pdf.

FORUM-ASIA. 2018. "Shrinking Democratic Space and Freedom of Expression in Bangladesh." December 26, 2018. https://www.forum-asia.org/?p=27911.

Hellmuth, Dorle. 2015. "Countering Jihadi Terrorists and Radicals the French Way." *Studies in Conflict & Terrorism* 38 (12): 979–997. https://doi.org/10.1080/1057610X.2015.1076277.

Hoffman, Paul. 2004. "Human Rights and Terrorism." *Human Rights Quarterly* 26 (4): 932–955. https://muse.jhu.edu/article/174729.

Hoskins, Andrew, Akil N Awan, and Ben O'Loughlin. 2011. *Radicalization and Media: Connectivity and Terrorism in the New Media Ecology*. London and New York: Routledge.

Human Rights Watch. 2018. "Bangladesh: New Law Will Silence Critics." Accessed May 5, 2020. https://www.hrw.org/news/2018/09/24/bangladesh-new-law-will-silence-critics.

International Federation of Human Rights. 2013. "Bangladesh: New Amendment to Anti-Terrorism Act Gags Freedom of Expression." Accessed June 25. https://www.fidh.org/en/region/asia/bangladesh/bangladesh-new-amendment-to-anti-terrorism-act-gags-freedom-of-expression-13457.

Islam, Zyma, and Muntakim Saad. 2020. "Digital Security Act: 11 Sued, Two Sent to Jail." *The Daily Star*, May 7, 2020. https://www.thedailystar.net/frontpage/news/digital-security-act-11-sued-two-sent-jail-1900228.

Jago News 2020. "Bangladeshi Journalist Jailed after Mysterious 53-day Disappearance." May 8, 2020. https://www.jagonews24.com/en/national/news/49612.

Laws of Bangladesh. 2009. "Anti-Terrorism Act 2009." Accessed August 20, 2020. http://bdlaws.minlaw.gov.bd/act-1009/section-39278.html?hl=1.

Mendel, Toby. 2010. "Restricting Freedom of Expression: Standards and Principles." *Background Paper for Meetings Hosted by the UN Special Rapporteur on Freedom of Opinion and Expression.* Accessed December 12, 2020. http://www.law-democracy.org/wp-content/uploads/2010/07/10.03.Paper-on-Restrictions-on-FOE.pdf.

Michaelsen, Christopher. 2006. "Balancing Civil Liberties against National Security—A Critique of Counterterrorism Rhetoric." *University of New South Wales Law Journal* 29 (2): 1–21.

MiekleJohn, Alexander. 1948. *Freedom of Speech and its Relation to Self-Government.* New York: Harper Brothers Publishers.

Mill, John Stuart. 1864. *On Liberty.* London: Longman Roberts & Green.

Office of the United Nations High Commissioner for Human Rights. n.d. "International Covenant on Civil and Political Rights." Accessed August 15, 2020. https://www.ohchr.org/Documents/ProfessionalInterest/ccpr.pdf.

PoKempner, Dinah. 2007. *A Shrinking Realm: Freedom of Expression since 9/11.* New York: Human Rights Watch.

Rashid, Muktadir. 2019. "Seven to Die for Holey Artisan Attack." *New Age*, November 28, 2019. https://www.newagebd.net/article/91895/seven-to-die-for-holey-artisan-attack.

Riaz, Ali. 2016. "Who Are the Bangladeshi 'Islamist Militants'?" *Perspectives of Terrorism* 10 (1): 1–18. http://www.terrorismanalysts.com/pt/index.php/pot/article/view/485.

Rozario, Rock Ronald, and Stephan Uttom. 2018. "Bangladesh's Digital Security Act: Old Wine in New Bottle?" *UCA News.* October 2, 2018. https://www.ucanews.com/news/bangladeshs-digital-security-act-old-wine-in-new-bottle/83471.

Shahabuddin, Mohammad. 2013. *The International Covenant on Civil and Political Rights: A Study on Bangladesh Compliance.* Dhaka: National Human Rights Commission, Bangladesh.

Sharma, Shudipta. 2014. "Environmental Movements and Social Networking Sites in Bangladesh. *International Journal of Innovation and Sustainable Development* 8 (4): 380–393.

Siapera, Eugenia. 2012. *Understanding New Media.* London: SAGE.
Siddique, Md. Abu Bakar, and Sharmin Akter. 2016. "Right to Privacy and Counter-terrorism in the Digital Age: A Critical Appraisal for Bangladesh." *IOSR Journal of Humanities and Social Science* 21 (7): 64–72.
The Daily Star. 2016. "Fakhrul, 25 Others Relieved of Explosive Case." *The Daily Star*, March 10, 2016. https://www.thedailystar.net/politics/fakhrul-25-others-relieved-explosive-case-789379.
———. 2018a. "Amend Nine Sections of Digital Security Act." October 16, 2018. https://www.thedailystar.net/city/digital-security-act-2018-amend-9-sections-editors-council-1647205.
———. 2018b. *Free speech will cease to exist.* Dhaka: The Daily Star, September 30, 2018. Accessed August 10, 2020. https://www.thedailystar.net/city/news/digital-security-act-abolish-freedom-expression-shahdeen-malik-1640332.
———. 2020. "3 Journalists in Narsingdi Arrested under Digital Security Act." May 3, 2020. https://www.thedailystar.net/country/news/3-journalists-narsingdi-arrested-under-digital-security-act-1898932.
The Financial Express. "BNP's Kushtia-4 Candidate Sued under Digital Security Act." December 18, 2018. https://thefinancialexpress.com.bd/public/national/crime/bnps-kushtia-4-candidate-sued-under-digital-security-act-1545133988.
TRT World. 2018. "Bangladesh Opposition Say Hundreds of Supporters Arrested." December 9, 2018. https://www.trtworld.com/asia/bangladesh-opposition-say-hundreds-of-supporters-arrested-22323.
Tsegaye, Molaligne. 2016. "Implications of the Anti-Terrorism Law of Ethiopia on Freedom of Expression and the Media." LLM Thesis, College of Law and Governance Studies, School of Law, Addis Ababa University.
Tura, Husen Ahmed. 2017. "The Impact of Ethiopia's Anti-Terrorism Law on Freedom of Expression." *5th International Conference of PhD Students and Young Researchers.* Vilnius, Lithuania: Vilnius University Faculty of Law.
United Nations. n.d. "The Universal Declaration of Human Rights." Accessed August 15, 2020. https://www.un.org/en/universal-declaration-human-rights/.
United Nations Security Council. 2003. "United Nations Security Council Resolution 1456." January 20, 2003. https://www.undocs.org/S/RES/1456%20.
———. 2004. "United Nations Security Council Resolution 1566." October 8, 2004. https://www.un.org/ruleoflaw/files/n0454282.pdf.
———. 2005. "United Nations Security Council Resolution 1624." September 14, 2005. https://www.un.org/en/ga/search/view_doc.asp?symbol=S/RES/1624%282005%29.
Wahiduzzaman, AKM. "Bangladesh is Suppressing Free Speech During the COVID-19 Pandemic." *The Diplomat*, April 29, 2020. https://thediplomat.com/2020/04/bangladesh-is-suppressing-free-speech-during-the-covid-19-pandemic/.
Zaif, Ahmed. 2020. "Digital nirapatta ain: Coronakaleo bereche mamla o greptar." *Prothom Alo*, May 11, 2020.

PART V

EPILOGUE

Chapter 19

Epilogue

Insights and Lessons Learned or Confirmed

Paul Haridakis and Téwodros Workneh

During times of societal conflict, such as the ongoing threat or proliferation of terrorism, the credibility, if not the legitimacy, of government is tested. The governed expect the government to protect not only national security but their safety. At the same time, government leaders have a competing interest to not only address the concerns of the public but also to display their ability to defend and protect the nation and its government from the challenge.

But there is no universal model for how these competing interests are met. This is due, in part, by the fact that governments reside on a continuum from authoritarian to democratic. Governments also reside on a continuum from stable to unstable. These factors affect how government officials can and do exercise their authority, the degree to which they recognize freedoms of the citizenry, and the extent to which the government considers citizens' rights in counter-terrorism actions it takes.

Accordingly, analyzing the tension between balancing governmental attempts to combat terrorism and preserve national security with freedom of speech and other civil liberties is an inexact social science. The analyses provided in the chapters in this book highlight differences in counter-terrorism approach taken across nations, but also striking similarities in the restrictions on freedoms in the interest of preserving national security, regardless of differences in the systems. Specifically, the analyses provided in the chapters included here provide insight, if not lessons, regarding similarities across systems in the way governments often fail to sufficiently protect these freedoms, or, worse, sometimes exploit the fight against terrorism in using laws, polices, and procedures to assault those freedoms, generally, or those of specific groups engaged in expressive activities unrelated to terrorism, but opposed by the government (e.g., dissent, public protest, criticism of the government).

Here, we conclude our review by considering some of those similarities that may shed light on the ways controls on communication have and are being used in ways that constrain expressive activities. Although some governments provide greater protections of freedom of speech than others, and therefore differ in the degree of control on communication activity, the above chapters suggest that when a nation is confronted with a crisis like terrorism, individual rights become more tenuous and constraints on expression have been heightened across systems.

Below we reference some commonalities in counter-terrorism mechanisms employed by governments in the fight against terrorism that have impinged freedom of speech. The discussion focuses on some general "takeaways" gleaned from the chapters, as specific examples of constraints on freedom of speech and other civil liberties in the nations spotlighted are contained in the individual chapters.

THE EXPLOITATION OF FEAR

Fear is a powerful motivator of government action to confront terrorist attacks. Contemporaneously, fear is a powerful force that affects the extent to which citizens are willing to accept certain controls on freedoms in exchange for government counter-terrorism efforts to combat terrorism and protect their safety. This provides an opportunity for governments to constrain freedoms in the name of preserving safety and security without garnering widespread citizen disapproval. The slippery slope of acquiescence to controls on communication is that greater freedom of communication is one of the strongest checks on governmental abuse. Though written outside of the context of controls on freedom of speech, over 300 years ago Benjamin Franklin, U.S. Diplomat, signer of the U.S. Declaration of Independence, and one of the United States' founding fathers, wrote that "those who would give up essential liberty, to purchase a little temporary safety, deserve neither liberty nor safety." Paraphrased on the Statue of Liberty that stands in the New York harbor, Franklin's words serve as a warning that freedom and safety are not mutually exclusive, and the former should not have to be compromised to secure the latter. And, in fact, if the governed do compromise, they may not get what they bargained for.

SURVEILLANCE/MONITORING

Although government surveillance and monitoring of individuals raises questions about violation of privacy, increased surveillance is designed to target communication activities. It is designed to uncover activities such as what people are seeing, reading, and doing—as well as the communication channels they are using individually, interpersonally, and collectively. It may be reasonable to expect the government to employ such preventive mechanisms to thwart terrorism before it occurs. However, there is a danger when counter-terrorism laws and/or practices grant the government greater authority to circumvent protections ordinarily in place to protect individuals' privacy from government monitoring. In addition, because government surveillance is by design conducted in secrecy, when employed it is difficult to ascertain when it is mis-applied to monitor non-terrorist-related communication of individuals with no connection to terrorism or terrorist organizations. Accordingly, ongoing analyses such as those conducted by authors of chapters in this book are necessary to subject government action to scrutiny in an effort to uncover abuse that government secrecy invites. This is particularly true when governments spy on their own citizens and prosecute them on the basis of secretly obtained communications.

CONTROLS ON COMMUNICATORS, CONTENT, AND COMMUNICATION CHANNELS

As noted in the above chapters, controls on communication have been amplified in response to the threat and proliferation of terrorist activity. But, even in "normal" times, when societal conflict is not as intense as a war on terror, certain types of communication content and channels arc regulated. For example, governments seldom accept or protect speech such as sedition, defamation, obscenity, hate speech, or incitement to violence, to reference just a few. Similarly, the media themselves (movies, print, television, telephony, the Internet) generally are subject to varying and different degrees of regulation. In addition, there is a wide array of communicators whose level of speech protection has varied historically based on their religious or political ideology, citizenship status, gender, age, and so on.

Counter-terrorism laws, however, provide new tools to distinguish the level of protection afforded media, specific content, and different communicators based on the classification of the individual. The chapters here have illuminated various ways governments have used these laws in opportunistic ways to target individuals and groups with which the respective nation or current government has had longstanding disputes or concerns. Those targeted have included government critics, political and social dissidents, members of certain religious groups or faiths, foreigners, members of certain ethnic groups, artists, and simply those government leaders fear to pose a risk to their rule. Government leaders and those acting on their behalf have even used these laws to target media, journalists, and other media professionals for legitimate media coverage of government action, and to target others simply for voicing their opinions regarding their government.

DETENTION

Regardless of the governmental system—democratic or authoritarian—during times of war or other threat of attack governments sometimes exercise the power of detention—to arrest and jail those individuals suspected to be perpetrators, associates, or accomplices without affording them the ordinary safeguards against arbitrary and capricious confinement. Counter-terrorism laws and procedures often abrogate normal protections afforded individuals prior to being arrested or jailed, and the chapters above indicate this enormous detention power has been being used extensively in the war on terror in the twenty-first century. This has ranged from the arrest and incarceration of individual journalists and dissidents, to large-scale imprisonment, such as that exercised by the U.S. government at Guantanamo Bay and the detention of Uyghurs in China.

Such practices must continue to be brought to light and monitored because of all the freedoms arguably highlighted in the chapters, they all pale in relation to the right to be free from unjustified confinement. There is no more complete way to control communication than to confine the communicator. The mere threat of arbitrary detention by the government can silence even its harshest critics.

THE CENTRALITY OF COMMUNICATION

This brings us to our assertion that analyses of terrorism and/or counter-terrorism must consider the centrality of communication. In chapter 1, we argued for the value of applying a communication approach to studying and analyzing terrorism and counter-terrorism activity. The chapters emphasize that focus. The evidence suggests the centrality of communication in both the promulgation of terrorism and in the focus of government to counter it.

Terrorists often engage in acts in ways that are theatrical, spectacular, and designed to garner media coverage. Terrorists also use all communication channels at their disposal—from mediated to interpersonal—to recruit members, plan and coordinate attacks, and gain publicity. But, more broadly, terrorism itself is communicative. Terrorism has been referred to as "propaganda by deed" (Barton 2015, 306). Applying a communication approach to studying propaganda, Jowett and O'Donnell (2018) defined it as "*the deliberate, systematic attempt to shape perceptions, manipulate cognitions, and direct behavior to achieve a response that furthers the desired intent of the propagandist*" (p. 6). One of the desired intents of terrorists is to terrorize—to instill fear in a wider audience beyond the particular victims of an attack. Without communication, terrorists could not achieve their goals. Therefore, it seems almost beyond debate to recognize the need for and propriety of the use mechanisms described above to circumvent terrorist communication and to use terrorists' communication to stop, arrest, and prosecute them.

At the same time, however, the power of a government to mobilize the nation's forces to wage war or confront threats to national security such as that posed by terrorism is immense. Such power requires checks on it, because even under the best of intentions such unbridled power runs the risk of abuse. The free flow of communication—to see what the government is doing, acquire information about it, and to be able to comment and debate it—is one of those important checks.

Thus, communication is at the crux of the tension between balancing the protection of national security with the protection of civil liberties. An imbalance in one direction can hamper the ability of the government to sufficiently protect national security and end a terrorist threat. An imbalance in the other direction—that fails to sufficiently protect freedom of speech—can undermine an important check on unbridled government power resulting in long-lasting repercussions on individual liberties for us all.

It is the latter problem on which we have focused here. The intent of this book and compilation of chapters documenting experiences of the application of counter-terrorism in various nations across continents was not to minimize the need for governments to confront terrorism, or their authority to do so. Governments need to respond to legitimate threats. But, they should not use them in opportunistic or inadvertent ways to unnecessarily adversely affect legitimate freedoms. When that may be happening, we must remain vigilant in uncovering it. We need to distinguish between appropriate exercise of authority and inappropriate exercise of authority when confronting terrorism. It is our hope that the chapters here have helped in that important scrutiny.

The chapters do not clear up the definitional vagueness of terrorism. This remains a problem. A terrorist frame behind counter-terrorism laws and vague and inconsistent interpretations of the term "terrorism" often permit governments to use these laws in ways that target those the government sees as a challenge to them, regardless of whether they are involved in acts of terrorism. What is most concerning, and tragic, is that those often targeted are innocent citizens who are most vulnerable for the simple reason that they are not in hiding or hard to find, but simply exercising what otherwise are their expressive freedoms. Thus, it is the exercise of their freedom that renders them visible.

It is that definitional vagueness combined with the communicator visibility that has permitted governments to harass, jail, and/or otherwise restrict free speech rights of journalists simply doing their jobs—a job that is particularly important—to inform the public, editorialize and help the public make sense of their environment, and transmit societal and cultural heritage; and to do the same with citizens who are simply engaging in debate and civic participation the government may not like.

When the exercise of their very freedom makes citizens and professional communicators vulnerable to government constraint and/or prosecution pursuant to vague laws and/or vague or overbroad interpretation and application of those laws, the laws deserve greater scrutiny than the communication. Without that scrutiny, true professional journalism and complete and robust civic debate and participation are threatened by the very governments that should be charged with protecting these rights.

REFERENCES

Barton, Mary S. 2015. "The Global War on Anarchism: The United States and International Anarchist Terrorism, 1898–1904*." *Diplomatic History* 39 (2): 303–330. https://doi.org/10.1093/dh/dhu004.

Jowett, Garth S., and Victoria O'Donnell. 2018. *Propaganda & Persuasion*. 7th ed. Los Angeles/London/New Delhi/Singapore/Washington DC/Melbourne: SAGE Publications.

Index

Note: Page numbers in *italics* refer to tables.

About the Editors and Contributors

EDITORS

Téwodros Workneh is an assistant professor of Global Communication at the School of Communication Studies, Kent State University. Dr. Workneh's studies explore global media industries and policies through critical political economy and postcolonial approaches. His most recent works focus on discourses telecommunications deregulation in Sub-Saharan Africa as they pertain to notions of universal access, information justice, and freedom of expression.

Paul Haridakis is a professor of Communication Studies at Kent State University. He conducts research on freedom of speech, media uses and effects, law, public policy, new communication technologies, sports communication, and the history of communication studies. His recent work has focused on the role of YouTube and other social media in political campaigns and interpersonal communication, user-generated content, mediated interactivity, and First Amendment issues related to the regulation of content in various media such as the Internet and television. He teaches courses in Freedom of Speech; Media Use and Effects; Political Communication; Communication in an Information Society; Sports Communication; Media, War & Propaganda; Research Methods; and Communication Theory.

CONTRIBUTORS

Rebecca Ananian-Welsh is a senior lecturer at the University of Queensland, School of Law, with a combined expertise in constitutional law and national security. Dr. Ananian-Welsh has published widely in these fields, and her research on fair trial rights and the impact of national security laws on press freedom was recognized in the Australian Academy of Social Sciences Paul Bourke Award. Prior to commencing her academic career, Rebecca held legal positions with DLA Piper Sydney and the Australian Government Attorney-General's Department.

Nazlı Bülay Doğan is interested in digital sociology and in STS. A graduate of Galatasaray University, she received her MA from Bogazici University. She holds a PhD in Design, Technology and Society from Graduate School of Social Sciences and Humanities in Koç University. In her doctoral studies, she studied crime frames about hacktivism in Turkey within the perspective of critical criminology. A Fulbright alumna, a former research fellow at the Annenberg School for Communication and a member of IAMCR and the Union for Democratic Communications, Dr. Doğan worked as a lecturer in Istanbul Bilgi University Department of Sociology. Currently, she works in Istanbul Planning Agency.

Peter Greste is an award-winning former foreign correspondent with twenty-five years' experience in Afghanistan, the Middle East, Latin America, and Africa, mainly for the BBC and Al Jazeera. He became a champion of media freedom after he was imprisoned in Egypt on spurious terrorism charges and released in 2015 after 400 days. He joined the University of Queensland as UNESCO Chair in Journalism and Communication in January 2018. He continues to work as a journalist, academic, and advocate.

Athina Karatzogianni is an associate professor in Media and Communication at the University of Leicester and researches the use of digital technologies by emerging sociopolitical and economic formations, social movements, protest, and insurgency groups.

Gabriela Martínez is a professor at the University of Oregon. She is a scholar who specializes in political economy of communication and international communication. Martinez's geographic area of expertise is the Latin American region where she conducts research on human rights, social movements, and their relationship to media content production and distribution. Other topics at the core of her research are telecom and media ownership, and the global circulation of technologies and cultural products. She is the author of the book "Latin American Telecommunications: Telefónica's Conquest," and co-editor of "Political Economy of Media Industries: Global Transformations and Challenges". Martínez is also an international award-winning documentary filmmaker who has produced, directed, or edited more than fifteen documentaries.

Richard Murray is a former journalist and foreign correspondent. He is currently a research fellow in press freedom and journalist safety at the University of Queensland.

Peter Tiako Ngangum is a member of the Centre de Recherche en Information et Communication (ReSIC) of the Université Libre de Bruxelles (ULB). He holds a PhD in Information and Communication Sciences from the ULB, an MA in Mass Communication from the University of Leicester, an MSc in Environmental Sciences from the University of Greenwich, London and a BA in English from the University of Yaoundé, Cameroon. His areas of expertise include media law and regulation, media ethics, media systems, professionalism, journalism, journalist safety, media and counterterrorism laws, press freedom and freedom of expression. He has published research articles and book chapters on the above themes. In addition to his academic career, he works as a media consultant and trainer.

Daniel Oppermann is a postdoctoral researcher and lecturer at the Institute for Strategic Studies at the Fluminense Federal University in Niterói, Brazil (INEST-UFF). He is a research coordinator at the NUPRI Research Center for International Relations at the University of São Paulo (NUPRI-USP) and editor of the book "Internet Governance in the Global South". Daniel studied Political Science at the Free University of Berlin and holds a PhD in International Relations from the University of Brasília (UnB). He was a researcher, fellow, and/or visiting scholar at the Institute of Economy of the Federal University of Rio de Janeiro (UFRJ), the School of Command and General Staff of the Army (ECEME) in Rio de Janeiro, the University of Los Andes in Bogotá and FGV Law School in Rio de Janeiro.

Daniel Ortner is a constitutional lawyer who fights for individual liberty including freedom of speech and freedom of religion. He graduated summa cum laude and top of his class from BYU Law School and after graduation clerked on the Utah Supreme Court and the Third Circuit Federal Court of Appeals. He now works for the Pacific Legal Foundation, a public interest law firm that opposes government overreach. He speaks Russian fluently after severing a two-year proselytizing mission in Novosibirsk for the Church of Jesus Christ of Latter-day Saints.

Mohammad Imran Parray is an assistant professor at the Department of Communication and Journalism, Institute of Home Economics, University of Delhi, India. He was an Indian Council of Social Science Research (ICSSR) doctoral candidate at Centre for Culture, Media and Governance, Jamia Millia Islamia, New Delhi, India. Prior to that, he worked as a journalist in Kashmir and is a recipient of International Committee of the Red Cross–Press Institute of India award for his reportage on humanitarian and under-reported issues from Kashmir's armed conflict. His research interests include media history, media anthropology, postcolonial media theory, and new media.

Rita Radostitz has been a human rights attorney and activist for more than twenty-five years. She has a BA and MS from the University of Oregon, and a JD from Villanova Law School. A mother of twin daughters, she has represented indigent clients as a public defender in the states of Washington and Oregon, and in the state of Texas where she represented death-sentenced clients in state and federal courts. She currently works for the Military Commissions Defense Organization defending a law of war detainee in the 9/11 trial in the Military Commissions at Guantanamo Bay, Cuba.

Andrew Robinson is an independent scholar working on critical theory, everyday life, and the politics of oppression and resistance. Recent work includes pieces on precarity, Deleuze and the social symptom, anarchism and war, a postcolonial critique of global justice theory and post-left anarchist utopianism.

Eunice Castro Seixas holds a PhD in sociology and is a researcher at the Center for Research in Economic and Organizational Sociology (SOCIUS), Lisboa School of Economics & Management (ISEG), in Portugal. She is currently the principal investigator of "Children and their right to the city: Tackling urban inequity through the participatory design of child friendly cities," a project funded by the Portuguese Foundation for Science and Technology. Dr. Castro Seixas has published peer-reviewed works on a variety of topics including development aid, human rights, terrorism, citizen participation in environmental issues, environmental governance, and political discourses.

Florence Namasinga Selnes recently completed her PhD in Media and Communication at the University of Oslo, Norway. She holds an MPhil in media studies (Norway) and Bachelor of Mass Communication (Uganda). She was a lecturer of journalism, media, and communication at Makerere University in Uganda. Currently, Dr. Selnes is an independent researcher. Her research interests include journalism in relation to ICTs, media and democracy, social media, political communication, gender in relation to social media.

Isabel Serrano Maillo is an associate professor of Constitutional Law and Information Law at the Complutense University of Madrid. Dr. Serrano Maillo has published widely on various subjects including freedom of expression, fundamental rights, protection of personal data, transparency, children rights, and so on. She has participated in numerous National (ACE, CIT, GIGGAP) and international academic conferences (IAMCR, AISOC) and has presented papers on these topics. She is the principal investigator of the Research Group Legal Regulation and Participation of the Digital Citizen.

Shudipta Sharma is an assistant professor of Communication and Journalism at the University of Chittagong. His research interests include new media and society, violent extremism, social movements, political communication, and critical communication studies. His recent works explore the role of social media in social movements and violent extremism in Bangladesh. He teaches courses in New Media Technologies, Communication Research Methods, Social and Political Processes and Institutions, and Advanced Reporting. Before joining the university, he worked as a journalist in leading newspapers in Bangladesh.

Wei Sun is faculty at the Department of Communication, Culture and Media Studies, Howard University, Washington, DC. Her research interests include intercultural communication, media studies, health communication, and minority invisibility. She teaches doctoral seminars in Intercultural Communication, Qualitative Research Methods, Social Media, Communication and Culture, Diversity and Leadership, Community and Public Health, and so on. Her publications have appeared in *The Howard Journal of Communications*, *Intercultural Communication Studies*, and *World Communication.* Her scholarly works on health communication, social media, crisis communication, and millennial studies have been included in several academic books.

Francesco Tamburini is an assistant professor in the Department of Political Science of the University of Pisa, where he teaches History of Afro-Asiatic countries, and Geopolitics of Africa and Asia. His main field of research is history, institutions, and foreign relations of North Africa, Islamic law, and Italian colonial history. He recently published a monography on diplomatic relations between Italy and Tunisia from 1956 to 1965.

www.ingramcontent.com/pod-product-compliance
Ingram Content Group UK Ltd.
Pitfield, Milton Keynes, MK11 3LW, UK
UKHW020838290926
15470UKWH00004B/1421

9 781793 622167